Pleyn Delit: Medieval Cookery for Modern Cooks

ROBERT KARL WHITEFORD II

Constance B. Hieatt & Sharon Butler

Pleyn Delit

Medieval Cookery for Modern Cooks

University of Toronto Press
Toronto Buffalo London

FOR OUR MOTHERS

© University of Toronto Press 1976
Toronto Buffalo London
Printed in Canada
Revised and reprinted 1979
First paperback edition 1979

Library of Congress Cataloging in Publication Data

Hieatt, Constance B
 Pleyn delit.

 Bibliography: p. 161
 Includes index.
 1. Cookery. I. Butler, Sharon, 1942-
 joint author. II. Title.
 TX652.H53   641.5   76-29734
 ISBN 0-8020-2252-9
 ISBN 0-8020-6366-7 pbk.

This book has been published
with the assistance of grants from the
Canada Council and the
Ontario Arts Council.

Contents

Preface

The idea for this book was born some six years ago, and gradually took form more clearly as we worked, on and off, testing recipes – sometimes together, sometimes independently, sometimes with others assisting. Constance Hieatt carried out most of the library research, on this continent and in England, as a sort of intermezzo sandwiched between other scholarly errands. Sharon Butler has done all the art work. The diverting chore of working out and testing recipes was shared, as was the writing.

We owe an incalculable debt to fellow cooks who have worked with our recipes over the years, especially Brenda Thaon and Brian Shaw. The adventurous trenchermen whose judicious comments were helpful are legion, but Paul Thaon deserves special mention, as do A. Kent Hieatt and John Lingard. We have reason to be grateful to various members of the staff of the University of Toronto Press for enthusiastic guidance and assistance: without Prudence Tracy's editorial acumen and Allan Fleming's talents as a designer the final result could never have been so pleasing to its authors.

But our most basic debt is to our mothers, who guided our early steps in the kitchen.

CBH SB

Introduction

A FRANKELEYN was in his compaignye.
Whit was his berd as is the dayes eye;
Of his complexioun he was sangwyn.
Wel loved he by the morwe a sop in wyn;
To lyven in delit was evere his wone,
For he was Epicurus owene sone,
That heeld opinioun that pleyn delit
Was verray felicitee parfit.

from the General Prologue to *The Canterbury Tales*

In the last decade or so a great many people, only a few of them students of the middle ages, have become intrigued with the idea of banqueting medieval-style; anyone who has travelled, or read tourist literature and advertisements, must know by now that medieval fare is available, and consumed at considerable cost, in an Irish castle, an expensive London restaurant, and other successful commercial establishments in Britain and the European continent. In both Britain and North America medieval 'feasts' are being held with ever increasing frequency, not only in academic communities but as church suppers and the like. Yet there has never been, and still is not, a medieval cookbook which could be safely used by anyone but an expert in Middle English with a great deal of experience as a cook. This book is intended to fill that gap.

Such medieval cookbooks as have been available fall into three rough categories. The first, and most useful because most complete, includes various scholarly editions of fourteenth and fifteenth century cookery rolls. The best-known of these is the *Two Fifteenth Century Cookery Books* published by the Early English Text Society.[1] Such editions were intended as background information for scholars specializing in the period, and certainly not to be used as cookbooks. The modern reader who wishes to turn such books to kitchen use is on his own in deciding how much of this or that to use, and often even to determine what the general effect should be: editors have been somewhat unreliable guides. A second category might be termed the coffee-table variety, intended to amuse and beguile, but rarely to be much use in the kitchen. Such books have tended to emphasize the exotic, and sometimes even to discourage readers from trying to cook the recipes presented. A third, if slightly overlapping, category is that of the historical cookbooks which present a selection of medieval recipes 'adapted' for modern tastes. Their selections are also often slanted towards the stranger and more exotic dishes, frequently so drastically adapted as to be a long way from authenticity. They invariably provide only a slender sampling of the fare of the period.

Our aim, then, has not been that of any previous editor. We intended to produce a large and representative collection for practical use in the kitchen, not — or not just — in the study or living room, for those who may enjoy recreating their culinary heritage on either a grand or a modest scale. Whether one wishes to give a do-it-yourself Medieval Feast or simply to vary the everyday repertoire, much can be learned from the medieval cooks whose notes were collected in the manuscripts from which we have drawn. The most cautious and conservative cook should find here appealingly economical and simple fare; the gourmet can discover something to titillate the most jaded palate. Even seasoned medievalists are likely to be surprised at the full range of the cookery of the period, a matter which has been sadly misunderstood. It is not nearly so difficult as most scholars assume or so displeasing to modern tastes, to reproduce the epicurean 'pleyn delit' which characterized Chaucer's Franklin's bounteous table.

Recipes selected for this volume are first given in their original form, though we have sometimes emended the punctuation, and, in the case of those taken from French sources, translated into English. Comments follow, where they seemed necessary or helpful; anyone interested in authenticity may thus compare and judge for himself the accuracy of the recipes below, given in standard modern kitchen terms. All our directions have been thoroughly kitchen-tested, except for a few variants which are appended for the reader's edification and amusement. Not that amusement is our primary purpose: nor even edification, in a truly scholarly sense.[2] Yet a certain amount of both, especially edification, is certainly desirable. For one thing, the number of still circulating misconceptions about the food of the period, even (even perhaps especially) among medievalists, is deplorable.

Almost everyone who has written on the subject has suggested that medieval people preferred rich, spicy foods drowned in outlandish sauces, and that they never ate simple fare, especially vegetables and salads, unless forced to by poverty. These and other commonplaces are simply false. Much medieval cooking was so bland as to seem dull today. Spices, to judge by extant household records of a year's supply, not to mention cost, were no doubt used as sparingly as a modern cook uses pepper: when a dish is meant to be strongly flavoured with a particular spice, the directions call for 'a great deal of ...' Logically, then, unless a 'great deal' is called for, frugality was the rule. The argument that many and lavish spices were necessary because so much meat and fish was salted down for the winter is unconvincing. Salt fish or meat can be soaked (or parboiled, as is frequently called for in medieval recipes) until it loses all its salty quality – which is not necessarily desirable.

Rich dishes in exotic sauces appear to be in the minority on actual medieval menus. The most elaborate multi-course feasts had a higher proportion of roasts and plain boiled meats, served with simple 'pottages' of vegetables, than of fancier dishes. And far more vegetables were grown and used, alone or in combination with meat, eggs, or fish, than is generally recognized: the treatises on gardening list dozens of varieties, often differentiating between those which should be cooked and those suitable for salads. The post-medieval revolution in tastes and cooking habits assumed by writers in this area is, we suspect, more a matter of emphases than of basic tastes and techniques. Many foods and flavourings which are ubiquitous today (such as tomatoes, coffee, and vanilla) had not yet been introduced into the British and European kitchen, and thus it is natural that more use was made of other available ingredients. But there has been much more continuity than has been realized.

'Green sauce,' for example, appears in accounts of European food at least as early as the twelfth century and was a standard favourite with fish throughout the period, and later: a recipe of around the turn of the seventeenth century is virtually identical with those of earlier centuries, and the same sauce is still served in modern France, and probably elsewhere, with only slight modifications. Almost everything which seems odd to British and North American tastes has modern descendants somewhere in European cuisine. Even the practice of 'gilding' poultry, and, sometimes, then replacing the feathered hide intact, has been reported to us from several quarters.

Some of the common misconceptions about medieval food are easily traceable to misunderstanding of the evidence presented by the cookery rolls and by the menus which have come down to us from various state occasions or as sample 'model' menus. Actually, when the two sources of evidence are placed side by side, they contradict (or supplement) each other in various ways. The idea that roasted meats, aside from poultry, were rare in the period goes back to Pegge, one of the early editors, who interpreted the preponderance of stews over roasts in the manuscripts as meaning that fewer roasts were consumed. But it is precisely because roasting is a simple, common procedure that no one would have thought it necessary to write down directions for performing it; knowledge of roasting procedures is assumed in some of the more elaborate recipes, which may tell us to roast the spiced meatballs, or sausages in the form of porcupines, or whatever, 'as one does pigs,' or something of the sort. And if Pegge had looked further into the recipe rolls he would have found a goodly number of recipes for sauces to accompany plain roasts. But also, as we have remarked above, menus for feasts

on grand state occasions show a far greater proportion of
roasts of various kinds than of more elaborate dishes. Even
the wedding feast of Henry IV offered such items as 'gross
char' – a large roast of meat so un-aristocratic, in comparison
with game, as not to deserve more precise description: probably this was roast beef, if it was to be really 'gross.'

The aristocratic menu, on the other hand, is misleading in
giving very few clear references to vegetables, and, as far as
we know, none at all to salads. There may have been a good
many vegetables lurking in the various pottages and other
dishes. The recipe rolls, which generally claim to emanate
from the royalty or the higher nobility, include many recipes
for simple vegetable dishes. Further, the various warnings
against eating salads and raw fruits, which have been cited as
proof that they were not eaten, prove quite the opposite:
who bothers to condemn a non-existent practice?

The menus also show a greater sense of order in the serving
of a multi-course meal than has usually been perceived. A
typical English feast menu for days on which meat was permissible started with pork (or boar) served with mustard or
pepper sauce and either bacon with pease pottage or venison
with frumenty, which were invariable combinations. The remainder of the first course consisted of the more common
roasts or boiled meats with, usually, one meat pie or pasty.
Two other courses generally followed on state occasions, in
each of which more roasts appeared, usually featuring game
birds, along with more complicated pottages of meats, poultry, and fish in various sauces; the last course was usually the
richest, with more pastries, fried dishes such as fritters, jellies,
and sweetened foods than occur in earlier courses. The same
general order prevails in the menus for fish days, which almost
invariably begin with red – smoked and/or pickled – herring:
still the standard way to begin a meal in Scandinavia and
hardly unknown elsewhere.

Thus it seems apparent that menu-planners followed the
advice which can be found in various sources to start with the
plainer foods and eat the delicacies afterwards. A last course
of fruit, nuts, wafers, and other small delicacies is not often

xii mentioned on English menus, but would appear to have been part of the normal routine, perhaps so much so that this was not thought worth noting on the menu of a major feast any more than was bread, which is never mentioned on any menu but was the indispensable part of any meal, simple or complex. In general, the French menu was much like those recorded in England except that the first course was often composed of pastries and elegant concoctions, with the plainer roasts postponed to the second course. Thus the French were already tending to give diners 'appetizers' before the more solid part of the meal.

It may well be asked what relation feast menus have to everyday eating. Probably the main meal of the day, a midday or late morning dinner, was a fairly lavish one in an aristocratic household, consisting of the equivalent of at least the first course of a feast menu. This would appear to be the model emulated by the bourgeoisie and country squires such as Chaucer's Franklin. Most people, of course, would have had to settle for rather less. In the case of the peasantry, we may note that the poor widow of the Nun's Priest's Tale subsisted almost entirely on bread and milk, with bacon and a few eggs to add variety. In a period of drought Piers Plowman complained that he did not even have any bacon – just some fresh cheese, the coarsest types of bread, and a supply of herbs and greens; but his almost equally poor neighbours responded by bringing gifts of peas, beans, fruits, and onions. Servants in a household of any standing did much better than that. The Ménagier de Paris admonished his young wife to be sure that her servants got the proper food and drink, and the morning breakfast order for the nursery given in an early sixteenth century source specifies a quart of beer and three boiled mutton bones to feed the nurse and her two infant charges; in Lent, of course, fish was substituted for the meat.

The lord and lady of the manor ate a really hearty breakfast. Between them, they were to be served one loaf of bread sliced into 'trenchers' – the medieval equivalent of plates; two small loaves of higher quality bread; a quart of beer; a quart of wine; and a good-sized piece of beef or boiled mutton. Yet we gather from Chaucer that a true gourmet's breakfast consisted simply of toast and wine: both the Franklin and January, the elderly knight of the Merchant's Tale, broke their fasts of a morning with a 'sop in wine.' Supper, the third meal of the day, consisted of dishes similar to those served for dinner, though probably in smaller quantities. Some of the feast menus combine dinner and supper, obviously suggesting that the party took time off from eating for other pastimes between courses, but also suggesting that supper menus may have featured less hearty, more 'delicate' foods.

Perhaps the best example of the kind of fare which 'snowed' upon the Franklin's table is a model menu given in John Russell's *Boke of Nurture* for a 'Feast for a Franklin.' The first course consists of 'brawn' (cold pork?) with mustard, bacon with pease pottage, stewed beef or mutton, boiled chicken or capon, roast goose or pork, and a capon pie or 'crustard' (a tart resembling a modern quiche): a total of six dishes, mostly simple ones. The second course started with either 'mortrewes' – ground meat or fish in a bland mixture nearer to soup than to paté in consistency – or a sort of savoury pudding made with bread crumbs, then went on to roasts: veal or lamb, kid or rabbit, chicken or pigeon; and some sort of meat pie or pasty. After this came fritters and mixtures thick enough to be served in slices. The feast was to end with apples and pears (possibly baked) with spices; bread and cheese; and, finally, spiced cakes and wafers, served with spiced ale and mead.

More aristocratic menus differ only in the number of dishes served and the substitution of spiced wine for spiced ale and mead. However, there was one more indispensable feature of feasts for great occasions: the 'subtlety' (usually spelled 'Sotiltee') which provided the climax of every course. Most festive subtilties appear to have been made of sugar, no doubt combined with other things, and were the sort of confectionary art that survives today in fancy cake decorations, especially the bride and groom which traditionally stand at the top of a wedding cake. Our ancestors had different ideas of suitable motifs for a wedding feast: the high point of one such occasion was a subtlety showing 'a wyf lying in childe-bed,' an obvious hint to the bride. Many subtleties appear to have been figures of birds or animals, often bearing suitable mottos, but they sometimes ran to minature castles or cathedrals, or figures of saints or of the dignitaries being honoured. One of the more intriguing known ones depicted Father, Son, and Holy Ghost in Trinity, which sounds like a pretty tricky job for the pastry cook. (See the appendix on subtleties.)

In our own menu planning we have tended to follow the French model when we have given feasts, since it lends itself to an order familiar to modern diners. For smaller meals, the English style is quite suitable, since there is always a simple pottage at or near the beginning of a meal – a tradition which lingers on in the archetypal English dinner today. We hope readers will scan the varied possibilities and put together their own menus according to their tastes and pocketbooks, but the menus which follow provide examples of combinations we found pleasing to various guests. (The quantities given with each recipe are sufficient to feed 4 to 6 people.)

1 *A simple but elegant dinner for 4-6*
Cold Chicken Livers (35)
Chicken with Orange Sauce (82), served with crusty bread
Salad (44)
Cream Junket with Blueberries (108)

2 *A gourmet meal for 4-6*
Green Almond Soup (2)
Chicken and Shellfish in Shellfish Sauce (104) with
bread or rice and Peapods (41)
Cheese Custard Tart (118, var. 2)

3 *A dinner for 8-12*
(double all quantities)
Oysters Stewed in Ale (7)
Mushroom Pasties (24)
Pork in Pepper Sauce (94), with Braised Spinach (40) and
Barley (22, var.)
Apple Fritters (119)

4 *A feast for about 20*
   (some quantities should be doubled)
   To be placed on the table before guests are seated: bread,
     butter, wine
   Hors d'œuvres: Brie Tarts (23), Shrimps (26), Gilded Meat-
     balls with Currants (28, var. 2)
   Main dishes and side dishes: Roast Beef with Garlic Pepper
     Sauce (70); Chicken in White Wine Sauce (84); Salmon
     and Leeks in Almond Sauce (50); Kidney Stew (103);
     Noodles (45); Buttered Greens (22); Green Peas (19);
     Parsnip Fritters (39)
   Dessert: Strawberry Pudding (107); Apple Tarts (116);
     Sweet Fritters (121); Nuts (preferably glazed or spiced);
     Spiced Wine (127)

5 *A feast for about 30*
   (most quantities should be doubled)
   Bread, butter, and wine on the tables, as above
   Hors d'œuvres: Fish in Jelly (27), Sausage Hedgehogs (29),
     Paris Pies (79)
   Main dishes and side dishes: Gilded Chicken (65); Loin of
     Pork in Boar's Tail Sauce (74); Grilled Fish with Yellow
     Sauce (62); Rice with Shellfish (58); Roast Tongue (77);
     Giblets (102); Peas (20); Savory Rice (21, var. 1);
     Creamed Leeks (13); Turnips with Chestnuts (17); Green
     Pancakes (37)
   Dessert: Strawberry Custard Tart (118); Pears in Wine
     Syrup (106); Fig Pudding (115); Sweet Fritters (119);
     Honey and Almond Candy (125); Wafers (126); Spiced
     Wine (127)

6 *A Chaucerian feast of dishes mentioned in Chaucer's poetry*
   (increase quantities as necessary, depending on the
   number to be served)
   On the table: Wastel (white) and Broun Breed; Boter;
     Whit and Reed Wyn; Mortreux (9 or 11)
   Main dishes and side dishes: Pyk in Galantyne (55);
     Blankmanger (58 or 89); Stubbel Goos with Percely
     (67, var. 1 or 2); Chiknes with the Marybones (83);

Pyes (79 or 81) and/or Pastees (24 or 78); Potages of
      Wortes (19), Pesene (20), and Lekes (13)
      Dessert: Peres, Appels, and Grapes White and Rede; Chese;
      Gyngebreed (122); Wafres (126); Ypocras (127)

In adjusting quantities, try to provide a taste of everything,
not a full helping, for every guest at a feast; thus, if you have
twenty guests and are serving Menu 4, you should have
twenty very small Brie tarts or two larger ones (each to be
cut into ten small slices); enough shrimps so that each diner
gets a tablespoon or two; and forty to sixty meatballs. One of
the most important considerations in planning any feast is
the tastes of those likely to sample the food. There should be
some familiar-looking dishes, as well as more exotic ones, not
a plethora of highly spiced stews. Following such principles is
more authentic as well as more pleasing to modern tastes.

For example, most menus should include some of the simple foods which will seem familiar to the most conservative
tastes, such as 20, 26, 42, 49, 64, 76, 114, and 118. Those
with an eye on costs should watch for such recipes as 10, 22,
28, 37, 45, 51, 80, 88, 102, 110, 112, and 122. Dishes with
special appeal for gourmets can be found everywhere but we
might draw special attention to 1, 39, 47, 54, 74, 91, 117,
and 121, as well as those mentioned on the first three menus
given above. Those who are watching for ways to use leftovers, including wilted flowers, will find some dishes which
demand such, including 11, 36, 52, 85, 87, 89, 95, 98, 100,
and 109.

Some may be shocked to hear that we usually serve sherry
before a feast, anachronistic as it may be when sack was,
apparently, not introduced into England until the sixteenth
century. As accompaniments to sherry, or simply set on the
table with the bread, butter, and table wine, we serve olives
and radishes, both of which are mentioned in some Continental menus as preceding the first course. We always serve a
table wine, or choice of table wines, with medieval food.
Those who prefer ale (or milk) will also be properly authentic, if not as aristocratic. Most commercially marketed mead

is too sweet to go with anything but a dessert course. And,
finally, for a proper feast we usually construct a proper subtlety. Any pastry cook, even a relatively inept one, can do
something in this line, although the more spectacular effects
can only be managed by those with plenty of experience at
producing elaborately decorated cakes.

The manner of service of a medieval meal does not really concern us as much as the authenticity (and tastiness) of the
food. Those who yearn for real authenticity may use 'trenchers' instead of plates and deny their guests forks, which were
only used for serving in the middle ages. We find it more
comfortable to use our customary plates and forks. For a
feast we try to set up tables festively, with the white table-
cloths prescribed by medieval authorities and candles to provide illumination. We also see no reason to use medieval
kitchen tools and methods when better ones have replaced
the numerous servants of a large medieval household. Thus
we see no point in straining eggs when we can reach for a
whisk or egg beater, and we find a blender better than a mortar and pestle for most grinding. A mortar is especially useful,
however, for certain jobs such as pulverizing saffron or caraway seeds, both difficult chores – unless you have an electric
coffee grinder. Those who have no grinder and neither blender
nor mortar will have to try rubbing saffron (with some salt or
sugar, depending on the recipe) in a saucer with a spoon. In
any case, we have found that saffron is much easier to grind
if you dry it in a warm oven first.
    Other substances which present special problems are galin-
gale (or ginger root) and bread crumbs. We advise grating
galingale – if you have any – or ginger root with a nutmeg
grater or the fine edge of a grater one uses for lemon peel.
Bread crumbs, the ubiquitous thickening agent of so many
medieval sauces, were no doubt favoured because this was a
way to use up the leftover crusts and broken pieces of bread;
they are also practical because there is no need to make a
roux, as we usually do for a modern flour thickening. But in
no case should one try to use the packaged toasted bread-

crumbs available in boxes at the market. The result will be terribly gritty, and not really very thick. If the recipe calls for toast, use toast, broken into pieces; otherwise, the best bread-crumbs are made from fairly stale bread, ground in a blender or mortar, if possible. They can be rolled with a rolling pin, if necessary. In any case – whether the recipe calls for crumbs or soaked bread or toast – the smoothness of the sauce will be immeasurably better if the sauce is blended in a blender; failing that, blend the crumbs and part of the sauce very thoroughly (preferably in a mortar) before proceeding to the final step: and use a whisk, if possible.

Sometimes our recipes may appear to depart from the original version printed. This is because we have compared different versions of the same dish and when we found a more appealing feature from another source chose to incorporate it. However, we have avoided adding or subtracting anything unless at least one source justified the change. Substitutions are another question. There seems, for example, no good reason why a modern cook should not substitute cornstarch for rice flour if he has no rice flour and does not have a blender in which to pulverize rice grains; the effect will be the same. Nor are we fussy about the bread we serve, as long as it is crusty and reasonably chewy. Round loaves, or large buns, are the most authentic in appearance. We have experimented with barley flour and other grains much used in the middle ages, but it is easiest to rely on a local Portuguese bakery, or others which bake relatively coarse bread in round loaves, and to concentrate our efforts on other foods.

Spices remain a vexed question. We cannot even be sure that we know what some of the common spices were: the 'grains of paradise' sometimes called for is particularly baffling. Information in dictionaries seems to indicate carda-mom, but this is questionable since both are occasionally called for in a single recipe. Cubebs and galingale are difficult to find today, but well worth trying if you can get any. It is hard to see why they ever went out of style, for both are delightfully aromatic. Those who cannot purchase them may substitute pepper and cloves and ginger and cinnamon, respectively: the result will not be all that different.

The evidence as to the nature of the various mixed spice 'powders' is even more confused. One recipe suggests ginger and white sugar as an alternative to 'powdor blanche' while another suggests ginger, cinnamon, and nutmeg – a very different mixture. Further, the latter is very close to the formula suggested elsewhere for 'powdor fort,' of ginger, cinnamon, and mace. Surely a *fort* powder must have been different from one that was *douce* (or *blanche*): some recipes call for a little of two different kinds. It may be thought that the *douce* varieties always contained sugar, but one must still be careful here, since some recipes call for sugar to be added as well as 'powdor douce.' Our general conclusion is that these mixtures must have varied with the individual cook or commercial supplier just as a modern 'curry powder' does – and that this is probably the most meaningful familiar parallel. Indian curries are often made with a particular blend made for the individual dish, and no two cooks are likely to use exactly the same blend, except that there are certain spices which are commonly found in a curry mixture – such as turmeric and chili peppers; another common Indian spice powder, garam masala, invariably excludes turmeric, whatever the proportions of other ingredients may be. The principle of making such powders is, clearly, to allow for the use of very small quantities of individual spices, mixed in a way that will suit the dish to be prepared, whether one buys the spices ready-mixed or grinds them oneself for a particular dish.

Thus, our advice to those making medieval dishes is to mix their own spices, either in a large batch from which a spoonful or two will be taken for this dish or that or in an individual mixture to compliment a particular dish. Mixed spices of the kind sold for apple pies may be used for many dishes, if one wishes. We have suggested particular combinations for each dish calling for unspecified 'powders,' but there is no reason why others should not vary our suggestions, as long as they aim at a stronger mixture for a fort powder as against a

xx douce one. We think, for example, that it would be inadvisable to add pepper or cubebs to a douce powder, or sugar to a fort one. If a recipe calls for sugar, pepper, or another spice – such as ginger – as well as a powdor douce or powdor fort, this does not necessarily mean that there is none in the powder itself; it may simply mean that additional seasoning of the particular type is called for. Again, we draw the reader's attention to the fact that a curry recipe may call for curry powder *and* a particular spice which is represented to a lesser degree in the curry powder.

The sources from which we have drawn recipes are indicated by abbreviations at the end of each original version. These are all from fourteenth and fifteen century sources, although some of the scanty earlier collections have also been consulted, as well as a few slightly later in date. Roman sources, although still in circulation in manuscript in the middle ages, do not seem to have influenced later cooks, and have, thus, been ignored. The collections we found most useful are both fourteenth century: *The Ménagier de Paris* (MP) and *The Forme of Cury* (FC). Other abbreviations signify the following: AC: 'Ancient Cookery,' a two-part collection appended to FC in the printed editions; N: Napier's *A Noble Boke of Cookry*; LCC: *Liber Cure Cocorum;* HARL: ms Harleian, both 279 and 4016 (which one is indicated by number). Other mss are designated by their usual names. Recipes from various mss appear in a number of the books listed in the bibliography, page 161.

NOTES

1 See the bibliography for further information on this and all other sources cited, as well as generally informative works.
2 Readers who may be skeptical about whether we have done our scholarly homework are referred to the annotated bibliography and to C.B. Hieatt's forthcoming article ' "To boille the chiknes with the marybones": Hodge's Kitchen Revisited,' which goes into some of the matters touched on in a more thorough, and thoroughly annotated, version.

Soppes and Potages

In this section are all the dishes most likely to be considered soups today, as well as vegetables in broth which may be served either as soups or as accompaniments to meat. Thicker meat and fish pottages are listed in the sections on fish and stews; salads and fried or sautéed vegetables, in the section on entremets.

1 Tredure

Take Brede and grate it. Make a lyre of rawe ayren and do þer=to Safron and powdor douce and lye it up with gode broth; and make it as a Cawdel, and do þerto a lytel verious.

FC 15

Golden Soup

4 cups chicken, lamb, or pork broth
1 cup breadcrumbs
2 eggs, beaten
optional: 1/8 tsp each cardamon, coriander; pinch saffron
1/2 tsp salt (or to taste)
2 tbsp lemon juice

Bring the broth to a boil. Meanwhile, beat the breadcrumbs together with the eggs and spices. Off the heat, beat egg mixture into broth; return to very low heat for a few minutes, stirring constantly, to thicken a bit; do not allow mixture to boil. Stir in lemon juice.

2 Jowtes of Almand Mylke

Take erbes; boile hem, hewe hem, and grynde hem smale; and drawe hem up with water. Set hem on the fire and seeþ the jowtes with the mylke; and cast þeron sugar & salt, & serue it forth. FC 88

Green Almond Soup

ca 2 cups spinach (tightly packed down whole leaves –
  about 1/2 lb – raw; if you wish to use leftover cooked
  spinach, use about 1 cup, drained; less if the cooked
  spinach is chopped)
3-4 scallions, cut in pieces
2-3 sprigs parsley
6 cups water
1 1/2 tsp salt (or to taste)
1 tsp sugar
8 oz ground almonds or 4 oz almonds plus 1 tbsp cornstarch,
  dissolved in 2 tbsp cold water

Bring the water to a boil, adding salt; put in spinach and scallions and boil about 4 minutes; then add parsley, boil for a few more seconds, then remove from the heat. Drain, reserving the cooking water. Chop the vegetables very fine – or put in a blender with the almonds and a little of the cooking water and blend. Stir together greens, almonds, and all the reserved water, adding the sugar, in the saucepan, and return to the stove. Simmer together gently for about five minutes. Then stir in cornstarch dissolved in water, and simmer for a few more minutes before serving.

VARIATIONS
1 The soup may be chilled and served cold.
2 Watercress, sorrel, or other greens may be substituted for the spinach. A few leaves of fresh herbs from the garden, if you are lucky enough to have some, would be a welcome

addition, providing they are not added in such strength as to overwhelm the delicate flavour of the basic soup. (For this reason, dried herbs may be a bit dangerous.)

3 𝔖𝔬𝔴𝔭𝔭𝔰 𝔇𝔬𝔯𝔯𝔭

𝔑𝔶𝔪 𝔬𝔫𝔶𝔬𝔫𝔰 𝔞𝔫𝔡 𝔪𝔶𝔫𝔠𝔢 𝔥𝔢𝔪 𝔰𝔪𝔞𝔩𝔢 𝔞𝔫𝔡 𝔣𝔯𝔶 𝔥𝔢𝔪 𝔦𝔫 𝔬𝔭𝔩 𝔡𝔬𝔩𝔶𝔣. 𝔑𝔶𝔪 𝔴𝔶𝔫 𝔞𝔫𝔡 𝔟𝔬𝔶𝔩𝔢 𝔶𝔱 𝔴𝔶𝔱𝔥 𝔱𝔥𝔢 𝔬𝔫𝔶𝔬𝔲𝔫𝔰; 𝔱𝔬𝔰𝔱𝔢 𝔴𝔶𝔱𝔢 𝔟𝔯𝔢𝔡 𝔞𝔫𝔡 𝔡𝔬 𝔶𝔱 𝔦𝔫 𝔡𝔦𝔰𝔠𝔥𝔦𝔰, 𝔞𝔫𝔡 𝔤𝔬𝔡 𝔄𝔩𝔪𝔞𝔫𝔡𝔢 𝔪𝔶𝔩𝔨 𝔞𝔩𝔰𝔬, 𝔞𝔫𝔡 𝔡𝔬 𝔱𝔥𝔢𝔯' 𝔞𝔟𝔬𝔳𝔢, 𝔞𝔫𝔡 𝔰𝔢𝔯𝔳𝔢 𝔶𝔱 𝔣𝔬𝔯𝔱𝔥𝔢. AC.II.6

Other recipes for this soup, under the title of 'Sowp Dorry' or 'Soupes Dorroy,' etc, do not always include the onions: without them, it is simply a soup of almonds and wine indistinguishable from Cawdel of Almand Mylk (6); with them, it becomes a forerunner of the modern type of onion soup; but still quite different. Austin (p 127, 'Dorre') glosses as 'endored,' gilded; but such 'Sops' were not notably golden. Perhaps the etymology here is, rather, *du roi*, royal; wine was not a cheap ingredient.

Onion Soup

3 or 4 large onions, minced or thinly sliced
1/4 cup olive oil
1 bottle dry white wine (or use half wine and half water)
4 tbsp ground almonds
bread, sliced and toasted
salt to taste

Heat the oil in a large stew-pan and stir the onions in; let them cook over low heat, stirring occasionally, for 5-10 minutes. Meanwhile, soak the almonds in 1/2 cup of the wine plus 1/2 cup boiling water. Then add the rest of the wine to the onions; cover the pot and let simmer for 15 minutes; add

almond mixture and cook for a few more minutes. Salt to taste.

   To serve in the true medieval style, place a slice of toasted bread in each serving bowl, and pour the soup over the toast. Such 'sops' give 'soup' its name.

4 Fenkel in Soppes

Take blades of Fenkel; shrede hem not to smale, do hem to seeþ in water and oile and oynons mynced þerwith. Do þerto safron and salt and powdor douce. Serue it forth; take brede ptosted and lay þe sewe onoward. FC 77

Fennel Soup

1 bunch fennel
2 onions, minced
4 cups water (more or less, depending on desired thickness
   and number to be served)
1/4 cup olive oil
optional: pinch saffron
1/8 tsp each ginger, pepper
1 tsp salt, or to taste

Cut the white part of the fennel into shreds – about one inch by 1/2 inch. (The green, feathery part of the fennel may be saved for salads or other uses – for example, see Spynoch Yfryed (40), and Salat (44).) Heat the oil in a heavy pot, and stir the onions and fennel in the oil over low heat until they are slightly wilted, but not browned. Add water, and seasonings, and bring to a boil. Simmer for about 20 minutes (or longer, if fennel does not seem tender). Place a slice of toasted bread in each bowl, and pour the soup over the toast.

VARIATION
Fennel cooked the same way, but with less water (1 cup is enough) may be served as a vegetable dish.

5 Blandissorpe

Take the ȝolkys of Eggs sodyn and temper it wyth mylk of a kow and do ther'to Compn and Safron and flowr' of ris or wastel bred mynced and grynd in a morter and temper it up wyth the milk and mak it boyle and do ther'to wit of Egg' corbyn smale and tak fat chese and kerf ther'to wan the li= cour is boylyd and serve it forth. AC II.19

Even the etymology of this dish is somewhat confusing, since many of the recipes include (as this one does) saffron, so that it is hardly *'blanc.'* Most contain chicken meat rather than eggs and cheese, and are thickened with almonds and rice flour, using water rather than milk; many advise sweetening with sugar. Anyone who wishes to try such variants is welcome, but we rather prefer this one. If you wish to serve it as a thick sauce or side dish, use half the recommended amount of milk.

Soup of Milk, Eggs, and Cheese

6 eggs, hard boiled
3 cups milk
1/2 - 1 cup bread crumbs (depending on how finely ground)
   or 3 tbsp rice flour or cornstarch
1/4 tsp each cumin and saffron, ground (if you must grind
   the saffron yourself, do it in a mortar or saucer with the
   salt)
1/2 tsp salt
ca 3/4 cup soft or semi-soft cheese, cut into fairly small
   pieces

Beat together the egg yolks, milk, and all other ingredients except egg whites and cheese: a blender is useful for this. Cook, stirring constantly, in a pan over medium heat until thick. Then add the egg whites, minced, and cheese, and stir for a few minutes more before serving.

6 Cawdel of Almand Mylk

Take almands blanched and drawe hem up with wyne; do perto powder of gynger and sugar, and color it with Safron. Boile it and serue it forth. FC 87

An otherwise similar recipe in the same collection calls for water rather than wine, omits saffron, and adds rice flour and salt. The Ménagier recommends making almond milk by mixing ground almonds with water in which onions have been cooked. All three sources have been drawn upon for the following recipe. If you wish to use this as a sauce, use somewhat less liquid (eg, 1 cup each white wine and water).

Almond Soup

2 oz (1/4 cup) ground almonds
2 tbsp rice flour or cornstarch
1 1/2 cups each white wine and water, preferably water in
   which onions have been parboiled
1/2 tsp salt
1/4 tsp each ginger, sugar
pinch ground saffron

Mix the almonds and rice flour or cornstarch with some of the wine (cold); add the ground spices and gradually stir in the rest of the liquids. Put over medium hot heat and bring to a boil, stirring. Simmer, stirring fairly frequently, for five to ten minutes, or until the soup seems thick enough. Serve hot.

VARIATION
For those who tire of the taste of saffron, try using rosé wine instead of white and omitting the saffron; it was not an invariable ingredient, as the notes above indicate, and rosé wine will give an equally interesting pastel colour — and slight flavour. (Remember, too, that for colour effects food colouring may be substituted for saffron.)

7 Oystrys in Bruette

Take an shele Oystrys, an kepe þe water þat cometh of hem, an strayne it, an put it in a potte, & Ale þer=to, an a lytil brede þer=to; put Gyngere, Canel, Pouder of Pepir þer=to, Safroun an Salt; an whan it is y=now al=moste, putte on þin Oystrys: loke þat þey ben wel y=wasshe for þe schullys: & þan serue forth. HARL 279.92

Oysters Stewed in Ale

8 oz oysters (use canned if you must, but fresh are much
    better)
12 oz ale
6 tbsp bread crumbs
1/8 tsp each ginger, cinnamon
1/4 tsp pepper
1/2 tsp salt
pinch of saffron (preferably ground)

Drain the liquid from shelled oysters (or the can, if using canned oysters) into a pan with the ale; add breadcrumbs and spices, and bring to a boil – carefully, as the ale is likely to foam over. Lower heat and stir for about five minutes, or until well blended and thickened to the consistency of a fairly thick soup. Then add oysters and stir a few minutes more. Serve hot. This amount will serve three generously, four more sparsely, as a first course; if you wish to serve as a main dish, allow this much for two.

8 Muscules in Broth

Take Muscules, And sith hem, and pike hem oute of the shell; And drawe the broth thorgh a strepnour into a faire vessell, And sette hit on the fire; And then take faire brede, and stepe hit with þe same broth, and draw hit thorgh a strepnour, And cast in=to a potte with þe sewe, and menge oynons, wyn, and pouder peper, and lete boyle; & cast there= to the Musculis and pouder ginger, and saffron, and salte; And then serue ye hit forthe. HARL 4016

Mussel Soup

1 qt fresh mussels, or at least 4 oz canned mussels (in brine)
1/4 cup breadcrumbs
2 onions, chopped, fried in a little oil or butter until soft but
  not brown
2 cups each white wine, mussel broth (add water to make up
  the necessary quantity, if using canned mussels)
1/4 tsp each pepper (white), ginger
pinch saffron

Scrub the mussels well and steam them in about 3 cups water, if using fresh mussels, for about 10 minutes. Remove from broth; allow to cool slightly and discard shells. Strain broth before proceeding. Moisten breadcrumbs with a little broth (brine from the can, if using canned mussels). While the crumbs steep for a few minutes, sauté onions. Blend crumb mixture in a blender or put through a strainer; then add to onions, together with wine, broth, and spices. Let simmer for at least 10 minutes before adding mussels; continue to heat just until mussels are heated through again.

VARIATIONS

Ale may be substituted for wine, or both omitted; a little vinegar may be added (preferably as a moistening for the crumbs), and/or other spices, such as cinnamon.

9 Whyte Mortrewes of Fysshe

Take codling, haddock oþ hake and lyveres with the rawnes and seeþ it well in water; pyke out þe bones, grynde smale the Fysshe, draw a lyour of almands & brede with the self broth; and do the Fysshe gronden þerto; and seeþ it and do þerto powdor fort, safron and salt, and make it stondyng.
FC 125

Other recipes for 'white' mortrews do not call for saffron, and we found it better to use other savory ingredients here.

Fish Soup or Pâté

1 lb cod or haddock, poached
2 cups water
1 cup white wine
1 slice onion
1 sprig parsley
1/4 cup each rice flour (or cornstarch), ground almonds
1 cup milk (or water, but in this case double the amount of almonds; cow's milk is cheaper than almond milk)
1 1/2 tsp salt (approximately)
1/4 tsp each white pepper, ginger
1/8 tsp nutmeg

Poach the fish in water and wine with the parsley, onion, and a little salt, for about ten minutes. Drain, straining broth. While fish is poaching, mix almonds and rice flour with milk and leave to steep. Put fish in blender (or use a mortar, followed by a strainer: blending is much easier) with enough of the strained broth to cover, and blend until smooth. Mix spices with a spoonful of water to completely dissolve. Then mix all ingredients together in a saucepan and simmer gently, for about five minutes, stirring. It should be a very thick soup. Taste for salt: underseasoning is inadvisable. It can be reheated later, but avoid boiling, as it may curdle.

VARIATION

To serve as a sort of paté rather than as soup, halve all liquid ingredients.

10 Roo Broth

Take the lire of the Deer oþer of the Roo; parboil it on smale peces. Seeþ it well, half in water and half in wyne. Take brede and bray it wiþ the self broth and drawe blode þer=to, and lat it seeth to=gedre with powdor fort of gynger oþer of cannell and macys, with a grete porcion of vinegar with Raysons of Corante. FC 14

This is a good way to use leftover bits of roast venison.

Venison Soup

ca 1 lb venison, cooked or parboiled, cut into small pieces
ca 1 1/2 cups each water, red wine
1/2 cup breadcrumbs (use wholewheat bread or rye – the
  darker the better)
1/4 tsp each ginger, cinnamon, mace
1 tsp salt
1/4 cup vinegar (preferably red wine vinegar)
1/4 cup currants
1 tsp Marmite, or other yeast-based gravy seasoning
  (in lieu of blood)

Cover the chopped venison with wine and water; simmer for about an hour. Steep the breadcrumbs in some of the broth (and the Marmite or other colouring), and stir into the pot, along with currants and seasonings. Simmer for about five minutes more, stirring occasionally, before serving.

11 Mortrews

𝔑ym hennyn and porke and seth hem togedere. 𝔑ym the lyre of the hennyn and the porke and hakkyth smale and grynd hit al to dust, and wyte bred therwyth, and temper it wyth the selve broth and with heyryn, and colore it with sa= fron; and boyle it and disch it, and cast thereon powder of peper and of gyngyner, and serve it forth. AC 5

Cream Soup of Pork and Chicken

ca 1 lb each (including bone) chicken and pork, or enough
   to yield around 2 cups cooked, chopped meat
2 slices bread (better if on the stale side)
2 eggs
large pinch saffron
1/4 tsp each ginger, white pepper
1 tsp salt (or more)

Cover the pork and chicken – or, if you are using leftover cooked meat, the bones and any odds and ends – with at least a quart of salted water. Wine (white) may be used for part of the cooking water, and a slice or two of onion adds to the flavour. Simmer for about an hour. Remove meat from broth, and discard all skin and bones. Strain broth and reserve. Cut the meat into small chunks and puree in a blender (or use a meat grinder or mortar: a blender is much the best, however) with bread, spices, eggs, and enough of the broth to cover amply. It should be very smooth. Stir into the rest of the broth, and cook over low heat, stirring constantly, until thick. If it curdles, blend again, or rub through a strainer. More water may be added if it is too thick, but it should be quite thick. Taste for salt: underseasoning is to be avoided.

VARIATIONS
1 Some recipes call for pork only.
2 A little ale (or beer) may be added at the moment when

the whole mixture comes to a boil; this helps to keep it from getting too hot and curdling. Try a half cup, if you wish. Sugar and/or cinnamon are sometimes added: 1 tsp sugar and 1/4 tsp cinnamon can be recommended.

See also Whyte Mortrewes of Fysshe (9): and note that with less liquid this can be served as a sort of paté.

12 Black Porray

Black porray is made with strips of spiced bacon. The porray should be picked over, washed, then cut up and blanched in boiling water, then fried in fat from the bacon slices; then you moisten it with boiling water—yet some say that if it is washed in cold water it is darker and more black—and you should set upon each bowl two slices of bacon. MP

The 'bowls' called for are probably servings for two though they may be individual bowls.

Greens braised with Bacon

2 lbs beet, dandelion, or other greens (such as spinach)
6-8 slices bacon

Pick over and wash the greens, then chop them and boil for three to five minutes in a large pot of boiling water; drain, and run cold water over them, then roll in paper towelling to dry as much as possible. Meanwhile, fry the bacon strips until brown and crisp, and set aside. Add the greens to the fat left in the frying pan and stir, over medium low heat, for several minutes, until well wilted and dark in colour. While the Ménagier calls for adding water at the moment before serving, this is not really necessary unless you wish to serve this as a soup. Serve with the bacon strips arranged over the top of the greens. If it is to be used as soup, add boiling water and crumble the bacon.

13 Blaunchyd Porray

Take thykke mylke of almondes dere
And leke hedes þou take with stalk in fere,
Þat is in peses þou stryke;
Put alle in pot, alye hit ilyke
With a lytel floure, and serve hit þenne
Wele soþun, in sale, before gode menne. LCC

Creamed Leeks

2 bunches of leeks, washed, trimmed, and sliced
2 tbsp ground almonds
2 tbsp flour (preferably instant-blending)
2 cups water, or 1 cup each water and milk
1 tsp salt

Mix the almonds and flour to a paste with a little of the
water, and gradually beat in the rest of the water. (A blender
is best, but it is not difficult to do by hand.) Bring to a boil,
stirring, until the sauce is very thick. Add salt and sliced leeks
and simmer for about ten minutes.

VARIATIONS
The Ménagier advises blanching (or parboiling, depending on
the season: winter leeks, he says, are older and require full
parboiling) the leeks; then adding them to some lightly fried
onions until they wilt before putting them in white sauce to
finish cooking. He recommends milk, except in Lent, when
almond milk was necessary, and suggests bread as a thickening. On meat days, he adds, they may be cooked in a broth of
pork or salted pork (ham, bacon) and served with bacon. If
using any of these variations involving blanching or parboiling,
cut the final cooking time in the sauce down to five minutes.

14 Caboches in Potage

Take Caboches and quarter hem and seeth hem in gode broth with Oynons y-mynced and the whyte of Lekes y-slit and corue smale, and do þer-to safron and salt, and force it with powdor douce. FC 4

After following these directions as exactly as possible, we concluded that the Ménagier of Paris is right in suggesting that it is a better idea to cut up cabbages before cooking them, rather than to cook them in such large pieces as quarters. Others may like it as well in the larger pieces, however.

Cabbage Stew

1 head cabbage, cut in quarters or shredded
2 onions, sliced thin or minced
2-3 leeks, washed and chopped
1/2 tsp salt (or less, if broth is well seasoned)
2 cups (approximately) meat broth or stock
1/8 tsp each cardamom and coriander (ground)
optional: 1 tsp sugar, pinch of saffron (scant)

Bring all ingredients to a boil and simmer for about 20 minutes (somewhat less if cabbage is shredded fine).

15 Gourdes in Potage

Take young Gowrds; pare hem and kerue hem on pecys; cast hem in gode broth, and do þer=to a gode party of Oynons mynced. Take Pork soden; grynd it and alye it þer=with and wiþ ȝolkes of ayren. Do þer=to safron and salt, and messe it forth with powder douce. FC 8

'Gourds' may mean gourds, squash, pumpkin, or even cucumbers. In this case, squash seems an appropriate choice, but pumpkin is perfectly feasible.

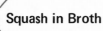

Squash in Broth

2 lbs squash or pumpkin, peeled, seeded, and cut into chunks
3-4 onions, minced
3 cups meat broth (approximately)
1/2-1 cup ground, cooked pork
2 egg yolks (or one whole egg), beaten
pinch saffron
salt to taste
1/8 tsp each cinnamon and ginger
1 tsp sugar

Boil the squash in the broth with the onions; stir in ground pork and seasonings when almost done. Take off the fire and beat in egg or egg yolks just before serving.

VARIATIONS
1 Parboil the squash in salted water for 20 minutes, or until soft; mash, and add beef or pork drippings rather than broth. Season with salt and saffron.
2 Prepare as in variation 1, but sprinkle the saffron over the cooked squash in threads as a decorative touch: the Ménagier says this is known as 'fringed with saffron.'

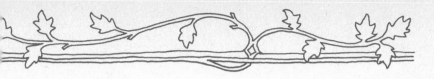

16 Rapes in Potage

Take rapus and make hem clene and waissh hem clene;
quare hem; parboile hem; take hem up, caste hem in a gode
broth and seeþ hem. Mynce Oynons and cast þer=to Safron
and Salt and messe it forth with powdor douce. In the wise
make of Pasturnakes and skyrwates. FC 5

Turnips in Broth

2 lbs white turnips, cut in quarters or chunks (after peeling)
2 cups meat broth
2 onions, minced
1/2 tsp salt
optional: pinch of saffron, and/or 1/8 tsp each cardamom
   and coriander; 1 tsp sugar

Parboil turnips in a pot of boiling, salted water for about 5
minutes; then drain, and put in a pan with onions, broth, and
seasonings, and simmer until tender (10-30 minutes, depending on the age and size of the turnips).

VARIATION
Cook parsnips, yellow turnips, or carrots the same way, or
try a mixture.

17 Tornep with Chestenne

Young, small turnips should be cooked in water without
wine for the first boiling. Then throw away the water
and cook slowly in water and wine, with chestnuts therein,
or, if one has no chestnuts, sage. MP

Even if one does have chestnuts, sage seems to improve the
dish.

Turnips with Chestnuts

2 lbs small white turnips, peeled (or use medium ones,
   peeled and quartered)
5 cups water
1 cup white wine
1/4 - 1/2 lb chestnuts, shelled (that is, as many as you
   have time and energy to shell), *and/or*
1/2 tsp dried sage, or a sprig of fresh sage (more if you are
   not using chestnuts)
salt

To shell chestnuts: one method is to pare off a strip of skin
from each chestnut (using a small, sharp knife), then drop
them, a few at a time, into boiling water. When they have
boiled a few minutes, remove from the water and peel off the
rest of the shell.

Parboil the turnips in 4 cups boiling, salted water for five
minutes. Drain and recover with remaining cup of water and
the wine; add shelled chestnuts and sage, as well as a little
more salt, and bring back to a boil. Lower the heat and simmer gently for about 30 minutes.

18 Funges

𝕿ake Funges and pare hem clene and dyce hem; take leke
and shred hym small and do hym to seeþ in gode broth. Color
it with safron and do þer=inne powdor fort. FC 10

Mushrooms

1 lb mushrooms, washed and sliced (not too thinly)
1 bunch leeks, washed and shredded
1-2 cups broth, preferably chicken

1/8 tsp each ginger, cardamom, allspice, white pepper
salt to taste
optional: pinch of saffron

Simmer vegetables and spices in the broth for 10-15 minutes. If you wish to serve this as a soup rather than as a vegetable dish, use more broth.

19 Buttered Wortes

Take al maner of good herbes that thou may gete, and do bi ham as is foresaid; putte hem on þe fire with faire water; put þere-to clarefied buttur a grete quantite. Whan thei ben boyled ynogh, salt hem; late none otemele come therein. Dise brede small in disshes, and powre on þe wortes, and serue hem forth. HARL 4016

The 'wortes' mentioned in the recipe occurring just before this in the ms include cabbage leaves, beet greens, borage, parsley, and leeks: in other words, use any combination of greens and vegetables of the onion family.

Buttered Greens

2-3 lbs mixed greens (spinach and parsley, if nothing else is in season)
2-3 leeks or onions
2 tbsp butter (or more)
4-6 slices bread, diced and lightly toasted

Blanch the greens and leeks or onions in a large pot of boiling, salted water for three or four minutes – no more. Drain, squeeze out excess water, and chop. Put in a pan with the butter and about 1/2 cup fresh water; stir, cover, and leave over very low heat for another five minutes. Salt to taste and serve, mixed with toasted bread cubes. (*more*)

Water may be decreased to 1/4 cup; on the other hand, if one desires to serve this as a soup, increase the water to 1 cup, or more – this is more probably the way it was served in the 15th century.

20 Grene Pesen

𝔗ake yonge grene pesen, and sethe hom with gode broth of beef, and take parsell, sage, saverap, and psope, and a lytel brede, and bray all this in a morter, and sume of the pesen therwyth, and tempur hit wyth the broth, and do hit in a pot to the other pesen, and let hit boyle togedur, and serve hit forth. ARUNDEL

Two closely related recipes advise only parsley and mint, or parsley and hyssop, so our feeling that these should be the preponderant herbs is strengthened.

Green Peas

3 lbs fresh green peas, shelled, or, if peas are out of season,
   2 packages of frozen peas
1 cup beef broth (or use chicken — it is just as good)
2 sprigs parsley
a few leaves of mint, or 1/2 tsp dried mint
1 or 2 sage leaves and a bit of savory
   (or 1/8 to 1/4 tsp each dried)
1 slice bread (slightly stale)

Boil the peas in broth until almost done (about 12 minutes). Grind herbs and bread in a mortar or blender with some of the broth; add about 1/2 cup of the cooked peas and continue to blend, adding more broth, until you have a smooth, fairly thick sauce. Drain the rest of the peas and reheat (gently) in this sauce.

21 Ryse of Flessh

Take Ryse and waisshe hem clene, and do hem in erthen pot with gode broth and lat hem seeþ wel. Afterward take Almand mylke and do þerto, and color it wiþ safron, and salt, and messe forth. FC 9

Rice in Meat Broth

1 cup raw rice
2 1/2 cups chicken or meat broth
2 tbsp ground almonds
1/2 tsp salt (or less, if broth is sufficiently salty)
pinch saffron

Put the rice in a pot with a well-fitting lid, and add 2 cups of the broth. Bring to a boil; cover and turn the heat down very low. Bring the rest of the broth to a boil separately; remove it from the heat and stir in almonds, saffron, and salt. Cover and let steep.

   When the rice has been cooking for about 15 minutes, add the almond mixture, cover again, and let it continue to cook over very low heat for another five minutes, or until it has absorbed most of the moisture.

VARIATIONS
1 For Ris engoulé in the French style, rice should be washed in several waters, then cooked in rather more water than is advised above for about ten minutes, drained, and spread out in a large, flat pan and left in a warm place to dry out. (A low, or barely on, oven is fine.) Then add meat drippings and saffron, and cook for another five or ten minutes.
2 Ris engoulé to go with fish is made the same way except that almond milk (as above, but use water instead of broth) is used in place of drippings; the Ménagier advises a little sugar instead of saffron.

22 Frumenty

𝔑ym clene 𝔚ete and bray it in a morter wel that the holys gon al of and seyth yt til it breste and nym yt up, and lat it kele and nym fayre fresch broth and swete mylk of Almandys or swete mylk of kyne and temper yt al, and nym the yolkys of eyryn; boyle it a lityl and set yt adon and messe yt forthe wyth fat venyson and fresh moton. AC 1

Modern packagers of cracked wheat (or Bulgur, a popular variety) relieve us of the tedious preprocessing here. Egg yolks are not always called for, nor need one use two or more of the recommended liquids. Sweetened and/or with milk, the effect is like a modern breakfast porridge, but in broth this is an excellent accompaniment to meats.

Cracked Wheat

1 cup cracked wheat
3 cups meat or chicken stock or bouillon, or use half milk
optional: pinch of saffron, 1 or 2 egg yolks

Bring the stock to a boil and stir in the wheat (and saffron, if desired). Cover the pan and turn the heat very low; let the frumenty cook for about 45 minutes. It may be served then as it is, or you can remove it from the heat, stir in beaten egg yolk, then return to very low heat and stir for a few minutes before serving.

VARIATION
Barley was also used this way, and is excellent. Small pearl barley takes about the same time to cook, or just a little longer. If using barley, saffron is particularly desirable, and the egg added at the end a vast improvement.

Entremets

This section includes specialities suitable for serving as hors d'oeuvres and side dishes (although some of the latter may be found in the section on soups and pottages) as well as eggs and cold dishes. At a medieval feast such dishes were sometimes served as a first course, but usually appeared after the simpler roasts and pottages.

23 Tart de Bry

𝔗ake a 𝔠rust ynche depe in a trap. 𝔗ake zolkes of 𝔄yren rawe and chese ruayn, & medle it & þe zolkes togyder; and do þerto powdor gynger, sugar, safron, and salt. 𝔇o it in a trap; bake it and serue it forth. FC 166

Brie Tart

pastry for one open tart shell or 2 dozen very small tarts
6 egg yolks (or 3 whole eggs)
5 oz soft, runny cheese, preferably Brie; rind pared off
1/4 tsp each ginger, salt
optional: 1/4 cup sugar (only if to be served as a dessert)
scant pinch saffron

Mash the cheese and beat in the eggs and seasonings; put in tart shell or shells and bake in a 375° oven for 15 to 20 minutes, or until *lightly* browned. Do not overcook, especially if they are to be reheated before serving (they should be served warm, if used as appetizers).

Ideally, mix this in a blender. If you have none, beat eggs well before adding mashed cheese, and beat until the whole mixture seems light, as well as thoroughly smooth. Do not overfill tart shells: about half-full is enough, as the mixture will puff during baking. This puffy effect may fall a bit when the tart is taken from the oven, but, if you are careful, there will still be a slightly rounded look to the top.

24 Mushroom Pasties

Mushrooms of one night are the best, if they are small, red inside, and closed at the top; and they should be peeled and then washed in hot water and parboiled, and if you wish to put them in a pasty add oil, cheese, and spice powder. MP

Perhaps it really was necessary to peel mushrooms and wash them in hot water in 14th century France, but we doubt that the kind of little button mushroom here described need be treated so today: a scrubbing in cold water should suffice. In making them into pasties, we prefer to use open tart shells, although medieval pasties were made like turnovers: one put the filling on top of a piece of rolled pastry, then doubled the pastry over and pinched the edges together. But this makes rather a lot of pastry in proportion to filling, particularly if you make them very small, as we do when serving a large number of people. We suspect medieval people also found all that pastry superfluous at a dinner with many courses, since the treatises on carving and serving at tables regularly advise the server to remove the top of the pasty and serve the contents.

Mushroom Pasties

One full recipe pastry (enough to make a two-crust pie),
   rolled and cut into pieces a little over twice the size of the
   desired pasties; *or* 12 small tart cases (made from your own
   pastry, or from the frozen food case at the supermarket)
3/4 lb small button mushrooms
1-2 oz cheese, grated: 1 oz each of cheddar and parmesan
   is excellent for this purpose
2 tbsp olive oil
1/2 tsp salt (approximately)
1/4 tsp ginger
1/8 tsp ground pepper

Wash mushrooms, and pare away the bottom of the stems, but leave whole. Parboil in salted water for 3-4 minutes. Drain, and mix with oil and seasonings; if you are using tart shells, rather than making a sort of turnover, reserve the cheese to sprinkle on top. Fill the tart shells or make turnovers; bake in a 425° oven for about 20 minutes, or until lightly browned.

VARIATION
A large open tart of mushrooms prepared in this way makes an excellent first-course dish for a dinner.

25 Tart in Ymbre Day

Take and parboile Oynons; presse out þe water & hewe hem smale; take brede & bray it in a mortar, and temper it up with Ayren; do þerto butter, saffron and salt, & raisons corans, & a litel sugar with powdor douce, and bake it in a trap, & serue it forth. FC 165

Tart for an Ember Day

2 large onions
1 tbsp melted butter
4 eggs
2 tbsp bread crumbs
pinch saffron
1/2 tsp salt
1/8 tsp sugar (plus, if you wish, a pinch of one or two mild spices, such as cardamom and mace)
ca 2 tbsp currants
unbaked pie shell

Parboil the onions for about five minutes; cool and chop (or

chop first, then parboil and strain: it is easier). Add butter to thoroughly drained onions. Mix remaining ingredients together in a bowl; add onions; pour into pie shell. Bake at 350° for 30 to 40 minutes, until the filling is set and the pastry lightly browned.

26 Creuʏce

𝕭oil in water and wine and eat with vinegar. MP

Crayfish

Other shellfish may be treated the same way — lobster tails make a fine substitute for crayfish, though the frozen ones are apt to be a bit tough. Crayfish, like shrimp, should be cleaned after cooking, to remove the intestinal tract. Medieval authorities counsel one to remove the flesh of crayfish or crab from the shell and cut the meat into strips; legs, however, can be served in the shell, with the shell cracked. Shrimps were served shelled. John Russell counsels,

Shrympes welle pyked, þe scales away ye cast,
Round abowt a sawcer ley ye þem in hast;
Þe vinegre in þe same sawcer, þat youre iord may attast,
Þan with þe said fische he may fede hym & of þem
   make no wast.

27 Gele of Fyssh

𝕿ake Tenches, pʏkes, eelʏs, turbot, and plaʏs; kerue hem to pecʏs. Scalde hem & waische hem clene. Drʏe hem with a cloth and do hem in a pane; do þerto half vʏnegar & half wʏne & seeth it wel; & take the Fʏsche and pike it clene; cole the broth thurgh a cloth into an erthen pane. Do þerto

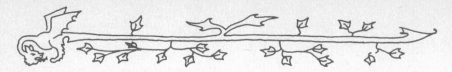

powdor of pepper and safron ynowh. Lat it seep and skym it wel whan it is ysode; dof þe grees clene; cowche fisshe on chargeors & cole the sewe thorow a cloth onoward, & serue it forth. FC 101

This particular recipe does not seem to be a cold, jellied dish, and those who so wish may serve it hot. However, comparison with similar recipes, which are explicit on this point, makes it clear that such dishes often were jelled: a version we prefer. The jelling was effected by the concentration of fish: other recipes tell us to add fish skins, etc, if the liquid will not 'catch.' Modern cooks will find it easier and safer to add powdered geletine. Later recipes often allowed for water, as well as wine and vinegar, in the cooking broth; a combination of these, with higher proportions of the wine and vinegar than is apt to be found in a more modern recipe, produced a highly satisfactory flavour.

The most attractive way to present this dish is to use one whole fish and cut other, smaller fish into slices (through the spine). This will produce a handsome dish if you have an oval dish a little longer than the whole fish in which to arrange the effect. Another consideration is that the jelly should cover the fish: so measure the content of your serving dish and calculate the amount of liquid needed to exactly cover the fish before you start, adjusting the quantities accordingly.

Fish in Jelly

1 whole fish, ca 1 1/2 to 2 lbs (pike, bass, trout, or pickerel are suitable; or try flounder, plaice, or a flatter fish, if you can get one with the skin on)
ca 1 lb smaller fish (eel is particularly suitable) cut into slices about an inch thick
2 cups each water, vinegar, and white wine – or more, if needed to cover fish while it poaches: if liquid must be increased, use the same proportions

1/4 tsp salt (or more, in proportion to liquid)
1/8 tsp ground white pepper
pinch saffron
1 envelope unflavoured gelatine, soaked in 1/4 cup cold water

Bring cooking broth (water, wine, and vinegar) to a boil; salt and turn down the heat. Poach the fish *gently* in this broth for 15-20 minutes, adding the cut-up pieces of fish after the whole fish has been cooking for 5-10 minutes. Be sure to remove the fish before it shows signs of beginning to fall apart. Put it aside and allow to cool. Add the pepper and saffron to the cooking broth and leave it to steep while the fish cools.

Skin the fish carefully and arrange in the serving dish, with the smaller pieces around the whole fish. Soak the gelatine, and let it stand while you strain the broth and bring 2 1/2 cups of the strained broth to a boil. (If you need to increase the amount of broth by more than a half cup, you will have to increase the amount of gelatine also.) Off the heat, stir the measured, hot broth into the soaked gelatine, stirring until well dissolved. Pour this over the fish in its dish.

If you wish to decorate the dish further, use sprigs of parsley and/or slivered blanched almonds. When cool, put in refrigerator or other cool place to chill until well set.

28 Pommeaulx

Take fayre buttys of Vele and hewe hem, and grynd hem in a morter, and wyth þe ȝolkes of eyroun, and with þe whyte of eyroun; and caste þer-to powder Peppyr, Canel, Gyngere, Clowys powþer, and datys y-mynced, Safroun, and raysonys of Coraunce, and sethe in a panne wyth fayre water, and let it boyle; þan wete þin handys in Raw eyroun, þan take it and rolle it in þin handys, smaller or gretter, as þow wolt haue it, an caste it in-to boyling water, an let boyle y-now; þan putte it on a Spete round and let hem rosty; þen take flowre an ȝolkes of eyroun, an þe whyte, and draw hem þorwe a straynowre, an caste þer-to pouder Gyngere, an make

þin þature grene with þe Ius of Percely, or Malwys, in tyme of ʒere Whete, an caste on þe pommys as þey turne a-boute, anð serve forth. HARL 279.46

Comparison with similar recipes indicates that, as usual, considerable leeway is available to the cook in making such meatballs. Sometimes the meat was boiled before it was chopped up; sometimes balls were poached in a sauce rather than grilled: the sauce specified for poaching Pumpes is a white sauce made with almond milk and rice flour, and seasoned with mace. We prefer our Pommeaulx small (no more than two inches in diameter). A composite recipe:

Meat Balls

2 lbs ground meat (veal, pork, lamb, beef, or a combination)
2 eggs, slightly beaten
1 tsp salt
1/2 tsp each ground ginger and mace
1/4 tsp each ground cardamom and cinnamon
1/8 tsp ground cloves
finely minced parsley, and/or flour, ginger

Moisten meat and seasoning with beaten eggs, mixing thoroughly. Shape into balls. Parboil in salted water: ca 10 minutes for pork, but 5 minutes is enough for small balls of other meats. Put on skewers and grill, turning regularly. When almost done, sprinkle with flour mixed with a little ginger and/ or finely minced parsley, or just the parsley. Do not overcook after adding one of these finishes, especially if meatballs are to be reheated before serving.

VARIATIONS
1 Pumpes: use ground, cooked pork, with chopped currants, as a base; season with ground cloves and mace, and, instead of eggs, moisten with a mixture of ground almonds and water or stock (ca 1/4 cup water, boiling, to a tbsp of almonds,

allowed to steep for at least 15 minutes before using) and add 1-2 tbsp rice flour or cornstarch to make it thick and cohesive enough to boil without losing shape.

2 Pome dorres: use ground raw pork and whites of eggs rather than whole eggs; gild by brushing on, in the last stages of cooking, a mixture of almond milk (made with ground almonds and water or broth) with flour, sugar, and eggs, with or without something to make the glaze green (parsley juice, for example – or green food colouring). *Or*: use raw ground beef and egg white, adding currents and seasoning with pepper. This variation advises simply gilding with egg yolk (cf Chicke Endored, 65).

29 Yrchouns

Take Piggis mawys & skalde hem wel; take groundyn Porke & knede it with Spicerye, with pouder Gyngere, and Salt and Sugre; do it on the mawe, but fille it nowt to fulle, þen sewe hem with a fayre þrede and putte hem in a Spete as men don piggys. Take blaunchid Almoundys & kerf hem long, smal, and scharpe, & frye hem in grece & sugre. Take a litel prycke & pryckke þe yrchons. An putte in þe holes the Almundys, every hole half, & leche fro oþer. Ley hem þen to the fyre; when they ben rostid, dore hem, sum wyth Whete Flowre & mylke of Almaundys, sum grene, sum blake wiþ Blode, and lat hem nowt browne to moche; & serue forth. HARL 279.20

This recipe calls for a giant sausage made of a pig's stomach stuffed with ground spiced pork (a sort of sausage meat) and decorated with slivered almonds to form the spines of the 'hedgehogs.' Partly because giant sausages are difficult for the amateur medieval cook to make and partly because the larger the sausage the more difficult it is to get the pork cooked thoroughly, we prefer to make these much smaller and serve them as appetizers. The final coloured decoration is not essential, but can easily be accomplished with the use of some

food colouring, mixed with thin flour paste, if the cook so desires.

Sausage Hedgehogs

2 lbs ground pork
2 tsp ginger
1 tsp each salt, sugar
2 oz almonds, blanched and slivered (not sliced)

Mix pork and spices and form into balls about 1 1/2 to 2 inches in diameter; then elongate the balls a little, into ovals shaped like large walnuts (and about the same size). It is not absolutely necessary to fry the slivered almonds before using them – and may be dangerous, since they have a tendency to get overdone and turn black in the later baking – but a few minutes of sautéing over low heat, with a sprinkling of sugar, may help to make them less brittle and thus easier to handle. Insert them into the 'hedgehogs' in a pattern suggesting quills – you will need at least eight small spines for each ball to achieve the proper effect. Bake on a cookie sheet in a 350° oven for about 30 minutes, or until a good shade of medium brown. To reheat (if necessary), put in a hot oven for only a few minutes. Drain on paper towelling for a minute or two before serving.

If you wish to add the coloured decoration suggested above, this should be done just before the last few minutes of cooking; if done earlier, it will, of course, discolour.

VARIATION
Hedgehogs may be made out of ready-made sausage meat, but the flavour will, of course, be more ordinary.

Note: 'Hedgehogs can be made out of mutton tripe, and it is a great expense and a great labour and little honour and profit.' (MP)

30 Charlet

𝕿𝖆𝖐𝖊 𝕻𝖔𝖗𝖐 𝖆𝖓𝖉 𝖘𝖊𝖊𝖕 𝖎𝖙 𝖜𝖊𝖑. 𝕳𝖊𝖜𝖊 𝖎𝖙 𝖘𝖒𝖆𝖑𝖊; 𝖈𝖆𝖘𝖙 𝖎𝖙 𝖎𝖓 𝖆 𝖕𝖆𝖓𝖓𝖊. 𝕭𝖗𝖊𝖐𝖊 𝖆𝖞𝖗𝖊𝖓 𝖆𝖓𝖉 𝖉𝖔 𝖕𝖊𝖗𝖙𝖔, 𝖆𝖓𝖉 𝖘𝖜𝖞𝖓𝖌 𝖎𝖙 𝖜𝖊𝖑 𝖙𝖔𝖌𝖞𝖉𝖊𝖗. 𝕯𝖔 𝖕𝖊𝖗𝖙𝖔 𝕮𝖔𝖜𝖊 𝖒𝖞𝖑𝖐𝖊 𝖆𝖓𝖉 𝕾𝖆𝖋𝖗𝖔𝖓, 𝖆𝖓𝖉 𝖇𝖔𝖎𝖑𝖊 𝖎𝖙 𝖙𝖔𝖌𝖞𝖉𝖊𝖗. 𝕾𝖆𝖑𝖙 𝖎𝖙 & 𝖒𝖊𝖘𝖘𝖊 𝖎𝖙 𝖋𝖔𝖗𝖙𝖍. FC 39

Pork Hash with Egg

ca 2 cups cooked pork, minced or coarsely ground
4 eggs, lightly beaten
1 cup milk
1/2 tsp salt, or to taste
small pinch saffron

Put the pork in a saucepan or skillet; mix in eggs beaten with milk and seasonings. Cook, stirring, over low to medium heat until the sauce is quite well set. If it is cooked too quickly the eggs will curdle a little, but since the effect is simply scrambling, this is not a disaster.

VARIATIONS
1 Veal may be used in place of pork.
2 A pinch of sage may be added; and/or stir in a little ale or beer at the moment when the mixture reaches the boiling point: this helps to prevent separation of the sauce.
3 For a Charlet y-forced (in sauce), make a separate sauce of milk or almond milk (ground almonds steeped in broth – or water or milk) and thicken with egg yolks. This should be seasoned with some or all of (but be sparing): ginger, mace, clove, galingale, sugar, saffron, cinnamon. Some recipes also call for the addition of wine. To serve, put the Charlet on a serving platter and pour the sauce over it.

31 Sawge Y-farced

Take Sawge; grynde it and temper it up with apren; a[nd] sawcystes & kerf hym to gobettes and cast it in a possynet; and do þerwiþ grece & frye it. Whan it is fryed ynowȝ, cast þerto sawge with apren — make it not to harde; cast þerto powdour douce, messe it forth. FC 160

Sausage with Sage-Flavoured Scrambled Egg Sauce

1 1/2 lb smoked sausage (comparison with the recipe for
   sausage given by the Ménagier suggests that medieval
   sausages were smoked)
1/2-1 tsp chopped sage, depending on freshness and strength
8 eggs, beaten
ca 1/4 tsp each sugar, ginger
ca 1/8 tsp cinnamon
1 tbsp lard or other cooking fat

Slice the sausage into chunks. Brown it in a frying pan in the fat; when it is well cooked, drain off excess fat (leaving no more than 2 tbsp), stir in eggs and sage, and continue to stir over low heat until eggs are set but still soft. Add spices and serve at once.

32 Erbolat

Take parsel, mynts, sauery, & sauge, tansey, beruayn, clarry, rew, ditayn, fenel, southrenwode; hewe hem & grinde hem smale; medle hem up with Ayren; do butter in a trap; & do þe fars þerto; & bake it & messe it forth. FC 172

Herb Custard

a small handful of whatever greens and herbs you can get:
    preferably including parsley, mint, sage, savory, and fennel
    leaves; in lieu of some of the less common ones, use a bit
    of spinach or other leafy greens – and in much larger pro-
    portion than the more strongly flavoured herbs
6 eggs, well beaten
1/2 tsp salt (or to taste)
1-2 tablespoons butter

Chop the greens and herbs as finely as possible and beat into the eggs; a blender will do it all at once, of course. Add salt. Melt the butter and pour it into a baking dish; tilt the dish around to coat it well with the butter before adding the egg and herb mixture. Bake in a 325° oven for 15 to 20 minutes, or until well set but not dried out. (Test by inserting a knife blade or toothpick.)

VARIATION

The Ménagier advises cooking this mixture in a frying pan as an omelet, sprinkling grated cheese on the top when the eggs are beginning to set on the bottom (he cautions that the cheese should not be mixed in because it will make the eggs stick to the bottom of the pan). His recipe also adds a bit of ginger, and specifies as quantities to mix with 16 eggs (for two very large omelets): half a leaf of rue, 2 leaves of dittany, four each of smallage (wild celery), tansey, mint, and sage; a little more in graduated steps upward, of marjoram, fennel, and parsley; and two large handfuls of such greens as beet

greens, violet leaves, spinach, lettuces, and clary (a member of the mint family, but not so strongly flavoured). These proportions can, at least, serve as a guide.

33 Eggys Ryal

𝕮𝖔𝖔𝖐 onions, parboiling them for a long time ... then fry them; afterwards empty the pan in which you have fried eggs so that nothing is left in it, and in it put water and onions and a quarter part of vinegar, so that the vinegar is a quarter of the whole quantity; and boil it and pour it over the eggs. MP

The name for this dish is borrowed from an early 15th century menu; no corresponding recipe seems to exist in English sources. But this is interesting enough to rate a very special name. Lovers of Eggs Benedict are urged to try this simpler, less rich, but subtly tangy dish.

Royal Eggs

6 eggs
2 medium large onions, peeled
1/3 cup olive oil
3 tbsp vinegar
1/2 tsp salt

Cover the whole onions with salted water to cover and parboil for ca 10 minutes; then drain, reserving the onion water. Part of it will be used in the sauce; the rest can be used for recipes in which an onion-flavoured water is appropriate, such as Cawdel of Almond Mylk (6). When the onions have cooled a little, slice them. Heat olive oil in a large frying pan and fry onions until wilted and slightly golden. Remove and

reserve; add eggs and fry them in the same oil. Remove eggs to a serving platter when done. Then put onions back in the pan with 1/3 cup of the water in which they were cooked, vinegar, and salt. Boil for a few minutes, then pour over the eggs and serve at once.

34 Pochee

Take Ayren and breke hem in scalding hoot water; and whan þei bene sode ynowh, take hem up and take ȝolkes of ayren and rawe mylke and swyng hem togydre; and do þerto powdor gynger, safron, and salt; set it ouer the fire, and lat it not boile, and take ayren isode & cast þe sew onoward; & serue it forth. FC 90

Poached Eggs with Cream Sauce

for 6-8 poached eggs
3 egg yolks or 1 whole egg plus 1 yolk
1 1/2 cups milk
optional: pinch ground saffron
1/8 tsp ginger
1/4 tsp salt

Poach the eggs in water just below the boiling point; when they are done, remove to serving platter or plates. Meanwhile, beat the egg yolks or remaining eggs; heat milk to scalding, and gradually beat into the egg mixture. Put this sauce in a pan over very low heat, stirring continually, until thick; do not allow to boil. Season and pour over the poached eggs.

35 A Disshe mete for Somere

Take garbage of capons, and of hennes, and of chekyns, and of dowes, and make hom clene, and sethe hem, and cut hom smal, and take parsel and hew hit smal, and dresse hit in platers, and poure vynegur thereon, and caste thereon pouder of gynger, and of canel, and serve hit forthe colde at nyght.

ARUNDEL

Cold Chicken Livers

1 lb chicken livers
1 cup (ca) chicken stock *or* a mixture of water and red wine
1/2 tsp salt
2-3 tbsp minced fresh parsley
2 tbsp wine vinegar
1/8 tsp each cinnamon and ginger, mixed with 1/4 tsp salt

Put the livers and the 1/2 tsp salt in a small saucepan and cover with stock or wine and water; bring to a boil and simmer for about 5 minutes. Drain livers and chill. Just before serving, mix with parsley and vinegar and sprinkle the spice powder over the top. This can be served with toothpicks as an hors d'œuvre, or on pieces of toast or bread as a canape.

36 Pigge in Sauge

Take a pigge; Draw him, smyte of his hede, kutte him in iiij. quarters, boyle him til he be ynow; take him vppe, and lete cole; smyte him in peces; take an hondefull or ij of Sauge; wassh hit, grynde it in a morter with hard yolkes of egges; then drawe hit vppe with goode vinegre, but make hit not to thyn; then seson hit with powder of Peper, ginger, and salt; then cowche thi pigge in disshes, and caste þe sirippe þer-vppon, and serue it forthe. HARL 4016

That this is a cold dish is evident in the French version, Froide Sauge.

Cold Pork with Sage Sauce

Cold, sliced roast (or boiled) pork, to serve 4-6 people: about 1 1/2 lbs. (We have used the leftovers from a previously cooked larger roast.)
2 tbsp dried sage or about 12 fresh leaves, chopped
1-2 tsp finely chopped parsley
  (may be omitted with fresh sage)
4 hardboiled eggs
1/4 cup vinegar (approximately)
1/2 tsp salt
1/8 tsp each pepper, ginger

Separate yolks and whites of boiled eggs. Mash the yolks with the sage and parsley – preferably in a morter; a blender may be used, but if so vinegar should be added at this point. Chop whites as finely as possible separately. Add to yolk and herb mixture with vinegar (if not already added) and other seasonings. If mixture seems too thick, add a little more vinegar.

Arrange the sliced pork on a suitable platter or dish for serving, and pour the sauce over it. (It is best to do this at the last minute: this sauce is not meant to be a marinade.)

VARIATIONS
Some similar recipes specify additional ingredients and/or alternate meats; for example:
1 other spices – galingale, cloves, cinnamon, cardamom – may be used;
2 a thickening of breadcrumbs steeped in broth, wine, or vinegar – but in this case use fewer eggs in the sauce and put a decorative garnish of hardboiled eggs around the dish.
3 Chicken or fish (either, skinned) may be used instead of pork.

37 Tansp Cake

Breke egges in bassyn and swyng hem sone,
Do powder of peper her to anone;
Hen grynde tansy, ho iuse owte wrynge,
To blynde with ho egges with owte lesynge.
In pan or skelet hou shalt hit frye,
In butter wele skymmet wyturly,
Or white grece hou make take her to,
Geder hit on a cake, henne hase hou do,
With platere of tre, and frye hit browne.
On brode leches serbe hit hou schalle,
With fraunche mele or oher metes with alle. LCC

Other recipes for tansy cakes seem to call for smaller cakes, thickened with breadcrumbs (and in a later period, flour), with spice added. Since small pancakes seem more attractive than a cut-up green omelet, we have adapted the recipe to follow other examples. Tansy is a bitter herb not much in use today, but other recipes indicate almost any green, leafy vegetable may be substituted – one specifies 'spinage,' which satisfies us, though tansy is a sharper, more bitter herb. Others may wish to try more exotic leaves.

Green Pancakes

1 cup blanched spinach (parboiled for 4-5 minutes)
1 cup light cream
3 eggs
1 cup fine breadcrumbs
1/8 tsp each ground nutmeg and ginger
butter for frying

Drain spinach and squeeze out excess water with your hand. If you have a blender, put in blender with all other ingredients and blend until smooth; otherwise, chop spinach as finely as possible, then beat together with eggs, cream, and

seasonings. If batter is too thick, thin with cream or milk; cook as small, thin pancakes.

As with other such crepes, you may put the cakes aside when they are done, refrigerate, and reheat later in a medium oven.

38 Frytor of Erbes

Take gode erbys; grynde hem and medle hem with flour and water, a lytel zest and salt, and frye hem in oyle; and ete hem with clere hony. FC 151

This makes a pleasant and unusual accompaniment for roast meats – but for this purpose the honey can well be omitted.

Herb Fritters

1 package yeast
1 1/4 cups water (lukewarm)
1 cup flour
3-4 tbsp mixed green herbs: eg, 3 tbsp fresh parsley plus
    1/2 tsp each dried thyme, savory, and marjoram
1/4 tsp salt

Dissolve yeast in 1/4 cup lukewarm water, stirring. Then mix in flour, rest of water, and finely chopped herbs. Cover (a bit of plastic wrap is fine) and set in a warm place (for example, the back of the stove, presuming you are cooking something else in the oven or on the front burners at the time) for about an hour. Then drop by spoonfuls into fairly hot oil and fry, turning over once if you are not using deep fat.

39 Frytours of Pasternakes

Take skyrwats and pasternaks and apples, & parboile hem; make a bator of floer and ayren; cast perto ale, safron & salt; wete hem in þe bator and frye hem in oile or in grece; do perto Almand Mylk, & serue it forth. FC 149

This is a savory, rather than a sweet, fritter, and we assume that one need not use more than one of the root vegetables suggested, let alone combine apples and root vegetables.

Parsnip Fritters

2-4 parsnips (depending on size), peeled and sliced
1 package yeast (optional), dissolved in 1/4 cup lukewarm
　　ale or beer
2/3 cup lukewarm ale or beer (in addition to any used to
　　dissolve yeast)
1 cup flour
2 beaten eggs
1/2 tsp salt
optional: pinch of saffron (for colour);
　　4 tbsp ground almonds (for sauce)

If using yeast, start by dissolving the yeast; let it sit a few minutes, then stir in the rest of the ale or beer, flour, salt, and egg. Put in a warm place (such as the back of the stove, if you are using the front burners) to rise for about an hour. Meanwhile, parboil the parsnips in salted water for about 20 minutes; drain, reserving cooking water if a sauce is desired. If you have not made a yeast batter, mix the rest of the ingredients for batter at this point.

　　Stir the parsnip slices into the bowl of batter, so as to coat each piece. Fry the fritters in deep fat, or in a little oil in a frying pan, turning them over as they brown; drain on paper. If a sauce is desired, beat some of the water in which the parsnips were cooked into the ground almonds until the desired

consistency is reached; season this with salt to taste, and add ground saffron if you wish to colour it.

VARIATION

Turnips, carrots, or apples may be substituted for the parsnips. Carrots should be parboiled for only 5 minutes, however, and apples not at all.

40 Spynoch Yfryed

𝕿ake Spynoches; parboile hem in sebyng water. 𝕿ake hem up and presse out þe water and hewe in two. 𝕱rye hem in oile clene, & do þer-to powder & serue forth. FC 180

This recipe for spinach is almost exactly what a contemporary French cook would specify.

Braised Spinach

2 lbs fresh spinach, washed and with excess stems and
   withered leaves removed
salted water for parboiling
ca 2-3 tbsp oil (preferably olive oil)
1/4 tsp salt
pinch each ginger, allspice

Parboil the spinach in a large pot of water for about 4 minutes; drain, press out excess water with your hands, and chop the spinach; put in a saucepan or small casserole with oil and seasonings. Stir, and leave to cook over very low heat for another 15 minutes or so; or put covered casserole in a low oven for about 20 minutes.

VARIATIONS

1 Beet or other greens may be cooked in the same way.
2 Add parsley and/or fennel with a little chicken or beef broth, instead of oil. (*more*)

3 Cook in water with a tbsp of vinegar added; then, instead of broth or oil, use 2 tbsp butter, and, if you wish, some grated cheese: the Ménagier suggests this.

41 𝕻𝖊𝖆𝖘𝖈𝖔𝖉𝖉𝖊𝖘

In cooking new peas to be eaten in the pod, one should put them in lard, on a meat=day; and on a fish day, when they have been cooked, pour away the water and put under them salted butter to melt, and then stir. MP

Jane Grigson informs us that in China street vendors sell peas cooked in their pods. The pod is picked up in the fingers, the peas which have been steamed inside sucked out, and the edible part of the pod then eaten, rather as we eat artichokes. The remaining fibrous part of the pod is discarded.

Peascoddes

2 lbs young peas in the pod
2 tbsp butter
water, salt

Leave the pods whole. If the stem end is cut off, the pods break open during cooking. Boil the peapods for 10-15 minutes, depending on size. Drain. Put into serving bowl or individual bowls, add butter, stir to coat.

Clearly, the original recipe calls for cooking the peapods with lard rather than butter whenever the fasts of the church

permit this; possibly, it is also meant that the cooking fluid on a 'meat day' ought to be meat (or chicken) broth. However, most modern diners ought to be content with the 'fasting' version of the dish.

42 Minces

𝕷ittle cabbages called minces are eaten with raw herbs in vinegar; and if one has plenty, they are good shelled, washed in hot water, and cooked whole with a little water; and when they are cooked, add some salt and oil and serve thick, without water, and put olive oil on them in 𝕷ent. MP

The last part of these directions suggest that something other than oil was normally used outside of Lent: presumably, then, butter or meat fats may be used in place of oil as a dressing. A very simple recipe.

Brussels Sprouts

2 lbs Brussel sprouts – or according to number to be served
water, oil, salt

Trim and wash the sprouts and cook them in a pot of salted water until tender (10 minutes, approximately). Drain and add about 1 tbsp oil per pound of sprouts; salt to taste. Serve at once. Substitute butter or other cooking fat for the oil if you wish, but the taste of real olive oil will give the vegetable a slightly different character from the familiar plain buttered sprouts.

43 Benes Yfryed

Take benes and seeþ hem almost til þey bersten; take and wryng out þis water clene; do þerto Oynons ysode and ymynced, and garlec þerwith; frye hem in oile oþer in grece, & do þerto powdor douce, & serue it forth. FC 181

Fried Beans

1 lb fresh shell beans, shelled and boiled until tender,
   or a large can of boiled, shelled beans, drained
2 onions
2 cloves of garlic, minced or crushed
oil or other cooking fat

If you are cooking fresh beans, parboil the onions with the beans for a few minutes, then remove them and allow them to cool before you proceed to mince them. Or, simply mince the onions and proceed without the step of parboiling them, if you wish. In any case, drain the beans thoroughly and mix with chopped onion and garlic; then sautee the vegetables, stirring to keep them from sticking or over-browning, for about five minutes.

44 Salat

Take parsel, sawge, garlec, chibollas, onyons, leeks, bor= age, myntes, porrectes, fenel, and ton tressis, rew, rose= marye, purslyne. Laue, and waishe hem clene; pike hem, pluk hem small with þyn honde and myng hem wel with rawe oile. Lay on vynegar and salt, and serue it forth.

FC 76

The greens and herbs called for in this recipe were un- doubtedly intended to be fresh from the garden (or field). Those modern cooks who must substitute dried herbs are

cautioned to use them sparingly. The general intention is, clearly, a green salad not very different from those we eat today, but with a rather larger component of the onion family than is usual in modern salads. It is advisable to be relatively sparing here, too: use only the smallest sort of leeks (if any are available) and onions. 'Garlic' may have meant the shoots or bulbs of wild garlic, which are much milder than the usual kind.

Green Salad

Salad greens: use an assortment of whatever greens are available, avoiding iceberg lettuce: in lieu of such rare greens as borage, you might try some spinach. Proportions of other ingredients below are predicated on a quantity of greens sufficient to fill one very large or two medium sized salad bowls.

1 tbsp each fresh (or 1 tsp dried) chopped parsley, sage, mint, and any other available, suitable herbs (eg, fennel, dill, savory)

1-2 bunches (depending on size and other ingredients) scallions, sliced

1-3 cloves garlic, minced

optional: 2-3 small leeks, well washed and finely sliced

optional: 2-3 tbsp chopped chives

1/2 cup salad oil (preferably olive oil)

3 tbsp vinegar

1 1/2 tsp salt

Wash and tear up greens. When well drained, put in bowl or bowls and add sliced scallions and leeks. Herbs, garlic, and oil may be added now, with the salt and vinegar reserved for the last minute, or, if you prefer, mix herbs, garlic, oil, vinegar, and salt as you normally would a salad dressing and add all at the same time just before serving: it comes to much the same thing. (It is the salt and vinegar which cause greens to wilt.) Mix and toss in the usual way.

45 Macrows

𝕿ake and make a thynne foyle of dowh, and kerve it on pieces, and cast hem on boilling water & seeþ it wele; take chese and grate it and butter cast bynethen and above as losyns, and serue forth. FC 92

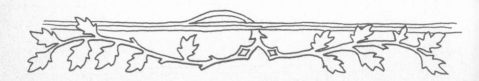

Noodles

1 lb broad noodles (homemade if you wish – see a standard cookbook)
1/4 cup (or more) grated cheese – cheddar, parmesan, or whatever you wish
2 tbsp butter (or more, to taste)

If your noodles are very long ones, break them into pieces a few inches in length. Boil in salted water until tender. In a serving dish or platter, put a layer of pieces of butter and half the cheese; put noodles on top of this; then add a second layer of butter and cheese, and serve hot.

VARIATION

Loseyns (lasagna) are made similarly, but presumably with larger noodles. FC 49 directs us to cook the Loseyns in broth (meat or chicken), then put them in a serving dish in several layers, with a layer of grated cheese and mild spices (eg, a mixture of cinnamon and mace – but be sparing with the spices) between layers. It is not clear whether any of the broth is poured over the completed arrangement, but it is probably not necessary and best omitted. If this does not seem much like a modern lasagna, remember that tomatoes were unknown in this period.

Fyssh

Some fish dishes have already been listed in the sections on soups and pottages and entremets; in this section we include primarily main-course dishes. The sauces given at the end may be used on almost any fish (steamed, fried, or broiled), as may those given with specific fishes in recipes; some of the sauces may also be used for meats and poultry.

46 Fyssh in Pottage

Take water and set it to boil with almonds in it; then peel and grind the almonds; moisten them with warm water; strain them and boil them with powdered ginger and saffron; and serve in bowls, and in each bowl put a slice of fried fish. MP

Most similar recipes call for broth or fish stock, which usually is laced with wine or vinegar. Such stock naturally gives the soup a lot more flavour.

Fish Soup

1 lb sliced fish (eg, cod or hake), plus some bones and
   trimming to make broth
4 cups water plus 1/4 cup vinegar, *or* 3 cups water plus
   1 cup white wine
1 tsp salt
1 oz ground almonds (or start with whole ones and blanch
   as directed in the recipe: it makes no difference)
1/4 tsp each ground ginger, saffron
2 tbsp olive oil

Cover the fish bones and trimmings with water, wine or vinegar, almonds, and seasonings, and simmer gently for about 20 minutes. Then fry the fish steaks in olive oil; they should be browned, but not overcooked to the point of becoming dry. Put a slice of fish in each serving bowl and strain the broth over it. Serve at once.

47 Ballok Brothe

'Pik and eles in ballok brothe/that muste our dame haue, or/els she will be wrothe.' To mak eles and pikes in ballok brothe take and splat a pik and shale hym and culpon eles smale and put them in a pot, do ther to grene onyons and quybibes and mince them and sesson them up with a liore of bread and put to it cloves maces pouder of cannell and saffron and put ther to a quantity of stock fisches like unto the eles and let the pik boile esely and serue the hole pik for a lord and quarto of a pik for comons... N

All Ballok Broth recipes call for eels, in various proportions and combinations, but since not all cooks will be able to get eel easily today we assume you may use whatever fish you can get. One ingredient is omitted here which is usual in other versions: brewer's yeast, clearly included for the flavour.

Fish in Broth

1 lb fresh fish fillets or skinned slices, preferably including some eel, plus pike, pickerel, or cod
1/2 lb (ca) salt cod, soaked in cold water for at least 8 hours, with any skin and bone removed
1 cup (at least) chopped onions and/or green onions or scallions
1/4 cup chopped parsley
3-4 slices bread (white or whole wheat)
1 cup white wine
1/8 tsp each ground mace and cubebs or pepper
pinch each saffron, ground cloves
1 tsp vinegar
1 tbsp brewers' yeast

Cut fish (including soaked salt cod) into chunks. Put in a pot with onions, parsley, saffron, and four cups water; bring to a

boil and simmer gently for ten to fifteen minutes. Meanwhile, soak the bread (torn up or ground into crumbs) in wine. When it is well softened add all remaining seasonings and blend in a blender or mortar or press through a strainer. Stir this mixture into the soup with the yeast and cook, stirring, for about five more minutes.

48 Samon Roste in Sauce

Take a Salmond and cut him rounde, chyne and all, and roste the peces on a gredirne; And take wyne, and pouder of Canell, and drawe it þorgh a strepnour; And take smale mynced oynons, and caste þere=to, and lete hem boyle; And þen take vynegre, or bergeous, and pouder ginger, and cast there=to; And þen ley þe samon in a dissh, and cast þe siryp þeron al hote, & serue it forth. HARL 4016

Grilled Salmon Steaks in Sauce

for 6 salmon steaks (around 3 lbs)
1 cup white wine
1/8 tsp (approximately) cinnamon
1 onion, or 3-4 green onions or scallions, finely minced
juice of 1/2 lemon or 1 tbsp vinegar
1/8 tsp (approximately) ginger
salt to taste

Broil the salmon steaks, after brushing them with some cooking oil or melted butter. Meanwhile, put onions or scallions in a saucepan with wine and cinnamon and bring to a boil; turn down heat and simmer gently. When salmon steaks are browned on both sides, add the lemon or vinegar and ginger to the sauce. Put salmon on a serving dish and pour the sauce over it.

49 Salmon Fressh Boiled

Take a fressh Salmon, and drawe him in þe bely; and
chyne him as a swyne, and leche him flatte with a knyfe; and
kutte the chyne in ii. or in iii. peces, and roste him on a faire
gredyrn; & make faire sauce of water, parcelly, and salt.
And whan hit begynneth to boyle, skem it clene, and cast þe
peces of salmon þere=to, and lete hem sethe; and þen take
hem vppe, and lete hem kele, and ley a pece or ii. in a dissh;
and wete faire foiles of parcely in vinegre, and caste hem
vppon þe salmon in the dissh; And þen ye shall serue hit
forthe colde. HARL 4016

The principal difference here from modern practice is that
the salmon is grilled before it is poached: cooks must be careful to do both steps briefly, or it will be overcooked.

Cold Poached Salmon

1 salmon, head and tail off; cleaned and split, but not fileted
water, parsley, salt, and vinegar: in quantities appropriate to
   the size of the fish

Lay the salmon flat on a cutting board and cut it into two or
three pieces (depending on size) crosswise. Grill it in a broiler
or on a grill pan for about 5 minutes – just enough to make it
golden, not brown. Meanwhile, fill a shallow pan large enough
to hold the pieces of fish with water, salt, and a few sprigs of
parsley (ca 1 tsp salt to a quart of water); bring this to a boil,
and put in the salmon. Turn down the heat so that the water
barely simmers. Remove the fish in five minutes and let it
cool before arranging on a dish or platter for serving. Cover
and chill. When ready to serve the dish, take a good number
of small sprigs of parsley – enough to really make an impressive appearance – and dip each sprig in vinegar before arranging the parsley over the cold salmon.

50 Cawdel of Samon

Take the gutts of Samon and make hem clene; parboile hem a lytell; take hem up and dyce hem. Slyt the white of Lekes and kerue hem smale. Cole the broth and do the lekes þerinne with oile, and lat it boile togyder. Do the Samon icorne þerin; make a lyor of Almand mylke & of brede & cast þerto spices, safron, and salt; seeþ it wel, and loke þat it be not stondyng. FC 111

Salmon and Leeks in Almond Sauce

a chunk of salmon, ca 2 lbs (the tail-piece is usually most
    economical)
3-4 leeks
2 tbsp olive oil
2 oz (1/4 cup) ground, blanched almonds
ca 5 tbsp breadcrumbs
1/4 tsp ginger
1/8 tsp cinnamon
1/2 tsp salt
optional: pinch ground saffron

Poach the salmon in enough water to barely cover (ca 2 cups) for about 15 minutes; remove and allow to cool. Strain broth and measure 2 cups into a saucepan. Wash the leeks, and slice the white part finely into the broth in which the salmon was cooked; stir in oil, and bring to a simmer. When the leeks have been cooking about 15 minutes, add the salmon, skinned and cut into chunks about 1-2 inches square. Stir about 1/2 cup of the broth into the almonds and breadcrumbs, and beat until thoroughly dissolved; then mix back into the pot. If the mixture is not thick enough, add more breadcrumbs. Season, and allow to simmer over low heat for a few more minutes before serving. The dish should be on the runny side, like a creamed salmon.

51 Makerel in Mynt Sawse

Take Makerels and smyte hem on pecys; cast hem on water and berious; seep hem with myntes and wip oþer erbes; color it grene or ȝelow, and messe it forth. FC 106

This recipe is especially recommended to those who think they do not care for mackerel: it has a subtly transforming effect on this inexpensive fish. While the recipe above calls for cutting the fish up, a later version leaves it whole, which may make a more attractive (if somewhat less convenient) dish.

Mackerel in Mint Sauce

2-3 mackerels, amounting to at least 2 lbs of fish
1 cup water, salted (use about 1/2 tsp salt)
1/4 cup vinegar (white vinegar has least discolouring effect)
4 large sprigs parsley and 3 or so of fresh mint
   (if you must use dried mint, ca 1 tbsp)
3-4 scallions or green onions

Mackerel should be cleaned and the head removed (though it may be left on if you wish to cook it whole). Leave whole or cut into pieces about two inches long. Put it in a cooking pot with the scallions, mint, and 3 of the parsley sprigs; pour salted water and vinegar over it and bring to a simmer. Cook gently for 15-20 minutes (depending on whether fish is whole or cut up). Remove fish to a serving dish. Sprinkle with remaining parsley, finely minced, and pour some of the cooking liquid, strained, over it. (Or use some sorrell, minced or ground with salt, in place of minced parsley for the sauce: this is specifically prescribed in the slightly later version.)

52 Rosepe of Fysshe

Take Almaunde Mylke an flowre of Rys, & Sugre, an
Safroun, an boyle hem y-fere; þan take Red Rosys, an
grynd fayre in a morter with Almaunde mylke; þan take
Loches, an toyle hem with Flowre, an frye hem, & ley hem
in dysshys; þan take gode pouder, and do in þe Sewe, and
cast þe Sewe a-bouyn þe lochys,& serue forth. HARL 279.100

The roses used in this recipe can be ones that are just a bit
too far gone to put (or keep) in a vase for decorative purposes; as long as they are not completely dried up, they will
do.

Fish in Rose Sauce

2 lbs small fish or fish fillets
flour for dredging fish
oil for frying

SAUCE
2 tbsp plus 2 tsp ground almonds
4 tsp cornstarch, rice flour, or potato flour
2 tsp sugar
small pinch saffron
ca 1/2 cup red rose petals (1-2 roses)
1 cup water
1/2 tsp salt
1/8 tsp ginger

Flour and fry the fish, removing to a serving dish when done;
keep warm. Make sauce at the last minute: it must not be
overcooked or rewarmed after the roses are added. Dissolve
starch in 2 tbsp cold water; add rest of water, sugar, 2 tbsp
almonds, and saffron; boil and stir until thick; set aside.
Grind rose petals with remaining almonds in morter (or use
blender, or improvise), adding a bit of the cooked sauce.

When all is blended into a smooth paste, stir into the sauce base and reheat gently, just to the boiling point. Season with ginger and salt and strain over the fried fish.

53 Turbut Roste Ensauce

Take a Turbut, and kut of þe vynnes in maner of a haste=lette, and broche him on a rounde broche, and roast him; And whan hit is half y=rosted, cast thereon smale salt as he rosteth. And take also as he rosteth, bergeous, or vinegre, wyne, pouder of Gynger, and a litull canell, and cast thereon as he rosteth, And holde a dissh vnderneth, fore spilling of the licour; And whan hit is rosted ynowe, hete þe same sauce ouer the fire, And caste hit in a dissh to þe fissh all hote, And serue it forth. HARL 4016

Roast Turbot in Sauce

1 large turbot, skinned, or 2 fillets
1 tsp salt
1/4 tsp ginger
pinch cinnamon
2 tbsp lemon juice or vinegar

Grill the turbot in a broiler, with a pan underneath to catch the juices. When it is about half done (ca 10 minutes), mix together salt and spices and sprinkle this powder over the fish; sprinkle with lemon juice or vinegar and continue broiling. When fish is done, remove to a serving platter; rewarm the pan drippings if necessary (it probably will not be, in a modern broiler) and pour them over the fish.

54 Pike in Rosemarye

Put them to roast well on the griddle so that they are well cooked. For the sauce to put on them: red wine, verjuice, a very little vinegar, and some ginger and some rosemary, and cook them all to boil together in an earthenware pot; and when the pike are cooked, pour it over.   MP, APP 5

Pike in Rosemary Sauce

1-2 whole pike (or pickerel), cleaned for roasting or split
  for broiling
1/2 cup red wine
2 tsp vinegar (wine or cider vinegar)
1/4 tsp each ginger, rosemary

Roast the pike by grilling in a broiler or over charcoal. While it cooks, mix the sauce ingredients and simmer over low heat for at least 10 minutes. (If too much of the wine evaporates, add a little water. But it should cook down a bit.) When the fish is done, salt it and pour the sauce over it on a serving platter.

55 Pike in Galentyne

Take browne brede, and stepe it in a quarte of vinegre, and a pynt of wyne for a pike, and quarteren of pouder canell, and drawe it thorgh a streynour skilfully thik, and cast it in a potte, and lete boyle; and cast there=to pouder peper, or ginger, or of clowes, and lete kele. And þen take a pike, and seth him in good sauce, and take him vp, and lete him kele a litul; and ley him in a boll for to cary him yn; and cast þe sauce vnder him and aboue him, that he be al y=hidde in þe sauce; and cary him wheþer euer þou wolt.   HARL 4016

None of the English recipes for this dish is entirely satisfactory: thus the recipe below is largely based on a 14th century

Italian source, but we thought we would spare our readers the Latin. What does emerge from a comparison of the various recipes and sources of information is that this was usually a cold, jellied dish.

Galantine of Pike

1 whole (or large unskinned chunk of) fish, preferably pike or pickerel; 2-3 lbs
1 1/2 cups each white wine and water (use a little more water if necessary to cover fish)
1 onion, peeled and chopped
2 sprigs parsley
1/2 tsp salt
2 thin slices wholewheat bread, toasted
1 tbsp each wine vinegar, white wine
1/8 tsp each cinnamon, ginger, pepper, and (if you have any) galingale
pinch of ground clove

Cover the fish, onion, and parsley with wine and water; salt, and bring to a simmer. Cook gently 15-20 minutes, then remove fish and leave to cool. Boil down broth to about half its original quantity. Meanwhile, soak the bread and spices in wine and vinegar. Put the bread mixture in a blender, add some of the reduced broth, and blend. (If you have no blender, use a mortar, or whisk vigorously, then press through a strainer.) Add this paste to the rest of the broth and boil for a few minutes, or until thick, then set aside to cool. Remove skin from fish and put it in a dish: preferably one just large enough to hold it with sides two or three inches deep. Pour broth mixture over fish, turning the fish very gently to ensure complete coverage. Cool and chill. If the fish is not completely covered by sauce (and it will not be, unless you have a dish of exactly the right size and shape) you will need to ladle the sauce over the fish several times during the cooling period to make sure it is completely coated.

56 Stokfissh in Sauce

Take faire broth of elys, or pike, or elles of fressh samond,
And streyn hit thorgh a strepnour; and take faire parcelly,
And hewe hem small, And putte the broth and þe parcelley
into an erthen potte, And caste þerto pouder ginger, and a
litul vergeous, And let hem boyle to-gidre; and þen take faire
sodden stokfissh, and ley hit in hote water; and whan þou
wilt serue it forth, take þe fissh fro þe water, and ley hit in a
dissh, And caste the sauce al hote there=on, and serue it
forth. HARL 4016

Salt Cod in Fish Stock

2 lbs dried salt cod (approximately)
bones and pieces of a white-fleshed fish or salmon to make
    fish stock (or use leftover stock from poaching salmon,
    pike, etc); about 1/4 lb, if you are buying pieces for the
    purpose, should be ample.
ca 1/4 cup finely minced parsley
1/4 tsp ground ginger
2 tbsp butter
2 tbsp lemon juice

Beat the dried cod by hitting against a table or counter top
about a dozen times; this helps to soften the tissues of the
fish when it is cooked. (Be thankful that you do not have to
follow the Ménagier's directions to beat it with a wooden
mallet for a full hour.) Soak the cod in water overnight – or
at least 12 hours. Drain and add fresh, cold water; bring
slowly to a boil and simmer gently for 5-10 minutes; then
turn off heat and leave the fish in the water while you prepare sauce – or, remove from water, and recover with hot
water for a few minutes to heat through just before serving.
    If you have no leftover fish stock, make some by covering
fish bones and pieces with water, boiling for about 20 minutes before straining. Measure one cup of this broth and put

it in a saucepan with the parsley, ginger, and butter. Bring to a boil, but cook for only a minute or two. Add lemon juice. Then drain the water from the cod, put it on a serving dish, and pour the sauce over it.

57 Cretone of Fyssh

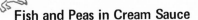

Fish and Peas in Cream Sauce

Follow the recipe for Checones in Critone (88), but substitute ca 2 lbs fried fish (fillets of sole, cod, etc) for the chicken; ground almonds may be used in place of breadcrumbs (MP).

58 Blamanger of Fysshe

Take Rys, an sethe hem tylle they brekyn, & late hem kele; þan caste þer-to mylke of Almaundys; nym Perche or Lop-stere & do þer-to, & melle it; þan nym sugre with pouder Gyngere, & caste þer-to, & make it chargeaunt, and þan serue it forth. HARL 279.98

Rice with Shellfish

4-6 lobster tails (depending on size)
1/2 lb raw medium shrimps
1 cup uncooked rice
4 oz (1/2 cup) ground blanched almonds
1/2 cup white wine
1 tsp sugar
1/2 tsp ginger
salt to taste

Cover the lobster tails and shrimps with salted, boiling water and parboil for 3-4 minutes. Pour the cooking water into another container and measure 1 cup of it; pour this cup of broth over the ground almonds and leave to steep 15-20 minutes.

Meanwhile, steam the rice in enough water to cover amply for 10-15 minutes; drain off any excess water. Shell the shrimps. Split the bottom of the lobster shells neatly in order to remove the meat but leave the shells in one piece. Cut the lobster meat and most of the shrimps into chunks, reserving a few of the shrimps and the lobster shells for later use. Stir the lobster and shrimp chunks into the rice with the seasonings and the almond milk and wine; add salt, if necessary. Stir this mixture over low heat for a few minutes. It should be thick and well-blended, but not dry. If it is on the dry side, add a little water. Pack into a ring-mold or casserole and cover with aluminum foil.

Just before serving, reheat in a moderate oven. Unmold onto a suitable tray or large plate, and decorate with the reserved lobster shells curling around the sides, or, if you have used a ring-mold, forming ribs from the middle to the outside; arrange the reserved shrimps between the lobster shells.

VARIATIONS

For an equally tasty, and far more economical, though obviously less spectacular, dish, use perch – or another kind of fish. One recipe suggests dried haddock, and, indeed, finnan haddie – or dried or smoked cod – will do very nicely. But when there are to be no lobster shells for decoration, there is little point in unmolding, and one might as well serve the dish from the casserole in which it is cooked.

59 Crustard of Eerbis

𝔗ake gode Eerbys and grynde hem smale with wallenots pycked clene, a grete portion; lye it up almost wiþ as myche berious as water; seeþ it wel with powdor and Safron withoute Salt; make a crust in a trap an do þe fyssh þerinne unstewed wiþ a litel oile & gode Powdors; whan it is half ybake do þe sewe þerto & bake it up. If þu wilt make it clere of Fyssh seeþ ayren harde take out þe ȝolks & grinde hem with gode powdors, and alye it up with gode stewes and serue it forth. FC 157

The recipe indicates that hardboiled egg yolks can be substituted for the fish, but should be mixed with the green sauce rather than put beneath it. This could be adapted in various ways: putting whole hardboiled eggs, or halves or quarters, under the sauce, for example. A sort of mixture seems, however, most appealing.

Quiche of Fish with Green Topping

about two handfuls (exact measurements are almost
   impossible for this small quantity of green stuff) of greens:
   a good combination is about 2/3 spinach, plus a few leafy
   tops of fennel (the bulb can be used separately – see, eg,
   Fenkel in Soppes (4), and the rest of the green part in
   salad), a few sprigs of parsley, and a green onion or scallion
   or two.
1/2 cup walnut meats
juice of 1 lemon
1 lb fish fillets (sole, flounder, perch, or what-have-you:
   the omission of salt in the 14th century directions indicates that stockfish (salt cod) was used, but for this recipe
   modern cooks will find fresh fish excellent.)
pastry to line a pie pan or baking dish
ca 1/8 tsp each ginger, cinnamon   (more)

1/2 tsp salt (or more, to taste)
1-2 tbsp olive oil or other cooking oil
2 yolks of hardboiled eggs

Line a suitable baking dish or piepan with pastry, fluting the top edge. Place the fish fillets in the bottom, and sprinkle oil and spices over them. Bake in a 350° oven for 10-15 minutes. Meanwhile, mince the greens and walnuts as finely as possible: it is best to put them through a meat grinder, or chop them in a blender with the lemon juice and an equal quantity of water. Put them in a saucepan with only this amount of liquid (that is, the juice of one lemon and an approximately equal quantity of water) and simmer for 4-5 minutes. Mash the egg yolks (or crush in a mortar); mix them into the cooked green sauce, and add salt to taste. Spread this mixture over the fish in the tart, and bake for another 10-15 minutes.

VARIATIONS

1 As suggested above, one could substitute hardboiled eggs for the fish for a dish with no fish or meat, with a larger proportion of greens.
2 Fish may be cooked this way in a shallow baking dish (oiled) without the crust.

60 Tart of Fysshe

Take Eelys and Samon and smyte hem on pecys; & stewe it in almand mylke and verious. Drawe up on almand mylk wiþ þe stewe. Pyke out the bons clene of þe fyssh, and save þe myddell pece hoole of þe Eelys, & grynde þat oþer fissh smale, and do þerto powdor, sugar, & salt and grated brede; & Fors þe Eelys þerwith þeras þe bonys were; medle þe oþer dele of the fars & þe mylk togider, and color it with sanders: make a crust in a trap as before, and bake it þerin and serue it forth. FC 170

Since eel is not always available in fishmarkets, we offer here an alternative version (as well as directions for using eel).

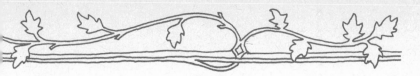

Fish Tart

ca 1 lb eel, sliced, or fillets of sole (any sort of flounder, etc,
    will do)
ca 1 lb salmon (slices or chunk: whatever is the cheapest)
pastry to line a *large* pie plate or other shallow baking dish
1 tsp salt
4 oz (1/2 cup) ground almonds
juice of one lemon
one slice white bread (or ca 1/4 cup crumbs of same)
1/8 tsp each cinnamon, ginger; pinch of nutmeg
1/2 tsp sugar

Put lemon juice, salt, and 2 tbsp of the almonds in a cooking
pot in which the fish will fit, and stir in a little water. Put the
salmon and eel (if used: fillets should not be poached at this
point) in the pot and add just enough more water to cover
the fish. Bring to a simmer and cook gently for about ten
minutes, then remove fish and allow to cool a few minutes.
Strain broth and measure 1 1/2 cups (add water if necessary);
stir the rest of the ground almonds into this broth and put it
aside to steep while you line the baking dish with pastry and
remove skin and bones from the poached fish. Put bread
(torn, or in crumbs) in a blender container or bowl, and pour
some of the almond milk over it (ca 1/2 cup); add the spices
to this, along with the skinned, boned salmon, and blend,
mash, or grind into a smooth thick paste.

If you are using fish fillets, cut them in half lengthwise to
make strips about 1 1/2 to 2 inches wide. Roll these strips
into round rings about 3 to 4 inches in diameter (with a hole
about an inch in diameter in the middle), arranging these
rings in the pastry crust. If using eel, it is easier to stuff the
centres of the pieces of eel before putting them in the pie
shell. In either case, then, stuff centres with salmon mixture.
Then add the rest of the almond milk to the salmon that is
left (which should be about half), and blend again. Pour this
over the fish in the tart. Bake at about 325° for 40-50 minutes. Serve hot.

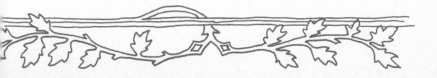

61 Verde Sawse

Take parsel, mynt, garlek, a litul serpell and sawge, a litul canel, gynger, piper, wyne, brede, vyneger & salt; grynde it smal with safron & messe it forth. FC 140

Green Sauce is the most common medieval (and later) accompaniment to fish: the recipes vary from very simple (parsley, ground with vinegar, bread, and salt) to infinite variations: besides the ingredients named in the 14th century recipe given here, recipes call for such other greens as sage, sorrel, ditteny, pellitory, and costmarye; spices may include cloves. The recipe suggested below can be varied infinitely, depending on what herbs you have on hand (and what spices you wish to try).

Green Sauce

2 tbsp fresh parsley, finely minced
2 tsp each fresh thyme, savory, and/or rosemary, finely
   minced (or, if need be, substitute rather less of dried herbs)
2 tbsp fine bread crumbs
1/2 tsp salt
1/8 tsp each ginger, pepper
1 tbsp lemon juice
1/4 cup white wine

Mix all ingredients together in a saucepan and stir over medium heat just long enough to thicken; do not overcook or sauce will loose its fresh, green quality. Or the sauce may be served without any cooking at all, if your crumbs are finely ground enough; since only a little sauce is needed, serving it cold will not cool the fish too much. Serve with poached, grilled, or sautéed fish.

62 Jance Sawce

**Grind ginger, garlic, almonds, and moisten with good ver=
juice, and then boil. And some put in a third part of wine.**

MP

The Ménagier recommends this sauce with cod and some
other fishes, as well as goose. Bread crumbs are an alternate
thickening; if you wish to omit them, increase the almonds.
Serve with steamed, fried, or broiled fish (cod, turbot, hali-
but, bluefish, etc).

Yellow Sauce

2 tbsp ground almonds
3 cloves garlic, mashed
1/2 tsp each ginger, salt
juice of 1/2 lemon
1 cup white wine
2 tbsp bread crumbs

Mix all ingredients together in a saucepan; boil gently, stirring
or whisking well, until it thickens. Leave it on very low heat
to keep warm and mellow in flavour while you cook the fish;
or, set it aside for at least fifteen minutes, then reheat.

   If your fish is to be cooked in wine and water, the stock
may be substituted for the white wine in the recipe; in this
case, the sauce may be made at the last minute and will not
need time to mellow.

63 Garlic Cameline

Grind ginger, garlic, and bits of white bread moistened with vinegar; and if you add liver to it it will be better. MP

The Ménagier recommends this sauce for fried ray or skate, but it can be used for other bland fried fish. It is quite possible that since this is called 'cameline,' cinnamon ought to be added: if you wish, add a pinch.

Garlic Cameline

1/2 tsp ground ginger
2 cloves garlic, mashed or put through a garlic press
1/4 cup bread crumbs (or 1 slice bread)
2 tbsp vinegar
1/4 tsp salt
optional: liver of the fish, chopped

Soak bread or bread crumbs with vinegar; put all ingredients in a small pan and cook, stirring, for a few minutes. If it seems too thick, add a little water or white wine. Serve hot with fried fish.

Rostes and
Bake Metes of Flessh

Since all cooks roast meat and poultry in standard ways, no directions will be given here for ordinary roasting procedures: medieval cookery books assume one knows that much. Follow your usual methods. The recipes included are for roasts with stuffings, sauces, etc; they include recipes for grilled meats, and meat pies, tarts, and 'crustards' – open tarts with a topping which crusts over in cooking.

64 Chik Y-rostyd with Sauce of Rose Water

In summer, the sauce for a roast chicken is half vinegar, half rosewater, and press ... orange juice is good added to this. MP

Oranges in the 14th century were bitter, not the sweet juice oranges familiar today. If you can get Seville oranges, they will be closest in flavour; otherwise, a combination of orange and lemon, or an adjustment in the amount of vinegar, is necessary. If you wish to make your own rosewater, the Ménagier directs us to dry the rose petals in the sun; afterwards, they are presumably boiled in distilled water. But, of course, you can buy rosewater in many shops.

Chicken with Rosewater Sauce

1 chicken, roasted
ca 1 tbsp each wine vinegar, rosewater, orange juice, and
   lemon juice (or whatever combination of the sweet and
   sharp you can muster)
salt to taste

Mix the sauce ingredients with juices from the roasting pan and pour over the chicken before serving.

65 Chike Endored

Take a chike, and drawe him, and roste him, and lete the fete be on, and take awey the hede; then make batur of yolkes of eyron and floure, and caste ther=to pouder of ginger, and peper, saffron, and salt, and pouder hit faire til hit be rosted ynogh. HARL 4016

The basic essential for gilding is yolk of egg, beaten. Any other ingredients are variable and optional; we find we prefer a plain egg-yolk gilding, as the taste of saffron, for example, can be a bit overwhelming.

Gilded Chicken

1 chicken, ca 3 lbs, dressed for roasting
2 egg yolks, beaten (do not substitute a whole egg here)
1/2 tsp salt
optional: small pinch of saffron

Roast the chicken, using a spit if you have one; baste with the pan drippings as the chicken roasts. About half an hour before the bird is done, brush it with beaten egg yolk seasoned with salt (plus the saffron, if desired); repeat the brushing once or twice, until chicken is done.

VARIATIONS

1 Chike Endored Y-farced: for a really impressive production – make a stuffing of a pound of ground veal or pork, or a mixture of the two, mixed with the minced (or ground) raw chicken liver from the chicken, plus a beaten egg, two tbsp grated cheese, and 1/8 tsp each pepper, ginger, and mace, plus 1/4 tsp salt. Put about half this mixture into the chicken and sew or skewer it closed. Form the rest into small meat balls, an inch or so in diameter. Poach the meatballs for about 10 minutes in a pot of simmering beef broth (or

chicken, if you have no beef). Remove from the broth carefully, and thread on skewers. Put the skewered meat balls by the cooking chicken when it is time to gild the chicken, and gild the meat balls at the same time. To serve, arrange the meat balls as a decorative edging around the chicken on its platter. The French source of this recipe advises adding some parsley for a further decorative touch: the intention is minced parsley sprinkled on the balls, but a few sprigs tucked around them may be even more appealing to the eye.

2 Any number of other roasts – especially poultry – were gilded in the same way. Use the technique on anything that appeals to you. We assume, though, you will not get around to trying it on a peacock, that pièce de résistance for the ultimate in medieval feasts. One recipe reads: 'Take and flee off the skynne with the fedurs, tayle, and the nekke, and the hed thereon; then take the skyne with all the fedurs and lay hit on a table aborde; and strawe thereon groundyn comyn; then take the pecokke, and roste him, and endore hym with raw yolkes of egges; and when he is roasted take hym of, and let hym cool awhile, and take hym and sowe hym in his skyn, and gilde his combe, and so serve hym forthe with the last cours.' Needless to say, we have not kitchen-tested this technique.

Note: Sir Kenelm Digby (d 1665) reported, on the subject of roast chicken, 'The Queen useth to baste such meat with yolks of fresh Eggs beaten thin ...' but we rather doubt that 17th century gentry frequented the kitchen the way today's Jet Set is said to.

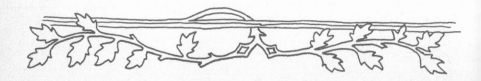

66 Capoun Y-rostyde with Black Sauce

Take þe Lyuer of capouns, and roste hit wel; take anyse, and grynde parysgingere, and canel, and a litil cruste of brede, and grynde hit well all to=gedre; tempre hit up wiþ verious, and þe grece of the capon, þanne boile it and serue forþe. ASHMOLE 1439

This recipe is just as good for chicken as for capon, but, since a chicken is smaller, quantities should be halved.

Roast Capon or Chicken with Black Sauce

1 capon (ca 6 lbs)
1 capon liver
1/4 tsp each anise, ginger, cardamom, and cinnamon –
  all ground
ca 1/4 cup bread crumbs
1/2 tsp salt
2 tsp vinegar or lemon juice
ca 1 cup drippings from capon: if the quantity of drippings
  is insufficient, add some chicken (or capon) broth

Roast the capon in the usual way. Separately, roast the capon liver, or sauté it in a frying pan, until it is fairly well cooked, but not dried out. Crush or grind the liver (using a mortar or blender, if possible) with bread, vinegar, and other seasonings; put in a saucepan with the drippings and bring to a boil, stirring. Serve in a sauce dish or gravy boat along with the capon.

67 Gees with Sawse Madame

Take sawge, parsel, ysope, and sauary; quinces and peers,
garlek and Grapes, and fylle the gees þerwith; and sowe þe
hole þat no grece come out. And roost hem wel, and kepe þe
grece þat fallith þerof. Take galyntyne and grece and do in
a possynet, whan þe gees buth rosted ynouh: take and
smyte hem on pecys, and þat tat is withinne and do in a
possynet and put þerinne wyne if it be to thyk. Do þerto
powdor of galyngale, powdor douce and salt; and boyle the
sawse, and dresse þe Gees in disshes, and lay þe sowe
onoward. FC 30

Goose with Sauce Madame

1 goose
1-2 tbsp each (less if dried) sage, parsley, hyssop (or mint),
   and savory
1 or 2 pears (hard; peeled, cored, and chopped)
1 or 2 quinces, if available (pared, cored, and chopped)
2-3 cloves garlic, mashed or finely minced
1 cup (approximately) seedless (or seeded) grapes
1/4 cup breadcrumbs
1/2 tsp cinnamon
1/4 tsp galingale or ginger
1/4 cup vinegar
1/4 cup red wine
1/2 tsp salt (or more, to taste)

Stuff the goose with a mixture of the fruits, herbs, and garlic;
sew or skewer closed, and roast on a rack in an open roasting
pan at 325° for 30 minutes per pound. Pour off the fat as it
accumulates, and set aside. When goose is about done, make a
sauce by blending together the breadcrumbs, vinegar, spices,
and wine, with a little of the accumulated fat (about 1/4 cup
is probably as much as most people would find palatable).

Pour the sauce over the goose, or serve separately.

VARIATIONS

1 Add chopped onions and the giblets of the goose to the stuffing. Omit quinces and garlic. When the goose is cooked, cut it up and arrange on a platter; put the stuffing in a pot with the other ingredients – using *white* wine and substituting, if you wish, several hardboiled yolks of eggs for the bread-crumbs; stir and simmer for a few minutes.

2 Omit quinces and pears. When goose is done, scoop out the stuffing and grind or mash it up with several yolks of hard-boiled eggs and enough vinegar or lemon juice to make a thickish sauce. Omit spices.

3 The following variation is not really Sauce Madame, but it is a similar idea. Roast the goose unstuffed. When it is almost done, take 1/4 cup of the goose fat, 1 cup of red wine, 2 tbsp vinegar, 2 onions, minced, and/or 2 cloves of mashed garlic, and put in a pot with the goose giblets (parboiled and chopped), 1/2 cup currents, pepper, ginger, cinnamon, clove, and mace. Boil, stirring, and serve as a sauce for the goose.

68 Chawdon

Take þe lyuer and þe offall of the Swanns & do it to seeþ in gode broth; take it up, take out þe bonys; take & hewe the flessh smale; make a Lyor of crust of brede & of þe blode of þe Swan ysoden, & do þerto powdor of clows & of piper & of wyne & salt, & seeþ it & cast þe flessh þerto iþewed, and messe it forth with þe Swan. FC 143

Since swans rarely appear on the dining tables of England and North America, we have adapted the recipe by substituting duck. We also suspect most cooks will not have a sufficient supply of duck blood for the sauce, and thus suggest broth – with, if desired, a little gravy colouring.

Duck with Chawdon Sauce

1 duck, ready to roast, with neck and giblets
2 tbsp bread crumbs (whole wheat or other dark bread is best)
1/2 cup red wine
1/2 tsp salt
1 cup stock or broth (preferably brown chicken stock)
1/4 tsp pepper
1/8 tsp ground cloves
optional: a little gravy colouring

Put the heart, liver, gizzard, neck, and any residue of blood from the duck into a saucepan; cover with 1 cup stock or broth and bring to a boil. Turn down the heat, cover, and simmer. Remove liver and heart after 10 minutes; let the rest cook another 20 minutes, then remove with a slotted spoon and allow to cool. If the broth has not already boiled down to about 1/2 cup, boil it down to about that amount; strain and reserve.

Roast the duck as you usually roast duck. When it is almost done, proceed with the sauce. Discard any bones from the neck and grind all the meat (including liver, etc) cooked in the broth; if you use a blender, the sauce can be made in one step. To ground meat, add all other ingredients, including the reduced stock; when well blended, cook, stirring, for about five minutes, or until nicely thickened. Serve separately as a sauce for the duck.

69 Ffesaunte Rosted

Lete a ffesaunte blode in þe mouthe as a crane, And lete him blede to dethe; pull him dry, kutte awey his hede and the necke by the body, and the legges by the kne, and putte the kneys in at the bente, and roste him: his sauce is Sugur and mustard. HARL 4016

Roast Pheasant

Sugar and mustard may sound a strange accompaniment to roast pheasant, and indeed some authorities of the period are firm that the pheasant should have no accompaniment but salt. However, the sugar and mustard combination may appeal to some tastes: if you wish to try it, mix powdered ground mustard with sugar and vinegar into a paste of fairly thin consistency. Or, substitute honey for sugar.

Pass separately with the roast pheasant: some diners are likely to prefer salt, alone, as advised by Wynken de Worde for roast fowl in general.

VARIATIONS
For game birds of all kinds, the *Modus Cenandi* recommends a cumin sauce. One given in the recipe for Checones in Critone (88 v1) would be suitable. Wynken de Worde suggests wine, ginger, and salt for partridge, and various combinations of wine or vinegar, ginger, pepper, mustard, and salt are specified elsewhere as sauces for game birds.

70 Rost Bef with Sauce Aliper

To mak sauce aliper for rostid bef take brown bred and stepe it in benygar and toiste it and strepne it and stampe garlic and put ther to pouder of pepper and salt and boile it a litill and serue it. N

This recipe has two defects: it reverses the order of toasting and steeping (it would be pretty hard to toast soaked bread) and it does not tell us to add any liquid except vinegar, although the sauce will have to be liquid enough to be boiled. But it has the great advantage of telling us what the sauce is to go with. The deficiencies are easily repaired by comparison with other recipes for the same sauce (which do not tell us what to serve it with), and other similar sauces.

Roast Beef with Garlic-Pepper Sauce

Roast beef (whatever cut you prefer and/or can afford, roasted as you like it)
2 slices wholewheat bread
2 tbsp wine vinegar
wine and/or stock, in quantities to produce desired consistency (see below)
2 cloves garlic, crushed
1/4 tsp each freshly ground black pepper, salt

When roast beef is almost ready to serve, toast the bread, then crumble it into a small bowl and pour the vinegar over it. Let this sit and soak for at least five minutes. Mash and put through a strainer, or blend in a blender. If you wish to make a boiled sauce (like a very thick gravy, with about 1 tbsp to be served with each slice of beef), add about 1 cup of beef stock and/or red wine; if, however, you wish to serve this as a very thick relish – rather like a modern horseradish sauce for beef – add only enough wine to make the paste of a soft consistency (up to 1/4 cup). Stir in garlic and seasonings,

tasting to see whether more salt seems called for. Serve as is if giving the thicker version, or, if making a thinner sauce, boil for a few minutes, and serve hot.

71 Venysoun Y-roste with Piper Sauce

Take brede, and frye it in grece, draw it up wiþ broþe and vinegre: caste þer=to poudre piper, and salt, sette on þe fire, boile it, and messe it forþ.   ASHMOLE 1439

This sauce is said to be a proper accompaniment to veal, goose, or venison – and some modern recipes for sauce for roast venison also make pepper a prominent spice. But John Russell advises salt and cinnamon with venison, and some of the modern recipes we have seen call for both pepper and cinnamon in a venison sauce. So we shall include both.

Roast Venison with Pepper Sauce

A roast of venison of ca 5 lbs (if unavailable, use veal)
3 slices white bread (crusts removed)
1 tbsp butter, lard, or beef fat
2 cups beef broth
1 tbsp wine vinegar
1 tsp salt
1/2 tsp each pepper, cinnamon

Roast the venison as you would beef, to the medium-well-done stage. (If the venison is old and tough, it should be marinated for several days beforehand, but young venison needs no marinade.) When it is about ready to serve, heat the butter (or other fat) in a frying pan and lightly fry the slices of bread. Pour over the bread a little of the broth (hot) and allow to soak for a few minutes. Then blend in remaining broth and all other ingredients – preferably in a blender. Boil the sauce, stirring, until thickened; serve separately.

72 Steykys of Venson or Bef

Take Venyson or Bef, & leche & gredyl it vp broun; þen take Vynegre & a litel berious, & a lytil Wyne, & putte pouder perpir þer=on y=now, and pouder Gyngere; & atte þe dressoure straw on pouder Canelle y=nowe, þat þe stekys be al y=helid þer=wyth, & but a litel Sawce; & þan serue it forth. HARL 279.II.31

Venison was obviously the preferable, aristocratic, meat: beef, a poor substitute. Most of us will have to make do with beef these days. It is probable, however, that this recipe does more for venison than it does for good beef; many modern recipes for venison still specify sweet, spicy seasonings not so far from this model. It is still a good recipe for beef steaks, however, if one is reasonably restrained in the matter of cinnamon: few 20th century diners would fancy their beefsteaks completely covered with cinnamon powder.

Venison or Beef Steaks

2 lbs beef (or venison) steaks; a thick piece of flank steak (London Broil) which can be sliced on the bias before saucing is ideal
1 tbsp vinegar
2 tbsp red wine
1/2 tsp salt
1/4 tsp pepper
1/8 tsp each ginger and cinnamon (use more cinnamon if you are using venison rather than beef – or if you yearn for more authenticity)

Grill the steak either in a grill pan (one with ridges) or a slightly greased frying pan or under a broiler. Grill as long as

necessary, according to size and thickness, and remove from the heat onto a serving platter as soon as brown. Then mix together the vinegar, wine, and seasonings, and spoon over the steaks. Serve at once.

This is obviously not a dish to do ahead of time and then heat up: it is better saved for one's smaller feast occasions. Those who choose to try a larger proportion of cinnamon may leave it out of the sauce mixture and, instead, sprinkle it directly on the meat before pouring on the sauce. If these are done in a grill pan, or under a broiler, the juices from cooking may be saved and used for final seasoning of a vegetable: Gourdes (15), for example.

VARIATION
Use a tougher cut of meat, such as a chuck steak; brown quickly in a frying pan with a little butter or other fat, then add seasonings, turn the heat down to barely warm, cover, and leave to finish cooking for about half an hour. This variety may be easier to reheat, if that is a consideration.

73 Alows de Beef

Take fayre Bef of þe quyschons, & motoun of þe bottes, & kytte in þe maner of Stekys; þan take raw Percely, & Oynonys smal y=scredde, & ȝolkys of Eyroun soþe hard, & Marow or swette, & hew alle þes to=geder smal; þan caste þer=on poudere of Gyngere & Saffroun, & tolle hem to=gederys with þin hond, & lay hem on þe Stekys al a=brode, & caste Salt þer=to; þen rolle to=gederys, & putte hem on a round spete, & roste hem til þey ben y=now. Þan lay hem in a dysshe and pore þer=on Vynegre & a lityl berious, & pouder Pepir þer=on y=now, & Gyngere, and Canelle, & a

fewe ȝolkys of harð Ƈyroun p-krempð þer=on; & serue forth.

HARL 279.II.30

Stuffed Beef Rolls

for 4 thin slices of steak (3/4 lb to 1 lb)
1 tbsp finely minced parsley
1 onion, minced
1 or 2 boiled eggs (or yolks only)
1 tbsp bone marrow, butter, or other cooking fat
1/4 tsp each ginger, salt
optional: small pinch ground saffron
juice of 1/2 lemon or 1 tbsp vinegar
sprinkling (scant) of pepper, ginger, cinnamon

Mix together parsley, onion, one egg yolk (mashed) or one whole boiled egg (chopped small) with marrow or fat, ginger, salt, and, if you wish, saffron. Spread this mixture on the steaks; then roll them up, securing with toothpicks and/or string (a combination is the best expedient). Put on skewers, for easy turning, and broil for about 10-15 minutes, turning to brown all sides of the rolls. When they are nicely browned, put them on a serving dish and sprinkle over them the lemon juice or vinegar, a dusting of pepper, ginger, and cinnamon, and crumbled yolk of hardboiled egg.

VARIATION

As the recipe suggests, lamb steaks may also be prepared in this fashion. Unless your butcher can provide you with boneless, thin lamb steaks, try using slices from a leg, removing the bone with a sharp knife. If slices of lamb leg are too thick to be rolled, they should be sliced into thinner slices: this is not difficult to do if the meat is partially frozen.

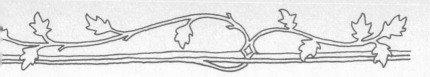

74 Bourbelier de Sanglier

First put the loin in boiling water, then take it out and stick it all over with cloves. Set it to roast, basting it with a sauce made from spices: that is, ginger, cinnamon, clove, grains, long pepper, and nutmeg, moistened with verjuice, wine, and vinegar; and baste with this without first boiling it. And when the roast is done, boil together. MP

This recipe apparently calls for a loin of wild boar; but, since wild boars will not be found in the average North American market, we have substituted pork. Those who want something which more closely approximates the flavour of wild boar can try marinating the pork for a few days in a marinade of wine, vinegar, oil, and herbs: which procedure is supposed to render the flavour more like that of wild boar. However, the roast is a very tasty one without such preliminaries.

Loin of Pork in Boar's Tail Sauce

4-6 lb loin roast of pork
cloves (enough to stud the roast at 1 or 2 inch intervals)
1/2 tsp each ground ginger, cardamom, pepper, salt
1/4 tsp each cinnamon, ground cloves, nutmeg
1/4 cup wine (preferably red)
1 cup vinegar

Stick whole cloves into the loin of pork; mix together all other ingredients and pour over the pork. Roast in the usual way, basting from time to time. When the roast is done, pour off pan juices and boil together to make the sauce.

Some recipes call for a thickening of breadcrumbs; if such a thickening is desired, use about 2 tbsp crumbs, stirred in as the sauce is boiling.

75 Cormarye

Take Colyandre, Caraway smalle gronden, Powdor of Peper and garlec ygronde in red wyne; medle alle þise togyder and salt it; take loyn of Pork rawe and fle of þe skyn, and pryk it wel with a knyf, and lay it in þe sawse; roost þerof what þu wilt, & kepe þat fallith þerfro in þe rosting and seeþ it in a possynet with faire broth, & serue it forth with þe roost anoon. FC 53

This recipe consists of a savory sauce, with which a loin of pork is to be basted, the dripping to be used as a sauce for the pork.

Roast Pork with Caraway Sauce

5-7 lb pork loin roast
2-3 cloves garlic, crushed
1/2 to 1 tsp each coriander and caraway seed
1 cup red wine (or 1/2 cup, if using a clay baker)
1/2 tsp salt
1/4 tsp pepper

Ideally, use a coffee grinder for grinding seeds. If you have none, use a mortar, a blender (not all blenders will do this well), or a rolling-pin, with the seeds between two sheets of waxed paper. When they are crushed, mix with all other sauce ingredients, preferably in a blender. The more finely the spices and garlic can be ground, the more effective the sauce will be.

Prick the loin of pork all over and place in a rack over a roasting pan. Pour the sauce over it and roast in the usual way, basting with the juices in the pan from time to time plus, if it seems desirable, wine. (You may, of course, adapt this to clay-baking procedures, if you have a clay baker.) When roast is done, pour off the drippings into a saucepan and add a small amount of broth or stock (chicken stock,

preferably – or broth made from pork bones). Stir and bring to a boil; thicken if you wish. Serve as a sauce for the pork.

76 Mouton Y-rosted with Sawse Camelyne

Take Raysons of Corance, & kyrnels of notys, & crusts of brede & powdor of gynger, clowes, flour of canel; bray it wel togyder and do it perto. Salt it, temper it up with vynegar, and serue it forth. FC 144

Cameline Sauce, like many other well-known dishes, varies from one recipe to another, though all contain cinnamon; this one is especially good, resembling a sort of chutney, which goes well with roast meat. The Ménagier suggests Cameline sauce with roast veal and rabbit, as well as with lamb, and tells us that both rabbit and veal should be parboiled and larded before roasting. It would be well to follow this advice if you wish to substitute one of them for the lamb.

Roast Lamb with Cameline Sauce

leg of lamb, roasted in the usual way
1/4 cup each currants and chopped nuts
   (walnuts are excellent)
2 tbsp breadcrumbs
1/2 tsp each ginger and cinnamon
1/4 tsp ground cloves
1/2 tsp salt (or more, to taste)
1/3 cup vinegar, preferably wine vinegar

If you have a blender, put all sauce ingredients in at once and blend until nuts and currants are finely chopped. Otherwise, a mortar may be used, or the currants and nuts chopped finely by hand and then mixed with other ingredients. Serve cold, in a separate dish. *(more)*

Some medieval directions call for sprinkling the roasting lamb with sage or thyme; others recommend dusting it with parsley as a finishing touch.

If a more liquid cameline is desired, add more vinegar. Or, for a simpler version, omit currants and nuts; wine may then be substituted for the vinegar, in which case the sauce should be boiled.

77 Longe de Buf

Nym the tonge of the rether and schalde and schawe yt wel and riȝt clene, and seth yt, and sethe nym a broche and larde yt wyth lardons and wyth clowys and gelofer, and do it rostyng, and drop yt wel yt rostyd wyth ȝolkes of eyrin and dresse it forth. AC 43

While the larding technique is probably a very good idea, it is one many modern cooks do not normally bother with, so our recipe is somewhat adapted here. Adepts with the larding needle are, however, urged to lard properly.

Roast Tongue

1 tongue, fresh or canned
ca 6 strips fresh fat pork; or, bacon, parboiled and drained
cloves (whole)
2 egg yolks (raw) – one will be enough for a small canned
    tongue

Parboil the tongue in water for about 2 hours, if fresh. Peel, stud with cloves, and wrap in the pork strips (or parboiled bacon). Roast in a 350° oven for about an hour. After 45 minutes, remove the pork and brush with beaten egg yolk.

(The tongue may be roasted on a spit instead, of course; in this case, the pork larding will have to be skewered on firmly, or tied with string.)

VARIATIONS
The French recipe is identical, but omits the gilding. It also recommends a cameline sauce as an accompaniment to tongue; the sort of sauce probably intended is made of ginger, cinnamon, nutmeg, and breadcrumbs, moistened with cold water and wine or vinegar, but the cameline recipe given here as an accompaniment to lamb would be very good with tongue, too. (See Mouton Y-rosted with Sawse Camelyne (76).) The Ménagier also notes that salted tongues may be simply boiled in wine and water and eaten with mustard.

78 Chicken Pasties Lombard

Chicken may be set in a pasty on their backs with the breast upward and large slices of bacon on the breast, and then covered. Item: in the Lombard manner, when the chickens are plucked and prepared, take beaten eggs, both the yolks and the whites, with verjuice and spice powder, and dip your chickens in this; and set them in the pasty with strips of bacon, as above. MP

As a whole chicken in pastry is a problem in carving – unless the chicken is boned, a chore few cooks are prepared to execute – we have limited ourselves to breasts of chicken for this dish. The pasties are much neater if the breasts are boned, but that is not particularly difficult. (Save the bones as an ingredient for broth or stock.) If it seems desirable to serve these as appetizers, simply cut the breasts in two or more portions.

Chicken Pasties Lombard

4 boned chicken breasts (for four main course portions)
1 egg, beaten
1 tbsp lemon juice
1/2 tsp ginger
pinch each cinnamon, cloves, cardamom
2-4 slices bacon
pastry, plain or puff: full recipe

If regular breakfast bacon is to be used, cook it partially first to take out some of the fat; or use back bacon (Canadian bacon), which has little fat. Roll out pastry and divide into 4 equal parts before it is completely rolled out; then try to make each portion as round as possible as you finish rolling it out piece by piece.

Mix beaten egg, lemon juice, and spices, and dip the pieces of chicken in this mixture. Lay each piece on one side of a round of pastry with a slice of bacon on top; bring other half of pastry round over to cover, and pinch edges together. For a neatly finished effect, press a fork around the edges to flute. Bake in a 350° oven for 30-40 minutes, depending on size; if using puff pastry, the oven should be hotter and the time not so long.

VARIATION

For a larger and much more spectacular dish, substitute a whole frozen boned turkey roll (thawed) for the chicken breasts; use puff pastry and glaze with beaten egg (or egg white). Do not cook the bacon very much beforehand, as the turkey needs the extra fat. Purists may object on the grounds that there were no turkeys in medieval Europe (the first ones arrived in the 16th century), but then perhaps purists will be prepared to bone their own chickens.

79 Pies of Parys

Take and smyte faire buttes of porke and buttes of vele togidre, and put hit in a faire potte, And putte thereto faire broth, And a quantite of Wyne, And lete all boile togedidre til hit be ynogh; And þen take hit fro the fire, and lete kele a litel, and cast ther-to raw yolkes of eyren, and pouudre of gyngeuere, sugre and salt, and mynced dates, reseyns of corence; make then coffyns of feyre past, and do it ther-ynne, and keuere it & lete bake y-nogh. HARL 4016

Other similar recipes suggest that the meats were variable, so we suspect a standard 'meat-loaf' mix, if your market carries one, will be fine. If you wish to serve as small hors d'œuvres, rather than as a main course, the same filling may be put into small tart shells, and, preferably, baked with a covering of aluminum foil, to be removed at the last moment, instead of a top crust: such small tarts will, of course, take less time to cook. In any case, however, it is advisable to do the parboiling of the meats well in advance of the rest of the cooking: modern tastes will prefer a de-fatted version, and it is a lot easier to remove the fat from the cooking juices if they are cooled for a time (even in a freezer, if you're in a real hurry).

Paris Pies

Pastry for a 9-inch pie pan (top and bottom) or
  ca 24 tart shells
1 1/2 lbs mixed ground meat, including at least two of
  pork, veal, beef
1 cup each meat stock or broth, red wine
3 egg yolks or 1 whole egg plus one yolk
1/2 tsp each ginger, sugar & salt
1/4 cup each minced dates, currants
optional: pinch of ground pepper or cubebs, and/or
  mace, ground clove

Put the ground raw meat in a saucepan and cover with the wine and water; bring to a boil and simmer for 10 minutes. Then drain all the cooking juices into a heatproof container, setting aside the meat. Let the cooking liquid cool (preferably in the refrigerator or freezer) until you can remove all the fat from the top.

When you are ready to assemble the pie, line a pie dish with pastry. Then bring the de-fatted juices to a boil; beat the egg yolks (or egg and yolk) in a bowl, and beat in a little of the hot (but not quite boiling) stock. Beat in the rest, still off the heat; then mix together meat, dried fruits, spices, and sauce, and stir over low heat for a few minutes to thicken slightly. Put in the prepared pie shell and cover with a top crust (unless you are making individual tarts). Bake in a pre-heated 350° oven for about one hour (less for individual tarts). As the mixture may tend to be pretty sloppy at first, be sure to slit the top crust to allow steam to escape; and it may also be wise to put a cookie sheet or piece of foil under the pie pan.

80 Mylates of Pork

Hewe Pork al to pecys and medle it with ayren & chese igrated. Do þerto powdor fort, safron, & pyneres with salt; make a crust in a trap, bake it wel þerinne, and serue it forth. FC 155

Pork Tart

1/2 lb minced or ground pork
4 eggs, beaten
1/4 cup grated cheese (parmesan is fine)
pinch each nutmeg, ginger, cardamom, pepper
scant pinch saffron
1/2 tsp salt
pastry tart shell (uncooked)

Mix together meat, cheese, eggs, and seasonings, and put in tart shell. Bake at 375° for 45 minutes. The tart may be served cold, but it is better hot.

81 Grete Pyes

Take faire yonge beef, And suet of a fatte beste, or of Motton, and hak all this on a borde small; And caste thereto pouder of peper and salt; And whan it is small hewen, put hit in a bolle, And medle hem well; then make a faire large Cofyn, and couche som of this stuffur in. Then take Capons, Hennes, Mallardes, Connynges, and parboile hem clene; take wodekokkes, teles, grete briddes, and plom hem in a boiling potte; And then couche al þis fowle in þe Coffyn, And put in euerych of hem a quantite of pouder of peper and salt. Then take mary, harde yolkes of egges, Dates cut in ii. peces, reisons of coraunce, prunes, hole clowes, hole maces, Canell, and saffron. But first, when thou hast cowched all thi foule, ley the remenaunt of thyne other stuffer of beef aboughte hem, as þou thenkest goode; and then strawe on hem this: dates, mary, and reysons, etc., And then close thi Coffyn with a lydde of the same, And putte hit in þe oven, And lete hit bake ynogh; but be ware, or thou close hit, that there come no saffron nygh the brinkes there=of, for then hit wol neuer close. HARL 4016

While few modern cooks will want to do anything on such a grand scale as this recipe suggests, even for feeding a mob, a scaled-down version is quite legitimate: Mrs Napier's recipe, for example, calls for capon or pheasant, not a whole lot of different fowls, whole or in pieces. The recipe below is for a fairly large pie (baked in a 9 to 10 inch dish), with ingredients selected from several recipes; those who wish to do something grander can add more poultry and, if they have a suitable dish, make a really 'great' pie.

Great Pies

Pastry to make two crusts for large pie pan
1 lb ground beef
1/3 cup red wine
2 Cornish game hens *or* one frying chicken, cut up; *or*
  2 chicken breasts (large), split
1/4 cup each chopped dates, currants, prunes
1/2 tsp salt
1/4 tsp each mace, cinnamon
1/8 tsp each ground cloves, cubebs or pepper
optional: pinch of saffron (or turmeric); marrow, egg yolks

Parboil the poultry for five minutes in salted, boiling water; allow to cool and remove skin. If using breasts of chicken, pull out as many bones as possible while leaving the pieces reasonably whole. Line pie pan with pastry. In a large mixing bowl, mix all remaining ingredients; if it seems too dry and crumbly, add a bit more wine; spread a layer of half this mixture on the bottom of the pie shell, then arrange the poultry on top; spread the rest of the meat mixture over the poultry, cover with a crust, and slit to let steam escape. Bake in a 325° oven for about 1 hour and 10 minutes, or until nicely browned. Glazing the top by brushing it with beaten egg white before baking produces a nice effect: and those who have been using recipes calling for egg yolks may find plenty of extra egg white for this purpose.

Stewes

Under this section are collected hearty, stewed, braised, and boiled dishes, all of which would have come under the vague heading of 'pottages' for our ancestors. At medieval feasts dishes of this kind were served along with roasts or in following courses, depending on the elaborateness of the menu. Fish stews can be found in the section on fish.

82 Lorengue de Pouchins

Take the oranges and slice them in white verjuice and white wine, and put them to boil, and put in ginger; and put your poultry to cook in this. MP, APP 5

Oranges were not much used in England at this period, but were apparently known there; since the oranges were bitter – of the Seville type – the normal oranges available in North America will need some extra tartness for this dish. The recipe does not tell us exactly how to cook the chicken (one doubts that the cooking is intended to be entirely accomplished in the sauce), so we shall take it as a way to finish partly roasted chicken.

Chicken in Orange Sauce

1 chicken, roasted (but not quite done)
2 oranges, sliced but not peeled
1 cup white wine
juice of 1/2 lemon (omit if you are using bitter oranges)
1/4 tsp ginger
1/2 tsp salt (or to taste)

When chicken is almost done, put sauce ingredients in a pan and cook together about 15 minutes. Cut up the chicken into serving pieces and arrange it in a heat-proof serving dish; pour the sauce over it, cover with aluminum foil (if your dish has no cover) and simmer for another 15 minutes before serving.

The recipe states that this is also a sauce for partridge or pigeons.

   If you prefer, the chicken or other poultry may be broiled or sautéed instead of roasted.

83 Schyconys with þe Bruesse

Take half a dosyn Chykonys, & putte hem in=to a potte; þen putte þer=to a gode gobet of fressh Beef, & lat hem boyle wel; putte þer=to Percely, Sawge leuys, Sauerey, noȝt to smal hakkyd; putte þer=to Safroun y=now; þen kytte þin Brewes & skalde hem with þe same broþe; Salt it wyl.

HARL 279.144

Comparison of this recipe with the Ménagier's Trumel de Beuf au Jaunet makes it evident that the beef to be used is the leg, and that this is, thus, chicken cooked with marrow-bones – the dish for which Chaucer's Cook was known. (The French recipe emphasizes the beef, but is otherwise the same.) Neither recipe calls for 'galengale' or 'pouder marchant,' but it would hardly be surprising if various spices were added by cooks. One almost indentical 16th century recipe calls for mace and ginger, among other things. In lieu of those mentioned in Chaucer's General Prologue, we feel a little experimentation with ginger and pepper is appropriate here. *Brewis* means toast used as a sop. Slices of toasted French bread are delicious with this dish – especially if it is really good French bread. The result is clearly the ancester of a modern Pot au feu, or potée Normande.

Chickens with Brewis

1 roasting chicken, tied to keep its shape
ca 2 lbs beef shin (cracked, ie, sliced by the butcher)

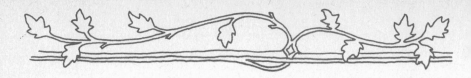

water to cover meats (but use a pot as small as possible)
1 onion, peeled
2-3 sprigs parsley
ca 2 sprigs each sage, savory (1/4-1/2 tsp dried)
pinch saffron (not too small; the saffron is really needed here)
1 tsp salt (or more, to taste); pepper, ginger, as desired
small loaf French bread, sliced and lightly toasted

Put chicken, beef, and all seasonings in a pot; cover with
water and simmer for about two hours. To serve, put slices
of toast on serving platter and chicken in the middle, with
beef around the chicken. Strain broth over the whole platter,
being sure to soak the brewis well.

84 Gelyne in Dubbatte

Take an Henne, and rost hure almoste y=now, an choppe
hyre in fayre pecys, an caste her on a potte; and caste þer=to
Freysshe broþe, & half Wyne; Clowes, Maces, Pepir,
Canelle; an stepe it with þe Same broþe fayre brede &
Vynegre: and whan it is y=now, serue it forth. HARL 279.41

Perhaps the title of this dish is equivalent to the modern term
'en daube.' Note that a hen is called for: if you wish to use an
older, tougher chicken, simply double the cooking time suggested, and increase (slightly) amounts of other ingredients,
since the chicken will be larger.

Chicken in White Wine Sauce

1 chicken
1 1/2 cups each chicken broth, white wine
1/4 tsp each mace, cinnamon
1/8 tsp (or less) each ground cloves, pepper

1/2 tsp salt, or to taste
1/4 cup bread crumbs
2 tsp vinegar

Roast the chicken in a hot oven (ca 450°) for half an hour,
then cut it into serving pieces; or, cut it up first, and brown
in a little fat in a frying pan. Then put the chicken pieces in
a cooking pot or casserole, and add wine, broth, and spices.
Simmer for half an hour; then take a little of the cooking
broth, plus the vinegar, and mix the breadcrumbs into a
smooth paste. Add this to the pot, and stir over medium heat
to thicken.

85 Mawmenny

Take þe chese and of Flessh of capons or of henns, &
bakke smal and grynde hem smale in a morter. Take mylke
of Almands with þe broth of freissh Beef, oþer freissh
flessh, & put the flessh in þe mylke oper in the broth and
set hem to þe fyre, & alye hem up with flour of Ryse or
gaftbon or ampdon as chargeant as þe blanke desire, &
with зolks of ayren and safron for to make it зelow. And
when it is dressit in disshes with blank desires styk aboue
clows de gilofre & strewe Powdor of galyngale aboue, and
serue it forth. FC 194

This recipe is presented in more than one source as to be
accompanied by what is here called 'blank desire' – variously
spelled elsewhere, but we shall call it Blandissorye: a sauce of
almonds mixed with broth, basically, though many other ingredients occur. But since the Mawmenny itself is made with
a similar sauce, most modern cooks will probably think the
extra sauce unnecessary. Those who wish to serve it in the
way here specified, however, should see the recipe for Blandissorye (5). They are advised to make the Mawmenny somewhat thicker than is specified here, so that it can be accompanied logically by the extra sauce.

Minced Chicken in Cheese and Almond Sauce

2-3 cups cold cooked chicken or capon, minced
1/2-2/3 cup minced or grated cheese (a mixture of
   Gruyere and Romano or Parmesan is pleasant)
2 tbsp ground almonds
2 cups chicken broth
2 tbsp rice flour or cornstarch
2 tbsp white wine
2 tbsp water
2 egg yolks (or one whole egg)
1/2 tsp salt
pinch of saffron
ca 1/4 tsp ground galengale or ginger

Steep the almonds in the broth for about 20 minutes. Dissolve rice flour or cornstarch in wine and water. Beat egg yolks (or egg). Heat the minced chicken and cheese in the almond milk; stir in rice flour mixture, with ground saffron, and stir until whole mixture is thick enough. Remove from heat and stir a little of the sauce into the beaten egg; then add this to the pot and stir, off the heat or over very low heat, for a few minutes. (Do not allow it to boil after adding the egg.)

Pour into a suitable serving dish and sprinkle with galingale or ginger, and, if you wish, ground cloves.

VARIATION

Omit cheese; this ingredient appears only in one early recipe. One cheese-less recipe also omits eggs, and adds further seasonings: sugar, cinnamon, mace, cubebs, and anise.

86 Chykens in Hocchee

Take parsel and sawge withoute eny oþer erbes; take garlec and grapes and stoppe þe Chikens ful, and seeþ hem in gode broth, so þat þey may esely be boyled þerinne. Messe hem and cast þerto powdor dowce. FC 34

Stuffed Boiled or Braised Chickens

1 roasting chicken
ca 1 cup (more-or-less: depending on the size of the chicken) seedless or seeded white grapes
ca 2 cloves garlic, mashed
ca 2 tbsp each parsley, sage (less sage if dried), finely minced
1-4 cups chicken broth (see below)
pinch each cinnamon, ginger, sugar, mixed with 1/2 tsp salt

The chicken may be boiled without any pre-browning, in which case you will need enough broth to cover it (up to 4 cups), but we advise browning it in a little oil or fat in a frying pan first, in lieu of the usual medieval practice of roasting the meat just long enough to brown it: or, even better, use an unglazed clay pot, which will boil and brown at the same time. In the latter case, use no more than 1 cup of broth.

In any case, mix together the grapes, garlic, parsley, and sage, and stuff the chicken with this mixture. Skewer or tie the chicken so that it is tightly closed and will hold its shape. Put it in a cooking pot in which it will barely fit – or a clay baker or a casserole – and pour the boiling broth over it. Simmer or bake (ca 350° oven, but you may adapt to your usual practice with a clay baker, if you are using one) for about an hour, or until done.

To serve, remove chicken from broth, and cut away string or remove skewers. If it has not been browned, remove skin. Sprinkle the spice powder over it and pour on a little of the broth as a sauce. A spoonful of stuffing should, of course, be served with every helping of meat.

87 Rosee of Hennys

𝕿ak the flowris of Rosys and wasch hem wel in water and after bray hem wel in a morter and than tak Almondys and temper hem and seth hem and after tak flesch of capons or of hennys and hac yt smale and than bray hem wel in a morter, and than do yt in the Rose so that the flesch accorde wyth the mylk and so that the mete be charchaunt, and after do yt to the fyre to boyle and do thereto sugur and safron that yt be wel ycolowrd and rosy of levys and of the forseyde flowrys and serve yt forth. AC 41

Exotic as this dish may sound, it is quite simple and pleasant, and to be recommended when you have some roses beginning to fade or wilt in the garden (or in a vase). We think it unwise to include saffron: the flavour can overwhelm the more delicate taste of the roses, and the colour added is more on the orange side than properly 'rosy.' If you want a more pronounced rose colour, add a drop or two of red food colouring.

Minced Chicken in Almond and Rosepetal Sauce

ca 3 cups diced cooked chicken
1 1/2 cups chicken broth
1 1/2 cups rose petals, red or pink (rinsed in cold water, dried gently, and with the white bases cut off; this amount means three or four roses of medium size)
2 oz (1/4 cup) chopped, slivered, or ground blanched almonds
1 tsp salt
optional: 1/2 tsp sugar, pinch of saffron

Put the rose petals in a mortar or coffee grinder with almonds – they are very difficult to grind by themselves. Since the average coffee grinder or small mortar will not hold this much, it will probably have to be done in 3 or more batches

of almonds and petals. Mix the resulting powder with the chicken broth (hot) and allow to steep for about ten minutes, or put in a saucepan and bring to a boil for a minute or two. Mince or grind the chicken as finely as possible and stir it into the sauce, or (preferably) blend it all together in a blender. Season and heat, stirring, for no more than five minutes. Do not overcook, or both flavour and colour will deteriorate.

To serve, mound on a serving dish or platter. It is good served with rice cooked in chicken broth with saffron, which can form a border on the serving dish. For an authentic decorative touch, garnish with a few more rose petals. (They taste like a really superior lettuce.)

This dish is also excellent cold, and may be served as a sort of paté.

88 Checones in Critone

Take checones and make hom clene, and chop hom on quarters, and sethe hom, and when thai byn half sothen take hom up and pylle of the skynne, and frie hom in faire grese and dress hom up, and cast thereon pouder of gynger ande sugur; then take iii pounde of almondes, and blaunche hom, and draw up a gode thik mylke with the brothe, and other gode brothe therewith, and do hit in a pot and sethe hit; and put thereto hole clowes, maces and pynes, and let hit boyle altogedur, and in the settynge down do thereto an ounce of pouder of gynger, and medel hit wyth vynegar, and serve hit forthe, and poure the syrip thereon, and cast thereon pouder of gynger and sugur; and a hole chekyn for a lorde.

ARUNDEL

This recipe (elsewhere in English cookery rolls given in a simplified form called Crayton, calling for cumin and omitting mace and cloves), is particularly remarkable in the helpful

statements of quantity: it is specified to be for 'ten messes,' ie, to serve 20 people; and if only a lord is to be served a whole chicken, we can assume that it is a recipe for five chickens (probably). However, difficulties remain: the French recipe, to which this is obviously related (Cretonée) calls for cow's milk, rather than almond milk, and a thickening of breadcrumbs and/or egg yolks. It also omits vinegar, and is vague about spices. But, most noticeably, it also features fresh peas as part of the sauce. We will therefore give two versions of this dish – one without peas in the English fashion, and one with, as prescribed by the Ménagier.

Chickens in Cream Sauce

ı the English version, with slight modifications from the French

1 frying chicken, quartered, or 4-6 chicken legs, cut in halves
2 tbsp ground almonds
lard, oil, or butter (or a combination) for frying
2-3 each whole cloves, peppercorns, maces
1/4 tsp each ground ginger, sugar
1 tsp vinegar
2 egg yolks (may be omitted: but in this case, the quantity
   of almonds should be tripled, or supplemented with breadcrumbs)

Parboil the chicken pieces in salted water to barely cover for about 15 minutes. Drain; remove the chicken skin if you wish to follow the recipe exactly, but it is not really necessary if you let the chicken dry thoroughly before proceeding. Brown the chicken in fat or oil. Meanwhile, add one cup of the broth to the almonds and whole spices and let them steep. When chicken is almost done, bring the sauce to a boil, stirring. Beat egg yolks (if used) in a bowl; pour the sauce onto

the yolks, stirring constantly. Return to the fire and stir over low heat for a few minutes to thicken. Then remove chicken to a serving platter; strain the sauce and add sugar, ground ginger, and vinegar, and pour it over the chicken.

II Checones in Critone with Peas

chicken, as above
2 lbs fresh, young peas, shelled (frozen peas are a poor substitute)
2 1/2 cups milk
1/4 cup (ca) breadcrumbs
1/4 tsp each ginger, sugar
pinch saffron
2 egg yolks or one whole egg (if omitted, increase quantity of breadcrumbs)
lard, oil, and/or butter for frying

Proceed to cook the chicken pieces as directed in the first recipe. Meanwhile, parboil the peas in salted water for 5-10 minutes, depending on size and age (skip this step if using frozen peas). While the chicken is frying, steep the bread-crumbs in 1/2 cup of the chicken broth and 1/2 cup milk. When peas have been parboiled, drain them and set aside. Stir the bread sauce over medium heat until it begins to thicken; add the rest of the milk and seasonings, and taste to see whether more salt is needed. Then add the peas and leave to simmer another five to ten minutes (but no more), while the chicken finishes browning.

When the chicken is done, remove to a serving platter. Strain the peas out of the sauce and scatter them over the chicken. Beat the egg or egg yolks (if used) in a bowl and gradually pour on the hot sauce, stirring constantly; return to the heat, stirring constantly, until sufficiently thick – do not allow to boil. Pour over the chicken and peas and serve at once. (This is not a dish to be completed in advance and re-heated.)

(more)

1 For the first version, all spices but ginger and pepper may be omitted, and cumin may be added (1/4 tsp is quite enough).

2 For the second type, veal, goose, or duck may be substituted for chicken, and lima beans or other shell beans may be used instead of peas.

89 Blamanger

Take Capons and seeþ hem; þenne take hem up. Take Almands blanched; grynd hem and alay hem up with þe same broth. Cast þe mylk in a pot. Waisshe rys and do þerto, and lat it seeþ. Þanne take brawn of Capons, teere it small, and do þerto. Take white grece, sugar and salt, and cast þerinne. Lat it seeþ. Þenne messe it forth and florissh it with aneys in confyt rede oþer whyt, and with Almands fryed in oyle, and serue it forth. FC 36

Rice with Capon or Chicken

1 chicken, or meat from a roast capon, cut up
1 cup raw rice
4 oz (1/2 cup) ground blanched almonds
1 tsp each salt and sugar, or to taste
1/4 tsp ginger
1 tbsp chicken fat or butter (or other cooking fat)
optional: 1/8 tsp cardamom
2-4 tbsp halved or sliced almonds, lightly browned
   in a little oil
1/4-1/2 tsp anise seeds

One capon has too much meat for a recipe on this scale, but the leftovers from a roast are fine; the bones can be used to produce the necessary broth. Of course, leftover roast chicken is also possible – if there is enough for the quantity of the dish desired.

Cover chicken or capon bones with a quart or so of salted water and simmer about 1 hour. Cover rice with cold water and leave to soak. Meanwhile, strain broth, skim off fat, and measure 3 cups of broth into a pan. Stir in almonds; cover and leave to steep about 15 minutes. Then drain water from rice and stir it into the almond broth; bring to a simmer, cover, and cook over low heat for about 15 minutes. Remove skin and bones from the chicken or capon, and cut the meat into small (ca 1-2 inch square) pieces. Stir into the rice along with butter or fat and remaining seasonings. Recover and leave to cook over low heat for 5-10 minutes, or put in a moderate oven for the same amount of time. If dish is to be reheated, undercook, and leave a little on the moist side – add more broth before reheating, if it seems dry. Serve in the casserole in which it was cooked, or mounded on a serving platter, or unmolded; garnish with the sautéed almonds and anise seed.

VARIATIONS
1 Some recipes call for other spices, such as cinnamon; at least one calls for saffron, which is pleasant here but probably inappropriate (a 'blancmanger' does not suggest the colour yellow).
2 Liver and/or giblets of the poultry may be added.
3 A later variant substitutes cream, eggs, and breadcrumbs for rice and broth, moving closer to the dish we know by this name today. Anyone who wishes to try this is reminded that almonds are still essential.
4 See also Blamanger of Fysshe (58).

90 Hoggepot

Take Gees and smyte hem on pecys. Cast hem in a Pot; do þerto half wyne and half water; and do þerto a gode quantite of Oynons and erbest. Set it ouer þe fyre and couer it fast. Make a layor of brede and blode and lay it þerwith. Do þerto powder fort and serue it forth. FC 31

The earliest version of this recipe calls for chicken, rather than goose, and, like many later versions, calls for the poultry to be browned before it is stewed. The following version combines features of several recipes of the period (mostly 14th century), some of which may sound odd – but the result is a really delicious dish.

Hodgepodge of Goose, Duck, or Chicken

1 goose, or 2 ducks, or 2 chickens, cut into pieces
2 cups each beef stock and red wine
4 medium onions, minced
2 tbsp minced parsley
2 tsp each (less if dried) minced sage, thyme, and savory
1/4 tsp each pepper, ginger, and cinnamon, ground (or mixed)
   with 1 tbsp lemon juice or cider (or wine) vinegar
1 tsp salt
4 slices bread, preferably whole wheat (ca 1 cup crumbs),
   lightly toasted

First brown the pieces of poultry. Chicken is best browned in a frying pan with a little oil or fat, but goose or duck is very fat in itself and it may be better to brown it, turning frequently, under a broiler, or in a hot oven. Reserve the liver or livers for a later stage: do not brown them. Fry the onions gently in some of the fat (or drippings) when the poultry is brown, but do not let the onions brown. Put poultry pieces

and onions in a dutch oven or other suitable covered pot or casserole; add stock, wine, and herbs; bring to a boil. Turn down the heat, cover tightly, and simmer (or bake in a 325° oven) for about an hour. Toward the end of this time, put the toasted bread (torn up or in crumbs) into a blender jar, bowl, or large mortar, along with uncooked poultry liver or livers and a few spoonfuls of the cooking sauce. With a duck or a goose, you will first have to skim excess fat off the sauce. Let bread soak for a few minutes, then blend, grind, or press through a strainer. Stir this thick paste back into the (degreased) sauce in the pot, along with the spice paste and salt; cook, stirring, for a few more minutes before serving.

VARIATIONS

1 Spices called for elsewhere include cumin, cloves, and mace; any of these may be substituted or added, but do not overdo it. This should not taste spicy.

2 Ale or beer may be substituted for the wine and stock; this will, of course, considerably modify the taste.

3 Since roasting was the usual way of pre-browning poultry, this is an excellent way to use up leftover roast goose, which will already have rendered its excess fat in the roasting and will thus be easier to handle than uncooked or partially cooked goose. Simply decrease all other ingredients in proportion to the amount of meat available, and cut the cooking time by about half.

91 Stwed Beeff

Take faire Ribbes of ffresh beef, And (if thou wilt) roste hit til hit be nygh ynowe; then put hit in a faire possenet; caste þer=to parcely and oynons mynced, reysons of corauns, powder peper, canel, clowes, saundres, safferon, and salt; then caste there=to wyn and a litull vynegre; sette a lyd on þe potte and lete hit boile sokingly on a faire charcole til hit be ynogh; þen lay the fflessh in disshes, and the sirippe there=vppon, And serve it forth. HARL 4016

Braised Beef Ribs

1 1/2 to 2 lbs boneless ribs of beef for braising, or about
  1 lb more of meat with the bone in
2-3 onions, minced
2 tbsp parsley, minced
2 tbsp currants
1/2 tsp cinnamon
1/4 tsp each pepper, allspice
1 tsp salt
optional: scant pinch of saffron
1 1/2 cups red wine
2 tsp vinegar (preferably wine vinegar)

Brown the beef by roasting it for about 30 minutes in an open pan in a hot oven, or brown it in a little cooking fat in a frying pan. Then put it in a stew-pot or casserole with all other ingredients. Cover and cook over low heat for about 45 minutes; or cook in a 325° oven for the same amount of time.

VARIATION
To cook in a clay baker, cook the beef by itself for about 45 minutes before adding other ingredients; cut the amount of wine by one half.

92 A Drye Stewe for Beeff

Take a fair urthen pot, and lay hit well with splentes in the bothum that the flessh neight hit not; then take rybbes of beef or faire leches, and couche hom above the splentes, and do therto onyons mynced, and clowes, and maces, and pouder of pepur and wyn, and stop hit well that no eyre goo oute, and sethe hit wyth esy fyre. ARUNDEL

This is an ideal dish to prepare in an unglazed clay baker, but it may also be done in another kind of covered casserole or roaster, using a rack (or improvised splints, as the 15th century recipe prescribes) to keep the beef from touching the bottom of the pot. If you cannot use an unglazed baker, however, you should brown the meat before proceeding with the recipe.

Pot Roast of Beef

a pot roast of beef, or some shortribs – ca 3 lbs
 (chuck is good)
1-2 onions, minced
ca 1/2 tsp each whole cloves, peppercorns, and whole mace
 (or a much smaller quantity of ground cloves, pepper,
 and mace)
1/2 cup red wine

Put the beef in the pot (on rack or splints if the pot does not have a ridged bottom, especially if it is not an unglazed baker) and scatter the onions and spices over it. Then pour over the red wine, close the pot tightly, and roast: about two hours at 325°, or follow whatever procedure you usually use for a pot roast of this size. (With an unglazed baker, many people prefer to bring the temperature nearer to 475°, cutting the cooking time somewhat.) To serve, put the beef on a serving platter and strain the pot juices over it. Thicken the juices if you wish, adding salt to taste.

93 Befe in Sirup

Take befe and sklice hit fayre and thynne,
Of þo luddock with owte or ellis with in;
Take mynsud onyouns, and powder also
Of peper, and suet and befe þerto
And cast þeron, rolle hit wele,
Enbroche hit overtwert, so have þou cele;
And rost hit browne as I þe kenne,
And take brothe of fresshe flesshe þenne,
And alye hit with bred er þou more do,
And mynsud onyons þou cast þer to,
With powder of peper and clowes in fere;
Boyle alle togeder, as I þe lere,
Þenne boylyd blode take þou shalle;
Strene hit þorowghe clothe, colour hit withalle;
Þenne take þy rost, and sklyce hit clene
In þe lengthe of a fynger; boyle hit by dene
In the same sewe; serve hit þou may
In a disshe togedur I say. LCC

Braised Stuffed Beef

ca 2 lbs round or rump steak (preferably in one piece)
2 medium onions, peeled and finely minced
ca 4 tbsp beef suet (use fat cut from the outer edge of the
   steak)
1/2 tsp ground black pepper
2 cups beef broth, stock, or boullion
1/4-1/2 cup breadcrumbs (whole wheat bread is appropriate)
pinch ground cloves
1 tsp meat glaze or commercial gravy colouring
   (substituting for blood, which was used for its colour)

Chop the suet and mix with half of the onions and pepper;

spread this mixture on the steak, roll it up, and fasten shut with skewers or string. Grill (in a broiler or on a spit) until brown. Meanwhile boil remaining ingredients, stirring until thick; strain. Slice the roasted beef and arrange neatly on a fireproof dish suitable for serving; pour the sauce over. Simmer for about five minutes, then serve.

94 Brawn en Peuerade

Take myghty brothe of Beef or of Capoun, an þenne take clene Freysshe Brawn, an sethe it, but not y=now; An ȝif it be Freysshe Brawn, roste it, but not I=now, an þan leche it in pecys an caste it to þe brothe. An þanne take hoole Oynonys, & pylle hem, and þanne take Vynagre þer=to, þen take Clowys, Maces, an powder Peppr, and caste þer= to and Canelle, and sette it on þe fyre, and draw yt þorw a straynoure, and caste þer=to, and a lytil Saunderys, and sette it on þe fyre, an let boyle tylle þe Oynonys an þe Brawn ben euyne sothyn, an nowt to moche; þan take lykoure y=mad of Bred an Vinegre an Wyne, an sesyn it vp an caste þer=to Saffroun to make þe coloure bryth, an Salt, and serue it forth. HARL 279.32

Pork in Pepper Sauce

3 lbs boneless pork tenderloin or 4 lbs of another lean, tender pork (not small chunks)
3 tsp wine vinegar
3 tbsp red wine
2 cups beef broth or stock (1 if using a clay baker)
24 very small onions (ca 1 inch) or fewer slightly larger ones, peeled

(*more*)

1/2 tsp each mace, freshly ground black pepper
1/8 tsp cinnamon
pinch ground cloves
optional: pinch saffron, sandalwood spice
1 tsp salt, or more
1/4 cup breadcrumbs or 1-2 slices bread, soaked in the wine

Brown the meat in a frying pan, unless you are using a clay baker or leftover roast pork. Put pork, onions, salt, spices, and 1 tsp of the vinegar into a clay baker or casserole. Pour the stock over and put in oven, preheated to 350° (if using clay baker, adjust accordingly). Cover tightly. Cook 1 1/4– 2 hours, depending on type of cooker and temperature; remove meat to a serving platter and slice neatly. Keep warm while making sauce.

Strain cooking juices into a bowl, reserving onions. Blend breadcrumbs or soaked bread with wine and 2 tsp vinegar until very smooth; beat in cooking juices and stir in a saucepan with the reserved onions until sauce is hot, smooth, and thick; then pour over the meat on its platter and serve.

This can also be prepared on top of the stove, but since pork takes long cooking the oven method is preferable – and the turned-off oven provides a place to keep the meat warm while the sauce is prepared.

95 Tartlett

Take pork ysode and grynde it small with safron, medle it with ayren and raisons of coraunce and powdor fort and salt; and make a foile of dowh3 and close the fars þerinne. Cast þe Tartlet in a Panne with faire water boillyng and salt; take of the clene Flessh withoute ayren and boile it in gode broth; cast þerto powdor douce and salt, and messe the tartlet in the dissh and helde the sewe þeronne. FC 50

Boiled Meat Dumplings in Broth

2 cups ground cooked pork
1/4 cup currants
1/4 tsp salt
pinch to 1/4 tsp of any or all of: ground cloves, ginger,
   pepper, cubebs, galingale (for powder fort)
1 egg
2 cups broth (meat or chicken)
pinch to 1/4 tsp of any or all of: cinnamon, cardamom,
   coriander, mace (for powdor douce)

In a small bowl mix one cup of ground cooked pork, the currants, salt, spices fort, and egg. Either make a paste of flour
and water/egg (use a noodle recipe) and roll it very thin, or
buy commercially made sheets of dough for eggrolls or won-
tons. Cut into 2 inch squares. Moisten the edge of the paste
with beaten egg or water, place a spoonful of the meat mixture in the middle, and fold over so the edges meet (to make
a triangle shape). Press edges together. Boil the tartlets in
salted water until the paste is cooked.

   Add the other cup of ground cooked pork to the broth,
with douce spices and salt. Heat the mixture, add the tartlets, and serve.

VARIATION
Like Won Tons, which they closely resemble, these dump-
lings may be fried rather than boiled.

96 Monchelet

Take Veel oþer Moton and smite it to gobetts; seeþ it in gode broth. Cast þerto erbes yhewe, gode wyne, and a quan= tite of Oynons, mynced. Powdor fort and Safron; and alye it with ayren and verjious: but lat not seeþ after. FC 16

This dish bears some resemblance to a modern Blanquette de Veau, but has a distinctive character of its own a bit different from any modern recipe. Since the primary purpose of the saffron appears to be colouring, we advise that this be omitted, or a drop of food colouring substituted.

A Veal or Lamb Stew

1 1/2 to 2 lbs veal stewing meat
1 1/2 to 2 cups chicken broth
1 cup white wine
2 medium onions, minced
1 tbsp minced parsley
1/2 to 1 tsp each (depending on whether fresh or dried
   herbs are used) thyme, rosemary, savory
1/4 tsp each ground ginger and coriander
salt to taste (depending on how well salted broth is)
1 egg
juice of 1/2 lemon (ca 2 tbsp; or use cider vinegar)
optional: pinch of saffron

Cut veal into pieces – about 2 inches square is ideal – and put in a cooking pot, preferably enamelled. Add onions, herbs, and spices, and cover with wine and broth. Simmer for about 45 minutes, covered. Beat egg together with lemon juice or vinegar. Pour a little of the hot (but not boiling) sauce into the egg and lemon mixture, stirring; then add this to the con- tents of the saucepan, off the heat. Stir off the heat or over very low heat to thicken; do not allow to boil after adding egg.

VARIATION

A similar dish, called Corat, calls for loin of veal, pork, or lamb (actually 'Noumbles,' but this may mean kidneys, or other organ meats), parboiled before it is cut up and put in broth to finish cooking. Otherwise, the recipe is identical.

97 Hericot de Mouton

Cut it up into little pieces, then put it to parboil in a first water. Then fry it in fresh lard; fry it with onions minced small, and add beef boullion, and put with it maces, parsley, hyssop, and sage; boil it together. MP

Later English recipes invariably call for turnips in a stew called Haricot. They may also have been a common ingredient earlier: early recipes are so few and far between that one cannot tell. By all means add turnips, if you like, to this recipe. We skip the parboiling as unnecessary for fresh young lamb: if you are using mutton, however, parboil it.

Lamb or Mutton Stew

3 lbs lamb (or mutton) stewing meat, cut into chunks
4 onions (ca), minced
lard, butter, or other cooking fat for browning (ca 1 tbsp)
2 cups beef stock, boullion, or other meat broth
1-2 tbsp fresh parsley, chopped
1 tsp salt (or to taste)
1/2 tsp each minced sage and mint (we did not find dried
    hyssop at all flavourful, and prefer to substitute mint,
    which is of the same family; if you grow hyssop, you may
    wish to try it)
1/4 tsp ground mace

Remove excess fat and bones from lamb. Brown over medium heat in a frying pan with fat, adding the minced onions after meat begins to brown. When meat and onions are both sufficiently brown, put in a pot or casserole with herbs, stock, mace, and salt; simmer for about an hour, or cook covered in a medium oven. If the sauce appears to be too thin, a thickening may be used (for example, cornstarch), but it should boil down to a good consistency.

98 Stwed Mutton

Take faire Mutton that hath ben roste, or elles Capons, or suche oþer flessh, and mynce it faire; put hit into a possenet or elles betwen ii. siluer disshes; caste thereto faire parcely, And oynons small mynced; then caste there=to wyn, and a litull vynegre or vergeous, pouder of peper, Canel, salt and saffron, and lete it stue on þe faire coles, And þen serue hit forthe; if he haue no wyne ne vynegre, take Ale, Mustard, and A quantite of vergeous, and do þis in þe stede of vyne or vinegre. HARL 4016

Reheated Lamb in Wine Sauce

2-3 cups leftover roast lamb or mutton, cut into fairly small chunks
2-3 onions, minced
ca 1/4 cup parsley, minced
1 tsp salt
1/4 tsp each pepper and cinnamon
optional: pinch of ground saffron
4 tsp vinegar or lemon juice
1 cup wine (preferably red)

Heat all ingredients together in a suitable pan, or in a shallow heatproof serving dish; the mixture should be simmered for at least 10 minutes to evaporate the alcohol sufficiently and cook the onions, but no more than 25 minutes, or the parsley will become overcooked. If a thickening is desired, stir in some cornstarch dissolved in cold water and stir a few minutes more.

VARIATIONS

1 Other roasted meats, such as chicken, may be substituted for the lamb. Some meats will, of course, do better with red wine – beef, for example; while white may be used with others.
2 Ale or beer may be substituted for wine. If mustard is added to this version, omit the cinnamon.

99 Egurdouce

Take Conynges or Kydde and smyte hem on pecys rawe, and frye hem in white grece. Take raysons of Corance and fry hem; take oynons, parboile hem and hew hem small and fry hem. Take rede wine, sugar, with powdor of peper, of gynger, of canel; salt; and cast þerto; and lat it seeþ with a gode quantite of white grece; and serue it forth. FC 21

'Egurdouce' (other spellings of the world include Egredouncye) means 'sweet-and-sour,' derived from French Aigredoux; oddly, about half the recipes omit one or the other essential aspect. This recipe omits the sour part; at least two others include vinegar but forget sugar. Etymology plus the few recipes that do include both vinegar and sugar suggest we should remedy the omission. Lamb is suggested as a reasonable substitute for kid, and breadcrumbs added as a thickener, as in most other recipes for the dish.

Sweet and Sour Lamb

2-3 lbs lamb stew meat, cut up in chunks (ca 2 inch)
butter or other cooking fat (about 2 tbsp)
1/4 cup currants
2-3 onions
1 1/2 cups red wine
1/2 cup vinegar
1/2 cup sugar
1/2 tsp each ginger and cinnamon
1/4 tsp pepper
1 tsp salt (or more: to taste)
ca 2 tbsp breadcrumbs

Melt butter or fat in a frying pan or dutch oven and brown the pieces of lamb in it; when lamb is almost brown enough, add currants. Meanwhile, cover onions with cold water and bring to a boil, then drain off the water and chop the onions; add them to the lamb and currants and fry a few minutes more. Then add wine, vinegar, sugar, and seasonings; cover, and let simmer for about 45 minutes. Thicken with the breadcrumbs, mixed to a paste with a few spoonfuls of the sauce first.

VARIATIONS
1 Use rabbit, pork, beef, or chicken instead of the lamb.
2 Add parsley, sage, and/or other herbs.
3 Add ground cloves, mace, and/or sandalwood spice.
4 Add a pinch of saffron.
5 Parboil the meat before browning; or brown the meat by broiling or roasting it; then chop and put in the broth, thus eliminating the fat from the recipe.

100 Gruelle A-forsydde

Take otemele an grynd it smal, an sethe it wyl, an porke þer-ynne, an pulle of þe swerde an pyke owt þe bonys, an þan hewe it, an grynd it smal in a morter; þan neme þin grwel and do þer-to; þan strayne it þorw a straynour, and put it in a potte an sethe it a lytel, an salt it euene; an colour it wyth saffroun, an serue forth rennyng. HARL 279.7

Another recipe for this dish calls for beef rather than pork, and suggests seasoning with sage and parsley rather than saffron. The latter seasoning is just as good with pork, and subtly transforms this admittedly simple and homely concoction. It seems an especially useful dish for using up the last bit of a roast: therefore the directions assume a piece of at least partly cooked meat.

Meat Porridge

Cooked piece of beef or pork, preferably with bone in,
   but enough meat on the bones to yield about 2 cups of
   chopped meat
5 cups water
one onion, peeled and chopped
ca 2 tbsp minced parsley
2-3 sage leaves, or about 1/4 tsp dried sage
1 tsp salt (or more, to taste)
1 1/2 cups quick-cooking oatmeal

Put onion and meat in a pan with the water and salt; simmer for about 15 minutes. Then remove meat; discard bone and any skin. Chop the meat finely, or put it through a grinder (or in a blender for a few seconds, with some of the broth). Then mix together in the pan meat, oatmeal, herbs, and broth, and bring to a boil. Boil, stirring, for about 3 minutes, then cover and leave, off the heat, for about five minutes before serving.

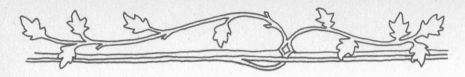

101 Cibey of Coney

To mak cony or malard in ceby tak cony henne or malard and rost them till they be almost enoughe or else chope them and fry them in freche grece and fry onyons mynced and put them in a pot and cast ther to freche brothe and half wyne clowes maces pouder of guinger and pepper and draw it with benygar and when it is boiled cast ther to thy licour and pouder of guingere and benygar and sesson it and serue it. N

This recipe omits, no doubt through someone's inadvertence, an important ingredient invariably called for elsewhere: a bread thickening, generally made with toasted bread.

Rabbit Stewed with Onions

1 rabbit, whole or cut into pieces
3-4 onions, sliced or chopped (1 1/2 to 2 cups chopped onion)
ca 2 tbsp cooking fat .
1 cup each chicken or meat broth, red wine
1/4 tsp each ginger, pepper (ginger may be slightly increased)
1/8 tsp mace; pinch of clove
1/2 tsp salt, or to taste (this depends on the broth)
2 slices bread (preferably wholewheat), toasted
1 tbsp wine vinegar

Roast the rabbit until brown, then cut it up, or start by browning pieces of rabbit in the fat. In either case, when pieces are brown, add onions to pan and cook together in fat until onions are soft. Meanwhile, soak the toast in broth. Then mash the toast through a strainer, or blend it with the broth in a blender. Add this bread paste to the rabbit and onions, along with the rest of the broth and wine, vinegar, and all seasonings. Let the meat stew in this sauce until done,

or at least long enough for the flavours to blend, if the rabbit is already roasted: this will take at least half an hour for rabbit that has only been browned in fat, and 10-15 minutes for roasted rabbit, but overcooking will not hurt this stew.

VARIATIONS

1 As the original recipe indicates, duck or chicken – among other meats – may be cooked the same way.

2 Some recipes substitute ale for wine, or use meat broth alone; we think the dish less interesting if only broth is used, but certainly ale or beer is a variant many may prefer.

3 Other spices sometimes called for include cinnamon and nutmeg. If you wish to add either one, do not overdo it: try adding 1/8 tsp of either or both. The most important seasoning is clearly the ginger (note that the whole spice mixture is simply referred to as 'ginger' the second time it is mentioned in the original recipe above); thus it may be appropriate to increase the amount of ginger to 1/2 tsp. Other seasonings sometimes called for are parsley and saffron. We do not see the point of saffron here, but think it a nice touch to sprinkle the stew with some minced parsley just before serving.

102 Garbage

𝕿ake fayre garbagys of chykonys, as þe hed, þe fete, þe lyuerys, an þe gysowrys; washe hem clene, an caste hem in a fayre potte, anð caste þer=to freysshe brothe of Beef or ellys of moton, an let it boyle; an a=lye it wyth brede, an ley on Pepir an Safroun, Maces, Clowyse, an a lytil verious an salt, an serue forth in þe maner as a Sewe.

HARL 279.17

Even the most enthusiastic of medievalists may feel qualms about serving or eating stewed chicken heads, so be selective about which 'garbage' you use. A dish made of livers alone is apt to be highest in general appeal, but hearts and gizzards

can also be used successfully. The recipe below calls for a mixture of these. Anyone who prefers to eliminate either the livers or the other giblets may adapt it accordingly.

Giblets

1 lb giblets (chicken hearts and gizzards)
1 lb chicken livers
1 cup (ca) brown stock, broth, or beef boullion
1 tsp salt
1/4 to 1/2 cup breadcrumbs
1/4 tsp each ground pepper, saffron (optional), and mace
1/8 tsp ground cloves
1 tsp verjuice (use cider vinegar or lemon juice)
1/2 tsp ground sage
2 tbsp chopped parsley

Put the gizzards and hearts in a saucepan with the stock and bring to a boil; simmer for 25-30 minutes. Then add livers, and simmer for another 5 minutes. Now stir in all seasonings (except the verjuice) and the breadcrumbs; stir until sauce seems well thickened. Add verjuice just before serving.

The sauce will be smoother if you can blend it in a blender, of course. Or you may use a thickener other than bread: flour, cornstarch, etc, observing the proper procedures for the thickener of your choice.

103 𝔑𝔬𝔲𝔪𝔟𝔩𝔢𝔰

𝔗𝔞𝔨𝔢 𝔫𝔬𝔲𝔪𝔟𝔩𝔢𝔰 𝔬𝔣 𝔇𝔢𝔢𝔯 𝔬𝔭𝔢𝔯 𝔬𝔣 𝔬𝔭𝔢𝔯 𝔟𝔢𝔢𝔰𝔱; 𝔭𝔞𝔯𝔟𝔬𝔦𝔩𝔢 𝔥𝔢𝔪; 𝔨𝔢𝔯𝔣 𝔥𝔢𝔪 𝔱𝔬 𝔡𝔶𝔠𝔢. 𝔗𝔞𝔨𝔢 𝔱𝔥𝔢 𝔰𝔢𝔩𝔣 𝔟𝔯𝔬𝔱𝔥 𝔬𝔯 𝔟𝔢𝔱𝔱𝔢𝔯; 𝔱𝔞𝔨𝔢 𝔟𝔯𝔢𝔡𝔢 𝔞𝔫𝔡 𝔤𝔯𝔶𝔫𝔡𝔢 𝔴𝔦𝔱𝔥 𝔱𝔥𝔢 𝔟𝔯𝔬𝔱𝔥, 𝔞𝔫𝔡 𝔱𝔢𝔪𝔭𝔢𝔯 𝔦𝔱 𝔲𝔭 𝔴𝔦𝔱𝔥 𝔞 𝔤𝔬𝔡𝔢 𝔮𝔲𝔞𝔫𝔱𝔦𝔱𝔢 𝔬𝔣 𝔳𝔶𝔫𝔢𝔤𝔞𝔯 𝔞𝔫𝔡 𝔴𝔶𝔫𝔢. 𝔗𝔞𝔨𝔢 𝔱𝔥𝔢 𝔬𝔶𝔫𝔬𝔫𝔰 𝔞𝔫𝔡 𝔭𝔞𝔯=

boyle hem, and mynce hem smale and do þer=to. Color it with blode and do þer=to powdor fort and salt, and boyle it wele, and serue it forth. FC 13

'Noumbles' is a confusing term because it is sometimes a word for loin meat and sometimes for organ meats. In reference to deer, however, it can be assumed that organ meats are intended – nor does this sort of recipe sound at all the normal way of cooking a loin, which would, of course, be roasted. We have assumed the kidney to be the best meat for the recipe, but liver or heart, or a combination of organ meats, could be substituted.

Kidney Stew

2 beef kidneys (ca 1 1/2-2 lbs)
3/4 cup beef broth or stock
1/4 cup breadcrumbs
2 tbsp vinegar
1/4 cup red wine
2-3 onions, peeled
1/4 tsp each ginger, mace, and pepper
1/2 tsp salt (or to taste)

Cover the kidneys with cold, salted water and bring to a boil; then pour off the water (or save it for broth, if you have no beef stock). Chop the kidneys into pieces about one inch square, or a little more. Beat the breadcrumbs into the broth (starting by moistening with just a tablespoon or two) and stir in the wine and vinegar.

Meanwhile, parboil onions in salted water for about five minutes. Drain, and chop the onions. Add them along with seasonings and chopped kidneys to the sauce and bring to a simmer; cover and cook gently for 25-30 minutes.

(more)

Substitute ale or beer for the wine and vinegar, using about half ale and half broth; season with 1/4 tsp pepper. Onions may be omitted.

104 A Tile of Meat

Take cooked crayfish and remove the meat from the tails; the rest, shells and carcase, should be ground for a very long time. Then take unpeeled almonds and have them shelled and washed in hot water like peas, then ground with the shells spoken of above, and with them grind bread browned on the grill. Then you should have capons, chickens, and pullets, broken into quarters raw, or veal broken into portions, cooked; and with the broth in which they are cooked moisten and dilute what you have ground and then put it through a strainer. Then grind what is left in the strainer again and strain again. Add ginger, cinnamon, clove, and long pepper, moistened with verjuice without vinegar, and boil all this together. Now let your meat be cooked in lard in gobbets or quarters, and serve it forth in bowls, and pour the sauce over it and on the sauce, in each bowl, set four or five crayfish tails, with powdered sugar over all. MP

This dish, a real *pièce de résistance*, should not be attempted without a blender, or, at the very least, a large mortar and pestle. With a blender it is much easier and faster, but still takes some time and patience. It is worth it. The quantity given here is for a main course for four people; to serve six or more (including presentation as one of several dishes to be sampled at a feast), cut the chicken into smaller pieces, but try to arrange the pieces into the same sort of patterned effect, which is no doubt the source of the name 'tile' here.

Chicken and Shellfish in Shellfish Sauce

1 frying chicken, cut into quarters
2-3 tbsp cooking fat
4 or 8 (depending on size) crayfish, lobster tails, or scampi;
   in a pinch, use shrimp (the largest you can find; at least
   half a pound)
1/4 cup blanched almonds (they need not be ground in
   advance)
1-2 slices (depending on size) white bread, toasted
2 cups chicken broth or stock (use neck and giblets of
   chicken to make some, if you have none on hand)
1 tsp lemon juice or cider vinegar
1/8 tsp ground ginger
pinch each cinnamon, clove, pepper
salt to taste

Cover the shellfish with wine and water plus a little salt and cook for about five minutes, depending on the size of the shellfish. Drain (but reserve broth for part of the stock) and shell, keeping crayfish, scampi, tails, or shrimp whole, and reserving shells and all debris (such as roe). Soak the toasted bread in a little broth. Dry the shells (and etc, if any) with paper towelling and put through a meat grinder or chop as finely as possible. Then put the shells in a blender (or mortar) with the almonds, bread, and enough broth to cover and blend until it is very finely pulverized and as smooth as possible. Rub through a strainer; then return what is left in the strainer to the blender, add a bit more broth, and repeat the process. Put the strained mixture in a saucepan and stir in any remaining broth. Add the spices, dissolved in the lemon juice or vinegar, and bring to a boil. Stir for about five minutes or until slightly thickened; then cover and put aside.

Sauté the chicken pieces in fat, turning to brown both sides; this will take about 45 minutes, but if you wish to do it in advance, undercook and reheat in a covered casserole at the last minutes. (We do not think it necessary to parboil chicken first, as it was in the 14th century: but you may if

you wish. It does tend to make it harder to brown the chicken, however, unless you let the chicken cool and dry out after it has been parboiled.)

When you are ready to serve the dish, reheat the shellfish gently in a little bit of the sauce, while also reheating the rest of the sauce (and, if necessary, the chicken). Arrange the chicken in a quartered circle on a fairly deep platter; pour the sauce over it. Then arrange the shellfish between the pieces of chicken (but on top) so that the whole dish will have an appropriate tile-like pattern, and serve.

Desserts

Most – although by no means all – medieval feasts ended with a sweet course; though the word 'dessert' was not common, it originated in this period and the concept was commonplace enough. Most such last courses consisted of simple offerings such as fruits (some of which, however, were also eaten as a first course, as modern diners eat melons or fruit cup), nuts, cheeses, candied spices (such as preserved, candied ginger), wafers, and sweet spiced wines. But there are many other medieval dishes which we would think of as desserts today.

105 Strawberyes with Creme Bastard

Take þe whyte of Eyroun a grete hepe, & putte it on a panne ful of Mylke, & let yt boyle; þen sesyn it so with Salt an hony a lytel; þen lat hit kele, & draw it þorw a straynoure, an take fayre Cowe mylke an draw yt with=all, & seson it with Sugre; & loke þat it be poynant & doucet: & serue it forth for a potage, or for a gode Bakyn mete, wheder þat þou wolt. HARL 279.151

This is a recipe for custard, but made in quite the opposite way from the usual modern sauce in that whites, instead of yolks, are used.

Strawberries with White Custard Sauce

1 qt strawberries, washed, hulled, and sprinkled with
 ca 1 tbsp sugar
2 egg whites
1 cup plus 2 tsp milk
2 tbsp honey
pinch salt
2 tsp sugar

Put egg whites in a sauce pan with 1 cup of the milk, and stir over medium heat as it comes to a boil. Let it simmer for about 5 minutes, stirring; then add the honey and salt. After simmering for another minute or two, remove from heat and strain or blend in a blender, adding remaining milk and sugar. Pour into a pitcher or serving dish and chill; it will thicken as it chills.

Serve over washed, hulled, slightly sweetened strawberries.

106 Wardonys in Syryp

Take wardonys, an caste on a potte, and boyle hem till þey ben tender; þan take hem vp and pare hem, and kytte hem in to pecys; take y=now of powder of canel, a good quantyte, an caste it on red wyne, an draw it þorw a straynour; caste sugre þer=to, and put it in an erþen pot, and let it boyle: an þanne caste þe perys þer=to, an let boyle to=gederys, an whan þey haue boyle a whyle, take pouder of gyngere and caste þer=to an a lytil venegre, an a lytil safron; an loke þat it be poynaunt an dowcet. HARL 279.10

Another early recipe is reported to include cloves, and to call for longer, slower cooking. We will thus offer alternative instructions in this matter.

Pears in Wine Syrup

2 lbs firm, ripe, unblemished pears
2 cups red wine (or, if preferred, 1 cup wine and 1 cup water)
1/2 cup sugar
1 tsp cinnamon
1/4 tsp ginger
optional spices: 6-8 whole cloves; pinch of saffron
1 tbsp lemon juice (or do as later cooks did and use a strip
of lemon or orange peel; or use vinegar)

Parboil the pears in a large pot of water for about 5 minutes; remove and peel. Pears will look most attractive if left whole, but if you cut them up, cut lengthwise into halves or quarters, retaining stems, if possible, but removing stem lines and cores. Mix cinnamon and red wine (or wine and water) and strain the mixture into a pan (enamelled, if pears are to be cooked in same vessel). Add sugar and stir over heat until the sugar is dissolved. Then, either:

1 add pears to syrup and poach gently for about 10 minutes, keeping the syrup just below the simmering point to keep the pears from falling apart. Add ginger, lemon juice (or vinegar or peel), and saffron and/or cloves, if desired, toward the end of the cooking period. Let pears cool in the syrup. Or:

2 Put pears in an enamelled or earthenware casserole, with remaining ingredients. Pour sugar syrup over them; cover casserole and bake in a 250° oven for about 5 hours, turning pears from time to time, or cook covered on the stove over very low heat 6-8 hours. Remove pears to dish in which they will be served. If the quantity of syrup is excessive, boil it down a bit to thicken it. Pour syrup over pears and store in a cool place, or in refrigerator, where they will keep well for several days. Serve them in their syrup.

107 Strawberye

Take Strawberys, & waysshe hem in tyme of ȝere in gode red wyne; þan strayne þorwe a cloþe, & do hem in a potte with gode Almaunde mylke, a-lye it with Amyndoun oþer with þe flowre of Rys, & make it chargeaunt and lat it boyle, and do þer-in Roysonys of coraunce, Safroun, Pepir, Sugre grete plente, pouder Gyngere, Canel, Galyngale; poynte it with Vynegre, & a lytil whyte grece put þer-to; coloure it with Alkenade, & droppe it abowte, plante it with þe graynys of Pome-garnad, & þan serue it forth.

HARL 279.123

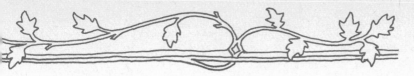

This recipe has been much maligned. Mead was among the writers horrified at the idea of so treating strawberries. But if one keeps a delicate touch with the spices (as most medieval cooks must have had to, considering their expense), the result is not unlike a modern strawberry mousse: it is, in fact, delicious.

Strawberry Pudding

1 pt fresh strawberries (if you must use the frozen kind, the juice should be substituted for some of the liquid in the recipe)
1/4-1/2 cup red wine
2 oz (1/4 cup) ground almonds
2 tbsp rice flour or cornstarch
1/3 cup sugar
1 1/4 cup water
pinch each pepper, ginger, cinnamon, salt
2 tbsp dried currants
1 tbsp lard or butter
2 tsp wine vinegar (or lemon juice)

Hull and pick over the strawberries, cutting out any bad places. Put in a bowl and pour the wine over them. Mix gently with your hand or a wood or plastic spoon; then pour off and discard the wine. Force strawberries through a sieve into a pot, and blend in remaining ingredients – or put them in a blender and blend everything together – except for the fat, vinegar, and currants. Bring mixture to a boil over medium heat, stirring constantly; let it boil for about two minutes to thicken, then remove at once and stir in, first, the fat, then the vinegar and currants. Pour into a large serving dish or individual serving dishes, and allow to cool. Chill before serving.

If you are as much of a perfectionist as the 15th century cook from whom this recipe comes apparently was, you may

beef up the colouring with red vegetable dye and/or garnish the pudding with pomegranate seeds, but it really is not necessary.

VARIATION

Turnesole, blackberry pudding, is made much the same way. Use blackberries instead of strawberries and omit spices, currants, lard, and vinegar. This is good hot, but some may wish to strain out the seeds at some point.

108 Ioncate with Hurtilberyes

Strawberie & hurtilberyes with the cold Ioncate

are mentioned in John Russell's *Boke of Nurture.* Russell lists Ioncate in conjunction with 'Milke, crayme, and cruddes.' He does not tell us how to make it, but another authority reports it to be 'a certaine spoone-meat made of creame, Rosewater, and Sugar,' and it is elsewhere said to be a species of cream cheese. The etymology of the word is generally accounted to derive from reed baskets in which this 'cream cheese' was drained of its whey. Later cookbooks – for example, the nineteenth-century editions of *Fanny Farmer* – invariably give a recipe for milk sweetened and thickened with rennet, which is, of course, what we call junket today. Rennet is a basic ingredient of both cheese and modern junkets. The question, then, is not what went into a medieval junket – that is clear enough; but whether it was set and served in the same dish, after one cooking procedure, as is the case with junkets today, or made into a cheese and drained. The latter seems more likely in the earlier period, but it is a great deal more trouble. We therefore prefer a recipe made as today's junket is made – but with medieval ingredients. Those who wish to try a variety more like cream cheese should consult the directions for cottage cheese which come with packets of plain rennet tablets, and adapt the procedure accordingly.

Junket with Blueberries

2 cups light cream

2 tsp rosewater (if your usual market does not stock this, try
a specialty store, delicatessen, health food store, or
pharmacy)

2 tbsp sugar

1 tablet plain, unflavoured rennet, dissolved in 1 tbsp
cold water

Blueberries, or, if in season, strawberries; if you must use
frozen berries, blueberries usually have a better texture

If your grocery store does not stock plain rennet tablets,
substitute vanilla junket powder for the rennet, water, and
sugar; but, of course, the flavour will be pronounced (and
anachronistic). If you can get liquid rennet, use the amount
advised for 2 cups of milk.

Mix cream, rosewater, and sugar in a saucepan and heat to
barely lukewarm, stirring occasionally to dissolve sugar. A
candy thermometer is helpful to assure reaching the best temperature, ca 100° F; no higher than 110°, for rennet mixtures
will be spoiled if they boil. Meanwhile, dissolve rennet tablet
in cold water. If cream overheats, allow it to cool before proceeding. Stir dissolved rennet into lukewarm cream as quickly
as possible: it takes only seconds. Pour *at once* into the individual dishes from which it will be eaten – custard cups, sher-
bet glasses, etc. For serving smaller helpings to guests at a
Feast, small stiff foil cases will do. Let it sit undisturbed for
10-15 minutes, then chill. To serve, put sweetened berries on
top.

109 Rede Rose

Take the same [ie, using roses, follow recipe for violets, boiled, pressed, and ground, cooked in milk or almond milk thickened with rice flour and sweetened with sugar], saue a=lye it with þe zolkes of eyroun. HARL 279.126

Red Rose Pudding

1 cup rose petals (use red roses that are just beginning to go,
   discarding any really wilted spots, as you would with greens)
2 tbsp rice flour or cornstarch
1/4 tsp salt
2 cups milk
1/4 cup sugar (scant; some may prefer to use only 3 tbsp)
3 egg yolks or one whole egg plus one yolk

Plunge the rose petals into boiling water and boil for about 5 minutes; drain away water and leave to dry on absorbant paper. The best way to dry them thoroughly is to put several layers of paper above and below the petals, then put a heavy weight, such as a cast-iron pan, on top. When petals are reasonably dry, mix the rice flour or starch into a paste with some of the milk. Then put this paste into a blender with the sugar and rose petals. (If you have no blender, you will have to pulverize the petals by some other method, such as grinding in a mortar with the sugar, before proceeding.) Blend, gradually adding the rest of the milk and the salt. Stir this mixture over medium heat until it has the consistency of a thick sauce – about 5 minutes. Remove from heat. Beat egg yolk (or egg and yolk), and then beat in a little of the warm pudding. Stir this back into the rest of the pudding, and stir over very low heat for another 5 minutes, or until very thick. The colour will be a pale violet: you may wish to add a drop or two of red food colouring to make it look rosier. Pour into a bowl or individual dishes and chill before serving.

VARIATION

Violets or hawthorne blossoms may be treated the same way, but the 15th century directions say to omit egg yolks for these flower puddings. It is thus advised that you substitute 2 oz (1/4 cup) ground almonds for the eggs and use one cup each milk and water; the whole pudding can be cooked in one step, since there is no need to worry about curdling.

110 Erbowle

𝕿ake bolas and scald hem with wyne and drawe hem with a strynor; do hem in a pot; clarify hony and do perto, with powdor fort and floer of Rhys. Salt it & florish it with whyte aneys, & serue it forth. FC 95

This fresh fruit pudding is like the modern Scandinavian berry and rhubarb puddings, and not to be confused with the traditional Christmas pudding.

Plum Pudding

1 lb ripe fresh plums
1 cup each red wine, water
1/4 cup clear honey
1/4 cup cornstarch or rice flour, dissolved in 1/4 cup cold
   water
1/2 tsp salt
1/4 tsp cinnamon
1/8 tsp each galingale or ginger, mace
ca 1/2 tsp anise seed

Put plums in a saucepan and cover with wine and water. Bring to a boil and simmer for about 5 minutes. Remove plums; peel them and discard pits. Press plums through a

strainer or blend in a blender; add honey and all spices (except anise) to the puréed plums, and stir this mixture back into the cooking liquid in the saucepan. Stir in the dissolved starch carefully: it must be thoroughly blended for about 5 minutes; it should be quite thick. If there are lumps, restrain or blend. Pour into a serving bowl; cool; then chill. Scatter anise seeds on top when the pudding is well set. It is good served with whipped cream or vanilla ice cream, if you do not object to a non-medieval touch.

111 Pomesmoille

Nym rys & bray hem in a morter, tempre hem vp with almande milke, boille hem: nym appelis & kerue hem as small as douste, cast hem yn after ye boillyng, & sugur: colour hit with safron, cast therto goud poudre, & ʒif hit forth. LAUD 553

Apple-Almond Pudding

1/4 cup rice flour (or cornstarch)
1/4 cup ground almonds
2 cups water, milk, or a combination of the two
1 lb cooking apples, pared, cored, and diced (fine)
pinch each ground clove, salt, nutmeg
1/2 cup sugar (less if apples are sweet)
1/2 tsp cinnamon
1/8 tsp ginger
optional: pinch of ground saffron or a drop of yellow
  food colouring

Mix sugar, rice flour, ground almonds, and water and/or milk in a saucepan; stir in apples and bring to a boil over medium heat. Stir and boil for about 5 minutes, or until pudding is

quite thick. Mix all seasonings except nutmeg in a small dish or cup with a spoonful of the pudding, then stir this into the rest of the pudding. When thoroughly blended, pour into a serving dish. Sprinkle nutmeg on top and cool and/or chill. This can be served as it is or, if preferred, with cream.

VARIATION

One recipe adds chopped or slivered almonds ('shere them smale'), which makes a pleasant variation in texture and can be strongly recommended; if desired, add about 1/4 cup finely slivered almonds along with the spices.

112 Chireseye

Tak Chiryes at the Fest of Seynt John the Baptist and do away the stonys; grynd hem in a morter, and after frot hem wel in a sebe so that the Jus be wel compn owt; and do than in a pot, and do therein feyr gres or Botor, and bred of wastrel ymincid, and of sugur a god party, and a porcion of wyn; and wan it is wel ysoden and ydressed in Dyschis, stik therein clowis of Gilofre and strew thereon sugur.

AC II.18

Cherry Bread Pudding

2 cups fresh, sour pie cherries, stoned; or 20 oz (2 cans) pie cherries, drained, plus the juice of 1/2 lemon
2 cups breadcrumbs
1/3 cup sugar
3/4 cup red wine (or 1/2 cup wine plus 1/4 cup water or juice from canned cherries)
1 tbsp butter

The easiest way to make this is with a blender: if you have one, put in all ingredients except butter and blend, then put

in pan, adding butter. If not, mash the cherries and force through a strainer, then mix with other ingredients before proceeding. Cook, stirring constantly, over a medium fire for about five minutes, or until well thickened. Pour into a serving dish, or individual dishes, and let cool – or chill in a refrigerator. Sprinkle with ground cloves (sparingly), if you wish, with or without extra sugar. This is particularly good served with cream – or with Creme Bastarde (105).

VARIATION
After stirring over heat for a moment or two, pour into a greased baking dish and bake in a 350° oven for about 20 minutes. Serve hot or cold.

113 Milkemete

Take faire mylke and floure, and draue hem þorgh a strepnour, and sette hem ouer þe fire, and lete hem boyle awhile; And then take hem vppe, and lete hem kele awhile. And þen take rawe yolkes of eyren and drawe hem thorgh a strepnour, and caste thereto a litull salt, And set it ouer þe fire til hit be som-what thik, And lete hit noʒt fully boyle, and stere it right well euermore. And put it in a dissh al abrode, And serue it forth for a gode potage in one maner; And then take Sugur a good quantite, And caste there-to, and serue it forth. HARL 4016

Milk Custard Pudding

2 cups milk
1/4 cup flour (instant-blending may be safest)
4 egg yolks or two whole eggs
1/8 tsp salt
1/4 cup brown sugar (either light or dark, but demerara,
    if you can get it, is best for this)

Mix the flour to a paste with the milk, gradually adding the rest of the milk – in a blender, if you have one. Bring to a boil in a saucepan, and let it simmer, stirring occasionally, until somewhat thickened. Meanwhile, beat yolks or eggs with the salt. Beat a little of the milk mixture into the eggs, then the rest; return to the pan, and cook over low heat, stirring continually, until well thickened. It is best not to let the mixture boil, but it is less apt to curdle than a normal modern custard because of the flour. Put in a bowl (or individual dishes) and sprinkle the sugar on top. Serve warm or cold. Chilled, it tastes rather like a crème caramel.

114 Rys

Take a porcyoun of Rys, & pyke hem clene, & sethe hem welle, & late hem kele; þen take gode Mylke of Almaundys & do þer-to, & seþe & stere hem wyl; & do þer-to Sugre an hony, & serue forth. HARL 279.86

Rice Pudding with Honey and Almonds

1/2 cup short grain rice
2 1/2 cups milk, water, or a combination
4 oz (1/2 cup) ground almonds blanched
1/4 cup sugar
2 tbsp honey
1 cup boiling water

Cover the rice with milk (or whatever combination you wish here) and bring to a simmer; cook over low heat, very gently, for at least 30 minutes, stirring occasionally and adding more water if it shows signs of drying out. It should be cooked until quite soft. Then remove from heat and put aside to cool, so that any remaining cooking liquid is absorbed.

Meanwhile, put the almonds, sugar, and honey in a pan and cover with boiling water. Stir and allow to steep. When rice has cooled, stir the almond mixture into the rice and put back on the heat; cook, stirring constantly, over medium low heat for about 5 minutes, or until pudding seems quite thick. Remove from heat and pour into serving dish; cool and chill.

The original recipe does not call for any spices. But on the assumption that the medieval cook often reached for powder douce (or something) almost automatically, as we do salt and pepper, it seems permissible to sprinkle the top of the pudding with cinnamon and/or nutmeg.

115 Fygey

Take Almands blanched; grynde hem and drawe hem up with water and wyne; quarter fygs, hole raisons. Cast þerto powdor gynger and hony clarified; seeþ it wel & salt it, and serue forth. FC 89

This is clearly the ancestor of the modern boiled fig (or plum) pudding, but less rich and far simpler to make.

Fig Pudding

4 oz (1/2 cup) ground blanched almonds
1/2 cup water
1/2 cup white wine (or, for a stronger flavour, madeira)
1 cup dried figs, cut into quarters and any stems removed
1 cup seeded (or seedless) raisins, whole
2 tbsp clear honey
1/2 tsp ginger
1/4 tsp salt

Mix the ground almonds into a paste in a saucepan with some of the wine and/or water, over medium heat; add rest of

liquid and allow to steep a few minutes over low heat while you cut up the figs. Stir in fruits and all seasonings and bring to a boil; cook, stirring, for about 5 minutes, or until the mixture is thick and well blended. Serve warm. If you wish to do this ahead of time, put the pudding in an ovenproof dish and cover it with foil, to be reheated in the oven.

116 Tartys in Applis

Tak gode Applys and gode Spycis and Figys and reysons and Perys and wan they are well ybrayed coloure wyth Safron wel and do yt in a cofyn, and do yt forth to bake wel.

AC II:23

Another similar recipe calls for prunes in place of figs, and directs that the fruits be minced rather than ground. Other variations occur in the second recipe (and elsewhere); our compromise here is the simplest version. The quantity is for a fairly large tart (ca 9-10 inches).

Apple Tarts

ca 2 lbs tart apples
optional: 1-2 very firm pears may be substituted for some of
  the apples, but not all varieties of pears are suitable: avoid
  Bartlett pears, which are too soft when they are ripe
ca 1/2 cup dried figs or prunes, stoned and chopped
1/3 cup raisins
1/2 cup sugar (brown, white, or a combination)
1/4 tsp each cinnamon, nutmeg, mace, salt
1/8 tsp ground cloves
pinch saffron
pastry for one pie shell

Peel and core apples (and pears, if used) and chop: pieces must be much smaller than the slices used in a normal apple pie today. Or, put all the fruit (fresh and dried) through the coarse blade of a meat grinder. Put the fruits in prepared pastry shell; mix sugar and spices and spread them over. Cover the tart with a sheet of aluminum foil; bake about 45 minutes at 375°, removing foil cover towards end of cooking time.

VARIATIONS

For a firmer filling, add up to 1/4 cup (2 oz) of ground almonds, dissolved in an equal quantity of water, plus (if you wish) 2 tbsp cooking oil. Or, for a 'flaune of Almayne' (Arundel), add cream beaten with eggs, and some butter.

117 Sambocade

𝕿ake & make a Crust in a trap & take cruddes and wryng out þe wheyʒe, and drawe hem þurgh a strynor, and put in þe strynor crusts. Do þerto suger þe þridde part & somdel whyte of Apren, & shake þerin bloms of elren, & bake it up with curose & mess it forth. FC 171

Elders are generally in bloom in late June and/or early July; their blossoms make a very nice flavouring for this simple cheese pie.

Elderflower Cheese Pie

pastry to line a pie dish
12 oz cottage cheese, drained of any watery whey
1/2 cup sugar
1/2 cup (or less, if bread is stale enough to make very fine crumbs) white bread crumbs
4 egg whites
ca 1/2 cup elder blossoms (3-4 clusters)

Leave your elder sprays in a glass of water until the crust is prepared: the blossoms are apt to discolour slightly if prepared too far in advance. When you are ready to prepare the filling, carefully strip off the white blossoms, trying not to include the little green stems. Then beat cottage cheese, sugar, crumbs, and egg whites together: a blender is ideal for the purpose. When this mixture is smooth, stir in the blossoms and pour the filling into the prepared shell. Bake about 45 minutes in a 350° oven. The pie is excellent either hot or cold.

118 Daryoles

Take Creme of Cowe mylke, oþer of Almands; do þerto ayren with suger, safron, and salt; medle it yfere; do it in a coffyn of ii. ynche depe; bake it wel and serue it forth.

FC 183

Custard Tarts

pastry to make an open pie shell or 12 tart shells
2 cups light cream, or a combination of cream and milk
4 eggs (or 8 egg yolks, if you prefer)
1/2 cup sugar
1/4 tsp salt
optional: pinch ground saffron (for colour); 1/4 tsp almond
    extract or a pinch each ground cloves, ginger, mace (or
    other spices: nutmeg and cinnamon, for example); or
    1/2-1 cup chopped dates or other dried fruit, or fresh
    strawberries

Beat eggs and sugar together, and then beat in cream and seasonings. Pour into prepared pie shell or tart shells, over fruit (if fruit is used). For one large tart, bake 10 minutes at 450°,

then about 30 at 300°-325°; for small tarts, about 20 minutes at 400°.

VARIATIONS
1 Custard Lumbarde: add prunes and dates (both cut up) to the basic mixture.
2 Cheese Daryoles: substitute drained cottage cheese, or a combination of dry cottage cheese (forced through a sieve, unless you are using a blender) with sour cream, for the cream, and use only 3 eggs or 6 egg yolks. Do not mix in spices, but sprinkle a bit of nutmeg and cinnamon over the top. This can be highly recommended to lovers of cheesecake.

119 Fretoure

Take whete Floure, Ale, ȝest, Safroun, & Salt, & bete alle togederys as þikke as þou schuldyst make oþer bature in fleyssche tyme, & þan take fayre Applys, & kut hem in maner of Fretourys, & wete hem in þe bature vp on downne, & frye hem in fayre Oyle, & caste hem in a dyssche, & caste Sugre þer-on & serue forth.

HARL 279.II.54

This recipe has the advantage of being a yeast recipe which calls for no special skill in handling yeast doughs; nor are skills in deep-fat frying necessary – the fritters may be cooked in a small amount of oil and turned over to brown both sides, if preferred. The flavour is very interesting indeed, too.

Apple Fritters

1 package dry yeast
1 1/4 cup ale or beer

1 cup flour
2 egg yolks or 1 egg
3-4 apples (Macintosh, for example, are suitable)
1/2 tsp salt
oil or shortening for frying

Heat the beer to lukewarm. Put the yeast in a medium-sized mixing bowl and add 1/4 cup of the beer; stir and let it sit for about 10 minutes. Then add flour, egg yolks or egg, salt, and remaining beer. Beat the mixture together, then cover the bowl and let it sit in a warm place (such as the back of the stove, while you use the front burners to cook the rest of the meal) for about an hour. It should at least double in bulk. Then peel the apples, core them, and cut in wedges. Put apple slices in the bowl of batter and stir to coat apples with batter. Fry quickly in oil or deep fat; drain the browned fritters on paper as you remove them from the pan. When all have been cooked, sprinkle with sugar and serve. To prepare ahead of time, simply be sure not to overcook; reheat for a few minutes in a moderate oven, and add the sugar just before serving.

VARIATION
A non-Lenten version calls for milk, rather than ale, omits yeast, and seasons with pepper and saffron. Aside from the pepper, this means something corresponding to more modern recipes for the dish, and we do not think it as interesting. The batter may also be simply flour and egg.

120 Rapeye

Take dow, & make þer-of a þinne kake; þanne take Fygys & raysonys smal y-grounde, & temper hem with Almaunde Milke; take pouder of Pepir, & of Galyngale, Clowes, & menge to-gederys, & ley on þin kake a-long as bene koddys; & over-caste þin kake to-gederys, & dewte on þe eggys, an frye in Oyle, & serue forth. HARL 279.II.47

Dumplings of Dried Fruit in Paste

4 dried figs
1/2 cup raisins
1 tbsp ground almonds
1 tbsp hot water
1/8 tsp each ground pepper, galingale (or ginger), cloves
fresh noodles, rolled very thin and cut in pieces 3-4 inches
long and 1 1/2-2 inches wide; or ready-made eggroll paste,
cut in two lengthwise

Mix the hot water and ground almonds. Let them stand while
you put the figs and raisins through a food grinder. Add the
almond mixture and spices to the figs and raisins; mix thoroughly. Put a thin line of the fruit mixture down the centre
of the pieces of dough. Moisten the edges with egg. Fold over
lengthwise, so the paste encloses the fig mixture in a long,
narrow case, similar in shape to a bean pod. Deep fry and
serve.

VARIATION
Risshewes is a similar recipe. The filling includes figs, pine-
nuts, currants, dates, sugar, saffron, ginger, and salt. These
are enclosed in a thin paste made with flour, sugar, and salt,
and then deep fried.

121 Cryspez

Take Whyte of Eyroun, Mylke, & Floure, & a lytel
Berme, & bete it to-gederys, & draw it þorw a straynoure,
so þat it be renneng, & not to styf, & caste Sugre þer=to, &
Salt; þanne take a chafer ful of freysshe grece boylyng, &
put þin hond in þe Bature, & lat þin bature renne dowun by
þin fyngerys in=to þe chafere; & whan it is ronne to-gedere
on þe chafere, & is y=now, take & nym a skymer, & take it
up, & lat al þe grece renne owt, & put it on a fayre dyssche,
& cast þer=on Sugre y=now, & serue forth. HARL 4016

Not all recipes for this dish call for yeast, and some appear to indicate something closer to a modern crêpe: those who wish to make the pancake type should see the variation below, but the more usual cryspez, given here are very good indeed.

Crisps

1/2 cup milk
1/2 tsp yeast (granular)
1 egg white
1/2 cup flour
2 tbsp sugar
dash salt

Dissolve the yeast in warm milk. Beat the other ingredients together (a wire whisk is best) and beat in yeast mixture; the batter should be runny. Fry in deep fat, dribbling the batter in with a spoon or fingers (as the original recipe suggests). Turn when browned on the bottom. Remove with a skimmer or slotted spoon and drain on absorbent paper. Sprinkle with sugar, or shake in a bag with the sugar. Some recipes say to 'serve them forth with fritters,' which they closely resemble; they could be mixed with apple fritters – see recipe for Fretoure (119).

VARIATION

The Ménagier's recipe calls for whole eggs, flour, salt, water, and wine, beaten together; this mixture is to be fried, preferably in butter, poured in so that it 'runs all around the pan' – which sounds like a way of making a single, thin pancake. This can be done successfully using about the same proportions as a modern French crêpe: eg, to a cup of flour, 2 eggs, 1/2 cup each water and white wine, and ca 1/4 tsp salt. Such crêpes may be served as a dessert course, with sugar sprinkled on (as the Ménagier recommends), or served rolled around a runny filling, such as Mawmenny (85).

122 Gyngere Brede

Take a quart of hony, & sethe it, & skeme it clene; take Safroun, pouder Pepir, & þrow þer-on; take gratyd Brede, & make it so chargeaunt þat it wol be y-lechyd; þen take pouder Canelle, & straw þer-on y-now; þen make yit square lyke as þou wolt leche yt; take when þou lechyst hyt, and caste Box leves a-bouen, y-styked þer-on, clowys. And ȝif þou wolt haue it Red, coloure it with Saunderys y-now.

HARL 279.II.4

Do not expect this gingerbread to resemble its modern spice-cake descendant. Both texture and flavour will be quite different, though equally delicious. But we must make up for the absent-mindedness of the scribe who neglected to tell us when to add ginger.

Gingerbread

1/2 cup clear honey
1 loaf bread (1 lb), at least 4 days old, grated or ground into fine crumbs; if bread is too fresh, it will not make sufficiently fine crumbs.
1 tsp each ginger, cinnamon
1/8 tsp ground white pepper
pinch saffron, if desired: it is not important here

Bring the honey to a boil and skim off any scum. Keeping the pan over very low heat, stir in breadcrumbs and spices. When it is a thick, well-blended mass, press firmly into a small greased (or teflon-lined) layer cake pan (8" is ideal for this quantity). Cover and leave in a cool place several hours or overnight before turning out on a cake plate. Cut into small slices to serve.

123 Cybele

Nym almandes, Sugur & salt, & payn de mayn, & bray hem in a morter; do therto eyren; frie hit in oylle or in grece; cast thereto sugur, & zif hit forth. LAUD 553

This sounds like a recipe for one good-sized cake, but it seems to work better as small cakes – which are more often specified by menus of the period.

Almond Cakes

1 cup (or more: depending on the freshness of the bread) breadcrumbs
4 oz (1/2 cup) ground almonds
1/4 cup plus 2 tbsp sugar
1/2 tsp salt
2 eggs
oil and/or fat for frying

Mix dry ingredients (reserving the extra sugar), preferably in a blender; add eggs, beaten, if not using a blender. Heat oil and/or other fat in a frying pan and drop the batter in in small spoonfuls, flattening with the spoon if necessary (which it will not be if you are using deep fat). Turn over once if not using deep fat. Drain on paper, and sprinkle with reserved sugar before serving – warm, preferably.

An alternative procedure which may be convenient and offers good results is to chill the batter for an hour or so, then divide it into balls (about twenty) and flatten into cakes; the cakes should be small and not too thick. One advantage is that much of the work can be done ahead of serving time; another is that the cakes will be of more uniform size, and less uneven in appearance.

124 Payn Pur-dew

Take fayre ȝolkes of Eyroun, & trye hem fro þe whyte, & draw hem þorw a straynoure, & take Salt and caste þer-to; þan take fayre brede, & kutte it as troundeȝ rounde; þan take fayre Boter þat is claryfiyd, or ellys fayre Freysshe grece, & putte it on a potte, & make it hote; þan take & wete wyl þin troundeȝ in þe ȝolkys, & putte hem in þe panne, and so frye hem uppe; but ware of cleuyng to the panne; & whan it is fryid, ley hem on a dysshe, & ley Sugre y-nowe þer-on, & þanne serue it forth.

HARL 279.II.43

This is a medieval version of what we call French toast, but it is richer – and if made with good French bread, of a more interesting texture. Those who hesitate to use all those yolks can substitute whole eggs (half as many) for some or all of the yolks.

Smothered Bread

8 slices (3/4-1 inch thick) French bread, crusts removed
12 egg yolks, beaten
1/4 tsp salt
1/2 cup sugar (light brown will do: the recipe does not
  specify white)
butter for frying: at least 3 tbsp, more if needed

Heat the butter in a frying pan, but do not allow to burn. Dip the bread slices in the beaten yolks (or put them in a baking pan in which they will barely fit and pour the egg yolks over them, turning, and allowing the egg to soak in a bit while you are heating the butter). Fry until golden brown on each side, turning carefully and adding more butter as needed. Put on a serving platter and sprinkle the sugar over the slices; serve hot.

125 Payn Ragon

Take hony sugar and clarifie it togydre and boile it with esy fyr, and kepe it wel from brenyng and whan it hath yboiled a while, take up a drope þer-of wiþ þy fynger and do it in a litel water and loke if it hong togyder, and take it fro the fyre and do þerto the thriddendele and powdor gyngen and stere it togyder til it bigynne to thik and cast it on a wete table; lesh it and serue it forth with fryed mete on flesh day or on fysshe dayes. FC 67

This recipe makes a fudge-type candy, complete with soft-ball test. The unspecified ingredient added during the beating stage would most probably be ground almonds, currants, pine nuts – the sort of ingredient used to stuff roasts, flavour stews, etc. Pegge suggests that the 'third part' must be bread ('payn'), but it seems more likely that this is one of the names which suggests an appearance rather than an ingredient. Just as 'yrchouns' are sausage made to look like hedgehogs, this is a sweet shaped and sliced like bread. Since this dish is recommended to accompany fried meat, it would provide the kind of contrast that a sweet sauce might.

Honey and Almond Candy

2 cups sugar
3 tbsp honey
2/3 cup water
2/3 cup ground almonds
1/4-1/2 tsp ginger

Cook the sugar, honey, and water together, stirring frequently, over fairly low heat, stirring, until the syrup reaches the soft-ball stage (approximately 234°). Cool it a little, then beat it until it begins to stiffen. Then add the almonds and ginger, stir together, and pour out onto waxed paper. When hardened, slice and serve.

126 𝔚afers

𝔚afers are made in fiïe ways. 𝔅y one method you beat the eggs in a bowl, then add salt and wine and throw in flour, and mix them; then put them on two irons, little by little, each time as much paste as the size of a slice or strip of cheese, and press them between the two irons and cook on both sides. MP

A krumcake iron is necessary to produce anything resembling a medieval wafer; these are available at many specialty kitchen shops, especially in areas where there are Scandinavian cooks. A modern waffle iron is too large to produce a thin wafer, but may be resorted to if you have no other recourse. Cheese is added in two of the Ménagier's five ways.

Wafers

2 eggs
1/4 cup flour
3 tbsp grated cheese (parmesan is fine)
1 tbsp sherry
1/2 tsp salt

Mix all ingredients together (but do not try to beat until light). Put by teaspoons onto krumcake iron and cook on both sides. They will come out on the limp side and need to dry: it is advisable to put them into a low oven to crisp them.

127 Ypocras

Treys Unces de canell, & iij unces de gyngener, spykenard de Spayn le pays dun deners: garyngale, clowes, gylofre, poiurs long, noiez mugadez, maziozame, cardemonii—de chescun quarter douce, grayne de paradys, floer de queynel—de chescun di unce; de toutes soit fait powdor &. FC 191

This Anglo-Norman recipe at least has the virtue of suggesting proportions: otherwise, it is not very clear. Comparison with a number of other recipes makes it clear that the essential ingredients are cinnamon, ginger, sugar, and red wine; the spices are to be mixed with hot wine, then strained. A problem is that the spice powder is very difficult to strain out: if an absolutely clear drink is desired, this must be done over a long period of time using cloth or filter paper. (Or, the mixture may be siphoned out.) This is an after-dinner wine, *not* a table wine. In medieval times it was served with wafers after the meal; it makes a very pleasant post-prandial drink.

Spiced Wine

3 bottles red wine: use *vin ordinaire*; that is, the cheapest
 red wine you can get that does not have a positively unpleasant taste that even the spices cannot mask
3/4 cup sugar
3 tbsp honey
1/4 cup cinnamon
2 tbsp ginger and/or galingale
1 tsp each nutmeg, mace, cardamom
1/2 tsp ground cloves

Heat the wine, and stir in sugar, honey, and spices, mixed into a paste with a little of the wine, over low heat. Stir until thoroughly dissolved, but avoid boiling. Let sit for a few minutes before straining through a fine mesh strainer. Repeat in a few minutes when wine has had time to settle a bit again. Then funnel into wine bottles and replace caps or corks.

Serve at room temperature.

VARIATIONS

Some recipes suggest a higher proportion of ginger (including the one given above), and some may wish to try a mixture of that sort; we have preferred to follow the advice of the majority of recipes, including those of the Ménagier, which call for a predominence of cinnamon and sugar. Other spices, such as galingale, may be added, but most of those called for are a bit mystifying. Sometimes 'tornsole' is called for; it is a vegetable dye added for colour rather than flavour. We have not tried gillyflower or spikenard because we do not have any, but perhaps others who are provided with these herbs may wish to try them.

A method not suggested in any medieval source, but which is easy and may appeal to those who prefer a clearer look to their ypocras, is to boil the spices whole, as for a modern hot punch, then strain them out.

On Subtleties

Bibliography

Glossary

Index

On Subtleties

While the term 'subtlety' can be applied to virtually any ingenious device or contrivance, in cookery it usually refers to an elaborate edible construction. The most notable exception occurs at the beginning of the *Liber Cure Cocorum*, where the ingenuity is directed towards practical jokes in the kitchen. We are given directions for making cooked meat appear to be raw, for making a pot boil over uncontrollably (by adding soap), and for making meat appear to be full of worms. We do not recommend any of these 'sly3tes of cure' for presentation at a feast, but they do share with more decorative subtleties the characteristic of a deceptive appearance, seeming to be other than what they are; and that is the essence of a subtlety. Though the most common festive subtlety is a representation in sugar of persons or objects, some were made of pastry or even of ground meat. Consider the recipe from *The Forme of Cury* for a pastry castle.

CHASTLETS. Take and make a foyle of gode past with a roller of a foot brode, & lynger by cumpas. Make iiii Coffyns of þe self past uppon þe rollers þe gretnesse of þe smale of þyn Arme, of vi ynche depnesse; make þe gretust in þe myddell. Fasten þe foile in þe mouth upwarde, & fasten þree oþer foure in euery syde. Kerue out keyntlich kyrnels above in þe maner of bataiwyng and drye hem harde in an Ovene, oþer in þe Sunne.

This castle has a huge pork pie for the central tower and the four smaller towers filled with almond cream, custard, ground fruit, etc; however, we feel that it is more practical to make a smaller unfilled version. The most satisfactory we have tried uses a cheese pastry, four round towers, and a square central section.

2 cups flour	1/2 oz each grated parmesan,
1/4 cup shortening	grated cheddar
1/4 cup butter	water

Blend the fat with the flour; add the grated cheese, mix
thoroughly, and add water to make a pastry the consistency
of pie crust. Divide the dough into five roughly equal portions. Roll each portion into a thin rectangle, approximately
6″ x 8″. Trim four of them evenly to fit the forms described
below, and cut crenelations into one long side. They are now
ready to mould into the shape of the four towers. To make
these towers, we used the cardboard tube around which wrap-
ping paper, aluminum foil, etc, is wrapped. Ours were 1 3/4″
in diameter and 4 1/2″ long. You can also make a cylinder
from lightweight cardboard. Cover each tube in aluminum
foil, butter it lightly, and wrap the pastry around, overlapping
and sealing the edges with eggwhite or water.

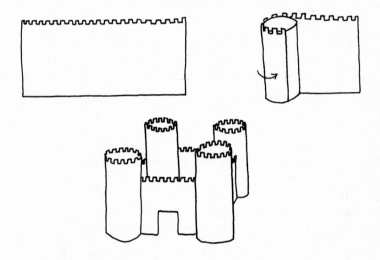

Prick the pastry with a fork so that it will not puff too much.
Stand the towers upright on a cookie sheet, and bake at 350°–
400° until lightly browned. Then carefully remove the cardboard centre and allow the towers to cool. The fifth portion
of pastry is cut into four equal pieces to form the walls between the towers, each approximately 3″ high and 2-4″ long.
Cut crenelations, prick with a fork, and cook flat on a cookie
sheet until the pastry is lightly browned. When all the pieces
are cooled, join them together, using eggwhite, flour and
water paste, or a soft cheese like Brie as glue. The castle is an

158 attractive centrepiece for a medieval table, and (if you can induce your guests to break it up at the end of the feast) it serves as a delicious conclusion to the feast.

More elaborate subtleties, and those designed for specific feast days, are usually constructed of icing made of stiffly beaten eggwhite and enough powdered sugar to make the icing firm enough to hold its shape after being forced through decorator tips. One such subtlety, which could be made by a relatively inexperienced cook, would be a Christmas tree. The first step is to make a cardboard cone the size and shape you want for the tree. Cover the cone with waxed paper. Make eggwhite icing and colour most of it green with food colouring. Starting at the bottom of the cone, force icing through an icing tip in loops (we use the leaf tip for this), gradually working your way to the top of the cone in slightly overlapping loops. Then use a flower tip to place 'decorations' on the tree in whatever colours you choose.

Leave the tree to dry for a day or two: this icing gets very hard, and the longer you can leave it the better. Then remove first the cone from inside the waxed paper and then the paper itself from the hardened icing shape. You can model a large star or angel to attach to the top of the tree with a little icing; icing will keep for days in the refrigerator in a sealed container. To mould a tiny angel, the icing must be very stiff so it can be moulded like clay.

We have used this icing and this basic technique to make very complicated subtleties. One of these was for a feast on St

Juliana's Day. It showed the saint in her prison with the devil looking on. The devil was modeled of icing brought to a clay-like consistency by the addition of extra icing sugar; the saint was constructed on a narrow cardboard cone (with head and hands modeled separately and allowed to dry several days in advance). The prison wall was made on a cardboard frame, with the frame removed when the icing had dried. The whole structure was placed on the bottom of a lightweight card-board box, with the interior of the prison represented by light gray icing, with lines drawn to represent stones. The exterior of the prison wall had vines with little roses, and green icing represented grass on the base.

The curved wall was strong enough to be anchored with the frosting, which dried and held it firmly in place. Similarly, Juliana's cone-form was held in place by having the edges of her dress trailing on the floor-icing. The devil was constructed with toothpicks protruding from his legs, so that he could be held in place by sticking them through the base and resting one arm against the prison wall. The first step in the con-struction of the subtlety was to make the devil, the hands and head of the saint, and the prison wall. Next, the prison wall was removed from the form and the concave face (smooth from contact with the waxed paper over the cardboard) was covered in icing with lines drawn to look like stone. Then the saint's body was made, the head and hands attached, and the whole allowed to dry. Next Juliana's hair was put on, using a very fine line tip, and her face painted. Finally the prison wall was put in place, with green icing outside and gray stone icing inside; the saint was put in place; holes were punched for the toothpicks and the devil put in place. The whole contruction was allowed to dry for several days before it was transported to the feast.

Be sure to allow enough time for complicated subtleties, and for experimentation when you are confronted with a difficult design. Every step of construction should be planned in advance, with plenty of time for drying – extra time may be required if something breaks or simply does not look right. Colour the icing *before* moulding faces, flowers, trees, walls, etc. You may wish to paint pinker cheeks with water colour or dilute food colouring when a head is dry, but an attempt to colour subtleties entirely by painting white icing is streaky, mottled, and generally unsatisfactory. Make duplicates of difficult or fragile parts – heads, wings, walls, etc – so that you can choose the best, and so that no time will be lost if something breaks. Allow at least two or three days for the whole construction to dry before the feast, but not months: the colours fade over a long period. Move the subtlety at least five or six hours in advance to the place where the feast will be held so that there will be time to make repairs if it breaks in transit. Reserve a small amount of icing to use in such repairs. It would be best for the aspiring subtlety-maker to begin with a relatively simple project: the Christmas tree, or a pastry or icing castle, for example. Before attempting a complicated combination of figures, try making a single human form. The complexity of the final production depends on the time, ingenuity, and ability of the subtlety-maker; with practice, almost anything can be attempted with pleasing results.

Bibliography

Aebischer, Paul 'Un manuscrit valaisan du "Viandier" attribué
à Taillevent' *Vallesia* 8 (Sion 1953) 73-100. Contains a very
early ms of the *Viandier*, which is usually dated ca 1380;
however, Aebischer gives evidence that this ms can be no
later than 1320, and concludes that Taillevent (qv below)
simply gave out his own version of an already established
text.

Anderson, John L., ed *A Fifteenth Century Cookry Boke*
(New York 1962). A handsomely illustrated selection from
the recipes printed by Austin (qv below), with an unusually
full glossary of cooking term; useful, if sometimes of questionable accuracy and rather flip in tone.

Aresty, Esther B. *The Delectable Past* (New York 1964). As
its very long subtitle indicates, this book runs the gamut
from ancient Greece to the late nineteenth century. The
brief section on medieval food contains a few rather drastically 'adapted' recipes.

Austin, Thomas, ed *Two Fifteenth Century Cookery Books*
EETS os 91 (London 1888). The two 'cookery books' meant
by the title are mss Harl 279 (ca 1430) and 4016 (ca 1450),
but Austin also includes parts of Ashmole 1439, Laud 553,
and Douce 55. The most generally available large collection
of fifteenth century recipes, this also contains some feast
menus of the period and other interesting information.

Barber, Richard *Cooking and Recipes from Rome to the
Renaissance* (London 1973). Barber's documentation is
sparse and he does not give his recipes in the original, only
his own adaptations; however, he gives much information –
usually if not invariably sound – and his recipes are usable.
About half the book (63 pp) is devoted to medieval food.

Buttes, Henry *Dyets Dry Dinner* (London 1599). Contains
many recipes almost (or entirely) identical to those of a
hundred or more years before.

162 Carter, Charles *The Compleat City and Country Cook, or,
Accomplish'd Housewife* (2nd ed London 1736). Even in
this eighteenth century work, much can be found that
echoes or illuminates medieval recipes. The newer dishes
represented here are more complicated and difficult.

Digby, Kenelm *The Closet of the Eminently Learned Sir
Kenelme Digbie Kt. Opened, Published by his Son's Consent*
(London 1669). Another indication that medieval cooking
habits were flourishing in the seventeenth century, this
makes amusing reading, for we are continually being informed of the culinary practices of various lords and ladies.

Furnivall, Frederick J., ed *The Babee's Book* EETS os 32 (London 1868, repr New York 1969). Contains several books on
manners, with emphasis on table manners, and other matters relating to medieval food, including the *Modus Cenandi*,
the *Bokes of Nurture* of Hugh Rhodes and John Russell,
Wynkyn de Worde's *Boke of Kervynge*, and a number of
Latin graces, as well as two pages of recipes. Almost all the
material here is fifteenth century, but the editor did not always indicate dates.

The Good Hus-wifes Handmaide for the Kitchen (London
1594). Among the recipes which are versions of earlier ones
is an informative version of chicken cooked with marrow-
bones and served with 'brewes.'

Lodge, Barton, ed *Palladius on Husbondrie* EETS os 52
(London 1873). A fifteenth century English ms translated
from a Latin one written in Italy, this lists many vegetables
which do not appear in menus or recipes of the period, such
as asparagus, but which must have been known in England
since their names appear in distinctly English forms.

Maino de' Maineri *De saporibus* ed Lynn Thorndike
'A Medieval Sauce-Book' *Speculum* 9 (1934) 183-90. Fourteenth century Italian versions of recipes found in English
and French mss.

Markham, Gervase *The English Housewife* (London 1649).
Another seventeenth century collection which contains instructive versions of medieval dishes such as chicken boiled
with marrowbones and gingerbread.

Mead, William Edward *The English Medieval Feast* (1931,
repr New York 1967). The standard and most informative
work on English food and its preparation and service in the
period, but one must put up with the author's lack of sympathy with his subject, imprecise documentation, and some
outright errors. Still very useful, but to be handled with care.
*Le Ménagier de Paris, composé vers 1393 par un Bourgeois
Parisien* ed Jérôme Pichon (2 vols, Paris 1896). The standard, complete edition of the most illuminating book from
medieval France. The second volume is almost entirely devoted to matters culinary.
Morris, R., ed *Liber Cure Cocorum* (London 1862). An early
fifteenth century collection of recipes given in doggerel
verse.
Napier, Mrs Alexander [Robina], ed *A Noble Boke of
Cookry ffor a Prynce Houssolde or eny other Estately
Houssolde* (London 1882). Prints a fifteenth century ms
from the Holkham collection.
Pegge, Samuel, ed *The Forme of Cury* (London 1780). The
title collection is attributed on the first page of the ms to
'the chef Maister cokes of kyng Richard the Secunde,' an
attribution no one has doubted; it has been dated 1390.
The volume also contains another late fourteenth century
roll, the two-part 'Ancient Cookery.'
Power, Eileen, trans *The Goodman of Paris* (London 1928).
An abridged translation of the *Ménagier de Paris*; unfortunately, it contains fewer than half the recipes.
Sass, Lorna J. *To the King's Taste: Richard II's Book of
Feasts and Recipes Adapted for Modern Cooking* (New
York: Metropolitan Museum of Art 1975). This adaptation
of the *Forme of Cury* is actually a selection (40 recipes; the
entire collection is 196), including some not from FC. It has
a strong preponderance of sweet, spicy, or 'odd' dishes and
is often rather freely adapted: sometimes downright wrong,
as is the case with the first recipe. But it has some interesting dishes we have not included, much information about
medieval kitchens and serving habits, an interesting bibliography, and other worthwhile apparatus. We cannot agree

164   with many of the pronouncements made about spices, for
       reasons sketched above in our introduction.

Serjeantson, M.S. 'The Vocabulary of Cookery in the Fif-
       teenth Century' in *Essays and Studies by Members of the
       English Association* 23 (1937) 25-37. A valuable check-list
       of cooking terms, though not always absolutely reliable; like
       others, the author tended to jump to conclusions about
       spices on insufficient evidence.

Simon, André L. *Guide to Good Foods and Wines* (rev ed
       London 1963). A good source of information about cooking
       terms, techniques, and ingredients which may be unusual to-
       day.

Taillevent *Le Viandier de Guillaume Tirel dit Taillevent* ed
       Jérôme Pichon and George Vicaire (Paris 1892). A standard
       fourteenth century work, drawing upon the same sources as
       the Ménagier, but often rather more confused (and confus-
       ing) than the latter. It is attributed to a master cook of the
       French royal kitchens of about the same time as FC.

Tannahill, Reay *Food in History* (London 1973). A survey
       running from pre-historic times to the nineteenth century,
       with primary emphasis on why people ate what they did in
       various times and places. The sections on the middle ages
       are limited but informative.

Warner, Richard, ed *Antiquitates Culinariae: Tracts on Culi-
       nary Affairs of the Old English* (London 1791). An edition
       of FC and other mss, including Arundel.

Wilson, C. Anne *Food and Drink in Britain* (London 1973).
       A very thorough and informative survey, well documented.

Wright, Thomas, ed *A Volume of Vocabularies* ([England]
       1857). Contains Alexander Neckham's twelfth century re-
       marks on matters culinary.

Cosman, Madeleine P. *Fabulous Feasts: Medieval Cookery
       and Ceremony* (New York 1976). 'Popular'; illustrated; no
       sources for recipes which appear to be free adaptations.

Henish, Bridget Ann *Fast and Feast: Food in Medieval
       Society* (University Park 1976). Interesting and scholarly
       discussion of medieval attitudes to preparation and presen-
       tation of food. Carefully documented.

Glossary

These are common terms; those which appear less frequently, or which should be easily understood, are not included, nor are all the variant spellings. Those who wish to consult more complete glossaries should check the bibliography.

ALAY, ALYE, LYE mix, dilute
AMYDON, AMYDONE, AMYNDOUN
  a wheat starch
ARAY dress, decorate

BRAY grind, crush
BROCCHE spit
BRUET sauce, broth

CANEL, CANELLE, CANNELL
  cinnamon
CAST add
CAWDEL thick soup or sauce
CHARGEANT thick
COFYN, COFFYN pastry shell
COLE usually strain, but some-
  times cool
COMYN (n) cumin
CONEY, CONNYNGE, CONY
  rabbit
COUCHE, COWCHE lay, arrange

DO: + ÞERTO add; + THEREABOVE
  pour over; + YT put it
DRAWE UP or THERTO mix with a
  liquid
DELE part

EYREN, EYROUN, AYREN,
  HEYREYN eggs

FARS mixture of ground
  ingredients
FLE flay, remove skin
FLOER, FLOWER, FLOWR (n)
  flour or flower
FLOER, FLORISSH (vb) decorate,
  garnish
FOIL, FOYLE leaf, often of
  rolled pastry
FORCE, FORS stuff or season
  (cf FARS)

GALYNTYN, GALYNTYNE spices,
  sometimes with breadcrumbs,
  as for a Pike in Galentine
GELOFLOR, GELOFRE, GILOFRE
  'gillyflower,' but almost always
  means 'cloves,' even in the
  phrase 'cloves of gilofre'
GREDERN gridiron

HELDE pour; Y-HELID covered
HEWE cut, chop

ICORNE, ICORUE cut (carved) up

KELE cool

LECHE, LESH, LESHE slice
LICOUR, LYCOUR, LYKOURE liquid

LIRE, LIORE, LYRE flesh
LYOR, LYOS, LYRE mixture
(see also LIRE)

MEDEL, MEDLE, MELLE mix;
sometimes, serve
MENGE, MYNG mix, mix in
MYLK, MYLKE unless cow's milk
('mylk of kyne,' eg) is specified,
ground almonds mixed with a
liquid

NENE, NYM take

OÞ, OÞER, OÞÞER or; sometimes,
other

PAST pastry
POSSYNET pan for sautéing or
stewing
POUDER, POWDER (etc) ground
spices; + DOUCE mild spices;
+ FORT strong spices

QUIBIBES, QUYBIBES cubebs

RAYSONS, REYSEYNS (etc) [of]
CORANCE, CORANTE (etc)
currants
RENNENG thin, runny, liquid

SANDERS, SAUNDERYS, SAUNDERS
sandalwood or red cedar, used
for colouring

SEETH, SEEÞ, SEÞE, SITH simmer
or boil (except in 77: 'after-
wards')
SEW, SEWE, SOWE broth, sauce
SIRIP, SIRRIPPE broth, sauce
SODEN, SOÞE, YSODE boiled; past
tense of SEETHE
STEPE steep, soak
STOCKFISH (variously spelled)
dried salt cod or similar fish
STONDYNG stiff, very thick
STREYNOUR strainer; 'wryng' or
'drawe' through a strainer:
beat, strain, pulverize
SWYNG beat

TEMPER, TEMPUR dilute, mix
TRAP baking dish

VERGEOUS, VERJUICE, VERIOUS
tart fruit juice, usually made
from grape juice too sour for
wine or from crabapples; the
Ménagier suggests bitter orange
juice as a substitute, which is
close to the lemon we generally
use

WASTEL, WASTREL white bread

YFERE, IN FERE together
YNOGH, Y-NOUHZ, YNOW enough;
done; or, nearly done

Index

Middle English titles (or translated French ones) are indicated by bold type. Sub-entries are indicated by italic. All numbers are recipe numbers.

JOHN STUART MILL was not only a great liberal thinker and writer of the nineteenth century—he was the acknowledged leader of the Utilitarian Movement. As a member of Parliament, he publicly fought for many of the democratic institutions we of the twentieth century take for granted. To his lasting credit were his work on Woman's Suffrage and his important role in the passage of the Great Reform Bill of 1867. Later, as Rector of St. Andrews University, he applied this same humanitarian faith to the problems of modern education.

———◆◆———

D1207722

THE SIX
GREAT
HUMANISTIC
ESSAYS
OF

JOHN STUART MILL

With an Introduction by
Albert William Levi

WSP
WASHINGTON SQUARE PRESS   NEW YORK

THE SIX GREAT HUMANISTIC ESSAYS
OF JOHN STUART MILL

A *Washington Square Press* edition

1st printing..........................May, 1963
2nd printing.....................January, 1969

L

Published by Washington Square Press,
a division of Simon & Schuster, Inc., 630 Fifth Avenue, New York, N.Y.

WASHINGTON SQUARE PRESS editions are distributed in the
U.S. by Simon & Schuster, Inc., 630 Fifth Avenue, New
York, N.Y. 10020 and in Canada by Simon & Schuster
of Canada, Ltd., Richmond Hill, Ontario, Canada.

CONTENTS

INTRODUCTION

JOHN STUART MILL is one of the truly great figures of the nineteenth century. Its most important British philosopher in the tradition of Berkeley and Hume, he was also a civil servant, member of the House of Commons, logician, political economist and moralist, asserter of the claims of labor and the rights of women, tentative socialist, commentator on the political issues of the day, ardent defender of civil liberties and an open mind in which many streams of eighteenth- and nineteenth-century culture met and were almost reconciled.

A careful and judicious thinker, he was forever involved with projects for social reform and defenses of political principle, so that his contemporaries saw him as a moral leader as well as an empirical philosopher. In many ways he is a more important representative of his age than Bradlaugh or Gladstone, Newman or Carlyle. If he is sometimes inconsistent, he is almost never dogmatic, and the scrupulous honesty of mind which he invariably exhibited (as well as an almost unimaginable intellectual generosity) makes him a brilliant paradigm of the best that English liberalism has produced.

It is, of course, as a social philosopher that his influence has been greatest. He and Marx were the great constructive social thinkers of the nineteenth century, and if Marx is responsible for Lenin and the Russian Revolution, Mill is no less responsible for the spirit of Fabian Socialism, the extension of the civil liberties in England, the root ideas in the social thought of Bertrand Russell and John Dewey and the liberal direction of the best minds of the British Labor Party. But Mill's liberal influence has not been confined to those exclusively on the social "left." Conservatives, too, have learned from his libertarian principles. It is characteristic that in our time two of his most profound British admirers have been Harold Laski, a former leader of the radical wing of the British Labor Party (who edited the Oxford edition of Mill's *Autobiography*) and Friedrich A. von Hayek, the conservative economist and opponent of state intervention (who edited the correspondence of Mill and his wife Harriet Taylor).

Although Mill is perhaps best known as a social philosopher, there is another—a more personal—respect in which he speaks specifically to us in the twentieth century. Many of the problems of our age; political, artistic, intellectual, have been set for us by the dialectic of the preceding two hundred years—by the confrontation of the rationalism of the eighteenth century (emphasizing the products of the logical intellect) with the irrationalism of the nineteenth (emphasizing the operations of emotion and of feeling). Mill himself knew the agony of this confrontation; knew it in his personal life as in the dilemmas of his thinking; knew it in the nervous breakdown which he suffered at twenty as in the problems of university education which he treated in "Inaugural Address At St. Andrews" not many years before his death. It penetrates his thinking and it runs like a persistent thread through the essays collected in this volume.

Mill's father, James, friend and disciple of Jeremy Bentham, was an oppressive, overbearing, domineering man (Elizabeth Barrett Browning also had such a father)—an exaggerated product of eighteenth-century enlightenment who mistrusted emotion, cared little for poetry and brought up his son sternly to be a man of pure rationality, a logical reformer of the social abuses of the time. John Stuart Mill has detailed this incredible and inhuman education in his *Autobiography*—how he was forced to undertake Greek at three, Latin at eight, Aristotelian formal logic at twelve and a complete course in Ricardian economics at thirteen. Without companions of his own age, constantly rebuked by his father for his "inattention, inobservance, and general slackness of mind," starved in his emotions and disciplined to feel ashamed in any expression of feeling, it is hardly remarkable that at twenty he suffered a nervous breakdown—what he himself termed "a crisis in my mental history."

Looking back over this period Mill blames the crisis upon the habit of analysis which completely supplanted his emotional life. Living after Freud, it is not difficult for us to surmise other unconscious factors in Mill's melancholy and dejection,[1] but what is most interesting is the turn in Mill's activities which this mental crisis provoked, for from this time onward "the cultivation of the feelings" became one of his chief preoccupations, and he turned deliberately to the imaginative arts. He derived extreme pleasure from the melodic gaiety of Weber's *Oberon,* and although his dogged reading of Byron had done little for his melancholy state, his first reading of Wordsworth in the autumn of 1828 was, as he acknowledges, an important event in his life. Wordsworth led him to Coleridge. Coleridge led him to Goethe and the Germans. Five years after his first acquaintance with Wordsworth (aged twenty-seven) he wrote for the *Monthly Repository* "Thoughts on Poetry and Its Varieties."

"Thoughts on Poetry and Its Varieties" is in its way (although quite unconsciously) as ironic a work as Thomas Mann's novel *Doctor Faustus* and for the same reason—the incongruity between its subject and the style in which that subject is treated. For despite Mill's insistence that poetry is passion, his treatment of it is dry and analytical. This has its internal pathos but it does not compromise the importance of Mill's insights. And in fairness it must perhaps be said that the essay improves in tone as it continues. Beginning with the logical task of defining poetry, it ends with the same reasoned defense of preferences and valuations as one might find today in Lionel Trilling or Edmund Wilson. For one who came late to poetry and the arts, it is surprising how original are Mill's impressions and this lies not so much in the Coleridgean distinction between science and poetry and in the emphasis upon the debt which the feelings owe to the imagination, as in the central distinction between poetry and eloquence, between the public and the private domain of feeling, between rhetoric and soliloquy. When Mill proceeds to generalize this contrast for all the arts (distinguishing, for example, between the garrulous passion of Rossini and the meditative glory of Mozart's "Dove sono," between a Holy Family of Raphael and the "fat, frouzy Dutch Venuses" of Rubens) we see the beginning of an aesthetics which Mill never bothered to complete. Those familiar with contemporary criticism will find in the second half of Mill's essay anticipa-

---

[1] See A. W. Levi, "The 'Mental Crisis' of John Stuart Mill," in *The Psychoanalytic Review* (January, 1945) pp. 86–101.

tions of the insights about "the dissociation of sensibility" which T. S. Eliot has made famous, and Mill's celebrated comparison of the poetic natures of Wordsworth and Shelley will interest even those whom it will fail to convince. The point is not that Mill is a brilliant literary critic, but that when one considers that such an essay as "Thoughts on Poetry and Its Varieties" would have been an absolute impossibility for James Mill or Jeremy Bentham even to attempt, one sees how far Mill has passed beyond the arid rationalism of his educational mentors.

"Thoughts on Poetry and Its Varieties" makes this point by implication. "Bentham," published in the *London and Westminster Review* in 1838, makes it explicitly. It is perhaps the most schizophrenic of all Mill's essays, torn between filial piety and temperamental incompatibility. He lauds Bentham— as his reason demanded—for his questioning spirit, his progressive and "subversive" attack upon English institutions and his introduction into morals and politics of those habits of thought which are derived from science. But he criticizes him too for his neglect of some of the strongest and most natural feelings of human nature, his deficiency of imagination, his "want of poetical culture" and his blindness to all those virtues which the self-consciousness of such writers as Byron and Wordsworth, Goethe and Chateaubriand had disclosed. Here also begins the first veiled criticism of Bentham's moral theory for its over-simplification and its abstractness which is to reach full expression in "Utilitarianism" published a quarter of a century later. Mill sees that the two deficiencies in Bentham are not unrelated. For Bentham's exclusively *moral* view of actions and characters, and his blindness to their *aesthetic* and *sympathetic* aspects has the same source as his peculiar "positivistic" opinions about poetry. Words, Bentham felt, are perverted from their proper use when employed in uttering anything but precise, logical truth. Thus all poetry is misrepresentation. To the Mill whose sanity had been in part restored by the poetry of Wordsworth, such one-sidedness was a *reductio ad absurdum*.

In the first few pages of the Bentham essay, Mill linked him with Coleridge and called them "the two great seminal minds of England in their age." Two years later his "Coleridge" was also published in the *London and Westminster Review.* They are companion pieces, yet are very different in spirit. "Bentham" is the better of the two, for while it displays the ambivalence of which I have spoken, it treats its subject intimately, from the inside. "Coleridge" is at once a colder and a more radical piece of work. Its ambiguity lies not in its content, but in the wonder that it was ever written at all. Coleridge was an arch-conservative. Mill was a philosophical and social radical. It is as if today an ideologist of the Communist Party should write an essay in praise of an arch-conservative or *The National Review*. Would this be an act of ideological treason or a demonstration of unbelievable intellectual generosity? Mill's philosophical co-believers must have felt something of the same perplexity.

Undoubtedly it was the latter. For Mill found in Coleridge a breadth which was more interested in expanding the area of meaning than in narrowing the domain of truth—a religious and cultural reaction against the rigidity of the eighteenth-century *philosophes*. And thus, although he admitted that on questions of metaphysics he was with Locke and Bentham rather than with Coleridge and the Germans, Mill owned to a real sympathy for a position which, however conservative in fact, was trying to work toward a philosophy of human culture based upon an intelligible reading of the philosophy of history. It may be, as Mill said later in the *Autobiography*, that the state of feeling into which he had emerged led him to exaggerate both Bentham's faults and Coleridge's virtues, but a mentality which could acknowledge an articulate debt to each of these opposite thinkers was steeped in the problematic issues of an authentic humanism.

"On Liberty," the greatest of all Mill's writings and his chief claim to fame, appeared at the height of his maturity, twenty years later—in 1859. Published at a moment of extreme reaction in the course of Western political history, it is easy to forget just how contrary was its message to the spirit of the times. Napoleon III was dictator of France. Serfdom still flourished in Russia and slavery in the United States. Most of the Balkans lay under the tyranny of Turkish rule, and in that same Italy where in 1855 Mill probably began the first draft of the essay, the prisons were filled with men who called themselves partisans of freedom. Mill's belief, as stated in the essay, that the problem of freedom was now one of social tyranny rather than political despotism is a conviction that we a hundred years later may well share, but it is hardly a valid conclusion from an observation of the age in which he lived.[2]

"On Liberty" is a statement of liberal principle so radical and at the same time so fundamental that it surely ranks with *The Social Contract* and *The Communist Manifesto* as a source for the political and social theory of the Western world. At any rate, it has had a checkered and by no means unambiguous history. In 1861 "On Liberty" was translated into Russian and became a thorn in the flesh of the Czar's secret police, but fifteen years later another Slav, Peter Karageorgevitch, later to become King of Serbia, painstakingly translated it himself into his native tongue. Prior to the second World War, at precisely the moment when Harold Laski and the intellectual leaders of the British Labor Party were appealing to it as a sacred text of political principle, the Japanese Emperor Hirohito, deeming it a potent source of the contagious disease *kikenshiso* (dangerous thoughts), banished it from the public domain.

The avowed intention of "On Liberty" is to examine the nature and limits of the power which society can legitimately exercise over the individual, and the reasonable conclusion to which it comes is that the sole end for which this power may rightfully be exercised is the protection of society. But as the argument proceeds, Mill finds it necessary to introduce two subordinate pleas which together really constitute the affirmative core of the entire essay: the first is for complete liberty of thought and discussion within the political order, the second is for the free development of individuality however and wherever it may need to flower. The two pleas seem at first sight to belong to different realms of discourse, for the chief restrictions against the absolute freedom of the intellect in thought and expression ordinarily come when church and state exercise their political powers, whereas the chief impediment to free experiment with different modes of life is the more informal tyranny of social pressure and public opinion and the strangling conformity which they seek to impose. But the political and the social are not, finally, so easily separated. The tyranny of the majority may express itself either in law or through the more subtle social pressures which society has

[2] See A. W. Levi, "The Value of Freedom: Mill's Liberty (1859–1959)" in *Ethics* (October, 1959), pp. 37–46.

learned to impose, and at the same time that liberty of conscience in the individual which is the condition of open and candid public expression of opinion is also the motivating power by which individuals frame the pattern of their tastes and the edifice of their individual life plan.

How does Mill justify the principle of freedom? The answer to this question shows that Mill is still nominally under the spell of the old Benthamite ethics which the essay "Bentham" had begun to criticize. For Mill's ultimate justification of the civil liberties is that "principle of utility" which he regarded as the final appeal on all ethical questions. Civil liberties promote the welfare of even that society which attempts blindly to suppress them: They are an absolute necessity for the achievement of the greatest happiness for the greatest number.

Mill's Benthamism commits him to a defense of freedom of thought and discussion which finds these to be primarily an instrument in the formation of the public mind and therefore shifts their justification from the self-determination of the individual to the self-determination of society. Interference with public discussion in an attempt to safeguard sacred institutions from attack is intrinsically an illegitimate power, and even when public opinion is itself on the side of coercive government in this attempt, it cannot be vindicated. And this because opinion is not merely the possession of its owner, but a public property either providing access to new truth or the occasion for the revivification of an old. The censorship of individual opinion is therefore in Mill's conception not a private injury but a public damage. It prevents social errors from being rectified and it puts an end to that democratic faith which holds that mistakes in social policy can be corrected by experience after being exposed within the arena of open public discussion. That "steady habit of correcting and completing opinion" is the only guarantee of success in perfecting public and private judgment. This is the culminating insight of Chapter II of "On Liberty."

Chapter III is a passionate defense of individuality. But here the line of defense shifts from Bentham to Aristotle—from a principle of "social utility" to a principle of "self-realization." It is "the proper condition of a human being arrived at the maturity of his faculties to use and interpret experience in his own way." And, "The human faculties of perception, judgment, discriminative feeling, mental activity, and even moral preference are exercised only in making a choice." And finally the famous: "Human nature is not a machine to be built after a model, and set to do exactly the work prescribed for it, but a tree, which requires to grow and develop itself on all sides, according to the tendency of the inward forces which make it a living thing."

The argument is distinctly and unmistakably Aristotelian. The external inducement to such acts as are not congruent with our feelings and our character renders us passive and dull. He who exercises deliberate decision employs all those faculties which are specifically human: observation, reasoning, judgment, purposive choice; and, once the choice is made, the firmness of will and self-control to hold fast to the decision. It might be a digest of the relevant portions of the *Nicomachean Ethics*.

Once the self-realization principle is established, it is possible to turn the argument toward its defense in a world threatening to independence and strength of character. Once it has become clear that "among the works of man which human life is rightly employed in perfecting and beautifying, the first in importance surely is man himself," Mill can state the case against a society which has finally gotten the better of individuality, which exercises over the individual life a hostile and dreaded censorship and which has established in the most respectable social positions those who give unquestioning allegiance to the cult of conformity.

The last half of Chapter III of "On Liberty" is perhaps the most rewarding and the most miraculous section in the entire essay to a contemporary audience newly sensitized to the dangers of "other-direction" and seeing before its very eyes that hatred of peculiarity of taste and eccentricity of conduct which "On Liberty" pointed out in 1859. When Mill goes on (as he clearly does) to recommend examples of non-conformity and eccentricity for their own sake, it is a great temptation to applaud his courage without, at the same time, paying marked attention to his aim. But the aim is of the essence of the prescription; it is to combat all of those modern influences which are hostile to pure individuality, and to score against that despotism of custom which is a perpetual threat to the self-determination of the independent self.

Four years after "On Liberty" appeared, Mill published

"Utilitarianism" in *Fraser's Magazine*. These two essays are his most famous ones and they have important characteristics in common. Both belong for their inception to an earlier period of his life, probably in the years 1854-1855 during which time Mill was gloomy and depressed about the state of his health—thinking, indeed, that he was dying of tuberculosis.[3] During this time, in addition to "Liberty," "Nature," and "The Utility of Religion," Mill wrote two other essays, "Utility" and "Justice," which with alterations and additions were combined together in 1863 to form "Utilitarianism."

Both essays also express the eternal strife of philosophical systems which comes to a head in Mill's own personal philosophical development, a strife which infects "Utilitarianism" with its qualitative distinction between pleasures as it does "On Liberty" with its utilitarian defense of the civil liberties. Both of these great works unfold with an undercurrent of confusion and inconsistency, and it is, I think, because of the quaint circumstance that Mill is at once a Benthamite by ruthless education and an Aristotelian by persuasion and natural election. Much of his most fruitful work is the consequence of this tension and it would be both dishonest and unrewarding to try to make it throughout consistent by the standards of exact logic. Therefore, of the general point of view expressed in "Utilitarianism" (as of that also in the essay "On Liberty") I think we may rightly say that it is a passionate and embattled Mill breaking from the vestigial wrappings of Benthamite doctrine toward the explicit standpoint of an Aristotelian moral philosophy.

Where Bentham had been abstract, consistent and uncompromising, Mill is refreshingly concrete although he makes concessions both to an ethics of conscience and an ethics of self-realization. Where Bentham had asserted that the motivation of every man is absolutely egoistic or selfish, Mill includes altruistic motives also, and this represents an important difference between the dominant psychology of the eighteenth and of the nineteenth century. For Mill, as for Aristotle, man is a social being and has by nature certain social feelings. Finally, whereas Bentham had seen pleasures and pains as the data of ethics—their precise calculation as the clue to moral wisdom and their chief characteristics such quantitative

[3] See A. W. Levi, "The Writing of Mill's Autobiography," in *Ethics* (July, 1951), pp. 284—96.

ones as intensity and duration—Mill finds that pleasures differ in rank and quality. On the central issue—that our acts are right as they tend to promote happiness and wrong as they tend to promote the reverse—Mill and Bentham are agreed, but the former sees that some *kinds* of pleasure are more desirable and more valuable than others. These are the pleasures of the higher faculties of man, not the pleasures of food and drink and bodily comfort (which Mill calls the pleasures of a satisfied pig), but the pleasures of knowledge, of beautiful objects, and of human companionship. And if one asks what is the proof that the so-called "higher" pleasures are more valuable than the so-called "lower," Mill falls back on an old argument which he has borrowed from Plato. The only proof lies in the preferences of those who have had experience of both, and that, he thinks, always favors the pleasures of man's higher faculties.

"Utilitarianism" is a somewhat diffuse essay, containing suggestions which have been a source of controversy to ethicists from Mill's day to our own. The controversy has been particularly severe in the last thirty years, when moral theory has been so largely treated from the standpoint of "logic" and "method." What Mill says about "the ultimate sanction of the principle of utility" and his idea about "what sort of proof" can be provided for it has been the subject of endless attack and defense. But this belongs to the quasi-scientific domain of method, and ordinary readers will do well to concentrate their attention upon the essay's importance as a humanistic document: for example, upon its careful treatment of the influence of "sympathy" on the moral life, upon its attempt (so like that of Aristotle) to show in what respects "happiness" is not an abstract idea but "a concrete whole," and upon the treatment of "justice" in terms of "legality" and "equality" (precisely what Aristotle does in Book V of his *Nicomachean Ethics*). Mill is one of the last great classical moralists—one of the last, that is, to consider ethics as a guide to life and not a mere exercise in the logic of moral discourse or an explication of the customary usages of ethical terms.

In 1867, two years after Mill's election to Parliament from Westminster and six years before his death, he was elected by the students to the honorary office of Lord Rector of the University of St. Andrews, and in accordance with custom, early in February delivered there his "Inaugural Address."

It was more a comprehensive essay on higher education than a speech, and since its delivery required well over three hours, it probably demanded more patience to hear than to read. Nevertheless it is a sober, comprehensive, humane treatment of the problem of liberal education in the University, and one of the great documents in British educational thought.

In the *Autobiography* Mill describes it thus: "In this Discourse I gave expression to many thoughts and opinions which had been accumulating in me through life, respecting the various studies which belong to a liberal education, their uses and influence, and the mode in which they should be pursued to render their influences most beneficial. The position I took up, vindicating the high educational value alike of the old classic and the new scientific studies, on even stronger grounds than are urged by most of their advocates, and insisting that it is only the stupid inefficiency of the usual teaching which makes those studies be regarded as competitors instead of allies, was, I think, calculated, not only to aid and stimulate the improvement which has happily commenced in the national institutions for higher education, but to diffuse juster ideas than we often find, even in highly educated men, on the conditions of the highest mental cultivation."

That Mill was over-optimistic about the improvement in British education, and about the diffusion of "juster ideas . . . on the conditions of the highest mental cultivation" is strikingly pointed up by the Rede Lecture, "The Two Cultures and the Scientific Revolution," which Sir Charles Snow delivered at Cambridge in 1959—almost a hundred years after Mill's "Inaugural Address." Clearly the problem of "the two cultures" has a long history, and Mill's efforts to reconcile "the old classic and the new scientific studies" represents a permanent problem for the humanistic imagination.

But this is not the only respect in which the "Inaugural Address" is prophetic. Mill wrestles with all the problems of educational humanism: that of providing general culture, of curtailing the dangers of a narrow specialization, of integrating the various branches of learning, of preserving somehow the wisdom of life expressed in the literature of the ancients. If these seem trite, it is only because they are perennial, and no one has expressed them more cogently than Mill.

But there is one thing more. That dialectic of intellect and feeling, of analysis and emotion which runs through Mill's entire life again shows itself here. Mill is clear in his advocacy of the educational value of scientific discipline, of semantic analysis, of verbal accuracy, of controlled reasoning, of the science of logic—there is no part of intellectual education, he says, which is of greater value. But the last few pages of the "Inaugural Address" is a final return to the subject of "Thoughts on Poetry and Its Varieties" which he had written thirty-five years before. Now he advocates a third division of education (to go with the intellectual and moral): the aesthetic branch, the culture which comes through poetry and art, which accomplishes the education of the feelings and the cultivation of the beautiful. He realizes that there is something quixotic in ranking Art with Science and Philosophy, but he has no hesitancy in doing so, and the reader who has persevered so far will find himself strangely pleased with the symmetry of the experience.

"Thoughts on Poetry and Its Varieties" was written by a young man of twenty-seven; the "Inaugural Address" by a mature one of sixty-one. The dualism of the mind and the feelings pervades Mill's life, but his humanistic response is constant. It is the witness to his depth, to his integrity.

ALBERT WILLIAM LEVI

BIBLIOGRAPHICAL NOTE

For Mill's life, the *Autobiography* (New York: Columbia University Press, 1924) is indispensible. The definitive modern work is Michael St. John Packe, *The Life of John Stuart Mill* (New York: The Macmillan Co., 1954). There is no work which adequately covers the whole of Mill's philosophy. Two relatively recent attempts are R. P. Anschutz, *The Philosophy of J. S. Mill* (Oxford University Press, 1953) and Karl Britton, *John Stuart Mill* (Penguin Books, 1953). Older, more leisurely, and also more literary than analytical is Leslie Stephen's *The English Utilitarians*, Vol. III. (London: Duckworth and Co., 1900).

BIBLIOGRAPHY OF TEXT REFERENCES

Bowring, John. (ed.). *The Works of Jeremy Bentham*. Edinburgh: W. Tate, 1843.

Gillman, James. *The Life of Samuel Taylor Coleridge*. London: W. Pickering, 1838.

Shedd, Professor. (ed.). *The Complete Works of Samuel Taylor Coleridge*. New York: Harper & Brothers, 1853.

Thoughts on Poetry and Its Varieties [1]

[1]*Monthly Repository*, January and October, 1833.

Yeats –

influenced / Sense
of debate with
oneself.

SECTION ONE

IT HAS OFTEN been asked, What is Poetry? And many
and various are the answers which have been returned.
The vulgarest of all—one with which no person possessed of
the faculties to which poetry addresses itself can ever have
been satisfied—is that which confounds poetry with metrical
composition; yet to this wretched mockery of a definition many
have been led back by the failure of all their attempts to
find any other that would distinguish what they have been
accustomed to call poetry from much which they have known
only under other names.

That, however, the word "poetry" imports something quite
peculiar in its nature; something which may exist in what is
called prose as well as in verse; something which does not
even require the instrument of words, but can speak through
the other audible symbols called musical sounds, and even
through the visible ones which are the language of sculpture,
painting, and architecture,—all this, we believe, is and must be
felt, though perhaps indistinctly, by all upon whom poetry
in any of its shapes produces any impression beyond that of
tickling the ear. The distinction between poetry and what is
not poetry, whether explained or not, is felt to be fundamental;
and, where every one feels a difference, a difference there
must be. All other appearances may be fallacious; but the
the appearance of a difference is a real difference. Appearances
too, like other things, must have a cause; and that which can
cause any thing, even an illusion, must be a reality. And hence,
while a half-philosophy disdains the classifications and distinctions indicated by popular language, philosophy carried
to its highest point frames new ones, but rarely sets aside
the old, content with correcting and regularizing them. It
cuts fresh channels for thought, but does not fill up such
as it finds ready-made: it traces, on the contrary, more

3

deeply, broadly, and distinctly, those into which the current has spontaneously flowed.

Let us then attempt, in the way of modest inquiry, not to coerce and confine Nature within the bounds of an arbitrary definition, but rather to find the boundaries which she herself has set, and erect a barrier round them; not calling mankind to account for having misapplied the word "poetry," but attempting to clear up the conception which they already attach to it, and to bring forward as a distinct principle that which, as a vague feeling, has really guided them in their employment of the term.

The object of poetry is confessedly to act upon the emotions;—and therein is poetry sufficiently distinguished from what Wordsworth affirms to be its logical opposite; namely, not prose, but matter of fact, or science. The one addresses itself to the belief; the other, to the feelings. The one does its work by convincing or persuading; the other, by moving. The one acts by presenting a proposition to the understanding; the other, by offering interesting objects of contemplation to the sensibilities.

This, however, leaves us very far from a definition of poetry. This distinguishes it from one thing; but we are bound to distinguish it from every thing. To bring thoughts or images before the mind, for the purpose of acting upon the emotions, does not belong to poetry alone. It is equally the province (for example) of the novelist: and yet the faculty of the poet and that of the novelist are as distinct as any other two faculties; as the faculties of the novelist and of the orator, or of the poet and the metaphysician. The two characters may be united, as characters the most disparate may; but they have no natural connection.

Many of the greatest poems are in the form of fictitious narratives; and, in almost all good serious fictions, there is true poetry. But there is a radical distinction between the interest felt in a story as such, and the interest excited by poetry; for the one is derived from incident, the other from the representation of feeling. In one, the source of the emotion excited is the exhibition of a state or states of human sensibility; in the other, of a series of states of mere outward circumstances. Now, all minds are capable of being affected more or less by representations of the latter kind, and all, or almost all, by those of the former; yet the two sources of interest correspond to two distinct and (as respects their greatest development) mutually exclusive characters of mind.

At what age is the passion for a story, for almost any kind of story, merely as a story, the most intense? In childhood. But that also is the age at which poetry, even of the simplest description, is least relished and least understood; because the feelings with which it is especially conversant are yet undeveloped, and, not having been even in the slightest degree experienced, cannot be sympathized with. In what stage of the progress of society, again, is story-telling most valued, and the story-teller in greatest request and honor? In a rude state like that of the Tartars and Arabs at this day, and of almost all nations in the earliest ages. But, in this state of society, there is little poetry except ballads, which are mostly narrative,—that is, essentially stories,—and derive their principal interest from the incidents. Considered as poetry, they are of the lowest and most elementary kind: the feelings depicted, or rather indicated, are the simplest our nature has; such joys and griefs as the immediate pressure of some outward event excites in rude minds, which live wholly immersed in outward things, and have never, either from choice or a force they could not resist, turned themselves to the contemplation of the world within. Passing now from childhood, and from the childhood of society, to the grown-up men and women of this most grown-up and un-child-like age, the minds and hearts of greatest depth and elevation are commonly those which take greatest delight in poetry: the shallowest and emptiest, on the contrary, are, at all events, not those least addicted to novel-reading. This accords, too, with all analogous experience of human nature. The sort of persons whom not merely in books, but in their lives, we find perpetually engaged in hunting for excitement from without, are invariably those who do not possess, either in the vigor of their intellectual powers or in the depth of their sensibilities, that which would enable them to find ample excitement nearer home. The most idle and frivolous persons take a natural delight in fictitious narrative: the excitement it affords is of the kind which comes from without. Such persons are rarely lovers of poetry, though they may fancy themselves so because they relish novels in verse. But poetry, which is the delineation of the deeper and more secret workings of human emotion, is interesting only to those to whom it recalls what they have felt, or whose imagination it stirs up to conceive what they could feel, or what they might have been able to feel, had their outward circumstances been different.

Poetry, when it is really such, is truth; and fiction also, if it is good for any thing, is truth: but they are different truths. The truth of poetry is to paint the human soul truly; the truth of fiction is to give a true picture of life. The two kinds of knowledge are different, and come by different ways,— come mostly to different persons. Great poets are often proverbially ignorant of life. What they know has come by observation of themselves: they have found within them one highly delicate and sensitive specimen of human nature, on which the laws of emotion are written in large characters, such as can be read off without much study. Other knowledge of mankind, such as comes to men of the world by outward experience, is not indispensable to them as poets: but, to the novelist, such knowledge is all in all; he has to describe outward things, not the inward man; actions and events, not feelings; and it will not do for him to be numbered among those, who, as Madame Roland said of Brissot, know man, but not *men*.

All this is no bar to the possibility of combining both elements, poetry and narrative or incident, in the same work, and calling it either a novel or a poem; but so may red and white combine on the same human features or on the same canvas. There is one order of composition which requires the union of poetry and incident, each in its highest kind,—the dramatic. Even there, the two elements are perfectly distinguishable, and may exist of unequal quality and in the most various proportion. The incidents of a dramatic poem may be scanty and ineffective, though the delineation of passion and character may be of the highest order, as in Goethe's admirable *Torquato Tasso;* or, again, the story as a mere story may be well got up for effect, as is the case with some of the most trashy productions of the Minerva press: it may even be, what those are not, a coherent and probable series of events, though there be scarcely a feeling exhibited which is not represented falsely, or in a manner absolutely commonplace. The combination of the two excellences is what renders Shakespeare so generally acceptable,—each sort of readers finding in him what is suitable to their faculties. To the many, he is great as a story-teller; to the few, as a poet.

In limiting poetry to the delineation of states of feeling, and denying the name where nothing is delineated but outward objects, we may be thought to have done what we promised to avoid,—to have not found, but made, a definition in opposition to the usage of language, since it is established by common consent that there is a poetry called descriptive. We deny the charge. Description is not poetry because there is descriptive poetry, no more than science is poetry because there is such a thing as a didactic poem. But an object which admits of being described, or a truth which may fill a place in a scientific treatise, may also furnish an occasion for the generation of poetry, which we thereupon choose to call descriptive or didactic. The poetry is not in the object itself, nor in the scientific truth itself, but in the state of mind in which the one and the other may be contemplated. The mere delineation of the dimensions and colors of external objects is not poetry, no more than a geometrical ground-plan of St. Peter's or Westminster Abbey is painting. Descriptive poetry consists, no doubt, in description, but in description of things as they appear, not as they are; and it paints them, not in their bare and natural lineaments, but seen through the medium and arrayed in the colors of the imagination set in action by the feelings. If a poet describes a lion, he does not describe him as a naturalist would, nor even as a traveller would, who was intent upon stating the truth, the whole truth, and nothing but the truth. He describes him by imagery, that is, by suggesting the most striking likenesses and contrasts which might occur to a mind contemplating a lion, in the state of awe, wonder, or terror, which the spectacle naturally excites, or is, on the occasion, supposed to excite. Now, this is describing the lion professedly, but the state of excitement of the spectator really. The lion may be described falsely or with exaggeration, and the poetry be all the better: but, if the human emotion be not painted with scrupulous truth, the poetry is bad poetry; i.e., is not poetry at all, but a failure.

Thus far, our progress towards a clear view of the essentials of poetry has brought us very close to the last two attempts at a definition of poetry which we happen to have seen in print, both of them by poets, and men of genius. The one is by Ebenezer Elliott, the author of "Corn-law Rhymes," and other poems of still greater merit. "Poetry," says he, "is impassioned truth." The other is by a writer in *Blackwood's Magazine*, and comes, we think, still nearer the mark. He defines poetry, "man's thoughts tinged by his feelings." There is in either definition a near approximation to what we are in search of. Every truth which a human being can enunciate, every thought, even every outward impression, which can enter into his consciousness, may become poetry, when shown through any impassioned medium; when invested with the coloring of joy, or grief, or pity, or affection, or admiration, or reverence, or awe, or even hatred or terror; and, unless so colored, nothing, be it as interesting as it may, is poetry. But both these definitions fail to discriminate between poetry and eloquence. Eloquence, as well as poetry, is impassioned truth; eloquence, as well as poetry, is thoughts colored by the feelings. Yet common apprehension and philosophic criticism alike recognize a distinction between the two: there is much that every one would call eloquence, which no one would think of classing as poetry. A question will sometimes arise, whether some particular author is a poet; and those who maintain the negative commonly allow, that though not a poet, he is a highly eloquent writer. The distinction between poetry and eloquence appears to us to be equally fundamental with the distinction between poetry and narrative, or between poetry and description, while it is still further from having been satisfactorily cleared up than either of the others.

Poetry and eloquence are both alike the expression or utterance of feeling: but, if we may be excused the antithesis, we should say that eloquence is *heard;* poetry is *over*heard. Eloquence supposes an audience. The peculiarity of poetry appears to us to lie in the poet's utter unconsciousness of a listener. Poetry is feeling confessing itself to itself in moments of solitude, and embodying itself in symbols which are the nearest possible representations of the feeling in the exact shape in which it exists in the poet's mind. Eloquence is feeling pouring itself out to other minds, courting their sympathy, or endeavoring to influence their belief, or move them to passion or to action.

All poetry is of the nature of soliloquy. It may be said that poetry which is printed on hot-pressed paper, and sold at a bookseller's shop, is a soliloquy in full dress and on the stage. It is so; but there is nothing absurd in the idea of such a mode of soliloquizing. What we have said to ourselves we may tell to others afterwards; what we have said or done in solitude we may voluntarily reproduce when we know that other eyes are upon us. But no trace of consciousness that any eyes are upon us must be visible in the work itself. The actor knows that there is an audience present but, if he act as though he knew it, he acts ill. A poet may write poetry, not only with the intention of printing it, but for the express purpose of being paid for it. That it should *be* poetry, being written under such influences, is less probable, not, however, impossible; but no otherwise possible than if he can succeed in excluding from his work every vestige of such lookings-forth into the outward and every-day world, and can express his emotions exactly as he has felt them in solitude, or as he is conscious that he should feel them, though they were to remain forever unuttered, or (at the lowest) as he knows that others feel them in similar circumstances of solitude. But when he turns round, and addresses himself to another person; when the act of utterance is not itself the end, but a means to an end,—viz., by the feelings he himself expresses, to work upon the feelings, or upon the belief or the will of another; when the expression of his emotions, or of his thoughts tinged by his emotions, is tinged also by that purpose, by that desire of making an impression upon another mind,—then it ceases to be poetry, and becomes eloquence.

Poetry, accordingly, is the natural fruit of solitude and meditation; eloquence, of intercourse with the world. The persons who have most feeling of their own, if intellectual culture has given them a language in which to express it, have the highest faculty of poetry: those who best understand the feelings of others are the most eloquent. The persons and the nations who commonly excel in poetry are those whose character and tastes render them least dependent upon the applause or sympathy or concurrence of the world in general. Those to whom that applause, that sympathy, that concurrence, are most necessary, generally excel most in eloquence. And hence, perhaps, the French, who are the least poetical of all great and intellectual nations, are among the most eloquent; the French also being the most sociable, the vainest, and the least self-dependent.

If the above be, as we believe, the true theory of the

distinction commonly admitted between eloquence and poetry, or even though it be not so, yet if, as we cannot doubt, the distinction above stated be a real *bonâfide* distinction, it will be found to hold, not merely in the language of words, but in all other language, and to intersect the whole domain of art.

Take, for example, music. We shall find in that art, so peculiarly the expression of passion, two perfectly distinct styles,—one of which may be called the poetry, the other the oratory, of music. This difference, being seized, would put an end to much musical sectarianism. There has been much contention whether the music of the modern Italian school, that of Rossini and his successors, be impassioned or not. Without doubt, the passion it expresses is not the musing, meditative tenderness or pathos or grief of Mozart or Beethoven; yet it is passion, but garrulous passion,—the passion which pours itself into other ears, and therein the better calculated for dramatic effect, having a natural adaptation for dialogue. Mozart also is great in musical oratory; but his most touching compositions are in the opposite style,—that of soliloquy. Who can imagine "Dove sono" *heard?* We imagine it *over*heard.

Purely pathetic music commonly partakes of soliloquy. The soul is absorbed in its distress; and, though there may be by-standers, it is not thinking of them. When the mind is looking within, and not without, its state does not often or rapidly vary; and hence the even, uninterrupted flow, approaching almost to monotony, which a good reader or a good singer will give to words or music of a pensive or melancholy cast. But grief, taking the form of a prayer or of a complaint, becomes oratorical: no longer low and even and subdued, it assumes a more emphatic rhythm, a more rapidly returning accent; instead of a few slow, equal notes, following one after another at regular intervals, it crowds note upon note, and often assumes a hurry and bustle like joy. Those who are familiar with some of the best of Rossini's serious compositions, such as the air "Tu che i miseri conforti," in the opera of *Tancredi,* or the duet "Ebben per mia memoria," in *La Gazza Ladra,* will at once understand and feel our meaning. Both are highly tragic and passionate: the passion of both is that of oratory, not poetry. The like may be said of that most moving invocation in Beethoven's *Fidelio,*—

Komm, Hoffnung, lass das letzte Stern
Der Müde nicht erbleichen,

in which Madame Schröder Devrient exhibited such consummate powers of pathetic expression. How different from Winter's beautiful "Paga fui," the very soul of melancholy exhaling itself in solitude! fuller of meaning, and therefore more profoundly poetical, than the words for which it was composed; for it seems to express, not simple melancholy, but the melancholy of remorse.

If from vocal music we now pass to instrumental, we may have a specimen of musical oratory in any fine military symphony or march; while the poetry of music seems to have attained its consummation in Beethoven's "Overture to Egmont," so wonderful in its mixed expression of grandeur and melancholy.

In the arts which speak to the eye, the same distinctions will be found to hold, not only between poetry and oratory, but between poetry, oratory, narrative, and simple imitation or description.

Pure description is exemplified in a mere portrait or a mere landscape,—productions of art, it is true, but of the mechanical rather than of the fine arts; being works of simple imitation, not creation. We say, a mere portrait or a mere landscape; because it is possible for a portrait or a landscape, without ceasing to be such, to be also a picture, like Turner's landscapes, and the great portraits by Titian or Vandyke.

Whatever in painting or sculpture expresses human feeling,—or character, which is only a certain state of feeling grown habitual,—may be called, according to circumstances, the poetry or the eloquence of the painter's or the sculptor's art: the poetry, if the feeling declares itself by such signs as escape from us when we are unconscious of being seen; the oratory, if the signs are those we use for the purpose of voluntary communication.

The narrative style answers to what is called historical painting, which it is the fashion among connoisseurs to treat as the climax of the pictorial art. That it is the most difficult branch of the art, we do not doubt, because, in its perfection, it includes the perfection of all the other branches; as, in like manner, an epic poem, though, in so far as it is epic (i.e., narrative), it is not poetry at all, is yet esteemed the greatest effort of poetic genius, because there is no kind whatever of poetry which may not appropriately find a place in it. But an historical picture as such, that is, as the representation of an incident, must necessarily, as it seems to us, be poor and ineffective. The narrative powers of painting are extremely limited. Scarcely any picture, scarcely even any series of pictures, tells its own story without the aid of an interpreter. But it is the single figures, which, to us, are the great charm even of an historical picture. It is in these that the power of the art is really seen. In the attempt to narrate, visible and permanent signs are too far behind the fugitive audible ones, which follow so fast one after another; while the faces and figures in a narrative picture, even though they be Titian's, stand still. Who would not prefer one "Virgin and Child" of Raphael to all the pictures which Rubens, with his fat, frouzy Dutch Venuses, ever painted?—though Rubens, besides excelling almost every one in his mastery over the mechanical parts of his art, often shows real genius in *grouping* his figures, the peculiar problem of historical painting. But then, who, except a mere student of drawing and coloring, ever cared to look twice at any of the figures themselves? The power of painting lies in poetry, of which Rubens had not the slightest tincture,—not in narrative, wherein he might have excelled.

The single figures, however, in an historical picture, are rather the eloquence of painting than the poetry. They mostly (unless they are quite out of place in the picture) express the feelings of one person as modified by the presence of others. Accordingly, the minds whose bent leads them rather to eloquence than to poetry rush to historical painting. The French painters, for instance, seldom attempt, because they could make nothing of, single heads, like those glorious ones of the Italian masters with which they might feed themselves day after day in their own Louvre. They must all be historical; and they are, almost to a man, attitudinizers. If we wished to give any young artist the most impressive warning our imagination could devise against that kind of vice in the pictorial which corresponds to rant in the histrionic art, we would advise him to walk once up and once down the gallery of the Luxembourg. Every figure in French painting or statuary seems to be showing itself off before spectators. They are not poetical, but in the worst style of corrupted eloquence.

SECTION TWO

"NASCITUR POËTA" is a maxim of classical antiquity, which has passed to these latter days with less questioning than most of the doctrines of that early age. When it originated, the human faculties were occupied, fortunately for posterity, less in examining how the works of genius are created than in creating them; and the adage probably had no higher source than the tendency common among mankind to consider all power which is not visibly the effect of practice, all skill which is not capable of being reduced to mechanical rules, as the result of a peculiar gift. Yet this aphorism, born in the infancy of psychology, will perhaps be found, now when that science is in its adolescence, to be as true as an epigram ever is; that is, to contain some truth,— truth, however, which has been so compressed, and bent out of shape, in order to tie it up into so small a knot of only two words, that it requires an almost infinite amount of unrolling and laying straight before it will resume its just proportions.

We are not now intending to remark upon the grosser misapplications of this ancient maxim, which have engendered so many races of poetasters. The days are gone by, when every raw youth, whose borrowed phantasies have set themselves to a borrowed tune, mistaking, as Coleridge says, an ardent desire of poetic reputation for poetic genius, while unable to disguise from himself that he had taken no means whereby he might *become* a poet, could fancy himself a born one. Those who would reap without sowing, and gain the victory without fighting the battle, are ambitious now of another sort of distinction, and are born novelists or public speakers, not poets; and the wiser thinkers understand and acknowledge that poetic excellence is subject to the same necessary conditions with any other mental endowment, and that to no one of the spiritual benefactors of mankind is a higher or a more assiduous intellectual culture needful than to the poet. It is true, he possesses this advantage over others who use the "instrument of words,"—that, of the truths which he utters, a larger proportion are derived from personal consciousness, and a smaller from philosophic investigation. But the power itself of discriminating between what really is consciousness and what is only a process of inference completed in a single instant, and the capacity of distinguishing whether that of which the mind is conscious be an eternal truth or but a dream, are among the last results of the most matured and perfect intellect. Not to mention that the poet, no more than any other person who writes, confines himself altogether to intuitive truths, nor has any means of communicating even these but by words, every one of which derives all its power of conveying a meaning from a whole host of acquired notions and facts learnt by study and experience.

Nevertheless, it seems undeniable in point of fact, and consistent with the principles of a sound metaphysics, that there are poetic *natures*. There is a mental and physical constitution or temperament peculiarly fitted for poetry. This temperament will not of itself make a poet, no more than the soil will the fruit; and as good fruit may be raised by culture from indifferent soils, so may good poetry from naturally unpoetical minds. But the poetry of one who is a poet by nature will be clearly and broadly distinguishable from the poetry of mere culture. It may not be truer; it may not be more useful; but it will be different: fewer will appreciate it, even though many should affect to do so; but in those few it will find a keener sympathy, and will yield them a deeper enjoyment.

One may write genuine poetry, and not be a poet; for whosoever writes out truly any human feeling, writes poetry. All persons, even the most unimaginative, in moments of strong emotion, speak poetry; and hence the drama is poetry, which else were always prose, except when a poet is one of the characters. What *is* poetry but the thoughts and words in which emotion spontaneously embodies itself? As there are few who are not, at least for some moments and in some situations, capable of some strong feeling, poetry is natural to most persons at some period of their lives; and any one whose feelings are genuine, though but of the average strength,—if he be not diverted by uncongenial thoughts or occupations from the indulgence of them, and if he acquire by culture, as all persons may, the faculty of delineating them correctly,—has it in his power to be a poet, so far as a life passed in writing unquestionable poetry may be considered to confer that title. But *ought* it to do so? Yes, perhaps, in a collection of "British poets." But "poet" is the name also of a variety of man, not solely of the author of a particular variety of book. Now, to have written whole volumes of real poetry is possible to almost all kinds of characters, and implies no greater peculiarity of mental construction than to be the author of a history or a novel.

Whom, then, shall we call poets? Those who are so constituted, that emotions are the links of association by which their ideas, both sensuous and spiritual, are connected together. This constitution belongs (within certain limits) to all in whom poetry is a pervading principle. In all others, poetry is something extraneous and superinduced; something out of themselves, foreign to the habitual course of their every-day lives and characters; a world to which they may make occasional visits, but where they are sojourners, not dwellers, and which, when out of it, or even when in it, they think of, peradventure, but as a phantom-world,—a place of *ignes fatui* and spectral illusions. Those only who have the peculiarity of association which we have mentioned, and which is a natural though not an universal consequence of intense sensibility, instead of seeming not themselves when they are uttering poetry, scarcely seem themselves when uttering any thing to which poetry is foreign. Whatever be the thing which they are contemplating, if it be capable of connecting itself with their emotions, the aspect under which it first and most naturally paints itself to them is its poetic aspect. The poet of culture sees his object in prose, and describes it in poetry: the poet of nature actually sees it in poetry.

This point is perhaps worth some little illustration; the rather as metaphysicians (the ultimate arbiters of all philosophical criticism), while they have busied themselves for two thousand years, more or less, about the few *universal* laws of human nature, have strangely neglected the analysis of its *diversities*. Of these, none lie deeper or reach further than the varieties which difference of nature and of education makes in what may be termed the habitual bond of association. In a mind entirely uncultivated, which is also without any strong feelings, objects whether of sense or of intellect arrange themselves in the mere casual order in which they have been seen, heard, or otherwise perceived. Persons of this sort may be said to think chronologically. If they remember a fact, it is by reason of a fortuitous coincidence with some trifling incident or circumstance which took place at the very time. If they have a story to tell, or testimony to deliver in a witness-box, their narrative must follow the exact order in which the events took place: *dodge* them, and the thread of association is broken; they cannot go on. Their associations, to use the language of philosophers, are chiefly of the successive, not the synchronous kind; and, whether successive or synchronous, are mostly casual.

To the man of science, again, or of business, objects group themselves according to the artificial classifications which the understanding has voluntarily made for the convenience of thought or of practice. But, where any of the impressions are vivid and intense, the associations into which these enter are the ruling ones; it being a well-known law of association, that, the stronger a feeling is, the more quickly and strongly it associates itself with any other object or feeling. Where, therefore, nature has given strong feelings, and education has not created factitious tendencies stronger than the natural ones, the prevailing associations will be those which connect objects and ideas with emotions, and with each other through the intervention of emotions. Thoughts and images will be linked together according to the similarity of the feelings which cling to them. A thought will introduce a thought by first introducing a feeling which is allied with it. At the centre of each group of thoughts or images will be found a feeling; and the thoughts or images will be there, only because the feeling was there. The combinations which the mind puts together, the pictures which it paints, the wholes which Imagination constructs out of the materials supplied by Fancy, will be indebted to some dominant *feeling*, not, as in other natures, to a dominant *thought,* for their unity and consistency of character,—for what distinguishes them from incoherences.

The difference, then, between the poetry of a poet, and the poetry of a cultivated but not naturally poetic mind, is, that in the latter, with however bright a halo of feeling the thought may be surrounded and glorified, the thought itself is always the conspicuous object; while the poetry of a poet is Feeling itself, employing Thought only as the medium of its expression. In the one, feeling waits upon thought; in the other, thought upon feeling. The one writer has a distinct aim, common to him with any other didactic author: he desires to convey the thought, and he conveys it clothed in the feelings which it excites in himself, or which he deems most appropriate to it. The other merely pours forth the overflowing of his feelings; and all the thoughts which those feelings suggest are floated promiscuously along the stream.

It may assist in rendering our meaning intelligible if we illustrate it by a parallel between the two English authors of our own day who have produced the greatest quantity of true and enduring poetry,—Wordsworth and Shelley. Apter instances could not be wished for: the one might be cited as the type, the *exemplar*, of what the poetry of culture may accomplish; the other, as perhaps the most striking example ever known of the poetic temperament. How different, accordingly, is the poetry of these two great writers! In Wordsworth, the poetry is almost always the mere setting of a thought. The thought may be more valuable than the setting, or it may be less valuable; but there can be no question as to which was first in his mind. What he is impressed with, and what he is anxious to impress, is some proposition more or less distinctly conceived; some truth, or something which he deems such. He lets the thought dwell in his mind, till it excites, as is the nature of thought, other thoughts, and also such feelings as the measure of his sensibility is adequate to supply. Among these thoughts and feelings, had he chosen a different walk of authorship (and there are many in which he might equally have excelled), he would probably have made a different selection of media for enforcing the parent thought: his habits, however, being those of poetic composition, he selects in preference the strongest feelings, and the thoughts with which most of feeling is naturally or habitually connected. His poetry, therefore, may be defined to be his thoughts, colored by, and impressing themselves by means of, emotions. Such poetry, Wordsworth has occupied a long life in producing; and well and wisely has he so done. Criticisms, no doubt, may be made occasionally both upon the thoughts themselves, and upon the skill he has demonstrated in the choice of his media; for an affair of skill and study, in the most rigorous sense, it evidently was. But he has not labored in vain: he has exercised, and continues to exercise, a powerful, and mostly a highly beneficial influence over the formation and growth of not a few of the most cultivated and vigorous of the youthful minds of our time, over whose heads poetry of the opposite description would have flown, for want of an original organization, physical or mental, in sympathy with it.

On the other hand, Wordsworth's poetry is never bounding, never ebullient; has little even of the appearance of spontaneousness: the well is never so full that it overflows. There is an air of calm deliberateness about all he writes, which is not characteristic of the poetic temperament. His poetry seems one thing; himself, another. He seems to be poetical because he wills to be so, not because he cannot help it. Did he will to dismiss poetry, he need never again, it might almost seem, have a poetical thought. He never seems *possessed* by any feeling: no emotion seems ever so strong as to have entire sway, for the time being, over the current of his thoughts. He never, even for the space of a few stanzas, appears entirely given up to exultation, or grief, or pity, or love, or admiration, or devotion, or even animal spirits. He now and then, though seldom, attempts to write as if he were; and never, we think, without leaving an impression of poverty: as the brook, which, on nearly level ground, quite fills its banks, appears but a thread when running rapidly down a precipitous declivity. He has feeling enough to form a decent, graceful, even beautiful, decoration to a thought which is in itself interesting and moving; but not so much as suffices to stir up the soul by mere sympathy with itself in its simplest manifestation, nor enough to summon up that array of "thoughts of power," which, in a richly stored mind, always attends the call of really intense feeling. It is for this reason, doubtless, that the genius of Wordsworth is essentially unlyrical. Lyric poetry, as it was the earliest kind, is also, if the view we are now taking of poetry be correct, more eminently and peculiarly poetry than any other: it is the poetry most natural to a really poetic temperament, and least capable of being successfully imitated by one not so endowed by nature.

Shelley is the very reverse of all this. Where Wordsworth is strong, he is weak: where Wordsworth is weak, he is strong.

Culture, that culture by which Wordsworth has reared from his own inward nature the richest harvest ever brought forth by a soil of so little depth, is precisely what was wanting to Shelley; or let us rather say, he had not, at the period of his deplorably early death, reached sufficiently far in that intellectual progression of which he was capable, and which, if it has done so much for greatly inferior natures, might have made of him the most perfect, as he was already the most gifted, of our poets. For him, voluntary mental discipline had done little: the vividness of his emotions and of his sensations had done all. He seldom follows up an idea: it starts into life, summons from the fairy-land of his inexhaustible fancy some three or four bold images, then vanishes, and straight he is off on the wings of some casual association into quite another sphere. He had scarcely yet acquired the consecutiveness of thought necessary for a long poem. His more ambitious compositions too often resemble the scattered fragments of a mirror,—colors brilliant as life, single images without end, but no picture. It is only when under the overruling influence of some one state of feeling, either actually experienced, or summoned up in the vividness of reality by a fervid imagination, that he writes as a great poet; unity of feeling being to him the harmonizing principle which a central idea is to minds of another class, and supplying the coherency and consistency which would else have been wanting. Thus it is in many of his smaller, and especially his lyrical poems. They are obviously written to exhale, perhaps to relieve, a state of feeling, or of conception of feeling, almost oppressive from its vividness. The thoughts and imagery are suggested by the feeling, and are such as it finds unsought. The state of feeling may be either of soul or of sense, or oftener (might we not say invariably?) of both; for the poetic temperament is usually, perhaps always, accompanied by exquisite senses. The exciting cause may be either an object or an idea. But whatever of sensation enters into the feeling must not be local, or consciously organic: it is a condition of the whole frame, not of a part only. Like the state of sensation produced by a fine climate, or indeed like all strongly pleasurable or painful sensations in an impassioned nature, it pervades the entire nervous system. States of feeling, whether sensuous or spiritual, which thus possess the whole being, are the fountains of that which we have called the poetry of poets, and which is little else than a pouring-forth of the thoughts and images that pass across the mind while some permanent state of feeling is occupying it.

To the same original fineness of organization, Shelley was doubtless indebted for another of his rarest gifts,—that exuberance of imagery, which, when unrepressed, as in many of his poems it is, amounts to a fault. The susceptibility of his nervous system, which made his emotions intense, made also the impressions of his external senses deep and clear; and agreeably to the law of association, by which, as already remarked, the strongest impressions are those which associate themselves the most easily and strongly, these vivid sensations were readily recalled to mind by all objects or thoughts which had co-existed with them, and by all feelings which in any degree resembled them. Never did a fancy so teem with sensuous imagery as Shelley's. Wordsworth economizes an image, and detains it until he has distilled all the poetry out of it, and it will not yield a drop more: Shelley lavishes his with a profusion which is unconscious because it is inexhaustible.

If, then, the maxim "Nascitur poëta" means, either that the power of producing poetical compositions is a peculiar faculty which the poet brings into the world with him, which grows like any of his bodily powers, and is as independent of culture as his height and his complexion; or that any natural peculiarity whatever is implied in producing poetry, real poetry, and in any quantity,—such poetry too, as, to the majority of educated and intelligent readers, shall appear quite as good as, or even better than, any other,—in either sense the doctrine is false. And, nevertheless, there *is* poetry which could not emanate but from a mental and physical constitution, peculiar, not in the kind, but in the degree, of its susceptibility; a constitution which makes its possessor capable of greater happiness than mankind in general, and also of greater unhappiness; and because greater, so also more various. And such poetry, to all who know enough of nature to own it as being in nature, is much more poetry, is poetry in a far higher sense, than any other; since the common element of all poetry, that which constitutes poetry,— human feeling,—enters far more largely into this than into the poetry of culture; not only because the natures which we have called poetical really feel more, and consequently have more feeling to express, but because, the capacity of feeling being so great, feeling, when excited and not voluntarily resisted, seizes the helm of their thoughts, and the succession of ideas and images becomes the mere utterance of an emotion; not, as in other natures, the emotion a mere ornamental coloring of the thought.

Ordinary education and the ordinary course of life are constantly at work counteracting this quality of mind, and substituting habits more suitable to their own ends: if, instead of substituting, they were content to superadd, there would be nothing to complain of. But when will education consist, not in repressing any mental faculty or power, from the uncontrolled action of which danger is apprehended, but in training up to its proper strength the corrective and antagonist power?

In whomsoever the quality which we have described exists, and is not stifled, that person is a poet. Doubtless he is a greater poet in proportion as the fineness of his perceptions, whether of sense or of internal consciousness, furnishes him with an ampler supply of lovely images, the vigor and richness of his intellect with a greater abundance of moving thoughts. For it is through these thoughts and images that the feeling speaks, and through their impressiveness that it impresses itself, and finds response in other hearts; and, from these media of transmitting it (contrary to the laws of physical nature), increase of intensity is reflected back upon the feeling itself. But all these it is possible to have, and not be a poet: they are mere materials, which the poet shares in common with other people. What constitutes the poet is not the imagery, nor the thoughts, nor even the feelings, but the law according to which they are called up. He is a poet, not because he has ideas of any particular kind, but because the succession of his ideas is subordinate to the course of his emotions.

Many who have never acknowledged this in theory bear testimony to it in their particular judgments. In listening to an oration, or reading a written discourse, not professedly poetical, when do we begin to feel that the speaker or author is putting off the character of the orator or the prose-writer, and is passing into the poet? Not when he begins to show strong feeling; *then* we merely say, he is in earnest; he feels what he says: still less when he expresses himself in imagery; then, unless illustration be manifestly his sole object, we are apt to say, this is affectation. It is when the feeling (instead of passing away, or, if it continue, letting the train of thoughts run on exactly as they would have done if there were no influence at work but the mere intellect) becomes itself the originator of another train of association, which expels, or blends with, the former; when (for example) either his words, or the mode of their arrangement, are such as we spontaneously use only when in a state of excitement, proving that the mind is at least as much occupied by a passive state of its own feelings as by the desire of attaining the premeditated end which the discourse has in view.[2]

Our judgments of authors who lay actual claim to the title of poets follow the same principle. Whenever, after a writer's meaning is fully understood, it is still matter of reasoning and discussion whether he is a poet or not, he will be found to be wanting in the characteristic peculiarity of association so often adverted to. When, on the contrary, after reading or hearing one or two passages, we instinctively and without hesitation cry out, "This is a poet!" the probability is that the passages are strongly marked with this peculiar quality. And we may add, that, in such case, a critic, who, not having sufficient feeling to respond to the poetry, is also without sufficient philosophy to understand it though he feel it not, will be apt to pronounce, not "This is prose," but "This is exaggeration," "This is mysticism," or "This is nonsense."

Although a philosopher cannot, by culture, make himself, in the peculiar sense in which we now use the term, a poet,— unless at least he have that peculiarity of nature which would probably have made poetry his earliest pursuit,—a poet may always, by culture, make himself a philosopher. The poetic laws of association are by no means such as *must* have their course, even though a deliberate purpose require their suspension. If the peculiarities of the poetic temperament were uncontrollable in any poet, they might be supposed so in Shelley; yet how powerfully, in the "Cenci," does he coerce

[2]And this, we may remark by the way, seems to point to the true theory of poetic diction, and to suggest the true answer to as much as is erroneous of Wordsworth's celebrated doctrine on that subject. For, on the one hand, *all* language which is the natural expression of feeling is really poetical, and will be felt as such, apart from conventional associations; but, on the other, whenever intellectual culture has afforded a choice between several modes of expressing the same emotion, the stronger the feeling is, the more naturally and certainly will it prefer the language which is most peculiarly appropriated to itself, and kept sacred from the contact of more vulgar objects of contemplation.

and restrain all the characteristic qualities of his genius! what severe simplicity, in place of his usual barbaric splendor! how rigidly does he keep the feelings and the imagery in subordination to the thought!

The investigation of nature requires no habits or qualities of mind but such as may always be acquired by industry and mental activity. Because, at one time, the mind may be so given up to a state of feeling, that the succession of its ideas is determined by the present enjoyment or suffering which pervades it, this is no reason but that in the calm retirement of study, when under no peculiar excitement either of the outward or of the inward sense, it may form any combinations, or pursue any trains of ideas, which are most conducive to the purposes of philosophic inquiry; and may, while in that state, form deliberate convictions, from which no excitement will afterwards make it swerve. Might we not go even further than this? We shall not pause to ask whether it be not a misunderstanding of the nature of passionate feeling to imagine that it is inconsistent with calmness; whether they who so deem of it do not mistake passion, in the militant or antagonistic state, for the type of passion universally,—do not confound passion struggling towards an outward object, with passion brooding over itself. But, without entering into this deeper investigation, that capacity of strong feeling which is supposed necessarily to disturb the judgment is also the material out of which all *motives* are made,—the motives, consequently, which lead human beings to the pursuit of truth. The greater the individual's capability of happiness and of misery, the stronger interest has that individual in arriving at truth; and, when once that interest is felt, an impassioned nature is sure to pursue this, as to pursue any other object, with greater ardor: for energy of character is commonly the offspring of strong feeling. If, therefore, the most impassioned natures do not ripen into the most powerful intellects, it is always from defect of culture, or something wrong in the circumstances by which the being has originally or successively been surrounded. Undoubtedly, strong feelings require a strong intellect to carry them, as more sail requires more ballast; and when, from neglect or bad education, that strength is wanting, no wonder if the grandest and swiftest vessels make the most utter wreck.

Where, as in some of our older poets, a poetic nature has

been united with logical and scientific culture, the peculiarity of association arising from the finer nature so perpetually alternates with the associations attainable by commoner natures trained to high perfection, that its own particular law is not so conspicuously characteristic of the result produced, as in a poet like Shelley, to whom systematic intellectual culture, in a measure proportioned to the intensity of his own nature, has been wanting. Whether the superiority will naturally be on the side of the philosopher-poet, or of the mere poet; whether the writings of the one ought, as a whole, to be truer, and their influence more beneficent, than those of the other,—is too obvious in principle to need statement: it would be absurd to doubt whether two endowments are better than one; whether truth is more certainly arrived at by two processes, verifying and correcting each other, than by one alone. Unfortunately, in practice, the matter is not quite so simple: there the question often is, Which is least prejudicial to the intellect,—uncultivation or malcultivation? For, as long as education consists chiefly of the mere inculcation of traditional opinions, many of which, from the mere fact that the human intellect has not yet reached perfection, must necessarily be false; so long as even those who are best taught are rather taught to know the thoughts of others than to think,—it is not always clear that the poet of acquired ideas has the advantage over him whose feeling has been his sole teacher. For the depth and durability of wrong as well as right impressions is proportional to the fineness of the material; and they who have the greatest capacity of natural feeling are generally those whose artificial feelings are the strongest. Hence, doubtless, among other reasons, it is, that, in an age of revolutions in opinion, the contemporary poets, those at least who deserve the name, those who have any individuality of character, if they are not before their age, are almost sure to be behind it; an observation curiously verified all over Europe in the present century. Nor let it be thought disparaging. However urgent may be the necessity for a breaking-up of old modes of belief, the most strong-minded and discerning, next to those who head the movement, are generally those who bring up the rear of it.

Bentham [1]

[1] *London and Westminster Review*, August, 1838.

THERE ARE TWO MEN, recently deceased, to whom their country is indebted not only for the greater part of the important ideas which have been thrown into circulation among its thinking men in their time, but for a revolution in its general modes of thought and investigation. These men, dissimilar in almost all else, agreed in being closet-students,— secluded in a peculiar degree, by circumstances and character, from the business and intercourse of the world; and both were, through a large portion of their lives, regarded by those who took the lead in opinion (when they happened to hear of them) with feelings akin to contempt. But they were destined to renew a lesson given to mankind by every age, and always disregarded,—to show that speculative philosophy, which to the superficial appears a thing so remote from the business of life and the outward interests of men, is in reality the thing on earth which most influences them, and, in the long-run, overbears every other influence save those which it must itself obey. The writers of whom we speak have never been read by the multitude; except for the more slight of their works, their readers have been few: but they have been the teachers of the teachers; there is hardly to be found in England an individual of any importance in the world of mind, who (whatever opinions he may have afterwards adopted) did not first learn to think from one of these two; and, though their influences have but begun to diffuse themselves through these intermediate channels over society at large, there is already scarcely a publication of any consequence, addressed to the educated classes, which, if these persons had not existed, would not have been different from what it is. These men are Jeremy Bentham and Samuel Taylor Coleridge,—the two great seminal minds of England in their age.

No comparison is intended here between the minds or influences of these remarkable men: this were impossible, unless there were first formed a complete judgment of each, considered apart. It is our intention to attempt, on the present occasion, an estimate of one of them; the only one, a complete edition of whose works is yet in progress, and who, in the classification which may be made of all writers into Progressive and Conservative, belongs to the same division with ourselves. For although they were far too great men to be correctly designated by either appellation exclusively, yet, in the main, Bentham was a Progressive philosopher; Coleridge, a Conservative one. The influence of the former has made itself felt chiefly on minds of the Progressive class; of the latter, on those of the Conservative: and the two systems of concentric circles which the shock given by them is spreading over the ocean of mind have only just begun to meet and intersect. The writings of both contain severe lessons, to their own side, on many of the errors and faults they are addicted to: but to Bentham it was given to discern more particularly those truths with which existing doctrines and institutions were at variance; to Coleridge, the neglected truths which lay *in* them.

A man of great knowledge of the world, and of the highest reputation for practical talent and sagacity among the official men of his time (himself no follower of Bentham, nor of any partial or exclusive school whatever), once said to us, as the result of his observation, that to Bentham more than to any other source might be traced the questioning spirit, the disposition to demand the *why* of every thing, which had gained so much ground and was producing such important consequences in these times. The more this assertion is examined, the more true it will be found. Bentham has been in this age and country the great questioner of things established. It is by the influence of the modes of thought with which his writings inoculated a considerable number of thinking men, that the yoke of authority has been broken, and innumerable opinions, formerly received on tradition as incontestable, are put upon their defence, and required to give an account of themselves. Who, before Bentham (whatever controversies might exist on points of detail), dared to speak disrespectfully, in express terms, of the British Constitution or the English law? He did so; and his arguments and his example together encouraged others. We do not mean that his writings caused the Reform Bill, or that the appropriation clause owns him as its parent: the changes which have been made, and the greater changes which will be made, in our institutions, are not the work of philosophers, but of the interests and instincts of large portions of society recently grown into strength. But Bentham gave voice to those interests and instincts: until he spoke out, those who found our institutions unsuited to them did not dare to say so, did not dare consciously to think so; they had never heard the excellence of those institutions questioned by cultivated men, by men of acknowledged intellect; and it is not in the nature of uninstructed minds to resist the united authority of the instructed. Bentham broke the spell. It was not Bentham by his own writings: it was Bentham through the minds and pens which those writings fed,—through the men in more direct contact with the world, into whom his spirit passed. If the superstition about ancestorial wisdom has fallen into decay; if the public are grown familiar with the idea that their laws and institutions are in great part, not the product of intellect and virtue, but of modern corruption grafted upon ancient barbarism; if the hardiest innovation is no longer scouted *because* it is an innovation,—establishments no longer considered sacred because they are establishments,—it will be found that those who have accustomed the public mind to these ideas have learnt them in Bentham's school, and that the assault on ancient institutions has been, and is, carried on for the most part with his weapons. It matters not, although these thinkers, or indeed thinkers of any description, have been but scantily found among the persons prominently and ostensibly at the head of the Reform movement. All movements, except directly revolutionary ones, are headed, not by those who originate them, but by those who know best how to compromise between the old opinions and the new. The father of English innovation, both in doctrines and in institutions, is Bentham: he is the great *subversive*, or, in the language of Continental philosophers, the great *critical*, thinker of his age and country.

We consider this, however, to be not his highest title to fame. Were this all, he were only to be ranked among the lowest order of the potentates of mind,—the negative or destructive philosophers; those who can perceive what is false, but not what is true; who awaken the human mind to the inconsistencies and absurdities of time-sanctioned opinions and institutions, but substitute nothing in the place of what they take away. We have no desire to undervalue the services of such persons: mankind have been deeply indebted to them; nor will there ever be a lack of work for them in a world in which so many false things are believed, in which so many which have been true are believed long after they have ceased to be true. The qualities, however, which fit men for perceiving anomalies, without perceiving the truths which would rectify them, are not among the rarest of endowments. Courage, verbal acuteness, command over the forms of argumentation, and a popular style, will make out of the shallowest man, with a sufficient lack of reverence, a considerable negative philosopher. Such men have never been wanting in periods of culture; and the period in which Bentham formed his early impressions was emphatically their reign, in proportion to its barrenness in the more noble products of the human mind. An age of formalism in the Church, and corruption in the State, when the most valuable part of the meaning of traditional doctrines had faded from the minds even of those who retained from habit a mechanical belief in them, was the time to raise up all kinds of sceptical philosophy. Accordingly, France had Voltaire, and his school of negative thinkers; and England (or rather Scotland) had the profoundest negative thinker on record,—David Hume; a man, the peculiarities of whose mind qualified him to detect failure of proof, and want of logical consistency, at a depth which French sceptics, with their comparatively feeble powers of analysis and abstraction, stopped far short of, and which German subtlety alone could thoroughly appreciate, or hope to rival.

If Bentham had merely continued the work of Hume, he would scarcely have been heard of in philosophy; for he was far inferior to Hume in Hume's qualities, and was in no respect fitted to excel as a metaphysician. We must not look for subtlety, or the power of recondite analysis, among his intellectual characteristics. In the former quality, few great thinkers have ever been so deficient; and to find the latter, in any considerable measure, in a mind acknowledging any kindred with his, we must have recourse to the late Mr. Mill,—a man who united the great qualities of the metaphysicians of the eighteenth century with others of a different complexion, admirably qualifying him to complete and correct their work. Bentham had not these peculiar gifts: but he possessed others, not inferior, which were not possessed by any of his precursors; which have made him a source of light to a generation which has far outgrown their influence, and, as we called him, the chief subversive thinker of an age which has long lost all that they could subvert.

To speak of him first as a merely negative philosopher,— as one who refutes illogical arguments, exposes sophistry, detects contradiction and absurdity: even in that capacity, there was a wide field left vacant for him by Hume, and which he has occupied to an unprecedented extent,—the field of practical abuses. This was Bentham's peculiar province,—to this he was called by the whole bent of his disposition—to carry the warfare against absurdity into things practical. His was an essentially practical mind. It was by practical abuses that his mind was first turned to speculation,—by the abuses of the profession which was chosen for him,—that of the law. He has himself stated what particular abuse first gave that shock to his mind, the recoil of which has made the whole mountain of abuse totter: it was the custom of making the client pay for three attendances in the office of a Master in Chancery, when only one was given. The law, he found on examination, was full of such things. But were these discoveries of his? No: they were known to every lawyer who practised, to every judge who sat on the bench; and neither before nor for long after did they cause any apparent uneasiness to the consciences of these learned persons, nor hinder them from asserting, whenever occasion offered, in books, in Parliament, or on the bench, that the law was the perfection of reason. During so many generations, in each of which thousands of well-educated young men were successively placed in Bentham's position and with Bentham's opportunities, he alone was found with sufficient moral sensibility and self-reliance to say to himself, that these things, however profitable they might be, were frauds, and that between them and himself there should be a gulf fixed. To this rare union of self-reliance and moral sensibility we are indebted for all that Bentham has done. Sent to Oxford by his father at the unusually early age of fifteen; required, on admission, to declare his belief in the Thirty-nine Articles,—he felt it necessary to examine them; and the examination suggested scruples, which he sought to get removed, but, instead of the satisfaction he expected, was told that it was not for boys like him to set up their judgment against the great men of the Church. After a struggle, he signed; but the impression that he had done an immoral act never left him: he considered himself to have committed a falsehood; and throughout life he never relaxed in his indignant denunciations of all laws which command such falsehoods, all institutions which attach rewards to them.

By thus carrying the war of criticism and refutation, the conflict with falsehood and absurdity, into the field of practical evils, Bentham, even if he had done nothing else, would have earned an important place in the history of intellect. He carried on the warfare without intermission. To this, not only many of his most piquant chapters, but some of the most finished of his entire works, are entirely devoted,—the "Defence of Usury;" the "Book of Fallacies;" and the onslaught upon Blackstone, published anonymously under the title of "A Fragment on Government," which, though a first production, and of a writer afterwards so much ridiculed for his style, excited the highest admiration no less for its composition than for its thoughts, and was attributed by turns to Lord Mansfield, to Lord Camden, and (by Dr. Johnson) to Dunning, one of the greatest masters of style among the lawyers of his day. These writings are altogether original: though of the negative school, they resemble nothing previously produced by negative philosophers; and would have sufficed to create for Bentham, among the subversive thinkers of modern Europe, a place peculiarly his own. But it is not these writings that constitute the real distinction between him and them. There was a deeper difference. It was that they were purely negative thinkers: he was positive. They only assailed error: he made it a point of conscience not to do so until he thought he could plant instead the corresponding truth. Their character was exclusively analytic: his was synthetic. They took for their starting-point the received opinion on any subject, dug round it with their logical implements, pronounced its foundations defective, and condemned it: he began *de novo*, laid his own foundations deeply and firmly, built up his own structure, and bade mankind compare the two. It was when he had solved the problem himself, or thought he had done so, that he declared all other solutions to be erroneous. Hence, what they produced will not last; it must perish, much of it has already perished, with the errors which it exploded: what he did has its own value, by which it must outlast all errors to which it is opposed. Though we may reject, as we often must, his practical conclusions, yet his premises, the collections of facts and observations from which his conclusions were drawn, remain for ever, a part of the materials of philosophy.

A place, therefore, must be assigned to Bentham among the masters of wisdom, the great teachers and permanent intellectual ornaments of the human race. He is among those who have enriched mankind with imperishable gifts; and although these do not transcend all other gifts, nor entitle him to those honors, "above all Greek, above all Roman fame," which, by a natural re-action against the neglect and contempt of the world, many of his admirers were once disposed to accumulate upon him, yet to refuse an admiring recognition of what he was, on account of what he was not, is a much worse error, and one which, pardonable in the vulgar, is no longer permitted to any cultivated and instructed mind.

If we were asked to say, in the fewest possible words, what we conceive to be Bentham's place among these great intellectual benefactors of humanity; what he was, and what he was not; what kind of service he did and did not render to truth,—we should say, he was not a great philosopher; but he was a great reformer in philosophy. He brought into philosophy something which it greatly needed, and for want of which it was at a stand. It was not his doctrines which did this: it was his mode of arriving at them. He introduced into morals and politics those habits of thought, and modes of investigation, which are essential to the idea of science, and the absence of which made those departments of inquiry, as physics had been before Bacon, a field of interminable discussion, leading to no result. It was not his opinions, in short, but his method, that constituted the novelty and the value of what he did,—a value beyond all price, even though we should reject the whole, as we unquestionably must a large part, of the opinions themselves.

Bentham's method may be shortly described as the method of detail; of treating wholes by separating them into their parts; abstractions, by resolving them into things; classes and generalities, by distinguishing them into the individuals of which they are made up; and breaking every question into pieces before attempting to solve it. The precise amount of originality of this process, considered as a logical conception,— its degree of connection with the methods of physical science, or with the previous labors of Bacon, Hobbes, or Locke,—is not an essential consideration in this place. Whatever originality there was in the method, in the subjects he applied it to, and in the rigidity with which he adhered to it, there was the greatest. Hence his interminable classifications; hence his elaborate demonstrations of the most acknowledged truths. That murder, incendiarism, robbery, are mischievous actions, he will not take for granted, without proof. Let the thing appear ever so self-evident, he will know the why and the how of it with the last degree of precision; he will distinguish all the different mischiefs of a crime, whether of the *first*, the *second*, or the *third* order; namely, 1. The evil to the sufferer, and to his personal connections; 2. The *danger* from example, and the *alarm* or painful feeling of insecurity; and, 3. The discouragement to industry and useful pursuits arising from the *alarm*, and the trouble and resources which must be expended in warding off the *danger*. After this enumeration, he will prove, from the laws of human feeling, that even the first of these evils, the sufferings of the immediate victim, will, on the average, greatly outweigh the pleasure reaped by the offender; much more when all the other evils are taken into account. Unless this could be proved, he would account the infliction of punishment unwarrantable; and, for taking the trouble to prove it formally, his defence is, "There are truths which it is necessary to prove, not for their own sakes, because they are acknowledged, but that an opening may be made for the reception of other truths which depend upon them. It is in this manner we provide for the reception of first principles, which, once received, prepare the way for admission of all other truths."[2] To which may be added, that in this manner also do we discipline the mind for practising the same sort of dissection upon questions more complicated and of more doubtful issue.

It is a sound maxim, and one which all close thinkers have felt, but which no one before Bentham ever so consistently

[2]Part I of the collected edition.

applied, that error lurks in generalities; that the human mind is not capable of embracing a complex whole, until it has surveyed and catalogued the parts of which that whole is made up; that abstractions are not realities *per se*, but an abridged mode of expressing facts; and that the only practical mode of dealing with them is to trace them back to the facts (whether of experience or of consciousness) of which they are the expression. Proceeding on this principle, Bentham makes short work with the ordinary modes of moral and political reasoning. These, it appeared to him, when hunted to their source, for the most part terminated in *phrases*. In politics, liberty, social order, constitution, law of nature, social compact, &c., were the catchwords: ethics had its analogous ones. Such were the arguments on which the gravest questions of morality and policy were made to turn; not reasons, but allusions to reasons; sacramental expressions, by which a summary appeal was made to some general sentiment of mankind, or to some maxim in familiar use, which might be true or not, but the limitations of which no one had ever critically examined. And this satisfied other people, but not Bentham. He required something more than opinion as a reason for opinion. Whenever he found a *phrase* used as an argument for or against any thing, he insisted upon knowing what it meant; whether it appealed to any standard, or gave intimation of any matter of fact relevant to the question; and, if he could not find that it did either, he treated it as an attempt on the part of the disputant to impose his own individual sentiment on other people, without giving them a reason for it,—a "contrivance for avoiding the obligation of appealing to any external standard, and for prevailing upon the reader to accept of the author's sentiment and opinion as a reason, and that a sufficient one, for itself." Bentham shall speak for himself on this subject. The passage is from his first systematic work, "Introduction to the Principles of Morals and Legislation;" and we could scarcely quote any thing more strongly exemplifying both the strength and weakness of his mode of philosophizing:—

It is curious enough to observe the variety of inventions men have hit upon, and the variety of phrases they have brought forward, in order to conceal from the world, and, if possible, from themselves, this very general, and therefore very pardonable, self-sufficiency.

1. One man says he has a thing made on purpose to tell him what is right and what is wrong; and that it is called a 'moral sense:' and then he goes to work at his ease, and says such a thing is right, and such a thing is wrong. Why? 'Because my moral sense tells me it is.'

2. Another man comes, and alters the phrase; leaving out *moral*, and putting in *common* in the room of it. He then tells you that his common sense tells him what is right and wrong as surely as the other's moral sense did: meaning, by common sense, a sense of some kind or other, which, he says, is possessed by all mankind: the sense of those whose sense is not the same as the author's being struck out, as not worth taking. This contrivance does better than the other; for, a moral sense being a new thing, a man may feel about him a good while without being able to find it out: but common sense is as old as the creation; and there is no man but would be ashamed to be thought not to have as much of it as his neighbors. It has another great advantage: by appearing to share power, it lessens envy; for, when a man gets up upon this ground in order to anathematize those who differ from him, it is not by a *sic volo sic jubeo*, but by a *velitis jubeatis*.

3. Another man comes, and says, that as to a moral sense indeed, he cannot find that he has any such thing; that, however, he has an *understanding*, which will do quite as well. This understanding, he says, is the standard of right and wrong: it tells him so and so. All good and wise men understand as he does: if other men's understandings differ in any part from his, so much the worse for them: it is a sure sign they are either defective or corrupt.

4. Another man says that there is an eternal and immutable rule of right; that that rule of right dictates so and so: and then he begins giving you his sentiments upon any thing that comes uppermost; and these sentiments (you are to take for granted) are so many branches of the eternal rule of right.

5. Another man, or perhaps the same man (it is no matter), says that there are certain practices conformable, and others repugnant, to the fitness of things: and then he tells you, at his leisure, what practices are

conformable, and what repugnant; just as he happens to like a practice or dislike it.

6. A great multitude of people are continually talking of the law of nature; and then they go on giving you their sentiments about what is right and what is wrong: and these sentiments, you are to understand, are so many chapters and sections of the law of nature.

7. Instead of the phrase, law of nature, you have sometimes law of reason, right reason, natural justice, natural equity, good order. Any of them will do equally well. This latter is most used in politics. The three last are much more tolerable than the others, because they do not very explicitly claim to be any thing more than phrases: they insist but feebly upon the being looked upon as so many positive standards of themselves, and seem content to be taken, upon occasion, for phrases expressive of the conformity of the thing in question to the proper standard, whatever that may be. On most occasions, however, it will be better to say *utility: utility is clearer*, as referring more explicitly to pain and pleasure.

8. We have one philosopher, who says there is no harm in any thing in the world but in telling a lie; and that, if, for example, you were to murder your own father, this would only be a particular way of saying he was not your father. Of course, when this philosopher sees any thing that he does not like, he says it is a particular way of telling a lie. It is saying that the act ought to be done, or may be done, when, *in truth*, it ought not be done.

9. The fairest and openest of them all is that sort of man who speaks out, and says, I am of the number of the elect: now God himself takes care to inform the elect what is right; and that with so good effect, that, let them strive ever so, they cannot help not only knowing it, but practising it. If, therefore, a man wants to know what is right and what is wrong, he has nothing to do but to come to me.

Few will contend that this is a perfectly fair representation of the *animus* of those who employ the various phrases so amusingly animadverted on; but that the phrases contain no argument, save what is grounded on the very feelings they are adduced to justify, is a truth which Bentham had the eminent merit of first pointing out.

It is the introduction into the philosophy of human conduct of this method of detail,—of this practise of never reasoning about wholes till they have been resolved into their parts, nor about abstractions till they have been translated into realities, —that constitutes the originality of Bentham in philosophy, and makes him the great reformer of the moral and political branch of it. To what he terms the "exhaustive method of classification," which is but one branch of this more general method, he himself ascribes every thing original in the systematic and elaborate work from which we have quoted. The generalities of his philosophy itself have little or no novelty: to ascribe any to the doctrine, that general utility is the foundation of morality, would imply great ignorance of the history of philosophy, of general literature, and of Bentham's own writings. He derived the idea, as he says himself, from Helvetius; and it was the doctrine no less of the religious philosophers of that age, prior to Reid and Beattie. We never saw an abler defence of the doctrine of utility than in a book written in refutation of Shaftesbury, and now little read,— Brown's[3] "Essays on the Characteristics;" and, in Johnson's celebrated review of Soame Jenyns, the same doctrine is set forth as that both of the author and of the reviewer. In all ages of philosophy, one of its schools has been utilitarian, not only from the time of Epicurus, but long before. It was by mere accident that this opinion became connected in Bentham with his peculiar method. The utilitarian philosophers antecedent to him had no more claims to the method than their antagonists. To refer, for instance, to the Epicurean philosophy, according to the most complete view we have of the moral part of it by the most accomplished scholar of antiquity, Cicero: we ask any one who has read his philosophical writings, the *De Finibus* for instance, whether the arguments of the Epicureans do not, just as much as those of the Stoics or Platonists, consist of mere rhetorical appeals to common notions, ἐικότα and σημεῖα instead of τεκμήρια, notions picked up, as it were, casually, and, when true at all, never so narrowly looked into as to ascertain in what sense, and under what limitations, they are true. The application of a real inductive philosophy to

[3]Author of another book, which made no little sensation when it first appeared, *An Estimate of the Manners of the Times.*

the problems of ethics is as unknown to the Epicurean moralists as to any of the other schools: they never take a question to pieces, and join issue on a definite point. Bentham certainly did not learn his sifting and anatomizing method from them.

This method Bentham has finally installed in philosophy; has made it, henceforth, imperative on philosophers of all schools. By it he has formed the intellects of many thinkers, who either never adopted, or have abandoned, many of his peculiar opinions. He has taught the method to men of the most opposite schools to his: he has made them perceive, that, if they do not test their doctrines by the method of detail, their adversaries will. He has thus, it is not too much to say, for the first time, introduced precision of thought into moral and political philosophy. Instead of taking up their opinions by intuition, or by ratiocination from premises adopted on a mere rough view, and couched in language so vague that it is impossible to say exactly whether they are true or false, philosophers are now forced to understand one another, to break down the generality of their propositions, and join a precise issue in every dispute. This is nothing less than a revolution in philosophy. Its effect is gradually becoming evident in the writings of English thinkers of every variety of opinion, and will be felt more and more in proportion as Bentham's writings are diffused, and as the number of minds to whose formations they contribute is multiplied.

It will naturally be presumed, that, of the fruits of this great philosophical improvement, some portion at least will have been reaped by its author. Armed with such a potent instrument, and wielding it with such singleness of aim; cultivating the field of practical philosophy with such unwearied and such consistent use of a method right in itself, and not adopted by his predecessors,—it cannot be but that Bentham by his own inquiries must have accomplished something considerable. And so, it will be found, he has; something not only considerable, but extraordinary; though but little compared with what he has left undone, and far short of what his sanguine and almost boyish fancy made him flatter himself that he had accomplished. His peculiar method, admirably calculated to make clear thinkers, and sure ones to the extent of their materials, has not equal efficacy for making those materials complete. It is a security for accuracy, but not for comprehensiveness; or, rather, it is a security for one sort of comprehensiveness, but not for another.

Bentham's method of laying out his subject is admirable as a preservative against one kind of narrow and partial views. He begins by placing before himself the whole of the field of inquiry to which the particular question belongs, and divides down till he arrives at the thing he is in search of; and thus, by successively rejecting all which is *not* the thing, he gradually works out a definition of what it *is*. This, which he calls the exhaustive method, is as old as philosophy itself. Plato owes every thing to it, and does every thing by it; and the use made of it by that great man in his Dialogues, Bacon, in one of those pregnant logical hints scattered through his writings, and so much neglected by most of his pretended followers, pronounces to be the nearest approach to a true inductive method in the ancient philosophy. Bentham was probably not aware that Plato had anticipated him in the process to which he, too, declared that he owed every thing. By the practice of it, his speculations are rendered eminently systematic and consistent: no question, with him, is ever an insulated one; he sees every subject in connection with all the other subjects with which in his view it is related, and from which it requires to be distinguished; and as all that he knows, in the least degree allied to the subject, has been marshalled in an orderly manner before him, he does not, like people who use a looser method, forget and overlook a thing on one occasion to remember it on another. Hence there is probably no philosopher, of so wide a range, in whom there are so few inconsistencies. If any of the truths which he did not see had come to be seen by him, he would have remembered it everywhere and at all times, and would have adjusted his whole system to it. And this is another admirable quality which he has impressed upon the best of the minds trained in his habits of thought: when those minds open to admit new truths, they digest them as fast as they receive them.

But this system, excellent for keeping before the mind of the thinker all that he knows, does not make him know enough; it does not make a knowledge of some of the properties of a thing suffice for the whole of it, nor render a rooted habit of surveying a complex object (though ever so carefully) in only one of its aspects tantamount to the power of contemplating it in all. To give this last power, other qualities are required: whether Bentham possessed those other qualities we now have to see.

Bentham's mind, as we have already said, was eminently synthetical. He begins all his inquiries by supposing nothing to be known on the subject; and reconstructs all philosophy *ab initio*, without reference to the opinions of his predecessors. But to build either a philosophy, or any thing else, there must be materials. For the philosophy of matter, the materials are the properties of matter; for moral and political philosophy, the properties of man, and of man's position in the world. The knowledge which any inquirer possesses of these properties constitutes a limit, beyond which, as a moralist or a political philosopher, whatever be his powers of mind, he cannot reach. Nobody's synthesis can be more complete than his analysis. If, in his survey of human nature and life, he has left any element out, then, wheresoever that element exerts any influence, his conclusions will fail, more or less, in their application. If he has left out many elements, and those very important, his labors may be highly valuable: he may have largely contributed to that body of partial truths, which, when completed and corrected by one another, constitute practical truth; but the applicability of his system to practise in its own proper shape will be of an exceedingly limited range.

Human nature and human life are wide subjects; and whoever would embark in an enterprise requiring a thorough knowledge of them has need both of large stores of his own, and of all aids and appliances from elsewhere. His qualifications for success will be proportional to two things,—the degree in which his own nature and circumstances furnish him with a correct and complete picture of man's nature and circumstances, and his capacity of deriving light from other minds.

Bentham failed in deriving light from other minds. His writings contain few traces of the accurate knowledge of any schools of thinking but his own; and many proofs of his entire conviction, that they could teach him nothing worth knowing. For some of the most illustrious of previous thinkers, his contempt was unmeasured. In almost the only passage of the *Deontology*, which from its style, and from its having before appeared in print, may be known to be Bentham's, Socrates and Plato are spoken of in terms distressing to his greatest admirers; and the incapacity to appreciate such men is a fact perfectly in unison with the general habits of Bentham's mind. He had a phrase, expressive of the view he took of all moral speculations to which his method had not been applied, or (which he considered as the same thing) not founded on a recognition of utility as the moral standard: this phrase was "vague generalities." Whatever presented itself to him in such a shape, he dismissed as unworthy of notice, or dwelt upon only to denounce as absurd. He did not heed, or rather the nature of his mind prevented it from occurring to him, that these generalities contained the whole unanalyzed experience of the human race.

Unless it can be asserted that mankind did not know any thing until logicians taught it to them; that, until the last hand has been put to a moral truth by giving it a metaphysically precise expression, all the previous rough-hewing which it has undergone by the common intellect, at the suggestion of common wants and common experience, is to go for nothing,—it must be allowed, that even the originality which can, and the courage which dares, think for itself, is not a more necessary part of the philosophical character than a thoughtful regard for previous thinkers, and for the collective mind of the human race. What has been the opinion of mankind, has been the opinion of persons of all tempers and dispositions, of all partialities and prepossessions, of all varieties in position, in education, in opportunities of observation and inquiry. No one inquirer is all this: every inquirer is either young or old, rich or poor, sickly or healthy, married or unmarried, meditative or active, a poet or a logician, an ancient or a modern, a man or a woman; and, if a thinking person, has, in addition, the accidental peculiarities of his individual modes of thought. Every circumstance which gives a character to the life of a human being carries with it its peculiar biasses,—its peculiar facilities for perceiving some things, and for missing or forgetting others. But, from points of view different from his, different things are perceptible; and none are more likely to have seen what he does not see than those who do not see what he sees. The general opinion of mankind is the average of the conclusions of all minds, stripped indeed of their choicest and most recondite thoughts, but freed from their twists and partialities; a net result, in which everybody's particular point of view is represented, nobody's predominant. The collective mind does not penetrate below the surface, but it sees all the surface: which profound thinkers, even by reason of their profundity, often fail to do; their intenser view of a thing in some of its aspects diverting their attention from others.

The hardiest assertor, therefore, of the freedom of private judgment; the keenest detector of the errors of his predecessors, and of the inaccuracies of current modes of thought, —is the very person who most needs to fortify the weak side of his own intellect by study of the opinions of mankind in all ages and nations, and of the speculations of philosophers of the modes of thought most opposite to his own. It is there that he will find the experiences denied to himself; the remainder of the truth of which he sees but half; the truths, of which the errors he detects are commonly but the exaggerations. If, like Bentham, he brings with him an improved instrument of investigation, the greater is the probability that he will find ready prepared a rich abundance of rough ore, which was merely waiting for that instrument. A man of clear ideas errs grievously if he imagines that whatever is seen confusedly does not exist: it belongs to him, when he meets with such a thing, to dispel the mist, and fix the outlines of the vague form which is looming through it.

Bentham's contempt, then, of all other schools of thinkers; his determination to create a philosophy wholly out of the materials furnished by his own mind, and by minds like his own,—was his first disqualification as a philosopher. His second was the incompleteness of his own mind as a representative of universal human nature. In many of the most natural and strongest feelings of human nature he had no sympathy; from many of its graver experiences he was altogether cut off; and the faculty by which one mind understands a mind different from itself, and throws itself into the feelings of that other mind, was denied him by his deficiency of imagination.

With imagination in the popular sense, command of imagery and metaphorical expression, Bentham was, to a certain degree, endowed. For want, indeed, of poetical culture, the images with which his fancy supplied him were seldom beautiful; but they were quaint and humorous, or bold, forcible, and intense: passages might be quoted from him, both of playful irony and of declamatory eloquence, seldom surpassed in the writings of philosophers. The imagination, which he had not, was that to which the name is *implied need for intuitive seeing into things.*

generally appropriated by the best writers of the present day; that which enables us, by a voluntary effort, to conceive the absent as if it were present, the imaginary as if it were real, and to clothe it in the feelings, which, if it were indeed real, it would bring along with it. This is the power by which one human being enters into the mind and circumstances of another. This power constitutes the poet, in so far as he does any thing but melodiously utter his own actual feelings. It constitutes the dramatist entirely. It is one of the constituents of the historian: by it we understand other times; by it Guizot interprets to us the middle ages; Nisard, in his beautiful Studies on the later Latin poets, places us in the Rome of the Cæsars; Michelet disengages the distinctive characters of the different races and generations of mankind from the facts of their history. Without it, nobody knows even his own nature, further than circumstances have actually tried it, and called it out; nor the nature of his fellow-creatures, beyond such generalizations as he may have been enabled to make from his observation of their outward conduct.

By these limits, accordingly, Bentham's knowledge of human nature is bounded. It is wholly empirical, and the empiricism of one who has had little experience. He had neither internal experience nor external: the quiet, even tenor of his life, and his healthiness of mind, conspired to exclude him from both. He never knew prosperity and adversity, passion nor satiety: he never had even the experiences which sickness gives; he lived from childhood to the age of eighty-five in boyish health. He knew no dejection, no heaviness of heart. He never felt life a sore and a weary burthen. He was a boy to the last. Self-consciousness, that demon of the men of genius of our time, from Wordsworth to Byron, from Goethe to Chateaubriand, and to which this age owes so much both of its cheerful and its mournful wisdom, never was awakened in him. How much of human nature slumbered in him he knew not, neither can we know. He had never been made alive to the unseen influences which were acting on himself, nor, consequently, on his fellow-creatures. Other ages and other nations were a blank to him for purposes of instruction. He measured them but by one standard,—their knowledge of facts, and their capability to take correct views of utility, and merge all other objects in it. His own lot was cast in a generation of the leanest and barrenest men whom England had yet produced; and he was an old man when a better race came in with the present century. He saw accordingly, in man, little but what the vulgarest eye can see; recognized no diversities of character but such as he who runs may read. Knowing so little of human feelings, he knew still less of the influences by which those feelings are formed: all the more subtle workings both of the mind upon itself, and of external things upon the mind, escaped him; and no one, probably, who, in a highly instructed age, ever attempted to give a rule to all human conduct, set out with a more limited conception either of the agencies by which human conduct *is*, or of those by which it *should* be, influenced.

This, then, is our idea of Bentham. He was a man both of remarkable endowments for philosophy, and of remarkable deficiencies for it; fitted beyond almost any man for drawing from his premises conclusions not only correct, but sufficiently precise and specific to be practical; but whose general conception of human nature and life furnished him with an unusually slender stock of premises. It is obvious what would be likely to be achieved by such a man; what a thinker, thus gifted and thus disqualified, could do in philosophy. He could, with close and accurate logic, hunt half-truths to their consequences and practical applications, on a scale both of greatness and of minuteness not previously exemplified; and this is the character which posterity will probably assign to Bentham.

We express our sincere and well-considered conviction when we say, that there is hardly any thing positive in Bentham's philosophy which is not true; that when his practical conclusions are erroneous, which, in our opinion, they are very often, it is not because the considerations which he urges are not rational and valid in themselves, but because some more important principle, which he did not perceive, supersedes those considerations, and turns the scale. The bad part of his writings is his resolute denial of all that he does not see, of all truths but those which he recognizes. By that alone has he exercised any bad influence upon his age; by that he has not created a school of deniers, for this is an ignorant prejudice, but put himself at the head of the school which exists always, though it does not always find a great man to give it the sanction of philosophy; thrown the mantle of intellect over the natural tendency of men in all ages to deny or disparage all feelings and mental states of which they have no consciousness in themselves.

The truths which are not Bentham's, which his philosophy takes no account of, are many and important; but his non-recognition of them does not put them out of existence: they are still with us; and it is a comparatively easy task that is reserved for us,—to harmonize those truths with his. To reject his half of the truth because he overlooked the other half would be to fall into his error without having his excuse. For our own part, we have a large tolerance for one-eyed men, provided their one eye is a penetrating one: if they saw more, they probably would not see so keenly, nor so eagerly pursue one course of inquiry. Almost all rich veins of original and striking speculation have been opened by systematic half-thinkers; though, whether these new thoughts drive out others as good, or are peacefully superadded to them, depends on whether these half-thinkers are or are not followed in the same track by complete thinkers. The field of man's nature and life cannot be too much worked, or in too many directions; until every clod is turned up, the work is imperfect: no whole truth is possible but by combining the points of view of all the fractional truths, nor, therefore, until it has been fully seen what each fractional truth can do by itself.

What Bentham's fractional truths could do there is no such good means of showing as by a review of his philosophy; and such a review, though inevitably a most brief and general one, it is now necessary to attempt.

The first question in regard to any man of speculation is, What is his theory of human life? In the minds of many philosophers, whatever theory they have of this sort is latent; and it would be a revelation to themselves to have it pointed out to them in their writings as others can see it, unconsciously moulding every thing to its own likeness. But Bentham always knew his own premises, and made his reader know them: it was not his custom to leave the theoretic grounds of his practical conclusions to conjecture. Few great thinkers have afforded the means of assigning with so much certainty the exact conception which they had formed of man and of man's life.

Man is conceived by Bentham as a being susceptible of

pleasures and pains, and governed in all his conduct partly
by the different modifications of self-interest, and the passions commonly classed as selfish, partly by sympathies, or
occasionally antipathies, towards other beings. And here
Bentham's conception of human nature stops. He does not
exclude religion: the prospect of divine rewards and punishments he includes under the head of "self-regarding interest;"
and the devotional feeling, under that of sympathy with God.
But the whole of the impelling or restraining principles,
whether of this or of another world, which he recognizes, are
either self-love, or love or hatred towards other sentient beings. That there might be no doubt of what he thought on
the subject, he has not left us to the general evidence of
his writings, but has drawn out a "Table of the Springs of
Action," an express enumeration and classification of human
motives, with their various names, laudatory, vituperative, and
neutral; and this table, to be found in Part I. of his collected
works, we recommend to the study of those who would understand his philosophy.

Man is never recognized by him as a being capable of
pursuing spiritual perfection as an end; of desiring, for its own
sake, the conformity of his own character to his standard
of excellence, without hope of good, or fear of evil, from other
source than his own inward consciousness. Even in the more
limited form of conscience, this great fact in human nature
escapes him. Nothing is more curious than the absence of
recognition, in any of his writings, of the existence of conscience, as a thing distinct from philanthropy, from affection
for God or man, and from self-interest in this world or in
the next. There is a studied abstinence from any of the
phrases, which, in the mouths of others, import the acknowledgment of such a fact.[4] If we find the words "conscience,"
"principle," "moral rectitude," "moral duty," in his "Table
of the Springs of Action," it is among the synonymes of the
"love of reputation;" with an intimation as to the two former
phrases, that they are also sometimes synonymous with the
religious motive, or the motive of *sympathy*. The feeling of
moral approbation or disapprobation, properly so called,
either towards ourselves or our fellow-creatures, he seems un-

---

[4] In a passage in the last volume of his book on Evidence, and possibly
in one or two other places, the "love of justice" is spoken of as a feeling
inherent in almost all mankind. It is impossible, without explanations now
unattainable, to ascertain what sense is to be put upon casual expressions so
inconsistent with the general tenor of his philosophy.

aware of the existence of; and neither the word *self-respect*, nor the idea to which that word is appropriated, occurs even once, so far as our recollection serves us, in his whole writings.

Nor is it only the moral part of man's nature, in the strict sense of the term,—the desire of perfection, or the feeling of an approving or of an accusing conscience,—that he overlooks: he but faintly recognizes, as a fact in human nature, the pursuit of any other ideal end for its own sake. The sense of *honor* and personal dignity,—that feeling of personal exaltation and degradation which acts independently of other people's opinion, or even in defiance of it; the love of *beauty*, the passion of the artist; the love of *order*, of congruity, of consistency in all things, and conformity to their end; the love of *power*, not in the limited form of power over other human beings, but abstract power, the power of making our volitions effectual; the love of *action*, the thirst for movement and activity, a principle scarcely of less influence in human life than its opposite, the love of ease,—none of these powerful constituents of human nature are thought worthy of a place among the "Springs of Action;" and though there is possibly no one of them, of the existence of which an acknowledgment might not be found in some corner of Bentham's writings, no conclusions are ever founded on the acknowledgment. Man, that most complex being, is a very simple one in his eyes. Even under the head of *sympathy*, his recognition does not extend to the more complex forms of the feeling,—the love of *loving*, the need of a sympathizing support, or of objects of admiration and reverence. If he thought at all of any of the deeper feelings of human nature, it was but as idiosyncrasies of taste, with which the moralist no more than the legislator had any concern, further than to prohibit such as were mischievous among the actions to which they might chance to lead. To say either that man should, or that he should not, take pleasure in one thing, displeasure in another, appeared to him as much an act of despotism in the moralist as in the political ruler.

It would be most unjust to Bentham to surmise (as narrow-minded and passionate adversaries are apt in such cases to do) that this picture of human nature was copied from himself; that all those constituents of humanity, which he rejected from his table of motives, were wanting in his own breast. The unusual strength of his early feelings of virtue was, as we have seen, the original cause of all his speculations; and a noble sense of morality, and especially of justice, guides and pervades them all. But having been early accustomed to keep before his mind's eye the happiness of mankind (or rather of the whole sentient world), as the only thing desirable in itself, or which rendered any thing else desirable, he confounded all disinterested feelings which he found in himself with the desire of general happiness; just as some religious writers, who loved virtue for its own sake, as much perhaps as men could do, habitually confounded their love of virtue with their fear of hell. It would have required greater subtlety than Bentham possessed to distinguish from each other feelings, which, from long habit, always acted in the same direction; and his want of imagination prevented him from reading the distinction, where it is legible enough, in the hearts of others.

Accordingly, he has not been followed in this grand oversight by any of the able men, who, from the extent of their intellectual obligations to him, have been regarded as his disciples. They may have followed him in his doctrine of utility, and in his rejection of a moral sense as the test of right and wrong; but, while repudiating it as such, they have, with Hartley, acknowledged it as a fact in human nature; they have endeavored to account for it, to assign its laws: nor are they justly chargeable either with undervaluing this part of our nature, or with any disposition to throw it into the background of their speculations. If any part of the influence of this cardinal error has extended itself to them, it is circuitously, and through the effect on their minds of other parts of Bentham's doctrines.

Sympathy, the only disinterested motive which Bentham recognized, he felt the inadequacy of, except in certain limited cases, as a security for virtuous action. Personal affection, he well knew, is as liable to operate to the injury of third parties, and require as much to be kept under government, as any other feeling whatever; and general philanthropy, considered as a motive influencing mankind in general, he estimated at its true value, when divorced from the feeling of duty,—as the very weakest and most unsteady of all feelings. There remained, as a motive by which mankind are influenced, and by which they may be guided to their good, only personal interest. Accordingly, Bentham's idea of the world is that of a

...on of persons pursuing each his separate interest or ...re, and the prevention of whom from jostling one an- ... more than is unavoidable may be attempted by hopes and fears derived from three sources,—the law, religion, and public opinion. To these three powers, considered as binding human conduct, he gave the name of *sanctions*,—the *political* sanction, operating by the rewards and penalties of the law; the *religious* sanction, by those expected from the Ruler of the universe; and the *popular* which he characteristically calls also the *moral* sanction, operating through the pains and pleasures arising from the favor or disfavor of our fellow-creatures.

Such is Bentham's theory of the world. And now, in a spirit neither of apology nor of censure, but of calm appreciation, we are to inquire how far this view of human nature and life will carry any one; how much it will accomplish in morals, and how much in political and social philosophy; what it will do for the individual, and what for society.

It will do nothing for the conduct of the individual, beyond prescribing some of the more obvious dictates of worldly prudence, and outward probity and beneficence. There is no need to expatiate on the deficiencies of a system of ethics which does not pretend to aid individuals in the formation of their own character; which recognizes no such wish as that of self-culture, we may even say, no such power, as existing in human nature; and, if it did recognize, could furnish little assistance to that great duty, because it overlooks the existence of about half of the whole number of mental feelings which human beings are capable of, including all those of which the direct objects are states of their own mind.

Morality consists of two parts. One of these is self-education,—the training, by the human being himself, of his affections and will. That department is a blank in Bentham's system. The other and co-equal part, the regulation of his outward actions, must be altogether halting and imperfect without the first; for how can we judge in what manner many an action will affect even the worldly interests of ourselves or others, unless we take in, as part of the question, its influence on the regulation of our or their affections and desires? A moralist on Bentham's principles may get as far as this, that he ought not to slay, burn, or steal; but what will be his qualifications for regulating the nicer shades of human behavior, or for laying down even the greater moralities as to those facts in human life which are liable to influence the depths of the character quite independently of any influence on worldly circumstances,—such, for instance, as the sexual relations, or those of family in general, or any other social and sympathetic connections of an intimate kind? The moralities of these questions depend essentially on considerations which Bentham never so much as took into the account; and, when he happened to be in the right, it was always, and necessarily, on wrong or insufficient grounds.

It is fortunate for the world that Bentham's taste lay rather in the direction of jurisprudential, than of properly ethical, inquiry. Nothing expressly of the latter kind has been published under his name, except the *Deontology*,— a book scarcely ever, in our experience, alluded to by any admirer of Bentham, without deep regret that it ever saw the light. We did not expect from Bentham correct systematic views of ethics, or a sound treatment of any question, the moralities of which require a profound knowledge of the human heart; but we did anticipate that the greater moral questions would have been boldly plunged into, and at least a searching criticism produced of the received opinions: we did not expect that the *petite morale* almost alone would have been treated, and that with the most pedantic minuteness, and on the *quid pro quo* principles which regulate trade. The book has not even the value which would belong to an authentic exhibition of the legitimate consequences of an erroneous line of thought; for the style proves it to have been so entirely rewritten, that it is impossible to tell how much or how little of it is Bentham's. The collected edition, now in progress, will not, it is said, include Bentham's religious writings: these, although we think most of them of exceedingly small value, are at least his; and the world has a right to whatever light they throw upon the constitution of his mind. But the omission of the *Deontology* would be an act of editorial discretion which we should deem entirely justifiable.

If Bentham's theory of life can do so little for the individual, what can it do for society?

It will enable a society which has attained a certain state

of spiritual development, and the maintenance of which in that state is otherwise provided for, to prescribe the rules by which it may protect its material interests. It will do nothing (except sometimes as an instrument in the hands of a higher doctrine) for the spiritual interests of society; nor does it suffice of itself even for the material interests. That which alone causes any material interests to exist, which alone enables any body of human beings to exist as a society, is national character: *that* it is which causes one nation to succeed in what it attempts, another to fail; one nation to understand and aspire to elevated things, another to grovel in mean ones; which makes the greatness of one nation lasting, and dooms another to early and rapid decay. The true teacher of the fitting social arrangements for England, France, or America, is the one who can point out how the English, French, or American character can be improved, and how it has been made what it is. A philosophy of laws and institutions, not founded on a philosophy of national character, is an absurdity. But what could Bentham's opinion be worth on national character? How could he, whose mind contained so few and so poor types of individual character, rise to that higher generalization? All he can do is but to indicate means by which, in any given state of the national mind, the material interests of society can be protected; saving the question, of which others must judge, whether the use of those means would have, on the national character, any injurious influence.

We have arrived, then, at a sort of estimate of what a philosophy like Bentham's can do. It can teach the means of organizing and regulating the merely *business* part of the social arrangements. Whatever can be understood, or whatever done, without reference to moral influences, his philosophy is equal to: where those influences require to be taken into account, it is at fault. He committed the mistake of supposing that the business part of human affairs was the whole of them; all, at least, that the legislator and the moralist had to do with. Not that he disregarded moral influences when he perceived them; but his want of imagination, small experience of human feelings, and ignorance of the filiation and connection of feelings with one another, made this rarely the case.

The business part is accordingly the only province of human affairs which Bentham has cultivated with any success; into which he has introduced any considerable number of comprehensive and luminous practical principles. That is the field of his greatness; and there he is indeed great. He has swept away the accumulated cobwebs of centuries; he has untied knots which the efforts of the ablest thinkers, age after age, had only drawn tighter; and it is no exaggeration to say of him, that, over a great part of the field, he was the first to shed the light of reason.

We turn with pleasure from what Bentham could not do to what he did. It is an ungracious task to call a great benefactor of mankind to account for not being a greater; to insist upon the errors of a man who has originated more new truths, has given to the world more sound practical lessons, than it ever received, except in a few glorious instances, from any other individual. The unpleasing part of our work is ended. We are now to show the greatness of the man; the grasp which his intellect took of the subjects with which it was fitted to deal; the giant's task which was before him; and the hero's courage and strength with which he achieved it. Nor let that which he did be deemed of small account because its province was limited: man has but the choice to go a little way in many paths, or a great way in only one. The field of Bentham's labors was like the space between two parallel lines,—narrow to excess in one direction; in another, it reached to infinity.

Bentham's speculations, as we are already aware, began with law; and in that department he accomplished his greatest triumphs. He found the philosophy of law a chaos: he left it a science. He found the practice of the law an Augean stable: he turned the river into it which is mining and sweeping away mound after mound of its rubbish.

Without joining in the exaggerated invectives against lawyers which Bentham sometimes permitted to himself, or making one portion of society alone accountable for the fault of all, we may say, that circumstances had made English lawyers, in a peculiar degree, liable to the reproach of Voltaire, who defines lawyers the "conservators of ancient barbarous usages." The basis of the English law was, and still is, the feudal system. That system, like all those which existed as custom before they were established as law, possessed a certain degree of suitableness to the wants of the society among whom it grew up; that is to say, of a tribe of rude soldiers, holding a conquered people in subjection, and dividing its spoils among themselves. Advancing civilization had, however, converted this armed encampment of barbarous warriors, in the midst of enemies reduced to slavery, into an industrious, commercial, rich, and free people. The laws which were suitable to the first of these states of society could have no manner of relation to the circumstances of the second; which could not even have come into existence, unless something had been done to adapt those laws to it. But the adaptation was not the result of thought and design: it arose not from any comprehensive consideration of the new state of society and its exigencies. What was done, was done by a struggle of centuries between the old barbarism and the new civilization; between the feudal aristocracy of conquerors holding fast to the rude system they had established, and the conquered effecting their emancipation. The last was the growing power, but was never strong enough to break its bonds, though ever and anon some weak point gave way. Hence the law came to be like the costume of a full-grown man who had never put off the clothes made for him when he first went to school. Band after band had burst; and as the rent widened, then, without removing any thing except what might drop off of itself, the hole was darned, or patches of fresh law were brought from the nearest shop, and stuck on. Hence all ages of English history have given one another rendezvous in English law: their several products may be seen all together, not interfused, but heaped one upon another, as many different ages of the earth may be read in some perpendicular section of its surface; the deposits of each successive period not substituted, but superimposed on those of the preceding. And in the world of law, no less than in the physical world, every commotion and conflict of the elements has left its mark behind in some break or irregularity of the strata. Every struggle which ever rent the bosom of society is apparent in the disjointed condition of the part of the field of law which covers the spot: nay, the very traps and pitfalls which one contending party set for another are still standing; and the teeth, not of hyenas only, but of foxes and all cunning animals, are imprinted on the curious remains found in these antediluvian caves.

In the English law, as in the Roman before it, the adaptations of barbarous laws to the growth of civilized society were made chiefly by stealth. They were generally made by the courts of justice, who could not help reading the new wants of mankind in the cases between man and man which came before them; but who, having no authority to make new laws for those new wants, were obliged to do the work covertly, and evade the jealousy and opposition of an ignorant, prejudiced, and, for the most part, brutal and tyrannical legislature. Some of the most necessary of these improvements, such as the giving force of law to trusts and the breaking-up of entails, were effected in actual opposition to the strongly declared will of Parliament, whose clumsy hands, no match for the astuteness of judges, could not, after repeated trials, manage to make any law which the judges could not find a trick for rendering inoperative. The whole history of the contest about trusts may still be read in the words of a conveyance, as could the contest about entails, till the abolition of fine and recovery by a bill of the present Attorney-General; but dearly did the client pay for the cabinet of historical curiosities which he was obliged to purchase every time that he made a settlement of his estate. The result of this mode of improving social institutions was, that whatever new things were done had to be done in consistency with old forms and names; and the laws were improved with much the same effect, as if, in the improvement of agriculture, the plough could only have been introduced by making it look like a spade; or as if, when the primeval practice of ploughing by the horse's tail gave way to the innovation of harness, the tail, for form's sake, had still remained attached to the plough.

When the conflicts were over, and the mixed mass settled down into something like a fixed state, and that state a very profitable and therefore a very agreeable one to lawyers, they, following the natural tendency of the human mind, began to theorize upon it, and, in obedience to necessity, had to digest it, and give it a systematic form. It was from this thing of shreds and patches, in which the only part that approached to order or system was the early barbarous part, already more than half superseded, that English lawyers had to construct, by induction and abstraction, their philosophy of law, and without the logical habits and general intellectual cultivation which the lawyers of the Roman empire brought to a similar task. Bentham found the philosophy of law what English practising lawyers had made it,—a jumble, in which *real* and *personal* property, *law* and *equity*, *felony*, *premunire*, *misprision*, and *misdemeanor*,—words without a vestige of meaning when detached from the history of English institutions; mere tide-marks to point out the line which the sea and the shore, in their secular struggles, had adjusted as their mutual boundary,—all passed for distinctions inherent in the nature of things; in which every absurdity, every lucrative abuse, had a reason found for it,—a reason which only now and then even pretended to be drawn from expediency; most commonly a technical reason, one of mere form, derived from the old barbarous system. While the theory of the law was in this state, to describe what the practice of it was would require the pen of a Swift, or of Bentham himself. The whole progress of a suit at law seemed like a series of contrivances for lawyers' profit, in which the suitors were regarded as the prey; and, if the poor were not the helpless victims of every Sir Giles Overreach who could pay the price, they might thank opinion and manners for it, not the law.

It may be fancied by some people, that Bentham did an easy thing in merely calling all this absurd, and proving it to be so. But he began the contest a young man, and he had grown old before he had any followers. History will one day refuse to give credit to the intensity of the superstition which, till very lately, protected this mischievous mess from examination or doubt,—passed off the charming representations of Blackstone for a just estimate of the English law, and proclaimed the shame of human reason to be the perfection of it. Glory to Bentham that he has dealt to this superstition its deathblow; that he has been the Hercules of this hydra, the St. George of this pestilent dragon! The honor is all his: nothing but his peculiar qualities could have done it. There were wanted his indefatigable perseverance; his firm self-reliance, needing no support from other men's opinion; his intensely practical turn of mind; his synthetical habits; above all, his peculiar method. Metaphysicians, armed with vague generalities, had often tried their hands at the subject, and left it no more advanced than they found it. Law is a matter of business; means and ends are the things to be considered in it, not abstractions: vagueness was not to be met by vagueness, but by definiteness and precision; details were not to be encountered with generalities, but with details. Nor could any progress be made on such a subject by

merely showing that existing things were bad: it was necessary also to show how they might be made better. No great
man whom we read of was qualified to do this thing, except
Bentham. He has done it, once and for ever.

Into the particulars of what Bentham has done we cannot
enter: many hundred pages would be required to give a
tolerable abstract of it. To sum up our estimate under a few
heads: First, He has expelled mysticism from the philosophy
of law, and set the example of viewing laws in a practical light,
as means to certain definite and precise ends. Secondly, He
has cleared up the confusion and vagueness attaching to the
idea of law in general, to the idea of a body of laws, and all
the general ideas therein involved. Thirdly, He demonstrated the necessity and practicability of *codification*, or
the conversion of all law into a written and systematically
arranged code; not like the Code Napoléon,—a code without
a single definition, requiring a constant reference to anterior
precedent for the meaning of its technical terms,—but one
containing within itself all that is necessary for its own interpretation, together with a perpetual provision for its own
emendation and improvement. He has shown of what parts
such a code would consist; the relation of those parts to one
another; and, by his distinctions and classifications, has done
very much towards showing what should be, or might be,
its nomenclature and arrangement. What he has left undone,
he has made it comparatively easy for others to do. Fourthly,
He has taken a systematic view[5] of the exigencies of society
for which the civil code is intended to provide, and of the
principles of human nature by which its provisions are to be
tested; and this view, defective (as we have already inti-
mated) wherever spiritual interests require to be taken into
account, is excellent for that large portion of the laws of any
country which are designed for the protection of material
interests. Fifthly (to say nothing of the subject of punishment, for which something considerable had been done before), He found the philosophy of judicial procedure, including that of judicial establishments and of evidence, in a more
wretched state than even any other part of the philosophy of
law: he carried it at once almost to perfection. He left it with
every one of its principles established, and little remaining

[5]See the "Principles of Civil Law," contained in his collected works.

to be done even in the suggestion of practical arrangements.

These assertions in behalf of Bentham may be left, without fear for the result, in the hands of those who are competent to judge of them. There are now, even in the highest seats of justice, men to whom the claims made for him will not appear extravagant. Principle after principle of those propounded by him is moreover making its way by infiltration into the understandings most shut against his influence, and driving nonsense and prejudice from one corner of them to another. The reform of the laws of any country, according to his principles, can only be gradual, and may be long ere it is accomplished; but the work is in progress, and both Parliament and the judges are every year doing something, and often something not inconsiderable, towards the forwarding of it.

It seems proper here to take notice of an accusation sometimes made both against Bentham and against the principle of codification,—as if they required one uniform suit of ready-made laws for all times and all states of society. The doctrine of codification, as the word imports, relates to the form only of the laws, not their substance: it does not concern itself with what the laws should be, but declares, that, whatever they are, they ought to be systematically arranged, and fixed down to a determinate form of words. To the accusation, so far as it affects Bentham, one of the essays in the collection of his works (then for the first time published in English) is a complete answer,—that "On the Influence of Time and Place in Matters of Legislation." It may there be seen that the different exigencies of different nations with respect to law occupied his attention as systematically as any other portion of the wants which render laws necessary; with the limitations, it is true, which were set to all his speculations by the imperfections of his theory of human nature. For, taking, as we have seen, next to no account of national character, and the causes which form and maintain it, he was precluded from considering, except to a very limited extent, the laws of a country as an instrument of national culture,—one of their most important aspects, and in which they must of course vary according to the degree and kind of culture already attained, as a tutor gives his pupil different lessons according to the progress already made in his education. The same laws would not have suited our wild ancestors, accustomed to rude in-

dependence, and a people of Asiatics bowed down by military
despotism: the slave needs to be trained to govern himself,
the savage to submit to the government of others. The same
laws will not suit the English, who distrust every thing which
emanates from general principles, and the French, who distrust whatever does not so emanate. Very different institutions
are needed to train to the perfection of their nature, or to
constitute into a united nation and social polity, an essentially
subjective people like the Germans, and an essentially *objective* people like those of Northern and Central Italy,—the
one affectionate and dreamy, the other passionate and
worldly; the one trustful and loyal, the other calculating and
suspicious; the one not practical enough, the other overmuch;
the one wanting individuality, the other fellow-feeling; the
one failing for want of exacting enough for itself, the other
for want of conceding enough to others. Bentham was little
accustomed to look at institutions in their relation to these
topics. The effects of this oversight must, of course, be perceptible throughout his speculations; but we do not think
the errors into which it led him very material in the greater
part of civil and penal law: it is in the department of constitutional legislation that they were fundamental.

The Benthamic theory of government has made so much
noise in the world of late years, it has held such a conspicuous
place among Radical philosophies, and Radical modes of
thinking have participated so much more largely than any
others in its spirit, that many worthy persons imagine there
is no other Radical philosophy extant. Leaving such people
to discover their mistake as they may, we shall expend a few
words in attempting to discriminate between the truth and
error of this celebrated theory.

There are three great questions in government. First, To
what authority is it for the good of the people that they should
be subject? Secondly, How are they to be induced to obey that
authority? The answers to these two questions vary indefinitely, according to the degree and kind of civilization and
cultivation already attained by a people, and their peculiar
aptitudes for receiving more. Comes next a third question,
not liable to so much variation; namely, By what means are
the abuses of this authority to be checked? This third question
is the only one of the three to which Bentham seriously applies himself; and he gives it the only answer it admits of,—

Responsibility; responsibility to persons whose interest, whose obvious and recognizable interest, accords with the end in view,—good government. This being granted, it is next to be asked, In what body of persons this identity of interest with good government (that is, with the interest of the whole community) is to be found? In nothing less, says Bentham, than the numerical majority; nor, say we, even in the numerical majority itself: of no portion of the community less than all will the interest coincide, at all times and in all respects, with the interest of all. But since power given to all, by a representative government, is, in fact, given to a majority, we are obliged to fall back upon the first of our three questions; namely, Under what authority is it for the good of the people that they be placed? And if to this the answer be, Under that of a majority among themselves, Bentham's system cannot be questioned. This one assumption being made, his "Constitutional Code" is admirable. That extraordinary power which he possessed, of at once seizing comprehensive principles, and scheming out minute details, is brought into play with surpassing vigor in devising means for preventing rulers from escaping from the control of the majority; for enabling and inducing the majority to exercise that control unremittingly; and for providing them with servants of every desirable endowment, moral and intellectual, compatible with entire subservience to their will.

But *is* this fundamental doctrine of Bentham's political philosophy an universal truth? Is it, at all times and places, good for mankind to be under the absolute authority of the majority of themselves? We say, the authority; not the political authority merely, because it is chimerical to suppose that whatever has absolute power over men's bodies will not arrogate it over their minds; will not seek to control (not perhaps by legal penalties, but by the persecutions of society) opinions and feelings which depart from its standard; will not attempt to shape the education of the young by its model, and to extinguish all books, all schools, all combinations of individuals for joint action upon society, which may be attempted for the purpose of keeping alive a spirit at variance with its own. Is it, we say, the proper condition of man, in all ages and nations, to be under the despotism of Public Opinion?

It is very conceivable that such a doctrine should find acceptance from some of the noblest spirits in a time of re-action against the aristocratic governments of modern Europe,—governments founded on the entire sacrifice (except so far as prudence, and sometimes humane feeling, interfere) of the community generally to the self-interest and ease of a few. European reformers have been accustomed to see the numerical majority everywhere unjustly depressed, everywhere trampled upon, or at the best overlooked, by governments; nowhere possessing power enough to extort redress of their most positive grievances, provision for their mental culture, or even to prevent themselves from being taxed avowedly for the pecuniary profit of the ruling classes. To see these things, and to seek to put an end to them by means (among other things) of giving more political power to the majority, constitutes Radicalism; and it is because so many in this age have felt this wish, and have felt that the realization of it was an object worthy of men's devoting their lives to it, that such a theory of government as Bentham's has found favor with them. But, though to pass from one form of bad government to another be the ordinary fate of mankind, philosophers ought not to make themselves parties to it by sacrificing one portion of important truth to another.

The numerical majority of any society whatever, must consist of persons all standing in the same social position, and having, in the main, the same pursuits; namely, unskilled manual laborers. And we mean no disparagement to them: whatever we say to their disadvantage, we say equally of a numerical majority of shopkeepers or of squires. Where there is identity of position and pursuits, there also will be identity of partialities, passions, and prejudices; and to give to any one set of partialities, passions, and prejudices, absolute power, without counter-balance from partialities, passions, and prejudices of a different sort, is the way to render the correction of any of those imperfections hopeless; to make one narrow, mean type of human nature universal and perpetual; and to crush every influence which tends to the further improvement of man's intellectual and moral nature. There must, we know, be some paramount power in society; and that the majority should be that power, is, on the whole, right, not as being just in itself, but as being less unjust than any other footing on which the matter can be placed. But it is necessary that the institutions of society should make provision for keeping up, in some form or other, as a corrective to partial views, and a shelter for freedom of thought and individuality of character, a perpetual and standing opposition to the will of the majority. All countries which have long continued progressive, or been durably great, have been so because there has been an organized opposition to the ruling power, of whatever kind that power was,—plebeians to patricians, clergy to kings, free-thinkers to clergy, kings to barons, commons to king and aristocracy. Almost all the greatest men who ever lived have formed part of such an opposition. Wherever some such quarrel has not been going on; wherever it has been terminated by the complete victory of one of the contending principles, and no new contest has taken the place of the old,—society has either hardened into Chinese stationariness, or fallen into dissolution. A centre of resistance, round which all the moral and social elements which the ruling power views with disfavor may cluster themselves, and behind whose bulwarks they may find shelter from the attempts of that power to hunt them out of existence, is as necessary where the opinion of the majority is sovereign, as where the ruling power is a hierarchy or an aristocracy. Where no such *point d'appui* exists, there the human race will inevitably degenerate; and the question, whether the United States, for instance, will in time sink into another China (also a most commercial and industrious nation), resolves itself, to us, into the question, whether such a centre of resistance will gradually evolve itself or not.

These things being considered, we cannot think that Bentham made the most useful employment which might have been made of his great powers, when, not content with enthroning the majority as sovereign, by means of universal suffrage, without king, or house of lords, he exhausted all the resources of ingenuity in devising means for riveting the yoke of public opinion closer and closer round the necks of all public functionaries, and excluding every possibility of the exercise of the slightest or most temporary influence either by a minority, or by the functionary's own notions of right. Surely, when any power has been made the strongest power, enough has been done for it: care is thenceforth wanted rather to prevent that strongest power from swallowing up all others. Wherever all the forces of society act in one single direction, the just claims of the individual human being are in extreme peril. The power of the majority is salutary so far as it is used defensively, not offensively,—as its exertion is tempered by respect for the personality of the individual, and deference to superiority of cultivated intelligence. If Bentham had employed himself in pointing out the means by which institutions fundamentally democratic might be best adapted to the preservation and strengthening of those two sentiments, he would have done something more permanently valuable, and more worthy of his great intellect. Montesquieu, with the lights of the present age, would have done it; and we are possibly destined to receive this benefit from the Montesquieu of our own times,—M. de Tocqueville.

Do we, then, consider Bentham's political speculations useless? Far from it. We consider them only one-sided. He has brought out into a strong light, has cleared from a thousand confusions and misconceptions, and pointed out with admirable skill the best means of promoting, one of the ideal qualities of a perfect government,—identity of interest between the trustees and the community for whom they hold their power in trust. This quality is not attainable in its ideal perfection, and must, moreover, be striven for with a perpetual eye to all other requisites: but those other requisites must still more be striven for, without losing sight of this; and, when the slightest postponement is made of it to any other end, the sacrifice, often necessary, is never unattended with evil. Bentham has pointed out how complete this sacrifice is in modern European societies; how exclusively, partial and sinister interests are the ruling power there, with only such check as is imposed by public opinion: which being thus, in the existing order of things, perpetually apparent as a source of good, he was led by natural partiality to exaggerate its intrinsic excellence. This sinister interest of rulers, Bentham hunted through all its disguises, and especially through those which hide it from the men themselves who are influenced by it. The greatest service rendered by him to the philosophy of universal human nature, is, perhaps, his illustration of what he terms "interest-begotten prejudice,"—the common tendency of man to make a duty and a virtue of following his self-interest. The idea, it is true, was far from being peculiarly Bentham's: the artifices by which we persuade ourselves that we are not yielding to our selfish inclinations when we are, had attracted the notice of all moralists, and had been probed by religious writers to a depth as much below Bentham's as their knowledge of the profundities and windings of the human heart was superior to his. But it is selfish interest in the form of class-interest, and the class-morality founded thereon, which Bentham has illustrated,—the manner in which any set of persons who mix much together, and have a common interest, are apt to make that common interest their standard of virtue, and the social feelings of the members of the class are made to play into the hands of their selfish ones; whence the union, so often exemplified in history, between the most heroic personal disinterestedness and the most odious class-selfishness. This was one of Bentham's leading ideas, and almost the only one by which he contributed to the elucidation of history; much of which, except so far as this explained it, must have been entirely inexplicable to him. The idea was given him by Helvetius, whose book, *De l'Esprit*, is one continued and most acute commentary on it; and together with the other great idea of Helvetius, the influence of circumstances on character, it will make his name live by the side of Rousseau, when most of the other French metaphysicians of the eighteenth century will be extant as such only in literary history.

In the brief view which we have been able to give of Bentham's philosophy, it may surprise the reader that we have said so little about the first principle of it, with which his name is more identified than with any thing else,—the "principle of utility," or, as he afterwards named it, "the greatest-happiness principle." It is a topic on which much were to be said, if there were room, or if it were in reality necessary for the just estimation of Bentham. On an occasion more suitable for a discussion of the metaphysics of morality, or on which the elucidations necessary to make an opinion on so abstract a subject intelligible could be conveniently given, we should be fully prepared to state what we think on this subject. At present, we shall only say, that while, under proper explanations, we entirely agree with Bentham in his principle, we do not hold with him that all right thinking on the details of morals depends on its express assertion. We think utility, or happiness, much too complex and indefinite an end to be sought, except through the medium of various secondary ends, concerning which there may be, and often is, agreement among persons who differ in their ultimate standard; and about which there does, in fact, prevail a much greater unanimity among thinking persons than might be supposed from their diametrical divergence on the great questions of moral metaphysics. As mankind are much more nearly of one nature, than of one opinion about their own nature, they are more easily brought to agree in their intermediate principles—*vera illa et media axiomata,* as Bacon says—than in their first principles; and the attempt to make the bearings of actions upon the ultimate end more evident than they can be made by referring them to the intermediate ends, and to estimate their value by a direct reference to human happiness, generally terminates in attaching most importance, not to those effects which are really the greatest, but to those which can most easily be pointed to, and individually identified. Those who adopt utility as a standard can seldom apply it truly, except through the secondary principles: those who reject it generally do no more than erect those secondary principles into first principles. It is when two or more of the secondary principles conflict, that a direct appeal to some first principle becomes necessary: and then commences the practical importance of the utilitarian controversy; which is, in other respects, a question of arrangement and logical subordination rather than of practise; important principally, in a purely scientific point of view, for the sake of the systematic unity and coherency of ethical philosophy. It is probable, however, that to the principle of utility we owe all that Bentham did; that it was necessary to him to find a first principle which he could receive as self-evident, and to which he could attach all his other doctrines as logical consequences; that to him systematic unity was an indispensable condition of his confidence in his own intellect. And there is something further to be remarked. Whether happiness be or be not the end to which morality should be referred,—that it be deferred to an *end* of some sort, and not left in the dominion of vague feeling, or inexplicable internal conviction; that it be made a matter of reason and calculation, and not merely of sentiment,—is essential to the very idea of moral philosophy; is, in fact, what renders argument or discussion on moral questions possible. That the morality of actions depends on the consequences which they tend to produce, is the doctrine of rational persons of all schools: that the good or evil of those consequences is measured solely by pleasure or pain, is all of the doctrine of the school of utility which is peculiar to it.

In so far as Bentham's adoption of the principle of utility

induced him to fix his attention upon the consequences of actions as the consideration determining their morality, so far he was indisputably in the right path; though, to go far in it without wandering, there was needed a greater knowledge of the formation of character, and of the consequences of actions upon the agent's own frame of mind, than Bentham possessed. His want of power to estimate this class of consequences, together with his want of the degree of modest deference, which, from those who have not competent experience of their own, is due to the experience of others on that part of the subject, greatly limit the value of his speculations on questions of practical ethics.

He is chargeable also with another error, which it would be improper to pass over, because nothing has tended more to place him in opposition to the common feelings of mankind, and to give to his philosophy that cold, mechanical, and ungenial air which characterizes the popular idea of a Benthamite. This error, or rather one-sidedness, belongs to him, not as a utilitarian, but as a moralist by profession, and in common with almost all professed moralists, whether religious or philosophical: it is that of treating the *moral* view of actions and characters, which is unquestionably the first and most important mode of looking at them, as if it were the sole one; whereas it is only one of three, by all of which our sentiments towards the human being may be, ought to be, and, without entirely crushing our own nature, cannot but be, materially influenced. Every human action has three aspects,—its *moral* aspect, or that of its *right* and *wrong;* its *aesthetic* aspect, or that of its *beauty;* its *sympathetic* aspect, or that of its *lovableness.* The first addresses itself to our reason and conscience; the second, to our imagination; the third, to our human fellow-feeling. According to the first, we approve or disapprove; according to the second, we admire or despise; according to the third, we love, pity, or dislike. The morality of an action depends on its foreseeable consequences: its beauty and its lovableness, or the reverse, depend on the qualities which it is evidence of. Thus a lie is *wrong,* because its effect is to mislead, and because it tends to destroy the confidence of man in man: it is also *mean,* because it is cowardly; because it proceeds from not daring to face the consequences of telling the truth; or, at best, is evidence of want of that *power* to compass our ends by straightforward means, which is conceived as properly belonging to every person not deficient in energy or in understanding. The action of Brutus in sentencing his sons was *right*, because it was executing a law, essential to the freedom of his country, against persons of whose guilt there was no doubt; it was *admirable*, because it evinced a rare degree of patriotism, courage, and self-control: but there was nothing *lovable* in it; it affords either no presumption in regard to lovable qualities, or a presumption of their deficiency. If one of the sons had engaged in the conspiracy from affection for the other, his action would have been lovable, though neither moral nor admirable. It is not possible for any sophistry to confound these three modes of viewing an action; but it is very possible to adhere to one of them exclusively, and lose sight of the rest. Sentimentality consists in setting the last two of the three above the first: the error of moralists in general, and of Bentham, is to sink the two latter entirely. This is pre-eminently the case with Bentham: he both wrote and felt as if the moral standard ought not only to be paramount (which it ought), but to be alone; as if it ought to be the sole master of all our actions, and even of all our sentiments; as if either to admire or like, or despise or dislike, a person for any action which neither does good nor harm, or which does not do a good or a harm proportioned to the sentiment entertained, were an injustice and a prejudice. He carried this so far, that there were certain phrases, which, being expressive of what he considered to be this groundless liking or aversion, he could not bear to hear pronounced in his presence. Among these phrases were those of *good* and *bad taste*. He thought it an insolent piece of dogmatism in one person to praise or condemn another in a matter of taste; as if men's likings and dislikings, on things in themselves indifferent, were not full of the most important inferences as to every point of their character; as if a person's tastes did not show him to be wise or a fool, cultivated or ignorant, gentle or rough, sensitive or callous, generous or sordid, benevolent or selfish, conscientious or depraved.

Connected with the same topic are Bentham's peculiar opinions on poetry. Much more has been said than there is any foundation for about his contempt for the pleasures of imagination and for the fine arts. Music was throughout life his favorite amusement: painting, sculpture, and the other arts addressed to the eye, he was so far from holding in any contempt, that he occasionally recognizes them as means employable for important social ends; though his ignorance of the deeper springs of human character prevented him (as it prevents most Englishmen) from suspecting how profoundly such things enter into the moral nature of man, and into the education both of the individual and of the race. But towards poetry in the narrower sense, that which employs the language of words, he entertained no favor. Words, he thought, were perverted from their proper office when they were employed in uttering any thing but precise logical truth. He says, somewhere in his works, that, "quantity of pleasure being equal, push-pin is as good as poetry;" but this is only a paradoxical way of stating what he would equally have said of the things which he most valued and admired. Another aphorism is attributed to him, which is much more characteristic of his view of this subject: "All poetry is misrepresentation." Poetry, he thought, consisted essentially in exaggeration for effect; in proclaiming some one view of a thing very emphatically, and suppressing all the limitations and qualifications. This trait of character seems to us a curious example of what Mr. Carlyle strikingly calls "the completeness of limited men." Here is a philosopher who is happy within his narrow boundary as no man of indefinite range ever was; who flatters himself that he is so completely emancipated from the essential law of poor human intellect, by which it can only see one thing at a time well, that he can even turn round upon the imperfection, and lay a solemn interdict upon it. Did Bentham really suppose that it is in poetry only that propositions cannot be exactly true,—cannot contain in themselves all the limitations and qualifications with which they require to be taken when applied to practice? We have seen how far his own prose propositions are from realizing this Utopia; and even the attempt to approach it would be incompatible, not with poetry merely, but with oratory, and popular writing of every kind. Bentham's charge is true to the fullest extent: all writing which undertakes to make men feel truths as well as see them does take up one point at a time,—does seek to impress that, to drive that home; to make it sink into and color the whole mind of the reader or hearer. It is justified in doing so, if the portion of truth which it thus enforces be that which is called for by the occasion. All writing addressed to the feelings has a natural tendency to exaggeration; but Bentham should have remembered, that in this, as in many things, we must aim at too much, to be assured of doing enough.

From the same principle in Bentham came the intricate and involved style, which makes his later writings books for the student only, not the general reader. It was from his perpetually aiming at impracticable precision. Nearly all his earlier and many parts of his later writings are models, as we have already observed, of light, playful, and popular style: a Benthamiana might be made of passages worthy of Addison or Goldsmith. But in his later years, and more advanced studies, he fell into a Latin or German structure of sentence, foreign to the genius of the English language. He could not bear, for the sake of clearness and the reader's ease, to say, as ordinary men are content to do, a little more than the truth in one sentence, and correct it in the next. The whole of the qualifying remarks which he intended to make he insisted upon embedding as parentheses in the very middle of the sentence itself; and thus, the sense being so long suspended, and attention being required to the accessory ideas before the principal idea had been properly seized, it became difficult, without some practice, to make out the train of thought. It is fortunate that so many of the most important parts of his writings are free from this defect. We regard it as a *reductio ad absurdum* of his objection to poetry. In trying to write in a manner against which the same objection should not lie, he could stop nowhere short of utter unreadableness; and, after all, attained no more accuracy than is compatible with opinions as imperfect and one-sided as those of any poet or sentimentalist breathing. Judge, then, in what state literature and philosophy would be, and what chance they would have of influencing the multitude, if his objection were allowed, and all styles of writing banished which would not stand his test.

We must here close this brief and imperfect view of Bentham and his doctrines; in which many parts of the subject have been entirely untouched, and no part done justice to, but which at least proceeds from an intimate familiarity with his writings, and is nearly the first attempt at an impartial estimate of his character as a philosopher, and of the result of his labors to the world.

After every abatement (and it has been seen whether we have made our abatements sparingly), there remains to Ben-

tham an indisputable place among the great intellectual benefactors of mankind. His writings will long form an indispensable part of the education of the highest order of practical
thinkers; and the collected edition of them ought to be in
the hands of every one who would either understand his age,
or take any beneficial part in the great business of it.[6]

---

[6]Since the first publication of this paper, Lord Brougham's brilliant series
of characters has been published, including a sketch of Bentham. Lord
Brougham's view of Bentham's characteristics agrees in the main points, so
far as it goes, with the result of our more minute examination; but there is
an imputation cast upon Bentham, of a jealous and splenetic disposition in
private life, of which we feel called upon to give at once a contradiction and
an explanation. It is indispensable to a correct estimate of any of Bentham's
dealings with the world, to bear in mind, that, in every thing except abstract
speculation, he was to the last, what we have called him, essentially a boy.
He had the freshness, the simplicity, the confidingness, the liveliness and
activity, all the delightful qualities of boyhood, and the weaknesses which
are the reverse side of those qualities,—the undue importance attached to
trifles, the habitual mismeasurement of the practical bearing and value of
things, the readiness to be either delighted or offended on inadequate cause.
These were the real sources of what was unreasonable in some of his attacks
on individuals, and in particular on Lord Brougham on the subject of his
Law Reforms: they were no more the effect of envy or malice, or any really
unamiable quality, than the freaks of a pettish child, and are scarcely a
fitter subject of censure or criticism.

Coleridge[1]

[1]*London and Westminster Review*, March, 1840.

THE NAME of Coleridge is one of the few English names of our time which are likely to be oftener pronounced, and to become symbolical of more important things, in proportion as the inward workings of the age manifest themselves more and more in outward facts. Bentham excepted, no Englishman of recent date has left his impress so deeply in the opinions and mental tendencies of those among us who attempt to enlighten their practice by philosophical meditation. If it be true, as Lord Bacon affirms, that a knowledge of the speculative opinions of the men between twenty and thirty years of age is the great source of political prophecy, the existence of Coleridge will show itself by no slight or ambiguous traces in the coming history of our country; for no one has contributed more to shape the opinions of those among its younger men, who can be said to have opinions at all.

The influence of Coleridge, like that of Bentham, extends far beyond those who share in the peculiarities of his religious or philosophical creed. He has been the great awakener in this country of the spirit of philosophy, within the bounds of traditional opinions. He has been, almost as truly as Bentham, "the great questioner of things established;" for a questioner needs not necessarily be an enemy. By Bentham, beyond all others, men have been led to ask themselves, in regard to any ancient or received opinion, Is it true? and by Coleridge, What is the meaning of it? The one took his stand *outside* the received opinion, and surveyed it as an entire stranger to it: the other looked at it from within, and endeavored to see it with the eyes of a believer in it; to discover by what apparent facts it was at first suggested, and by what ap-

pearances it has ever since been rendered continually credible,—has seemed, to a succession of persons, to be a faithful
interpretation of their experience. Bentham judged a proposition true or false as it accorded or not with the result of
his own inquiries; and did not search very curiously into
what might be meant by the proposition, when it obviously
did not mean what he thought true. With Coleridge, on the
contrary, the very fact that any doctrine had been believed
by thoughtful men, and received by whole nations or generations of mankind, was part of the problem to be solved; was
one of the phenomena to be accounted for. And, as Bentham's short and easy method of referring all to the selfish
interests of aristocracies or priests or lawyers, or some other
species of impostors, could not satisfy a man who saw so much
farther into the complexities of the human intellect and
feelings, he considered the long or extensive prevalence of any
opinion as a presumption that it was not altogether a fallacy;
that, to its first authors at least, it was the result of a struggle
to express in words something which had a reality to them,
though perhaps not to many of those who have since received
the doctrine by mere tradition. The long duration of a belief,
he thought, is at least proof of an adaptation in it to some portion or other of the human mind: and if, on digging down
to the root, we do not find, as is generally the case, some
truth, we shall find some natural want or requirement of
human nature which the doctrine in question is fitted to
satisfy; among which wants the instincts of selfishness and of
credulity have a place, but by no means an exclusive one.
From this difference in the points of view of the two philosophers, and from the too rigid adherence of each to his
own, it was to be expected that Bentham should continually
miss the truth which is in the traditional opinions, and Coleridge that which is out of them and at variance with them.
But it was also likely that each would find, or show the way
to finding, much of what the other missed.

It is hardly possible to speak of Coleridge, and his position
among his contemporaries, without reverting to Bentham:
they are connected by two of the closest bonds of association,
—resemblance and contrast. It would be difficult to find two
persons of philosophic eminence more exactly the contrary
of one another. Compare their modes of treatment of any
subject, and you might fancy them inhabitants of different

worlds. They seem to have scarcely a principle or a premise in common. Each of them sees scarcely any thing but what the other does not see. Bentham would have regarded Coleridge with a peculiar measure of the good-humored contempt with which he was accustomed to regard all modes of philosophizing different from his own. Coleridge would probably have made Bentham one of the exceptions to the enlarged and liberal appreciation which (to the credit of *his* mode of philosophizing) he extended to most thinkers of any eminence from whom he differed. But contraries, as logicians say, are but *quæ in eodem genere maxime distant,*—the things which are farthest from one another in the same kind. These two agreed in being the men, who, in their age and country, did most to enforce, by precept and example, the necessity of a philosophy. They agreed in making it their occupation to recall opinions to first principles; taking no proposition for granted without examining into the grounds of it, and ascertaining that it possessed the kind and degree of evidence suitable to its nature. They agreed in recognizing that sound theory is the only foundation for sound practice; and that whoever despises theory, let him give himself what airs of wisdom he may, is self-convicted of being a quack. If a book were to be compiled containing all the best things ever said on the rule-of-thumb school of political craftsmanship, and on the insufficiency for practical purposes of what the mere practical man calls experience, it is difficult to say whether the collection would be more indebted to the writings of Bentham or of Coleridge. They agreed, too, in perceiving that the groundwork of all other philosophy must be laid in the philosophy of the mind. To lay this foundation deeply and strongly, and to raise a superstructure in accordance with it, were the objects to which their lives were devoted. They employed, indeed, for the most part, different materials; but as the materials of both were real observations, the genuine product of experience, the results will, in the end, be found, not hostile, but supplementary, to one another. Of their methods of philosophizing, the same thing may be said: they were different, yet both were legitimate logical processes. In every respect, the two men are each other's "completing counterpart:" the strong points of each correspond to the weak points of the other. Whoever could master the premises and combine the methods of both would possess the entire

English philosophy of his age. Coleridge used to say that
every one is born either a Platonist or an Aristotelian: it may
be similarly affirmed, that every Englishman of the present
day is by implication either a Benthamite or a Coleridgian;
holds views of human affairs which can only be proved true
on the principles either of Bentham or of Coleridge. In one
respect, indeed, the parallel fails. Bentham so improved and
added to the system of philosophy he adopted, that, for his
successors, he may almost be accounted its founder; while
Coleridge, though he has left, on the system he inculcated,
such traces of himself as cannot fail to be left by any mind
of original powers, was anticipated in all the essentials of
his doctrine by the great Germans of the latter half of the
last century, and was accompanied in it by the remarkable series of their French expositors and followers. Hence,
although Coleridge is to Englishmen the type and the main
source of that doctrine, he is the creator rather of the shape in
which it has appeared among us than of the doctrine itself.

The time is yet far distant, when, in the estimation of
Coleridge, and of his influence upon the intellect of our
time, any thing like unanimity can be looked for. As a poet,
Coleridge has taken his place. The healthier taste, and more
intelligent canons of poetic criticism, which he was himself
mainly instrumental in diffusing, have at length assigned to
him his proper rank, as one among the great (and, if we
look to the powers shown rather than to the amount of actual
achievement, among the greatest) names in our literature.
But, as a philosopher, the class of thinkers has scarcely yet
arisen by whom he is to be judged. The limited philosophical
public of this country is as yet too exclusively divided between
those to whom Coleridge and the views which he promulgated
or defended are every thing, and those to whom they are
nothing. A true thinker can only be justly estimated when
his thoughts have worked their way into minds formed in
a different school; have been wrought and moulded into
consistency with all other true and relevant thoughts; when
the noisy conflict of half-truths, angrily denying one another,
has subsided, and ideas which seemed mutually incompatible
have been found only to require mutual limitations. This
time has not yet come for Coleridge. The spirit of philosophy
in England, like that of religion, is still rootedly sectarian.
Conservative thinkers and Liberals, transcendentalists and

admirers of Hobbes and Locke, regard each other as out of the pale of philosophical intercourse; look upon each other's speculations as vitiated by an original taint, which makes all study of them, except for purposes of attack, useless, if not mischievous. An error much the same as if Kepler had refused to profit by Ptolemy's or Tycho's observations, because those astronomers believed that the sun moved round the earth; or as if Priestley and Lavoisier, because they differed on the doctrine of phlogiston, had rejected each other's chemical experiments. It is even a still greater error than either of these. For among the truths long recognized by Continental philosophers, but which very few Englishmen have yet arrived at, one is, the importance, in the present imperfect state of mental and social science, of antagonist modes of thought; which, it will one day be felt, are as necessary to one another in speculation, as mutually checking powers are in a political constitution. A clear insight, indeed, into this necessity, is the only rational or enduring basis of philosophical tolerance; the only condition under which liberality in matters of opinion can be any thing better than a polite synonyme for indifference between one opinion and another.

All students of man and society who possess that first requisite for so difficult a study, a due sense of its difficulties, are aware that the besetting danger is not so much of embracing falsehood for truth, as of mistaking part of the truth for the whole. It might be plausibly maintained, that in almost every one of the leading controversies, past or present, in social philosophy, both sides were in the right in what they affirmed, though wrong in what they denied; and that, if either could have been made to take the other's views in addition to its own, little more would have been needed to make its doctrine correct. Take, for instance, the question, how far mankind have gained by civilization. One observer is forcibly struck by the multiplication of physical comforts; the advancement and diffusion of knowledge; the decay of superstition; the facilities of mutual intercourse; the softening of manners; the decline of war and personal conflict; the progressive limitation of the tyranny of the strong over the weak; the great works accomplished throughout the globe by the co-operation of multitudes: and he becomes that very common character, the worshipper of "our enlightened age." Another fixes his attention, not upon the value of these ad-

vantages, but upon the high price which is paid for them;
the relaxation of individual energy and courage; the loss of
proud and self-relying independence; the slavery of so large
a portion of mankind to artificial wants; their effeminate
shrinking from even the shadow of pain; the dull, unexciting
monotony of their lives, and the passionless insipidity, and
absence of any marked individuality, in their characters;
the contrast between the narrow mechanical understanding,
produced by a life spent in executing by fixed rules a fixed
task, and the varied powers of the man of the woods, whose
subsistence and safety depend at each instant upon his capacity of extemporarily adapting means to ends; the demoralizing effect of great inequalities in wealth and social rank; and
the sufferings of the great mass of the people of civilized
countries, whose wants are scarcely better provided for than
those of the savage, while they are bound by a thousand
fetters in lieu of the freedom and excitement which are his
compensations. One who attends to these things, and to these
exclusively, will be apt to infer that savage life is preferable
to civilized; that the work of civilization should as far as
possible be undone; and, from the premises of Rousseau, he
will not improbably be led to the practical conclusions of
Rousseau's disciple, Robespierre. No two thinkers can be more
entirely at variance than the two we have supposed,—the
worshippers of civilization and of independence, of the present
and of the remote past. Yet all that is positive in the opinions
of either of them is true: and we see how easy it would be to
choose one's path, if either half of the truth were the whole
of it; and how great may be the difficulty of framing, as it is
necessary to do, a set of practical maxims which combine
both.

So, again, one person sees in a very strong light the need
which the great mass of mankind have of being ruled over by
a degree of intelligence and virtue superior to their own. He
is deeply impressed with the mischief done to the uneducated
and uncultivated by weaning them of all habits of reverence,
appealing to them as a competent tribunal to decide the most
intricate questions, and making them think themselves capable, not only of being a light to themselves, but of giving
the law to their superiors in culture. He sees, further, that
cultivation, to be carried beyond a certain point, requires
leisure; that leisure is the natural attribute of a hereditary

aristocracy; that such a body has all the means of acquiring intellectual and moral superiority: and he needs be at no loss to endow them with abundant motives to it. An aristocracy indeed, being human, are, as he cannot but see, not exempt, any more than their inferiors, from the common need of being controlled and enlightened by a still greater wisdom and goodness than their own. For this, however, his reliance is upon reverence for a Higher above them, sedulously inculcated and fostered by the course of their education. We thus see brought together all the elements of a conscientious zealot for an aristocratic government, supporting and supported by an established Christian church. There is truth, and important truth, in this thinker's premises. But there is a thinker of a very different description, in whose premises there is an equal portion of truth. This is he who says, that an average man, even an average member of an aristocracy, if he can postpone the interests of other people to his own calculations or instincts of self-interest, will do so; that all governments in all ages have done so, as far as they were permitted, and generally to a ruinous extent; and that the only possible remedy is a pure democracy, in which the people are their own governors, and can have no selfish interest in oppressing themselves.

Thus it is in regard to every important partial truth: there are always two conflicting modes of thought,—one tending to give to that truth too large, the other to give it too small, a place; and the history of opinion is generally an oscillation between these extremes. From the imperfection of the human faculties, it seldom happens, that, even in the minds of eminent thinkers, each partial view of their subject passes for its worth, and none for more than its worth. But, even if this just balance exist in the mind of the wiser teacher, it will not exist in his disciples, far less in the general mind. He cannot prevent that which is new in his doctrine, and on which, being new, he is forced to insist the most strongly, from making a disproportionate impression. The impetus necessary to overcome the obstacles which resist all novelties of opinion seldom fails to carry the public mind almost as far on the contrary side of the perpendicular. Thus every excess in either direction determines a corresponding re-action; improvement consisting only in this,—that the oscillation, each time, departs rather less widely from the centre, and an ever-increasing tendency is manifested to settle finally in it.

Now, the Germano-Coleridgian doctrine is, in our view of the matter, the result of such a re-action. It expresses the revolt of the human mind against the philosophy of the eighteenth century. It is ontological, because that was experimental; conservative, because that was innovative; religious, because so much of that was infidel; concrete and historical, because that was abstract and metaphysical; poetical, because that was matter-of-fact and prosaic. In every respect, it flies off in the contrary direction to its predecessor: yet, faithful to the general law of improvement last noticed, it is less extreme in its opposition, it denies less of what is true in the doctrine it wars against, than had been the case in any previous philosophic re-action; and, in particular, far less than when the philosophy of the eighteenth century triumphed, and so memorably abused its victory, over that which preceded it.

We may begin our consideration of the two systems either at one extreme or the other,—with their highest philosophical generalizations, or with their practical conclusions. The former seems preferable, because it is in their highest generalities that the difference between the two systems is most familiarly known.

Every consistent scheme of philosophy requires, as its starting-point, a theory respecting the sources of human knowledge, and the objects which the human faculties are capable of taking cognizance of. The prevailing theory in the eighteenth century, on this most comprehensive of questions, was that proclaimed by Locke, and commonly attributed to Aristotle,—that all knowledge consists of generalizations from experience. Of nature, or any thing whatever external to ourselves, we know, according to this theory, nothing, except the facts which present themselves to our senses, and such other facts as may, by analogy, be inferred from these. There is no knowledge *à priori;* no truths cognizable by the mind's inward light, and grounded on intuitive evidence. Sensation, and the mind's consciousness of its own acts, are not only the exclusive sources, but the sole materials, of our knowledge. From this doctrine, Coleridge, with the German philosophers since Kant (not to go farther back), and most of the English since Reid, strongly dissents. He claims for the human mind a capacity, within certain limits, of perceiving the nature and properties of "things in themselves." He distinguishes in the human intellect two faculties, which, in the technical language common to him with the Germans, he calls Understanding and Reason. The former faculty judges of phenomena, or the appearances of things, and forms generalizations from these: to the latter it belongs, by direct intuition, to perceive things, and recognize truths, not cognizable by our senses. These perceptions are not indeed innate, nor could ever have been awakened in us without experience; but they are not copies of it: experience is not their prototype; it is only the occasion by which they are irresistibly suggested. The appearances in nature excite in us, by an inherent law, ideas of those invisible things which are the causes of the visible appearances, and on whose laws those appearances depend; and we then perceive that these things must have pre-existed to render the appearances possible; just as (to use a frequent illustration of Coleridge's) we see, before we know that we have eyes: but, when once this is known to us, we perceive that eyes must have pre-existed to enable us to see. Among the truths which are thus known *à priori*, by occasion of experience, but not themselves the subjects of experience, Coleridge includes the fundamental doctrines of religion and morals, the principles of mathematics, and the ultimate laws even of physical nature; which he contends cannot be proved by experience, though they must necessarily be consistent with it, and would, if we knew them perfectly, enable us to account for all observed facts, and to predict all those which are as yet unobserved.

It is not necessary to remind any one who concerns himself with such subjects, that between the partisan of these two opposite doctrines there reigns a *bellum internecinum*. Neither side is sparing in the imputation of intellectual and moral obliquity to the perceptions, and of pernicious consequences to the creed, of its antagonists. Sensualism is the common term of abuse for the one philosophy; mysticism, for the other. The one doctrine is accused of making men beasts; the other, lunatics. It is the unaffected belief of numbers on one side of the controversy, that their adversaries are actuated by a desire to break loose from moral and religious obligation; and of numbers on the other, that their opponents are either men fit for Bedlam, or who cunningly pander to the interests of hierarchies and aristocracies by manufacturing superfine new arguments in favor of old prejudices. It is almost needless to say, that those who are freest with these mutual accusations are seldom those who are most at home in the real intricacies of the question, or who are best acquainted with the argumentative strength of the opposite side, or even of their own. But, without going to these extreme lengths, even sober men on both sides take no charitable view of the tendencies of each other's opinions.

It is affirmed that the doctrine of Locke and his followers, that all knowledge is experience generalized, leads by strict logical consequence to atheism; that Hume and other sceptics were right when they contended that it is impossible to prove a God on grounds of experience; and Coleridge (like Kant) maintains positively, that the ordinary argument for a Deity, from marks of design in the universe, or, in other words, from the resemblance of the order in nature to the effects of human skill and contrivance, is not tenable. It is further said, that the same doctrine annihilates moral obligation; reducing morality either to the blind impulses of animal sensibility, or to a calculation of prudential consequences, both equally fatal to its essence. Even science, it is affirmed, loses the character of science in this view of it, and becomes empiricism,—a mere enumeration and arrangement of facts, not explaining nor accounting for them: since a fact is only then accounted for, when we are made to see in it the manifestation of laws, which, as soon as they are perceived at all, are perceived to be *necessary*. These are the charges brought by the transcendental philosophers against the school of Locke, Hartley, and Bentham. They, in their turn, allege that the transcendentalists make imagination, and not observation, the criterion of truth; that they lay down principles under which a man may enthrone his wildest dreams in the chair of philosophy, and impose them on mankind as intuitions of the pure reason: which has, in fact, been done in all ages, by all manner of mystical enthusiasts. And even if, with gross inconsistency, the private revelations of any individual Behmen or Swedenborg be disowned, or, in other words, outvoted (the only means of discrimination, which, it is contended, the theory admits of), this is still only substituting, as the test of truth, the dreams of the majority for the dreams of each individual. Whoever form a strong enough party may at any time set up the immediate perceptions of *their* reason, that is to say, any reigning prejudice, as a truth independent of experience,—a truth not only requiring no proof, but to be believed in opposition to all that appears proof to the mere understanding; nay, the more to be believed, because it cannot be put into words and into the logical form of a proposition without a contradiction in terms: for no less authority than this is claimed by some transcendentalists for their *à priori* truths. And thus a ready mode is provided, by which whoever is on the strongest side may dogmatize at his ease, and, instead of proving his propositions, may rail at all who deny them, as bereft of "the vision and the faculty divine," or blinded to its plainest revelations by a corrupt heart.

This is a very temperate statement of what is charged by these two classes of thinkers against each other. How much of either representation is correct cannot conveniently be discussed in this place. In truth, a system of consequences from an opinion, drawn by an adversary, is seldom of much worth. Disputants are rarely sufficiently masters of each other's doctrines to be good judges what is fairly deducible from them, or how a consequence which seems to flow from one part of the theory may or may not be defeated by another part. To combine the different parts of a doctrine with one another, and with all admitted truths, is not indeed a small trouble, nor one which a person is often inclined to take for other people's opinions. Enough if each does it for his own, which he has a greater interest in, and is more disposed to be just to. Were we to search among men's recorded thoughts for the choicest manifestations of human imbecility and prejudice, our specimens would be mostly taken from their opinions of the opinions of one another. Imputations of horrid consequences ought not to bias the judgment of any person capable of independent thought. Coleridge himself says (in the twenty-fifth Aphorism of his "Aids to Reflection"), "He who begins by loving Christianity better than truth will proceed by loving his own sect or church better than Christianity, and end in loving himself better than all."

As to the fundamental difference of opinion respecting the sources of our knowledge (apart from the corollaries which either party may have drawn from its own principle, or imputed to its opponent's), the question lies far too deep in the recesses of psychology for us to discuss it here. The lists having been open ever since the dawn of philosophy, it is not wonderful that the two parties should have been forced to put on their strongest armor both of attack and of defence. The question would not so long have remained a question, if the more obvious arguments on either side had been unanswerable. Each party has been able to urge in its own favor numerous and striking facts, to reconcile which with the opposite theory has required all the metaphysical resources which that theory could command. It will not be wondered at, then, that we here content ourselves with a bare statement of our opinion. It is, that the truth on this much-debated question lies with the school of Locke and of Bentham. The nature and laws of things in themselves, or of the hidden causes of the phenomena which are the objects of experience, appear to us radically inaccessible to the human faculties. We see no ground for believing that any thing can be the object of our knowledge except our experience, and what can be inferred from our experience by the analogies of experience itself; nor that there is any idea, feeling, or power, in the human mind, which, in order to account for it, requires that its origin should be referred to any other source. We are therefore at issue with Coleridge on the central idea of his philosophy; and we find no need of, and no use for, the peculiar technical terminology which he and his masters the Germans have introduced into philosophy for the double purpose of giving logical precision to doctrines which we do not admit, and of marking a relation between those abstract doctrines and many concrete experimental truths, which this language, in our judgment, serves, not to elucidate, but to disguise and obscure. Indeed, but for these peculiarities of language, it would be difficult to understand how the reproach of mysticism (by which nothing is meant in common parlance but unintelligibleness) has been fixed upon Coleridge and the Germans in the minds of many, to whom doctrines substantially the same, when taught in a manner more superficial, and less fenced round against objections, by Reid and Dugald Stewart, have appeared the plain dictates of "common sense," successfully asserted against the subtleties of metaphysics.

Yet, though we think the doctrines of Coleridge and the Germans, in the pure science of mind, erroneous, and have no taste for their peculiar terminology, we are far from thinking, that even in respect of this, the least valuable part of their

intellectual exertions, those philosophers have lived in vain.
The doctrines of the school of Locke stood in need of an entire renovation: to borrow a physiological illustration from
Coleridge, they required, like certain secretions of the human
body, to be re-absorbed into the system, and secreted afresh.
In what form did that philosophy generally prevail throughout
Europe? In that of the shallowest set of doctrines, which, perhaps, were ever passed off upon a cultivated age as a complete
psychological system,—the ideology of Condillac and his
school; a system which affected to resolve all the phenomena
of the human mind into sensation, by a process which essentially consisted in merely *calling* all states of mind, however heterogeneous, by that name; a philosophy now acknowledged to consist solely of a set of verbal generalizations, explaining nothing, distinguishing nothing, leading to nothing.
That men should begin by sweeping this away was the first
sign that the age of real psychology was about to commence.
In England, the case, though different, was scarcely better.
The philosophy of Locke, as a popular doctrine, had remained nearly as it stood in his own book; which, as its title
implies, did not pretend to give an account of any but the
intellectual part of our nature; which, even within that limited
sphere, was but the commencement of a system; and, though
its errors and defects as such have been exaggerated beyond
all just bounds, it did expose many vulnerable points to the
searching criticism of the new school. The least imperfect
part of it, the purely logical part, had almost dropped out of
sight. With respect to those of Locke's doctrines which are
properly metaphysical,—however the sceptical part of them
may have been followed up by others, and carried beyond
the point at which he stopped,—the only one of his successors
who attempted and achieved any considerable improvement
and extension of the analytical part, and thereby added any
thing to the explanation of the human mind on Locke's principles, was Hartley. But Hartley's doctrines, so far as they are
true, were so much in advance of the age, and the way had
been so little prepared for them by the general tone of thinking which yet prevailed, even under the influence of Locke's
writings, that the philosophic world did not deem them
worthy of being attended to. Reid and Stewart were allowed
to run them down uncontradicted; Brown, though a man of a
kindred genius, had evidently never read them; and but for the

accident of their being taken up by Priestley, who transmitted them as a kind of heirloom to his Unitarian followers, the name of Hartley might have perished, or survived only as that of a visionary physician, the author of an exploded physiological hypothesis. It perhaps required all the violence of the assaults made by Reid and the German school upon Locke's system to recall men's minds to Hartley's principles, as alone adequate to the solution, upon that system, of the peculiar difficulties which those assailants pressed upon men's attention as altogether insoluble by it. We may here notice, that Coleridge, before he adopted his later philosophical views, was an enthusiastic Hartleian; so that his abandonment of the philosophy of Locke cannot be imputed to unacquaintance with the highest form of that philosophy which had yet appeared. That he should pass through that highest form without stopping at it is itself a strong presumption that there were more difficulties in the question than Hartley had solved. That any thing has since been done to solve them, we probably owe to the revolution in opinion, of which Coleridge was one of the organs; and, even in abstract metaphysics, his writings, and those of his school of thinkers, are the richest mine from whence the opposite school can draw the materials for what has yet to be done to perfect their own theory.

If we now pass from the purely abstract to the concrete and practical doctrines of the two schools, we shall see still more clearly the necessity of the re-action, and the great service rendered to philosophy by its authors. This will be best manifested by a survey of the state of practical philosophy in Europe, as Coleridge and his compeers found it, towards the close of the last century.

The state of opinion in the latter half of the eighteenth century was by no means the same on the Continent of Europe and in our own island; and the difference was still greater in appearance than it was in reality. In the more advanced nations of the Continent, the prevailing philosophy had done its work completely: it had spread itself over every department of human knowledge; it had taken possession of the whole Continental mind; and scarcely one educated person was left who retained any allegiance to the opinions or the institutions of ancient times. In England, the native country of compromise, things had stopped far short of this; the philosophical movement had been brought to a halt in

an early stage; and a peace had been patched up, by concessions on both sides, between the philosophy of the time
and its traditional institutions and creeds. Hence the aberrations of the age were generally, on the Continent, at that
period, the extravagances of new opinions; in England, the
corruptions of old ones.

To insist upon the deficiencies of the Continental philosophy of the last century, or, as it is commonly termed, the
French philosophy, is almost superfluous. That philosophy
is indeed as unpopular in this country as its bitterest enemy
could desire. If its faults were as well understood as they
are much railed at, criticism might be considered to have
finished its work. But that this is not yet the case, the nature
of the imputations currently made upon the French philosophers sufficiently proves; many of these being as inconsistent
with a just philosophic comprehension of their system of
opinions as with charity towards the men themselves. It is
not true, for example, that any of them denied moral obligation, or sought to weaken its force. So far were they from
meriting this accusation, that they could not even tolerate the
writers, who, like Helvetius, ascribed a selfish origin to the
feelings of morality, resolving them into a sense of interest.
Those writers were as much cried down among the *philosophes*
themselves, and what was true and good in them (and there
is much that is so) met with as little appreciation, then as
now. The error of the philosophers was rather that they
trusted too much to those feelings; believed them to be more
deeply rooted in human nature than they are; to be not so
dependent, as in fact they are, upon collateral influences. They
thought them the natural and spontaneous growth of the human heart; so firmly fixed in it, that they would subsist un-
impaired, nay, invigorated, when the whole system of opinions
and observances with which they were habitually inter-
twined was violently torn away.

To tear away, was, indeed, all that these philosophers, for
the most part, aimed at: they had no conception that any thing
else was needed. At their millennium, superstition, priest-
craft, error, and prejudice of every kind, were to be annihi-
lated: some of them gradually added, that despotism and
hereditary privileges must share the same fate; and, this accomplished, they never for a moment suspected that all the
virtues and graces of humanity could fail to flourish, or that,

when the noxious weeds were once rooted out, the soil would stand in any need of tillage.

In this they committed the very common error of mistaking the state of things with which they had always been familiar, for the universal and natural condition of mankind. They were accustomed to see the human race agglomerated in large nations, all (except here and there a madman or a malefactor) yielding obedience more or less strict to a set of laws prescribed by a few of their own number, and to a set of moral rules prescribed by each other's opinion; renouncing the exercise of individual will and judgment, except within the limits imposed by these laws and rules; and acquiescing in the sacrifice of their individual wishes, when the point was decided against them by lawful authority; or persevering only in hopes of altering the opinion of the ruling powers. Finding matters to be so generally in this condition, the philosophers apparently concluded that they could not possibly be in any other; and were ignorant by what a host of civilizing and restraining influences a state of things so repugnant to man's self-will, and love of independence, has been brought about, and how imperatively it demands the continuance of those influences as the condition of its own existence. The very first element of the social union, obedience to a government of some sort, has not been found so easy a thing to establish in the world. Among a timid and spiritless race, like the inhabitants of the vast plains of tropical countries, passive obedience may be of natural growth; though even there we doubt whether it has ever been found among any people with whom fatalism, or, in other words, submission to the pressure of circumstances as the decree of God, did not prevail as a religious doctrine. But the difficulty of inducing a brave and warlike race to submit their individual *arbitrium* to any common umpire has always been felt to be so great, that nothing short of supernatural power has been deemed adequate to overcome it; and such tribes have always assigned to the first institution of civil society a divine origin. So differently did those judge who knew savage man by actual experience from those who had no acquaintance with him except in the civilized state. In modern Europe itself, after the fall of the Roman Empire, to subdue the feudal anarchy, and bring the whole people of any European nation into subjection to government (although Christianity in the most concentrated form of its influence was co-operating in the work), required thrice as many centuries as have elapsed since that time.

Now, if these philosophers had known human nature under any other type than that of their own age, and of the particular classes of society among whom they lived, it would have occurred to them, that wherever this habitual submission to law and government has been firmly and durably established, and yet the vigor and manliness of character which resisted its establishment have been in any degree preserved, certain requisites have existed, certain conditions have been fulfilled, of which the following may be regarded as the principle.

First, there has existed, for all who were accounted citizens, —for all who were not slaves, kept down by brute force,— a system of *education*, beginning with infancy and continued through life, of which, whatever else it might include, one main and incessant ingredient was *restraining discipline*. To train the human being in the habit, and thence the power, of subordinating his personal impulses and aims to what were considered the ends of society; of adhering, against all temptation, to the course of conduct which those ends prescribed; of controlling in himself all the feelings which were liable to militate against those ends, and encouraging all such as tended towards them,—this was the purpose, to which every outward motive that the authority directing the system could command, and every inward power or principle which its knowledge of human nature enabled it to evoke, were endeavored to be rendered instrumental. The entire civil and military policy of the ancient commonwealths was such a system of training: in modern nations, its place has been attempted to be supplied principally by religious teaching. And whenever and in proportion as the strictness of the restraining discipline was relaxed, the natural tendency of mankind to anarchy re-asserted itself; the State became disorganized from within; mutual conflict for selfish ends neutralized the energies which were required to keep up the contest against natural causes of evil; and the nation, after a longer or briefer interval of progressive decline, became either the slave of a despotism, or the prey of a foreign invader.

The second condition of permanent political society has been found to be, the existence, in some form or other, of the feeling of allegiance, or loyalty. This feeling may vary in its objects, and is not confined to any particular form of government: but, whether in a democracy or in a monarchy, its essence is always the same; viz., that there be in the constitution of the State *something* which is settled, something permanent, and not to be called in question,—something which, by general agreement, has a right to be where it is, and to be secure against disturbance, whatever else may change. This feeling may attach itself, as among the Jews (and, indeed, in most of the commonwealths of antiquity), to a common God or gods, the protectors and guardians of their State; or it may attach itself to certain persons, who are deemed to be, whether by divine appointment, by long prescription, or by the general recognition of their superior capacity and worthiness, the rightful guides and guardians of the rest; or it may attach itself to laws, to ancient liberties, or ordinances; or, finally (and this is the only shape in which the feeling is likely to exist hereafter), it may attach itself to the principles of individual freedom and political and social equality, as realized in institutions which as yet exist nowhere, or exist only in a rudimentary state. But, in all political societies which have had a durable existence, there has been some fixed point; something which men agreed in holding sacred; which, wherever freedom of discussion was a recognized principle, it was of course lawful to contest in theory, but which no one could either fear or hope to see shaken in practice; which, in short (except perhaps during some temporary crisis), was, in the common estimation, placed beyond discussion. And the necessity of this may easily be made evident. A State never is, nor, until mankind are vastly improved, can hope to be, for any long time, exempt from internal dissension; for there neither is, nor has ever been, any state of society in which collisions did not occur between the immediate interests and passions of powerful sections of the people. What, then, enables society to weather these storms, and pass through turbulent times without any permanent weakening of the securities for peaceable existence? Precisely this,—that, however important the interests about which men fall out, the conflict did not affect the fundamental principles of the system of social union which happened to exist; nor threaten large portions of the community with the subversion of that on which they had built their calculations, and with which their hopes and aims had become identified.

But when the questioning of these fundamental principles is, not the occasional disease or salutary medicine, but the habitual condition of the body politic, and when all the violent animosities are called forth which spring naturally from such a situation, the State is virtually in a position of civil war, and can never long remain free from it in act and fact.

The third essential condition of stability in political society is a strong and active principle of cohesion among the members of the same community or state. We need scarcely say that we do not mean nationality, in the vulgar sense of the term,—a senseless antipathy to foreigners; an indifference to the general welfare of the human race, or an unjust preference of the supposed interests of our own country; a cherishing of bad peculiarities because they are national; or a refusal to adopt what has been found good by other countries. We mean a principle of sympathy, not of hostility; of union, not of separation. We mean a feeling of common interest among those who live under the same government, and are contained within the same natural or historical boundaries. We mean, that one part of the community do not consider themselves as foreigners with regard to another part; that they set a value on their connection; feel that they are one people; that their lot is cast together; that evil to any of their fellow-countrymen is evil to themselves; and do not desire selfishly to free themselves from their share of any common inconvenience by severing the connection. How strong this feeling was in those ancient commonwealths which attained any durable greatness, every one knows. How happily Rome, in spite of all her tyranny, succeeded in establishing the feeling of a common country among the provinces of her vast and divided empire, will appear when any one who has given due attention to the subject shall take the trouble to point it out.[2]

---

[2]We are glad to quote a striking passage from Coleridge on this very subject. He is speaking of the misdeeds of England in Ireland; toward which misdeeds, this Tory, as he is called (for the Tories, who neglected him in his lifetime, show no little eagerness to give themselves the credit of his name after his death), entertained feelings scarcely surpassed by those which are excited by the masterly exposure for which we have recently been indebted to M. de Beaumont.

"Let us discharge," he says, "what may well be deemed a debt of justice from every well-educated Englishman to his Roman-Catholic fellow-subjects of the Sister Island. At least, let us ourselves understand the true cause of the evil as it now exists. To what and to whom is the present state of Ireland mainly to be attributed? This should be the question: and to this I answer aloud, that it is mainly attributable to those, who, during a period of little less than a whole century, used as a substitute what Providence had given into their hand as an opportunity; who chose to consider as superseding the most sacred duty a code of law, which could be excused only on the plea that it enabled them to perform it; to the sloth and improvidence, the weak-

In modern times, the countries which have had that feeling in the strongest degree have been the most powerful countries, —England, France, and, in proportion to their territory and resources, Holland and Switzerland; while England, in her connection with Ireland, is one of the most signal examples of the consequences of its absence. Every Italian knows why Italy is under a foreign yoke; every German knows what maintains despotism in the Austrian Empire; the evils of Spain flow as much from the absence of nationality among the Spaniards themselves as from the presence of it in their relations with foreigners; while the completest illustration of all is afforded by the republics of South America, where the parts of one and the same State adhere so slightly together, that no sooner does any province think itself aggrieved by the general government, than it proclaims itself a separate nation.

These essential requisites of civil society the French philosophers of the eighteenth century unfortunately overlooked. They found, indeed, all three—at least the first and second, and most of what nourishes and invigorates the third—already undermined by the vices of the institutions and of the men that were set up as the guardians and bulwarks of them. If innovators, in their theories, disregarded the elementary principles of the social union, conservatives, in their practice, had set the first example. The existing order of things had

ness and wickedness, of the gentry, clergy, and governors of Ireland, who persevered in preferring intrigue, violence, and selfish expatriation, to a system of preventive and remedial measures, the efficacy of which had been warranted for them alike by the whole provincial history of ancient Rome, *cui pacare subactos summa erat sapientia,* and by the happy results of the few exceptions to the contrary scheme unhappily pursued by their and our ancestors.

"I can imagine no work of genius that would more appropriately decorate the dome or wall of a senate-house than an abstract of Irish history from the landing of Strongbow to the battle of the Boyne, or to a yet later period, embodied in intelligible emblems,—an allegorical history-piece designed in the spirit of a Rubens or a Buonarotti, and with the wild lights, portentous shades, and saturated colors, of a Rembrandt, Caravaggio, and Spagnoletti. To complete the great moral and political lesson by the historic contrast, nothing more would be required than by some equally effective means to possess the mind of the spectator with the state and condition of ancient Spain at less than half a century from the final conclusion of an obstinate and almost unremitting conflict of two hundred years by Agrippa's subjugation of the Cantabrians, *omnibus Hispaniæ populis devictis et pacatis.* At the breaking-up of the empire, the West Goths conquered the country and made division of the lands. Then came eight centuries of Moorish domination. Yet so deeply had Roman wisdom impressed the fairest characters of the Roman mind, that at this very hour, if we except a comparatively insignificant portion of Arabic derivatives, the natives throughout the whole Peninsula speak a language less differing from the *Romana rustica,* or provincial Latin of the times of Lucan and Seneca, than any two of its dialects from each other. The time approaches, I trust, when our political economists may study the science of the provincial policy of the ancients in detail, under the auspices of hope, for immediate and practical purposes."—*Church and State.*

ceased to realize those first principles: from the force of circumstances, and from the short-sighted selfishness of its administrators, it had ceased to possess the essential conditions of permanent society, and was therefore tottering to its fall. But the philosophers did not see this. Bad as the existing system was in the days of its decrepitude, according to them it was still worse when it actually did what it now only pretended to do. Instead of feeling that the effect of a bad social order, in sapping the necessary foundations of society itself, is one of the worst of its many mischiefs, the philosophers saw only, and saw with joy, that it was sapping its own foundations. In the weakening of all government, they saw only the weakening of bad government, and thought they could not better employ themselves than in finishing the task so well begun; in discrediting all that still remained of restraining discipline, because it rested on the ancient and decayed creeds against which they made war; in unsettling every thing which was still considered settled, making men doubtful of the few things of which they still felt certain; and in uprooting what little remained in the people's minds of reverence for any thing above them, of respect to any of the limits which custom and prescription had set to the indulgence of each man's fancies or inclinations, or of attachment to any of the things which belonged to them as a nation, and which made them feel their unity as such.

Much of all this was, no doubt, unavoidable, and not justly matter of blame. When the vices of all constituted authorities, added to natural causes of decay, have eaten the heart out of old institutions and beliefs, while at the same time the growth of knowledge, and the altered circumstances of the age, would have required institutions and creeds different from these, even if they had remained uncorrupt, we are far from saying that any degree of wisdom on the part of speculative thinkers could avert the political catastrophes, and the subsequent moral anarchy and unsettledness, which we have witnessed and are witnessing. Still less do we pretend that those principles and influences which we have spoken of as the conditions of the permanent existence of the social union, once lost, can ever be, or should be attempted to be, revived in connection with the same institutions or the same doctrines as before. When society requires to be rebuilt, there is no use in attempting to rebuild it on the old plan. By the

union of the enlarged views and analytic powers of speculative
men with the observation and contriving sagacity of men of
practice, better institutions and better doctrines must be
elaborated; and, until this is done, we cannot hope for much
improvement in our present condition. The effort to do it in
the eighteenth century would have been premature, as the
attempts of the Economistes (who, of all persons then living,
came nearest to it, and who were the first to form clearly the
idea of a social science) sufficiently testify. The time was not
ripe for doing effectually any other work than that of de-
struction. But the work of the day should have been so performed as not to impede that of the morrow. No one can
calculate what struggles, which the cause of improvement has
yet to undergo, might have been spared, if the philosophers
of the eighteenth century had done any thing like justice
to the past. Their mistake was, that they did not acknowledge
the historical value of much which had ceased to be useful, nor saw that institutions and creeds, now effete, had
rendered essential services to civilization, and still filled a
place in the human mind, and in the arrangements of society,
which could not without great peril be left vacant. Their mistake was, that they did not recognize, in many of the errors
which they assailed, corruptions of important truths, and,
in many of the institutions most cankered with abuse, necessary elements of civilized society, though in a form and
vesture no longer suited to the age; and hence they involved,
as far as in them lay, many great truths in a common discredit with the errors which had grown up around them. They
threw away the shell, without preserving the kernel; and,
attempting to new-model society without the binding forces
which hold society together, met with such success as might
have been anticipated.

Now, we claim, in behalf of the philosophers of the reactionary school,—of the school to which Coleridge belongs,
—that exactly what we blame the philosophers of the eighteenth century for not doing, they have done.

Every re-action in opinion, of course, brings into view
that portion of the truth which was overlooked before. It
was natural that a philosophy which anathematized all that
had been going on in Europe from Constantine to Luther, or
even to Voltaire, should be succeeded by another, at once a
severe critic of the new tendencies of society, and an impas-

sioned vindicator of what was good in the past. This is the easy merit of all Tory and Royalist writers. But the peculiarity of the Germano-Coleridgian school is, that they saw beyond the immediate controversy, to the fundamental principles involved in all such controversies. They were the first (except a solitary thinker here and there) who inquired, with any comprehensiveness or depth, into the inductive laws of the existence and growth of human society. They were the first to bring prominently forward the three requisites which we have enumerated as essential principles of all permanent forms of social existence; as principles, we say, and not as mere accidental advantages, inherent in the particular polity or religion which the writer happened to patronize. They were the first who pursued, philosophically and in the spirit of Baconian investigation, not only this inquiry, but others ulterior and collateral to it. They thus produced, not a piece of party advocacy, but a philosophy of society, in the only form in which it is yet possible,—that of a philosophy of history; not a defence of particular ethical or religious doctrines, but a contribution, the largest made by any class of thinkers, towards the philosophy of human culture.

The brilliant light which has been thrown upon history during the last half-century has proceeded almost wholly from this school. The disrespect in which history was held by the *philosophes* is notorious: one of the soberest of them (D'Alembert, we believe) was the author of the wish, that all record whatever of past events could be blotted out. And, indeed, the ordinary mode of writing history, and the ordinary mode of drawing lessons from it, were almost sufficient to excuse this contempt. But the *philosophes* saw, as usual, what was not true, not what was. It is no wonder that they who looked on the greater part of what had been handed down from the past as sheer hinderances to man's attaining a well-being, which would otherwise be of easy attainment, should content themselves with a very superficial study of history. But the case was otherwise with those who regarded the maintenance of society at all, and especially its maintenance in a state of progressive advancement, as a very difficult task actually achieved, in however imperfect a manner, for a number of centuries, against the strongest obstacles. It was natural that they should feel a deep interest in ascertaining how this had been effected; and should be led to inquire, both what were the requisites of the permanent existence of the body politic, and what were the conditions which had rendered the preservation of these permanent requisites compatible with perpetual and progressive improvement. And hence that series of great writers and thinkers, from Herder to Michelet, by whom history, which was till then "a tale told by an idiot, full of sound and fury, signifying nothing," has been made a science of causes and effects; who, by making the facts and events of the past have a meaning and an intelligible place in the gradual evolution of humanity, have at once given history, even to the imagination, an interest like romance, and afforded the only means of predicting and guiding the future, by unfolding the agencies which have produced, and still maintain, the present.[3]

The same causes have naturally led the same class of thinkers to do what their predecessors never could have done for the philosophy of human culture. For the tendency of their speculations compelled them to see, in the character of the national education existing in any political society, at once the principle cause of its permanence as a society, and the chief source of its progressiveness; the former by the extent to which that education operated as a system of restraining discipline, the latter by the degree in which it called forth and invigorated the active faculties. Besides, not to have looked upon the culture of the inward man as the problem of problems would have been incompatible with the belief which many of these philosophers entertained in Christianity, and the recognition by all of them of its historical value, and the prime part which it has acted in the progress of mankind. But here too, let us not fail to observe, they rose to

---

[3]There is something at once ridiculous and discouraging in the signs which daily meet us, of the Cimmerian darkness still prevailing in England (wherever recent foreign literature or the speculations of the Coleridgians have not penetrated) concerning the very existence of the views of general history which have been received throughout the continent of Europe for the last twenty or thirty years. A writer in *Blackwood's Magazine*—certainly not the least able publication of our day, nor this the least able writer in it—lately announced, with all the pomp and heraldry of triumphant genius, a discovery which was to disabuse the world of an universal prejudice, and create "the philosophy of Roman history." This is, that the Roman Empire perished, not from outward violence, but from inward decay; and that the barbarian conquerors were the renovators, not the destroyers, of its civilization. Why, there is not a schoolboy in France or Germany who did not possess this writer's discovery before him: the contrary opinion has receded so far into the past, that it must be rather a learned Frenchman or German who remembers that it was ever held. If the writer in *Blackwood* had read a line of Guizot (to go no further than the most obvious sources), he would probably have abstained from making himself very ridiculous, and his country, so far as depends upon him, the laughing-stock of Europe.

principles, and did not stick in the particular case. The culture of the human being had been carried to no ordinary height, and human nature had exhibited many of its noblest manifestations, not in Christian countries only, but in the ancient world,—in Athens, Sparta, Rome: nay, even barbarians, as the Germans, or still more unmitigated savages, the wild Indians, and again the Chinese, the Egyptians, the Arabs, all had their own education, their own culture,—a culture which, whatever might be its tendency upon the whole, had been successful in some respect or other. Every form of polity, every condition of society, whatever else it had done, had formed its type of national character. What that type was, and how it had been made what it was, were questions which the metaphysician might overlook: the historical philosopher could not. Accordingly, the views respecting the various elements of human culture, and the causes influencing the formation of national character, which pervade the writings of the Germano-Coleridgian school, throw into the shade every thing which had been effected before, or which has been attempted simultaneously by any other school. Such views are, more than any thing else, the characteristic feature of the Goethian period of German literature; and are richly diffused through the historical and critical writings of the new French school, as well as of Coleridge and his followers.

In this long though most compressed dissertation on the Continental philosophy preceding the re-action, and on the nature of the re-action so far as directed against that philosophy, we have unavoidably been led to speak rather of the movement itself than of Coleridge's particular share in it; which, from his posteriority in date, was necessarily a subordinate one. And it would be useless, even did our limits permit, to bring together, from the scattered writings of a man who produced no systematic work, any of the fragments which he may have contributed to an edifice still incomplete, and even the general character of which we can have rendered very imperfectly intelligible to those who are not acquainted with the theory itself. Our object is to invite to the study of the original sources, not to supply the place of such a study. What was peculiar to Coleridge will be better manifested when we now proceed to review the state of popular philosophy immediately preceding him in our own island;

which was different, in some material respects, from the contemporaneous Continental philosophy.

In England, the philosophical speculations of the age had not, except in a few highly metaphysical minds (whose example rather served to deter than to invite others), taken so audacious a flight, nor achieved any thing like so complete a victory over the counteracting influences, as on the Continent. There is in the English mind, both in speculation and in practice, a highly salutary shrinking from all extremes; but, as this shrinking is rather an instinct of caution than a result of insight, it is too ready to satisfy itself with any medium merely because it is a medium, and to acquiesce in a union of the disadvantages of both extremes instead of their advantages. The circumstances of the age, too, were unfavorable to decided opinions. The repose which followed the great struggles of the Reformation and the Commonwealth; the final victory over Popery and Puritanism, Jacobitism and Republicanism, and the lulling of the controversies which kept speculation and spiritual consciousness alive; the lethargy which came upon all governors and teachers, after their position in society became fixed; and the growing absorption of all classes in material interests,—caused a state of mind to diffuse itself, with less of deep inward workings, and less capable of interpreting those it had, than had existed for centuries. The age seemed smitten with an incapacity of producing deep or strong feelings, such as at least could ally itself with meditative habits. There were few poets, and none of a high order; and philosophy fell mostly into the hands of men of a dry prosaic nature, who had not enough of the materials of human feeling in them to be able to imagine any of its more complex and mysterious manifestations; all of which they either left out of their theories, or introduced them with such explanations as no one who had experienced the feelings could receive as adequate. An age like this, an age without earnestness, was the natural era of compromises and half-convictions.

To make out a case for the feudal and ecclesiastical institutions of modern Europe was by no means impossible: they had a meaning, had existed for honest ends, and an honest theory of them might be made. But the administration of those institutions had long ceased to accord with any honest theory. It was impossible to justify them in principle, except on grounds which condemned them in practice; and grounds of which there was, at any rate, little or no recognition in the philosophy of the eighteenth century. The natural tendency, therefore, of that philosophy, everywhere but in England, was to seek the extinction of those institutions. In England, it would doubtless have done the same, had it been strong enough; but, as this was beyond its strength, an adjustment was come to between the rival powers. What neither party cared about, the *ends* of existing institutions, the work that was to be done by teachers and governors, was flung overboard. The wages of that work the teachers and governors did care about; and those wages were secured to them. The existing institutions in Church and State were to be preserved inviolate, in outward semblance at least; but were required to be, practically, as much a nullity as possible. The Church continued to "rear her mitred front in courts and palaces," but not, as in the days of Hildebrand or Becket, as the champion of arts against arms, of the serf against the seigneur, peace against war, or spiritual principles and powers against the domination of animal force; nor even (as in the days of Latimer and John Knox) as a body divinely commissioned to train the nation in a knowledge of God, and obedience to his laws, whatever became of temporal principalities and powers; and whether this end might most effectually be compassed by their assistance, or by trampling them under foot. No; but the people of England liked old things, and nobody knew how the place might be filled which the doing-away with so conspicuous an institution would leave vacant, and *quieta ne movere* was the favorite doctrine of those times: therefore, on condition of not making too much noise about religion, or taking it too much in earnest, the Church was supported, even by philosophers,—as a "bulwark against fanaticism," a sedative to the religious spirit, to prevent it from disturbing the harmony of society or the tranquillity of states. The clergy of the Establishment thought they had a good bargain on these terms, and kept its conditions very faithfully.

The State, again, was no longer considered, according to the old ideal, as a concentration of the force of all the individuals of the nation in the hands of certain of its members, in order to the accomplishment of whatever could be best accomplished by systematic co-operation. It was found that the State was a bad judge of the wants of society; that it in reality cared very little for them: and when it attempted any thing beyond that police against crime, and arbitration of disputes, which are indispensable to social existence, the private sinister interest of some class or individual was usually the prompter of its proceedings. The natural inference would have been, that the constitution of the State was somehow not suited to the existing wants of society; having indeed descended, with scarcely any modifications that could be avoided, from a time when the most prominent exigencies of society were quite different. This conclusion, however, was shrunk from; and it required the peculiarities of very recent times, and the speculations of the Bentham school, to produce even any considerable tendency that way. The existing Constitution, and all the arrangements of existing society, continued to be applauded as the best possible. The celebrated theory of the three powers was got up, which made the excellence of our Constitution consist in doing less harm than would be done by any other form of government. Government altogether was regarded as a necessary evil, and was required to hide itself,—to make itself as little felt as possible. The cry of the people was not, "Help us;" "Guide us;" "Do for us the things we cannot do; and instruct us, that we may do well those which we can" (and truly such requirements from such rulers would have been a bitter jest): the cry was, "Let us alone." Power to decide questions of *meum* and *tuum*, to protect society from open violence, and from some of the most dangerous modes of fraud, could not be withheld: these functions the Government was left in possession of; and to these it became the expectation of the public that it should confine itself.

Such was the prevailing tone of English belief in temporals. What was it in spirituals? Here, too, a similar system of compromise had been at work. Those who pushed their philosophical speculations to the denial of the received religious belief, whether they went to the extent of infidelity or only of heterodoxy, met with little encouragement: neither religion itself, nor the received forms of it, were at all shaken by the few attacks which were made upon them from without. The philosophy, however, of the time, made itself felt as effectually in another fashion: it pushed its way *into* religion. The *à priori* arguments for a God were first dismissed. This was indeed inevitable. The internal evidences of Christianity shared nearly the same fate: if not absolutely thrown aside, they fell into the background, and were little thought of. The doctrine of

Locke, that we have no *innate* moral sense, perverted into the doctrine that we have no moral sense at all, made it appear that we had not any capacity of judging, from the doctrine itself, whether it was worthy to have come from a righteous Being. In forgetfulness of the most solemn warnings of the Author of Christianity, as well as of the apostle who was the main diffuser of it through the world, belief in his religion was left to stand upon miracles,—a species of evidence, which, according to the universal belief of the early Christians themselves, was by no means peculiar to true religion; and it is melancholy to see on what frail reeds able defenders of Christianity preferred to rest, rather than upon that better evidence which alone gave to their so-called evidences any value as a collateral confirmation. In the interpretation of Christianity, the palpablest *bibliolatry* prevailed,—if (with Coleridge) we may so term that superstitious worship of particular texts, which persecuted Galileo, and, in our own day, anathematized the discoveries of geology. Men whose faith in Christianity rested on the literal infallibility of the sacred volume shrank in terror from the idea that it could have been included in the scheme of Providence, that the human opinions and mental habits of the particular writers should be allowed to mix with and color their mode of conceiving and of narrating the divine transactions. Yet this slavery to the letter has not only raised every difficulty which envelops the most unimportant passage in the Bible into an objection to revelation, but has paralyzed many a well-meant effort to bring Christianity home, as a consistent scheme, to human experience, and capacities of apprehension; as if there was much of it which it was more prudent to leave *in nubibus,* lest, in the attempt to make the mind seize hold of it as a reality, some text might be found to stand in the way. It might have been expected that this idolatry of the words of Scripture would at least have saved its doctrines from being tampered with by human notions: but the contrary proved to be the effect; for the vague and sophistical mode of interpreting texts, which was necessary in order to reconcile what was manifestly irreconcilable, engendered a habit of playing fast and loose with Scripture, and finding in, or leaving out of it, whatever one pleased. Hence, while Christianity was, in theory and in intention, received and submitted to, with even "prostration of the understanding" before it, much alacrity was in fact displayed in *accommodating* it to the received philosophy, and even to the popular notions of the time. To take only one example, but so signal a one as to be *instar omnium*. If there is any one requirement of Christianity less doubtful than another, it is that of being spiritually-minded; of loving and practising good from a pure love, simply because it is good. But one of the crotchets of the philosophy of the age was, that all virtue is self-interest; and accordingly, in the text-book adopted by the Church (in one of its universities) for instruction in moral philosophy, the reason for doing good is declared to be, that God is stronger than we are, and is able to damn us if we do not. This is no exaggeration of the sentiments of Paley, and hardly even of the crudity of his language.

Thus, on the whole, England had neither the benefits, such as they were, of the new ideas, nor of the old. We were just sufficiently under the influences of each to render the other powerless. We had a Government, which we respected too much to attempt to change it, but not enough to trust it with any power, or look to it for any services that were not compelled. We had a Church, which had ceased to fulfil the honest purposes of a church, but which we made a great point of keeping up as the pretence or *simulacrum* of one. We had a highly spiritual religion (which we were instructed to obey from selfish motives), and the most mechanical and worldly notions on every other subject; and we were so much afraid of being wanting in reverence to each particular syllable of the book which contained our religion, that we let its most important meanings slip through our fingers, and entertained the most grovelling conceptions of its spirit and general purposes. This was not a state of things which could recommend itself to any earnest mind. It was sure, in no great length of time, to call forth two sorts of men: the one demanding the extinction of the institutions and creeds which had hitherto existed; the other, that they be made a reality: the one pressing the new doctrines to their utmost consequences, the other re-asserting the best meaning and purposes of the old. The first type attained its greatest height in Bentham; the last, in Coleridge.

We hold that these two sorts of men, who seem to be, and believe themselves to be, enemies, are in reality allies. The powers they wield are opposite poles of one great force of progression. What was really hateful and contemptible was the state which preceded them, and which each, in its way, has been striving now for many years to improve. Each ought to hail with rejoicing the advent of the other. But most of all ought an enlightened Radical or Liberal to rejoice over such a Conservative as Coleridge. For such a Radical must know, that the Constitution and Church of England, and the religious opinions and political maxims professed by their supporters, are not mere frauds, nor sheer nonsense; have not been got up originally, and all along maintained, for the sole purpose of picking people's pockets; without aiming at, or being found conducive to, any honest end during the whole process. Nothing, of which this is a sufficient account, would have lasted a tithe of five, eight, or ten centuries, in the most improving period and (during much of that period) the most improving nation in the world. These things, we may depend upon it, were not always without much good in them, however little of it may now be left: and reformers ought to hail the man as a brother-reformer who points out what this good is; what it is which we have a right to expect from things established; which they are bound to do for us, as the justification of their being established; so that they may be recalled to it, and compelled to do it, or the impossibility of their any longer doing it may be conclusively manifested. What is any case for reform good for, until it has passed this test? What mode is there of determining whether a thing is fit to exist, without first considering what purposes it exists for, and whether it be still capable of fulfilling them?

We have not room here to consider Coleridge's Conservative philosophy in all its aspects, or in relation to all the quarters from which objections might be raised against it. We shall consider it with relation to Reformers, and especially to Benthamites. We would assist them to determine whether they would have to do with Conservative philosophers, or with Conservative dunces; and whether, since there are Tories, it be better that they should learn their Toryism from Lord Eldon, or even Sir Robert Peel, or from Coleridge.

Take, for instance, Coleridge's view of the grounds of a Church Establishment. His mode of treating any institution is to investigate what he terms the idea of it, or what in common parlance would be called the principle involved in it. The idea or principle of a national church, and of the Church of England in that character, is, according to him, the reservation of a portion of the land, or of a right to a portion of its produce, as a fund,—for what purpose? For the worship of God? For the performance of religious ceremonies? No; for the advancement of knowledge, and the civilization and cultivation of the community. This fund he does not term "church-property," but "the nationalty," or national property. He considers it as destined for "the support and maintenance of a permanent class or order, with the following duties:—

A certain smaller number were to remain at the fountainheads of the humanities, in cultivating and enlarging the knowledge already possessed, and in watching over the interests of physical and moral science; being likewise the instructors of such as constituted, or were to constitute, the remaining more numerous classes of the order. The members of this latter and far more numerous body were to be distributed throughout the country, so as not to leave even the smallest integral part or division without a resident guide, guardian, and instructor; the objects and final intention of the whole order being these,—to preserve the stores and to guard the treasures of past civilization, and thus to bind the present with the past; to perfect and add to the same, and thus to connect the present with the future; but especially to diffuse through the whole community, and to every native entitled to its laws and rights, that quantity and quality of knowledge which was indispensable both for the understanding of those rights, and for the performance of the duties correspondent; finally, to secure for the nation, if not a superiority over the neighboring States, yet an equality at least, in that character of general civilization, which, equally with, or rather more than, fleets, armies, and revenue, forms the ground of its defensive and offensive power.

This organized body, set apart and endowed for the cultivation and diffusion of knowledge, is not, in Coleridge's view, necessarily a religious corporation.

Religion may be an indispensable ally, but is not the essential constitutive end, of that national institute, which is unfortunately, at least improperly, styled the Church; a name which, in its best sense, is exclusively appropriate to

the Church of Christ. . . . The *clerisy* of the nation, or national church in its primary acceptation and original intention, comprehended the learned of all denominations,
the sages and professors of the law and jurisprudence, of
medicine and physiology, of music, of military and civil
architecture, with the mathematical as the common organ
of the preceding; in short, all the so-called liberal arts and
sciences, the possession and application of which constitute the civilization of a country, as well as the theological. The last was, indeed, placed at the head of all; and of
good right did it claim the precedence. But why? Because
under the name of theology or divinity were contained
the interpretation of languages; the conservation and tradition of past events; the momentous epochs and revolutions of the race and nation; the continuation of the records, logic, ethics, and the determination of ethical science, in application to the rights and duties of men in all
their various relations, social and civil; and, lastly, the
ground-knowledge, the *prima scientia,* as it was named,—
philosophy, or the doctrine and discipline of ideas.

Theology formed only a part of the objects, the
theologians formed only a portion of the clerks or clergy,
of the national church. The theological order had precedency indeed, and deservedly; but not because its
members were priests, whose office was to conciliate the
invisible powers, and to superintend the interests that
survive the grave; nor as being exclusively, or even principally, sacerdotal or templar, which, when it did occur,
is to be considered as an accident of the age, a misgrowth
of ignorance and oppression, a falsification of the constitutive principle, not a constituent part of the same. No:
the theologians took the lead, because the science of
theology was the root and the trunk of the knowledge of
civilized man; because it gave unity and the circulating
sap of life to all other sciences, by virtue of which alone
they could be contemplated as forming collectively the
living tree of knowledge. It had the precedency, because
under the name Theology were comprised all the main
aids, instruments, and materials of national education, the
nisus formativus of the body politic, the shaping and informing spirit, which, educing or eliciting the latent man
in all the natives of the soil, trains them up to be citizens

of the country, free subjects of the realm. And, lastly, because to divinity belong those fundamental truths which are the common groundwork of our civil and our religious duties, not less indispensable to a right view of our temporal concerns than to a rational faith respecting our immortal well-being. Not without celestial observations can even terrestrial charts be accurately constructed.—

Church and State, chap.v

The nationalty, or national property, according to Coleridge, "cannot rightfully be, and without foul wrong to the nation never has been, alienated from its original purposes," from the promotion of "a continuing and progressive civilization," to the benefit of individuals, or any public purpose of merely economical or material interest. But the State may withdraw the fund from its actual holders for the better execution of its purposes. There is no sanctity attached to the means, but only to the ends. The fund is not dedicated to any particular scheme of religion, nor even to religion at all: religion has only to do with it in the character of an instrument of civilization, and in common with all the other instruments.

I do not assert that the proceeds from the nationalty cannot be rightfully vested, except in what we now mean by clergymen and the established clergy. I have everywhere implied the contrary. . . . In relation to the national church, Christianity, or the Church of Christ, is a blessed accident, a providential boon, a grace of God. . . . As the olive-tree is said in its growth to fertilize the surrounding soil, to invigorate the roots of the vines in its immediate neighborhood, and to improve the strength and flavor of the wines; such is the relation of the Christian and the national Church. But as the olive is not the same plant with the vine, or with the elm or poplar (that is, the State) with which the vine is wedded; and as the vine, with its prop, may exist, though in less perfection, without the olive, or previously to its implantation: even so is Christianity, and *à fortiori* any particular scheme of theology derived, and supposed by its partisans to be deduced, from Christianity, no essential part of the being of the national Church, however conducive or even indispensable it may be to its well-being.—

Church and State, chap.vi

What would Sir Robert Inglis, or Sir Robert Peel, or Mr. Spooner, say to such a doctrine as this? Will they thank Coleridge for this advocacy of Toryism? What would become of the three-years' debates on the Appropriation Clause, which so disgraced this country before the face of Europe? Will the ends of practical Toryism be much served by a theory under which the Royal Society might claim a part of the church-property with as good right as the bench of bishops, if, by endowing that body like the French Institute, science could be better promoted? a theory by which the State, in the conscientious exercise of its judgment, having decided that the Church of England does not fulfil the object for which the nationalty was intended, might transfer its endowments to any other ecclesiastical body, or to any other body not ecclesiastical, which it deemed more competent to fulfil those objects; might establish any other sect, or all sects, or no sect at all, if it should deem, that, in the divided condition of religious opinion in this country, the State can no longer with advantage attempt the complete religious instruction of its people, but must for the present content itself with providing secular instruction, and such religious teaching, if any, as all can take part in; leaving each sect to apply to its own communion that which they all agree in considering as the keystone of the arch. We believe this to be the true state of affairs in Great Britain at the present time. We are far from thinking it other than a serious evil. We entirely acknowledge, that, in any person fit to be a teacher, the view he takes of religion will be intimately connected with the view he will take of all the greatest things which he has to teach. Unless the same teachers who give instruction on those other subjects are at liberty to enter freely on religion, the scheme of education will be, to a certain degree, fragmentary and incoherent. But the State at present has only the option of such an imperfect scheme, or of intrusting the whole business to perhaps the most unfit body for the exclusive charge of it that could be found among persons of any intellectual attainments; namely, the established clergy as at present trained and composed. Such a body would have no chance of being selected as the exclusive administrators of the nationalty on any foundation but that of divine right; the ground avowedly taken by the only other school of Conservative philosophy which is attempting to raise its head in this country,—that of the new Oxford theologians.

Coleridge's merit in this matter consists, as it seems to us, in two things. First, that by setting in a clear light what a national-church establishment ought to be, and what, by the very fact of its existence, it must be held to pretend to be, he has pronounced the severest satire upon what in fact it is. There is some difference, truly, between Coleridge's church, in which the schoolmaster forms the first step in the hierarchy, "who in due time, and under condition of a faithful performance of his arduous duties, should succeed to the pastorate,"[4] and the Church of England such as we now see. But to say the Church, and mean only the clergy, "constituted," according to Coleridge's conviction, "the first and fundamental apostasy."[5] He, and the thoughts which have proceeded from him, have done more than would have been effected in thrice the time by Dissenters and Radicals to make the Church ashamed of the evil of her ways, and to determine that movement of improvement from within, which has begun where it ought to begin, at the universities and among the younger clergy, and which, if this sect-ridden country is ever to be really taught, must proceed, *pari passu,* with the assault carried on from without.

Secondly, we honor Coleridge for having rescued from the discredit in which the corruptions of the English Church had involved every thing connected with it, and for having vindicated against Bentham and Adam Smith and the whole eighteenth century, the principle of an endowed class, for the cultivation of learning, and for diffusing its results among the community. That such a class is likely to be behind, instead of before, the progress of knowledge, is an induction erroneously drawn from the peculiar circumstances of the last two centuries, and in contradiction to all the rest of modern history. If we have seen much of the abuses of endowments, we have not seen what this country might be made by a proper administration of them, as we trust we shall not see what it would be without them. On this subject we are entirely at one with Coleridge, and with the other great defender of endowed establishments, Dr. Chalmers; and we consider the definitive establishment of this fundamental principle to be one of the permanent benefits which political science owes to the Conservative philosophers.

[4]*Church and State*
[5]*Literary Remains.*

Coleridge's theory of the Constitution is not less worthy of notice than his theory of the Church. The Delolme and Blackstone doctrine, the balance of the three powers, he declares he never could elicit one ray of common sense from, no more than from the balance of trade.[6] There is, however, according to him, an Idea of the Constitution, of which he says,—

> Because our whole history, from Alfred onwards, demonstrates the continued influence of such an idea, or ultimate aim, in the minds of our forefathers, in their characters and functions as public men, alike in what they resisted and what they claimed; in the institutions and forms of polity which they established, and with regard to those against which they more or less successfully contended; and because the result has been a progressive, though not always a direct or equable, advance in the gradual realization of the idea; and because it is actually, though (even because it is an idea) not adequately, represented in a correspondent scheme of means really existing,—we speak, and have a right to speak, of the idea itself as actually existing; that is, as a principle existing in the only way in which a principle can exist,—in the minds and consciences of the persons whose duties it prescribes, and whose rights it determines. This fundamental idea is at the same time the final criterion by which all particular frames of government must be tried: for here only can we find the great constructive principles of our representative system,—those principles in the light of which it can alone be ascertained what are excrescences, symptoms of distemperature, and marks of degeneration, and what are native growths, or changes naturally attendant on the progressive development of the original germ; symptoms of immaturity, perhaps, but not of disease; or, at worst, modifications of the growth by the defective or faulty, but remediless, or only gradually remediable, qualities of the soil and surrounding elements."[7]

Of these principles he gives the following account:—

> It is the chief of many blessings derived from the insular character and circumstances of our country, that

---
[6]*The Friend.*
[7]*Church and State.*

our social institutions have formed themselves out of our proper needs and interests; that, long and fierce as the birth-struggle and growing pains have been, the antagonist powers have been of our own system, and have been allowed to work out their final balance with less disturbance from external forces than was possible in the Continental States. . . . Now, in every country of civilized men, or acknowledging the rights of property, and by means of determined boundaries and common laws united into one people or nation, the two antagonist powers or opposite interests of the State, under which all other State interests are comprised, are those of *permanence* and of *progression*.

The interest of permanence, or the Conservative interest, he considers to be naturally connected with the land and with landed property. This doctrine, false in our opinion as an universal principle, is true of England, and of all countries where landed property is accumulated in large masses.

"On the other hand," he says, "the progression of a State in the arts and comforts of life, in the diffusion of the information and knowledge useful or necessary for all; in short, all advances in civilization, and the rights and privileges of citizens,—are especially connected with, and derived from, the four classes,—the mercantile, the manufacturing, the distributive, and the professional." (We must omit the interesting historical illustrations of this maxim.) "These four last-mentioned classes I will designate by the name of the Personal Interest, as the exponent of all movable and personal possessions, including skill and acquired knowledge, the moral and intellectual stock in trade of the professional man and the artist, no less than the raw materials, and the means of elaborating, transporting, and distributing them."[8]

The interest of permanence, then, is provided for by a representation of the landed proprietors; that of progression, by a representation of personal property and of intellectual acquirement: and while one branch of the Legislature, the Peerage, is essentially given over to the former, he considers it a part both of the general theory, and of the actual English Constitution, that the representatives of the latter should form "the clear and effectual majority of the Lower House;" or, if

[8]*Church and State.*

not, that at least, by the added influence of public opinion, they should exercise an effective preponderance there. That "the very weight intended for the effectual counterpoise of the great landholders" has, "in the course of events, been shifted into the opposite scale;" that the members for the towns "now constitute a large proportion of the political power and influence of the very class of men whose personal cupidity, and whose partial views of the landed interest at large, they were meant to keep in check,"—these things he acknowledges; and only suggests a doubt, whether roads, canals, machinery, the press, and other influences favorable to the popular side, do not constitute an equivalent force to supply the deficiency.[9]

How much better a Parliamentary Reformer, then, is Coleridge, than Lord John Russell, or any Whig who stickles for maintaining this unconstitutional omnipotence of the landed interest! If these became the principles of Tories, we should not wait long for further reform, even in our organic institutions. It is true, Coleridge disapproved of the Reform Bill, or rather of the principle, or the no-principle, on which it was supported. He saw in it (as we may surmise) the dangers of a change amounting almost to a revolution, without any real tendency to remove those defects in the machine which alone could justify a change so extensive. And, that this is nearly a true view of the matter, all parties seem to be now agreed. The Reform Bill was not calculated materially to improve the general composition of the Legislature. The good it has done, which is considerable, consists chiefly in this, that, being so great a change, it has weakened the superstitious feeling against great changes. Any good, which is contrary to the selfish interest of the dominant class, is still only to be effected by a long and arduous struggle; but improvements, which threaten no powerful body in their social importance or in their pecuniary emoluments, are no longer resisted as they once were, because of their greatness,—because of the very benefit which they promised. Witness the speedy passing of the Poor-law Amendment and the Penny-postage Acts.

Meanwhile, though Coleridge's theory is but a mere commencement, not amounting to the first lines of a political philosophy, has the age produced any other theory of government which can stand a comparison with it as to its first principles?

[9] *Church and State.*

Let us take, for example, the Benthamic theory. The principle of this may be said to be, that, since the <u>general interest is the object of government</u>, a complete control over the government ought to be given to those whose interest is identical with the general interest. The authors and propounders of this theory were men of extraordinary intellectual powers, and the greater part of what they meant by it is true and important. But, when considered as the foundation of a science, it would be difficult to find, among theories proceeding from philosophers, one less like a philosophical theory, or, in the works of analytical minds, any thing more entirely unanalytical. What can a philosopher make of such complex notions as "interest" and "general interest," without breaking them down into the elements of which they are composed? If by men's interest be meant what would appear such to a calculating bystander, judging what would be good for a man during his whole life, and making no account, or but little, of the gratification of his present passions,—his pride, his envy, his vanity, his cupidity, his love of pleasure, his love of ease,—it may be questioned, whether, in this sense, the interest of an aristocracy, and still more that of a monarch, would not be as accordant with the general interest as that of either the middle or the poorer classes; and if men's interest, in this understanding of it, usually governed their conduct, absolute monarchy would probably be the best form of government. But since men usually do what they like, often being perfectly aware that it is not for their ultimate interest, still more often that it is not for the interest of their posterity; and when they do believe that the object they are seeking is permanently good for them, almost always overrating its value,—it is necessary to consider, not who are they whose permanent interest, but who are they whose immediate interests and habitual feelings, are likely to be most in accordance with the end we seek to obtain. And, as that end (the general good) is a very complex state of things,—comprising as its component elements many requisites which are neither of one and the same nature, nor attainable by one and the same means,—political philosophy must begin by a classification of these elements, in order to distinguish those of them which go naturally together (so that the provision made for one will suffice for the rest) from those which are ordinarily in a state of antagonism, or at least of separation, and require to be provided for apart. This preliminary classification being supposed, things would, in a perfect government, be so ordered, that, corresponding to each of the great interests of society, there would be some branch or some integral part of the governing body so constituted that it should not be merely deemed by philosophers, but actually and constantly deem itself, to have its strongest interests involved in the maintenance of that one of the ends of society which it is intended to be the guardian of. This, we say, is the thing to be aimed at,—the type of perfection in a political constitution. Not that there is a possibility of making more than a limited approach to it in practice: a government must be composed out of the elements already existing in society; and the distribution of power in the constitution cannot vary much or long from the distribution of it in society itself. But wherever the circumstances of society allow any choice, wherever wisdom and contrivance are at all available, this, we conceive, is the principle of guidance; and whatever anywhere exists is imperfect and a failure, just so far as it recedes from this type.

Such a philosophy of government, we need hardly say, is in its infancy: the first step to it, the classification of the exigencies of society, has not been made. Bentham, in his "Principles of Civil Law," has given a specimen, very useful for many other purposes, but not available, nor intended to be so, for founding a theory of representation upon it. For that particular purpose we have seen nothing comparable, as far as it goes, notwithstanding its manifest insufficiency, to Coleridge's division of the interests of society into the two antagonist interests of Permanence and Progression. The Continental philosophers have, by a different path, arrived at the same division; and this is about as far, probably, as the science of political institutions has yet reached.

In the details of Coleridge's political opinions there is much good, and much that is questionable, or worse. In political economy especially, he writes like an arrant driveller; and it would have been well for his reputation, had he never meddled with the subject.[10] But this department of knowledge can now take care of itself. On other points we meet with far-reaching remarks, and a tone of general feeling sufficient to make a

[10]Yet even on this subject he has occasionally a just thought, happily expressed; as this: "Instead of the position that all things find, it would be less equivocal and far more descriptive of the fact to say, that things are always finding their level; which might be taken as the paraphrase or ironical definition of a storm."—*Second Lay Sermon.*

Tory's hair stand on end. Thus, in the work from which we have most quoted, he calls the State policy of the last half-century "a Cyclops with one eye, and that in the back of the head;" its measures "either a series of anachronisms, or a truckling to events instead of the science that should command them."[11] He styles the great Commonwealthsmen "the stars of that narrow interspace of blue sky between the black clouds of the First and Second Charles's reigns."[12] The *Literary Remains* are full of disparaging remarks on many of the heroes of Toryism and Church-of-Englandism. He sees, for instance, no difference between Whitgift and Bancroft, and Bonner and Gardiner, except that the last were the most consistent; that the former sinned against better knowledge:[13] and one of the most poignant of his writings is a character of Pitt, the very reverse of panegyrical.[14] As a specimen of his practical views, we have mentioned his recommendation that the parochial clergy should begin by being schoolmasters. He urges "a different division and subdivision of the kingdom," instead of "the present barbarism, which forms an obstacle to the improvement of the country, of much greater magnitude than men are generally aware."[15] But we must confine ourselves to instances in which he has helped to bring forward great principles, either implied in the old English opinions and institutions, or at least opposed to the new tendencies.

For example: he is at issue with the *let-alone* doctrine, or the theory that governments can do no better than to do nothing,—a doctrine generated by the manifest selfishness and incompetence of modern European governments, but of which, as a general theory, we may now be permitted to say, that one half of it is true, and the other half false. All who are on a level with their age now readily admit that government ought not to *interdict* men from publishing their opinions, pursuing their employments, or buying and selling their goods, in whatever place or manner they deem the most advantageous. Beyond suppressing force and fraud, governments can seldom, without doing more harm than good, attempt to chain up the free agency of individuals. But does it follow from this that government cannot exercise a free agency of its

[11]*Church and State.*
[12]*Church and State.*
[13]*Literary Remains.*
[14]Written in the *Morning Post,* and now (as we rejoice to see) reprinted in Mr. Gillman's biographical memoir.
[15]*Literary Remains.*

own?—that it cannot beneficially employ its powers, its means of information, and its pecuniary resources (so far surpassing those of any other association or of any individual), in promoting the public welfare by a thousand means which individuals would never think of, would have no sufficient motives to attempt, or no sufficient powers to accomplish? To confine ourselves to one, and that a limited, view of the subject: a State ought to be considered as a great benefit-society, or mutual-insurance company, for helping (under the necessary regulations for preventing abuse) that large proportion of its members who cannot help themselves.

"Let us suppose," says Coleridge, "the negative ends of a State already attained,—namely, its own safety by means of its own strength, and the protection of person and property for all its members: there will then remain its positive ends,— 1. To make the means of subsistence more easy to each individual. 2. To secure to each of its members the hope of bettering his own condition, or that of his children. 3. The development of those faculties which are essential to his humanity; that is, to his rational and moral being."[16]

In regard to the two former ends, he of course does not mean that they can be accomplished merely by making laws to that effect; or that, according to the wild doctrines now afloat, it is the fault of the government if every one has not enough to eat and drink. But he means that government can do something directly, and very much indirectly, to promote even the physical comfort of the people; and that, if, besides making a proper use of its own powers, it would exert itself to teach the people what is in theirs, indigence would soon disappear from the face of the earth.

Perhaps, however, the greatest service which Coleridge has rendered to politics in his capacity of a Conservative philosopher, though its fruits are mostly yet to come, is in reviving the idea of a *trust* inherent in landed property. The land, the gift of nature, the source of subsistence to all, and the foundation of every thing that influences our physical well-being, cannot be considered a subject of *property* in the same absolute sense in which men are deemed proprietors of that in which no one has any interest but themselves,—that which

[16] *Second Lay Sermon.*

they have actually called into existence by their own bodily exertion. As Coleridge points out, such a notion is altogether of modern growth.

> The very idea of individual or private property in our present acceptation of the term, and according to the current notion of the right to it, was originally confined to movable things; and the more movable, the more susceptible of the nature of property.[17]

By the early institutions of Europe, property in land was a public function, created for certain public purposes, and held under condition of their fulfilment; and as such, we predict, under the modifications suited to modern society, it will again come to be considered. In this age, when every thing is called in question, and when the foundation of private property itself needs to be argumentatively maintained against plausible and persuasive sophisms, one may easily see the danger of mixing up what is not really tenable with what is; and the impossibility of maintaining an absolute right in an individual to an unrestricted control, a *jus utendi et abutendi,* over an unlimited quantity of the mere raw material of the globe, to which every other person could originally make out as good a natural title as himself. It will certainly not be much longer tolerated, that agriculture should be carried on (as Coleridge expresses it) on the same principles as those of trade; "that a gentleman should regard his estate as a merchant his cargo, or a shopkeeper his stock;"[18] that he should be allowed to deal with it as if it only existed to yield rent to him, not food to the numbers whose hands till it; and should have a right, and a right possessing all the sacredness of property, to turn them out by hundreds, and make them perish on the high road, as has been done before now by Irish landlords. We believe it will soon be thought, that a mode of property in land, which has brought things to this pass, has existed long enough.

We shall not be suspected (we hope) of recommending a general resumption of landed possessions, or the depriving any one, without compensation, of any thing which the law gives him. But we say, that, when the State allows any one

[17]*Second Lay Sermon.*
[18]*Second Lay Sermon.*

to exercise ownership over more land than suffices to raise by his own labor his subsistence and that of his family, it confers on him power over other human beings,—power affecting them in their most vital interests; and that no notion of private property can bar the right which the State inherently possesses, to require that the power which it has so given shall not be abused. We say also, that, by giving this direct power over so large a portion of the community, indirect power is necessarily conferred over all the remaining portion; and this, too, it is the duty of the State to place under proper control. Further, the tenure of land, the various rights connected with it, and the system on which its cultivation is carried on, are points of the utmost importance both to the economical and to the moral well-being of the whole community. And the State fails in one of its highest obligations, unless it takes these points under its particular superintendence; unless, to the full extent of its power, it takes means of providing that the manner in which land is held, the mode and degree of its division, and every other peculiarity which influences the mode of its cultivation, shall be the most favorable possible for making the best use of the land, for drawing the greatest benefit from its productive resources, for securing the happiest existence to those employed on it, and for setting the greatest number of hands free to employ their labor for the benefit of the community in other ways. We believe that these opinions will become, in no very long period, universal throughout Europe; and we gratefully bear testimony to the fact, that the first among us who has given the sanction of philosophy to so great a reform in the popular and current notions is a Conservative philosopher.

Of Coleridge as a moral and religious philosopher (the character which he presents most prominently in his principal works), there is neither room, nor would it be expedient for us, to speak more than generally. On both subjects, few men have ever combined so much earnestness with so catholic and unsectarian a spirit. "We have imprisoned," says he, "our own conceptions by the lines which we have drawn in order to exclude the conceptions of others. *J'ai trouvé que la plupart des sectes ont raison dans une bonne partie de ce qu'elles avancent, mais non pas tant en ce qu'elles nient.*"[19] That almost all sects, both in philosophy and religion, are right in the posi-

---

[19]*Biographia Literaria.*

tive part of their tenets, though commonly wrong in the negative, is a doctrine which he professes as strongly as the eclectic
school in France. Almost all errors he holds to be "truths misunderstood," "half-truths taken as the whole," though not
the less, but the more, dangerous on that account.[20] Both the
theory and practice of enlightened tolerance, in matters of
opinion, might be exhibited in extracts from his writings, more
copiously than in those of any other writer we know; though
there are a few (and but a few) exceptions to his own practice of it. In the theory of ethics, he contends against the doctrine of general consequences, and holds, that *for man* "to
obey the simple unconditional commandment of eschewing
every act that implies a self-contradiction;" so to act as to "be
able, without involving any contradiction, to will that the
maxim of thy conduct should be the law of all intelligent beings,—is the one universal and sufficient principle and guide
of morality."[21] Yet even a utilitarian can have little complaint
to make of a philosopher who lays it down that "the *outward*
object of virtue" is "the greatest producible sum of happiness
of all men," and that "happiness in its proper sense is but the
continuity and sum-total of the pleasure which is allotted or
happens to a man."[22]

But his greatest object was to bring into harmony religion
and philosophy. He labored incessantly to establish, that "the
Christian faith—in which," says he, "I include every article
of belief and doctrine professed by the first reformers in common"—is not only divine truth, but also "the perfection of
human intelligence."[23] All that Christianity has revealed,
philosophy, according to him, can prove, though there is much
which it could never have discovered: human reason, once
strengthened by Christianity, can evolve all the Christian doctrines from its own sources.[24] Moreover, "if infidelity is not to
overspread England as well as France,[25] the Scripture, and
every passage of Scripture, must be submitted to this test;
inasmuch as "the compatibility of á document with the conclusions of self-evident reason, and with the laws of conscience, is a condition *à priori* of any evidence adequate to the
proof of its having been revealed by God;" and this, he says,

[20]*Literary Remains.*
[21]*The Friend.*
[22]*Aids to Reflection.*
[23]Preface to the *Aids to Reflection.*
[24]*Literary Remains.*
[25]*Literary Remains.*

is no philosophical novelty, but a principle "clearly laid down both by Moses and St. Paul."[26] He thus goes quite as far as the Unitarians in making man's reason and moral feelings a test of revelation; but differs *toto cœlo* from them in their rejection of its mysteries, which he regards as the highest philosophic truths; and says, that "the Christian to whom, after a long profession of Christianity, the mysteries remain as much mysteries as before, is in the same state as a schoolboy with regard to his arithmetic; to whom the *facit* at the end of the examples in his ciphering-book is the whole ground for his assuming that such and such figures amount to so and so."

These opinions are not likely to be popular in the religious world, and Coleridge knew it: "I quite calculate,"[27] said he once, "on my being one day or other holden in worse repute by many Christians than the 'Unitarians' and even 'Infidels.' It must be undergone by every one who loves the truth, for its own sake, beyond all other things." For our part, we are not bound to defend him; and we must admit, that, in his attempt to arrive at theology by way of philosophy, we see much straining, and most frequently, as it appears to us, total failure. The question, however, is, not whether Coleridge's attempts are successful, but whether it is desirable or not that such attempts should be made. Whatever some religious people may think, philosophy will and must go on, ever seeking to understand whatever can be made understandable; and, whatever some philosophers may think, there is little prospect at present that philosophy will take the place of religion, or that any philosophy will be speedily received in this country, unless supposed not only to be consistent with, but even to yield collateral support to, Christianity. What is the use, then, of treating with contempt the idea of a religious philosophy? Religious philosophies are among the things to be looked for; and our main hope ought to be, that they may be such as fulfil the conditions of a philosophy,—the very foremost of which is unrestricted freedom of thought. There is no philosophy possible where fear of consequences is a stronger principle than love of truth; where speculation is paralyzed, either by the belief that conclusions honestly arrived at will be punished by a just and good Being with eternal damnation, or by seeing in every text of Scripture a foregone conclusion, with

[26]*Literary Remains.*
[27]*Table Talk.*

which the results of inquiry must, at any expense of sophistry and self-deception, be made to quadrate.

From both these withering influences, that have so often made the acutest intellects exhibit specimens of obliquity and imbecility in their theological speculations which have made them the pity of subsequent generations, Coleridge's mind was perfectly free. Faith—the faith which is placed among religious duties—was, in his view, a state of the will and of the affections, not of the understanding. Heresy, in "the literal sense and scriptural import of the word," is, according to him, "wilful error, or belief originating in some perversion of the will." He says, therefore, that there may be orthodox heretics, since indifference to truth may as well be shown on the right side of the question as on the wrong; and denounces, in strong language, the contrary doctrine of the "pseudo-Athanasius," who "interprets catholic faith by belief," an act of the understanding alone. The "true Lutheran doctrine," he says, is that "neither will truth, as a mere conviction of the understanding, save, nor error condemn. To love truth sincerely is spiritually to have truth; and an error becomes a personal error, not by its aberration from logic or history, but so far as the causes of such error are in the heart, or may be traced back to some antecedent unchristian wish or habit."[28] "The unmistakable passions of a factionary and a schismatic, the ostentatious display, the ambitious and dishonest arts, of a sect-founder, must be superinduced on the false doctrine before the heresy makes the man a heretic."[29]

Against the other terror, so fatal to the unshackled exercise of reason on the greatest questions, the view which Coleridge took of the authority of the Scriptures was a preservative. He drew the strongest distinction between the inspiration which he owned in the various writers, and an express dictation by the Almighty of every word they wrote. "The notion of the absolute truth and divinity of every syllable of the text of the books of the Old and New Testament as we have it," he again and again asserts to be unsupported by the Scripture itself; to be one of those superstitions in which "there is a heart of unbelief," to be, "if possible, still more extravagant" than the Papal infallibility; and declares that the very same arguments are used for both doctrines. God, he believes, informed the

[28]*Literary Remains.*
[29]*Literary Remains.*

minds of the writers with the truths he meant to reveal, and
left the rest to their human faculties. He pleaded most earnestly, says his nephew and editor, for this liberty of criticism
with respect to the Scriptures, as "the only middle path of
safety and peace between a godless disregard of the unique
and transcendent character of the Bible, taken generally, and
that scheme of interpretation, scarcely less adverse to the
pure spirit of Christian wisdom, which wildly arrays our faith
in opposition to our reason, and inculcates the sacrifice of
the latter to the former: for he threw up his hands in dismay
at the language of some of our modern divinity on this point;
as if a faith not founded on insight were aught else than a
specious name for wilful positiveness! as if the Father of lights
could require, or would accept, from the only one of his creatures whom he had endowed with reason, the sacrifice of
fools! . . . Of the aweless doctrine, that God might, if he had
so pleased, have given to man a religion which to human intelligence should not be rational, and exacted his faith in it,
Coleridge's whole middle and later life was one deep and
solemn denial. He bewails "bibliolatry" as the pervading error of modern Protestant divinity, and the great stumbling-
block of Christianity; and exclaims,[30] "Oh! might I live but to
utter all my meditations on this most concerning point, . . . in
what sense the Bible may be called the word of God, and how
and under what conditions the unity of the Spirit is translucent
through the letter, which, read as the letter merely, is the
word of this and that pious but fallible and imperfect man."
It is known that he did live to write down these meditations;
and speculations so important will one day, it is devoutly to
be hoped, be given to the world.[31]

Theological discussion is beyond our province; and it is
not for us, in this place, to judge these sentiments of Coleridge:
but it is clear enough that they are not the sentiments of a
bigot, or of one who is to be dreaded by Liberals, lest he
should illiberalize the minds of the rising generation of Tories
and High-Churchmen. We think the danger is, rather, lest
they should find him vastly too liberal. And yet, now, when
the most orthodox divines, both in the Church and out of it,
find it necessary to explain away the obvious sense of the whole

[30]*Literary Remains*
[31]This wish has, to a certain extent, been fulfilled by the publication of
the series of letters on the Inspiration of the Scriptures, which bears the not
very appropriate name of "Confessions of an Inquiring Spirit."

first chapter of Genesis, or, failing to do that, consent to disbelieve it provisionally, on the speculation that there may hereafter be discovered a sense in which it can be believed, one would think the time gone by for expecting to learn from the Bible what it never could have been intended to communicate, and to find in all its statements a literal truth, neither necessary nor conducive to what the volume itself declares to be the ends of revelation. Such, at least, was Coleridge's opinion; and, whatever influence such an opinion may have over Conservatives, it cannot do other than make them less bigots, and better philosophers.

But we must close this long essay,—long in itself, though short in its relation to its subject, and to the multitude of topics involved in it. We do not pretend to have given any sufficient account of Coleridge; but we hope we may have proved to some, not previously aware of it, that there is something, both in him and in the school to which he belongs, not unworthy of their better knowledge. We may have done something to show, that a Tory philosopher cannot be wholly a Tory, but must often be a better Liberal than Liberals themselves; while he is the natural means of rescuing from oblivion truths which Tories have forgotten, and which the prevailing schools of Liberalism never knew.

And, even if a Conservative philosophy were an absurdity, it is well calculated to drive out a hundred absurdities worse than itself. Let no one think that it is nothing to accustom people to give a reason for their opinion, be the opinion ever so untenable, the reason ever so insufficient. A person accustomed to submit his fundamental tenets to the test of reason will be more open to the dictates of reason on every other point. Not from him shall we have to apprehend the owl-like dread of light, the drudge-like aversion to change, which were the characteristics of the old unreasoning race of bigots. A man accustomed to contemplate the fair side of Toryism (the side that every attempt at a philosophy of it must bring to view), and to defend the existing system by the display of its capabilities as an engine of public good,—such a man, when he comes to administer the system, will be more anxious than another person to realize those capabilities, to bring the fact a little nearer to the specious theory. "Lord, enlighten thou our enemies," should be the prayer of every true reformer; sharpen their wits, give acuteness to their perceptions, and consecutiveness and clearness to their reasoning powers. We are in danger from their folly, not from their wisdom: their weakness is what fills us with apprehension, not their strength.

For ourselves, we are not so blinded by our particular opinions as to be ignorant that in this, and every other country of Europe, the great mass of the owners of large property, and of all the classes intimately connected with the owners of large property, are, and must be expected to be, in the main, Conservative. To suppose that so mighty a body can be without immense influence in the commonwealth, or to lay plans for effecting great changes, either spiritual or temporal, in which they are left out of the question, would be the height of absurdity. Let those who desire such changes ask themselves if they are content that these classes should be, and remain, to a man, banded against them; and what progress they expect to make, or by what means, unless a process of preparation shall be going on in the minds of these very classes, not by the impracticable method of converting them from Conservatives into Liberals, but by their being led to adopt one liberal opinion after another as a part of Conservatism itself. The first step to this is to inspire them with the desire to systematize and rationalize their own actual creed: and the feeblest attempt to do this has an intrinsic value; far more, then, one which has so much in it, both of moral goodness and true insight, as the philosophy of Coleridge.

On Liberty

CHAPTER I

INTRODUCTORY

THE SUBJECT of this Essay is not the so-called Liberty of the Will, so unfortunately opposed to the misnamed doctrine of Philosophical Necessity; but Civil, or Social Liberty: the nature and limits of the power which can be legitimately exercised by society over the individual. A question seldom stated, and hardly ever discussed, in general terms, but which profoundly influences the practical controversies of the age by its latent presence, and is likely soon to make itself recognized as the vital question of the future. It is so far from being new, that, in a certain sense, it has divided mankind, almost from the remotest ages, but in the stage of progress into which the more civilized portions of the species have now entered, it presents itself under new conditions, and requires a different and more fundamental treatment.

The struggle between Liberty and Authority is the most conspicuous feature in the portions of history with which we are earliest familiar, particularly in that of Greece, Rome, and England. But in old times this contest was between subjects, or some classes of subjects, and the government. By liberty, was meant protection against the tyranny of the political rulers. The rulers were conceived (except in some of the popular governments of Greece) as in a necessarily antagonistic position to the people whom they ruled. They consisted of a governing One, or a governing tribe or caste, who derived their authority from inheritance or conquest; who, at all events, did not hold it at the pleasure of the governed, and whose supremacy men did not venture, perhaps did not desire, to contest, whatever precautions might be taken against its oppressive exercise. Their power was regarded as necessary, but also as highly dangerous; as a weapon which they would attempt to use against their subjects, no less than

127

against external enemies. To prevent the weaker members of the community from being preyed upon by innumerable vultures, it was needful that there should be an animal of prey stronger than the rest, commissioned to keep them down. But as the king of the vultures would be no less bent upon preying on the flock than any of the minor harpies, it was indispensable to be in a perpetual attitude of defence against his beak and claws. The aim, therefore, of patriots, was to set limits to the power which the ruler should be suffered to exercise over the community; and this limitation was what they meant by liberty. It was attempted in two ways. First, by obtaining a recognition of certain immunities, called political liberties or rights, which it was to be regarded as a breach of duty in the ruler to infringe, and which, if he did infringe, specific resistance, or general rebellion, was held to be justifiable. A second, and generally a later expedient, was the establishment of constitutional checks; by which the consent of the community, or of a body of some sort supposed to represent its interests, was made a necessary condition to some of the more important acts of the governing power. To the first of these modes of limitation, the ruling power, in most European countries, was compelled, more or less, to submit. It was not so with the second; and to attain this, or when already in some degree possessed, to attain it more completely, became everywhere the principal object of the lovers of liberty. And so long as mankind were content to combat one enemy by another, and to be ruled by a master, on condition of being guaranteed more or less efficaciously against his tyranny, they did not carry their aspirations beyond this point.

A time, however, came, in the progress of human affairs, when men ceased to think it a necessity of nature that their governors should be an independent power, opposed in interest to themselves. It appeared to them much better that the various magistrates of the State should be their tenants or delegates, revocable at their pleasure. In that way alone, it seemed, could they have complete security that the powers of government would never be abused to their disadvantage. By degrees, this new demand for elective and temporary rulers became the prominent object of the exertions of the popular party, wherever any such party existed; and superseded, to a considerable extent, the previous efforts to limit the power of rulers. As the struggle proceeded for making the ruling power emanate from the periodical choice of the ruled, some persons began to think that too much importance had been attached to the limitation of the power itself. *That* (it might seem) was a resource against rulers whose interests were habitually opposed to those of the people. What was now wanted was, that the rulers should be identified with the people; that their interest and will should be the interest and will of the nation. The nation did not need to be protected against its own will. There was no fear of its tyrannizing over itself. Let the rulers be effectually responsible to it, promptly removable by it, and it could afford to trust them with power of which it could itself dictate the use to be made. Their power was but the nation's own power, concentrated, and in a form convenient for exercise. This mode of thought, or rather perhaps of feeling, was common among the last generation of European liberalism, in the Continental section of which, it still apparently predominates. Those who admit any limit to what a government may do, except in the case of such governments as they think ought not to exist, stand out as brilliant exceptions among the political thinkers of the Continent. A similar tone of sentiment might by this time have been prevalent in our own country, if the circumstances which for a time encouraged it had continued unaltered.

But, in political and philosophical theories, as well as in persons, success discloses faults and infirmities which failure might have concealed from observation. The notion, that the people have no need to limit their power over themselves, might seem axiomatic, when popular government was a thing only dreamed about, or read of as having existed at some distant period of the past. Neither was that notion necessarily disturbed by such temporary aberrations as those of the French Revolution, the worst of which were the work of an usurping few, and which, in any case, belonged, not to the permanent working of popular institutions, but to a sudden and convulsive outbreak against monarchical and aristocratic despotism. In time, however, a democratic republic came to occupy a large portion of the earth's surface, and made itself felt as one of the most powerful members of the community of nations; and elective and responsible government became subject to the observations and criticisms which wait upon a great existing fact. It was now perceived that such phrases as "self-government," and "the power of the people over themselves," do not express the true state of the case. The "people" who exercise the power, are not always the same people with those over whom it is exercised, and the "self-government" spoken of, is not the government of each by himself, but of each by all the rest. The will of the people, moreover, practically means, the will of the most numerous or the most active *part* of the people; the majority, or those who succeed in making themselves accepted as the majority: the people, consequently, *may* desire to oppress a part of their number; and precautions are as much needed against this, as against any other abuse of power. The limitation, therefore, of the power of government over individuals, loses none of its importance when the holders of power are regularly accountable to the community, that is, to the strongest party therein. This view of things, recommending itself equally to the intelligence of thinkers and to the inclination of those important classes in European society to whose real or supposed interests democracy is adverse, has had no difficulty in establishing itself; and in political speculations "the tyranny of the majority" is now generally included among the evils against which society requires to be on its guard.

Like other tyrannies, the tyranny of the majority was at first, and is still vulgarly, held in dread, chiefly as operating through the acts of the public authorities. But reflecting persons perceived that when society is itself the tyrant—society collectively, over the separate individuals who compose it—its means of tyrannizing are not restricted to the acts which it may do by the hands of its political functionaries. Society can and does execute its own mandates: and if it issues wrong mandates instead of right, or any mandates at all in things with which it ought not to meddle, it practises a social tyranny more formidable than many kinds of political oppression, since, though not usually upheld by such extreme penalties, it leaves fewer means of escape, penetrating much more deeply into the details of life, and enslaving the soul itself. Protection, therefore, against the tyranny of the magistrate is not enough; there needs protection also against the tyranny of the prevailing opinion and feeling; against the tendency of society to impose, by other means than civil penalties, its own ideas and practices as rules of conduct on those who dissent from them; to fetter the development, and, if possible, prevent the formation, of any individuality not in harmony with its ways, and compel all characters to fashion themselves upon the model of its own. There is a limit to the legitimate interference of collective opinion with individual independence; and to find that limit, and maintain it against encroachment, is as indispensable to a good condition of human affairs, as protection against political despotism.

But though this proposition is not likely to be contested in general terms, the practical question, where to place the limit—how to make the fitting adjustment between individual independence and social control—is a subject on which nearly everything remains to be done. All that makes existence valuable to any one, depends on the enforcement of restraints upon the actions of other people. Some rules of conduct, therefore, must be imposed, by law in the first place, and by opinion on many things which are not fit subjects for the operation of law. What these rules should be, is the principal question in human affairs; but if we except a few of the most obvious cases, it is one of those which least progress has been made in resolving. No two ages, and scarcely any two countries, have decided it alike; and the decision of one age or country is a wonder to another. Yet the people of any given age and country no more suspect any difficulty in it, than if it were a subject on which mankind had always been agreed. The rules which obtain among themselves appear to them self-evident and self-justifying. This all but universal illusion is one of the examples of the magical influence of custom, which is not only, as the proverb says, a second nature, but is continually mistaken for the first. The effect of custom, in preventing any misgiving respecting the rules of conduct which mankind impose on one another, is all the more complete because the subject is one on which it is not generally considered necessary that reasons should be given, either by one person to others, or by each to himself. People are accustomed to believe, and have been encouraged in the belief by some who aspire to the character of philosophers, that their feelings, on subjects of this nature, are better than reasons, and render reasons unnecessary. The practical principle which guides them to their opinions on the regulation of human conduct, is the feeling in each person's mind that everybody should be required to act as he, and those with whom he sympathizes, would like them to act. No one, indeed, acknowledges to himself that his standard of judgment is his own liking; but an opinion on a point of conduct, not supported by reasons, can only count as one person's preference; and if the reasons, when given, are a mere appeal to a similar preference felt by other people, it is still only many people's liking instead of one. To an ordinary man, however, his own preference, thus supported, is not only a perfectly satisfactory reason, but the only one he generally has for any of his notions of morality, taste, or propriety, which are not expressly written in his religious creed; and his chief guide in the interpretation even of that. Men's opinions, accordingly, on what is laudable or blameable, are affected by all the multifarious causes which influence their wishes in regard to the conduct of others, and which are as numerous as those which determine their wishes on any other subject. Sometimes their reason—at other times their prejudices or superstitions: often their social affections, not seldom their antisocial ones, their envy or jealousy, their arrogance or contemptuousness: but most commonly, their desires or fears for themselves—their legitimate or illegitimate self-interest. Whenever there is an ascendant class, a large portion of the morality of the country emanates from its class interests, and its feelings of class superiority. The morality between Spartans and Helots, between planters and negroes, between princes and subjects, between nobles and roturiers, between men and women, has been for the most part the creation of these class interests and feelings: and the sentiments thus generated, react in turn upon the moral feelings of the members of the ascendant class, in their relations among themselves. Where, on the other hand, a class, formerly ascendant, has lost its ascendency, or where its ascendency is unpopular, the prevailing moral sentiments frequently bear the impress of an impatient dislike of superiority. Another grand determining principle of the rules of conduct, both in act and forbearance which have been enforced by law or opinion, has been the servility of mankind towards the supposed preferences or aversions of their temporal masters, or of their gods. This servility, though essentially selfish, is not hypocrisy; it gives rise to perfectly genuine sentiments of abhorrence; it made men burn magicians and heretics. Among so many baser influences, the general and obvious interests of society have of course had a share, and a large one, in the direction of the moral sentiments: less, however, as a matter of reason, and on their own account, than as a consequence of the sympathies and antipathies which grew out of them: and sympathies and antipathies which had little or nothing to do with the interests of society, have made themselves felt in the establishment of moralities with quite as great force.

The likings and dislikings of society, or of some powerful portion of it, are thus the main thing which has practically determined the rules laid down for general observance, under the penalties of law or opinion. And in general, those who have been in advance of society in thought and feeling, have left this condition of things unassailed in principle, however they may have come into conflict with it in some of its details. They have occupied themselves rather in inquiring what things society ought to like or dislike, than in questioning whether its likings or dislikings should be a law to individuals. They preferred endeavoring to alter the feelings of mankind on the particular points on which they were themselves heretical, rather than make common cause in defence of freedom, with heretics generally. The only case in which the higher ground has been taken on principle and maintained with consistency, by any but an individual here and there, is that of religious belief: a case instructive in many ways, and not least so as forming a most striking instance of the fallibility of what is called the moral sense: for the *odium theologicum*, in a sincere bigot, is one of the most unequivocal cases of moral feeling. Those who first broke the yoke of what called itself the Universal Church, were in general as little willing to permit difference of religious opinion as that church itself. But when the heat of the conflict was over, without giving a complete victory to any party, and each church or sect was reduced to limit its hopes to retaining possession of the ground it already occupied; minorities, seeing that they had no chance of becoming majorities, were under the necessity of pleading to those whom they could not convert, for permission to differ. It is accordingly on this battle-field, almost solely, that the rights of the individual against society have been asserted on broad grounds of principle, and the claim of society to exercise authority over dissentients openly controverted. The great writers to whom the world owes what religious liberty it possesses, have mostly asserted freedom of conscience as an indefeasible right, and denied absolutely that a human being is accountable to others for his religious belief. Yet so natural to mankind is intolerance in whatever they really care about, that religious freedom has hardly anywhere been practically realized, except where religious indifference, which dislikes to have its peace disturbed by theological quarrels, has added its weight to the scale. In the minds of almost all religious persons, even in the most tolerant countries, the duty of toleration is admitted with tacit reserves. One person will bear with dissent in matters of church government, but not of dogma; another can tolerate everybody, short of a Papist or an Unitarian; another, every one who believes in revealed religion; a few extend their charity a little further, but stop at the belief in a God and in a future state. Wherever the sentiment of the majority is still genuine and intense, it is found to have abated little of its claim to be obeyed.

In England, from the peculiar circumstances of our political history, though the yoke of opinion is perhaps heavier, that of law is lighter, than in most other countries of Europe; and there is considerable jealousy of direct interference, by the legislative or the executive power with private conduct; not so much from any just regard for the independence of the individual, as from the still subsisting habit of looking on the government as representing an opposite interest to the public. The majority have not yet learnt to feel the power of the government their power, or its opinions their opinions. When they do so, individual liberty will probably be as much exposed to invasion from the government, as it already is from public opinion. But, as yet, there is a considerable amount of feeling ready to be called forth against any attempt of the law to control individuals in things in which they have not hitherto been accustomed to be controlled by it; and this with very little discrimination as to whether the matter is, or is not, within the legitimate sphere of legal control; insomuch that the feeling, highly salutary on the whole, is perhaps quite as often misplaced as well grounded in the particular instances of its application. There is, in fact, no recognized principle by which the propriety or impropriety of government interference is customarily tested. People decide according to their personal preferences. Some, whenever they see any good to be done, or evil to be remedied, would willingly instigate the government to undertake the business; while others prefer to bear almost any amount of social evil, rather than add one to the departments of human interests amenable to governmental control. And men range themselves on one or the other side in any particular case, according to this general direction of their sentiments; or according to the degree of interest which they feel in the particular thing which it is proposed that the government should do; or according to the belief they entertain that the government would, or would not, do it in the manner they prefer; but very rarely on account of any opinion to which they consistently adhere, as to what things are fit to be done by a government. And it seems to me that, in consequence of this absence of rule or principle, one side is at present as often wrong as the other; the interference of government is, with about equal frequency, improperly invoked and improperly condemned.

The object of this Essay is to assert one very simple principle, as entitled to govern absolutely the dealings of society with the individual in the way of compulsion and control, whether the means used be physical force in the form of legal penalties, or the moral coercion of public opinion. That principle is, that the sole end for which mankind are warranted, individually or collectively, in interfering with the liberty of action of any of their number, is self-protection. That the only purpose for which power can be rightfully exercised over any member of a civilized community, against his will, is to prevent harm to others. His own good, either physical or moral, is not a sufficient warrant. He cannot rightfully be compelled to do or forbear because it will be better for him to do so, because it will make him happier, because, in the opinions of others, to do so would be wise, or even right. These are good reasons for remonstrating with him, or reasoning with him, or persuading him or entreating him, but not for compelling him, or visiting him with any evil, in case he do otherwise. To justify that, the conduct from which it is desired to deter him must be calculated to produce evil to someone else. The only part of the conduct of any one, for which he is amenable to society, is that which concerns others. In the part which merely concerns himself, his independence is, of right, absolute. Over himself, over his own body and mind, the individual is sovereign.

It is, perhaps, hardly necessary to say that this doctrine is meant to apply only to human beings in the maturity of their faculties. We are not speaking of children, or of young persons below the age which the law may fix as that of manhood or womanhood. Those who are still in a state to require being taken care of by others, must be protected against their own actions as well as against external injury. For the same reason, we may leave out of consideration those backward states of society in which the race itself may be considered as in its nonage. The early difficulties in the way of spontaneous progress are so great, that there is seldom any choice of means for overcoming them; and a ruler full of the spirit of improvement is warranted in the use of any expedients that will attain an end, perhaps otherwise unattainable. Despotism is a legitimate mode of government in dealing with barbarians, provided the end be their improvement, and the means justified by actually effecting that end. Liberty, as a principle, has no application to any state of things anterior to the time when mankind have become capable of being improved by free and equal discussion. Until then, there is nothing for them but implicit obedience to an Akbar or a Charlemagne, if they are so fortunate as to find one. But as soon as mankind have attained the capacity of being guided to their own improvement by conviction or persuasion (a period long since reached in all nations with whom we need here concern ourselves), compulsion, either in the direct form or in that of pains and penalties for non-compliance, is no longer admissible as a means to their own good, and justifiable only for the security of others.

It is proper to state that I forego any advantage which could be derived to my argument from the idea of abstract right, as a thing independent of utility. I regard utility as the ultimate appeal on all ethical questions; but it must be utility in the largest sense, grounded on the permanent interests of man as a progressive being. Those interests, I contend, authorize the subjection of individual spontaneity to external control, only in respect to those actions of each, which concern the interest of other people. If any one does an act hurtful to others, there is a *primâ facie* case for punishing him, by law, or, where legal penalties are not safely applicable, by general disapprobation. There are also many positive acts for the benefit of others, which he may rightfully be compelled to perform; such as, to give evidence in a court of justice; to bear his fair share in the common defence, or in any other joint work necessary to the interest of the society of which he enjoys the protection; and to perform certain acts of individual beneficence, such as saving a fellow creature's life, or interposing to protect the defenceless against ill-usage, things which whenever it is obviously a man's duty to do, he may rightfully be made responsible to society for not doing. A person may cause evil to others not only by his actions but by his inaction, and in either case he is justly accountable to them for the injury. The latter case, it is true, requires a much more cautious exercise of compulsion than the former. To make any one answerable for doing evil to others, is the rule; to make him answerable for not preventing evil, is, comparatively speaking, the exception. Yet there are many cases clear enough and grave enough to justify that exception. In all things which regard the external relations of the individual, he is *de jure* amenable to those whose interests are concerned, and if need be, to society as their protector. There are often good reasons for not holding him to the responsibility; but these reasons must arise from the special expediencies of the case: either because it is a kind of case in which he is on the whole likely to act better, when left to his own discretion, than when controlled in any way in which society have it in their power to control him; or because the attempt to exercise control would produce other evils, greater than those which it would prevent. When such reasons as these preclude the enforcement of responsibility, the conscience of the agent himself should step into the vacant judgment-seat, and protect those interests of others which have no external protection; judging himself all the more rigidly, because the case does not admit of his being made accountable to the judgment of his fellow-creatures.

But there is a sphere of action in which society, as distinguished from the individual, has, if any, only an indirect interest; comprehending all that portion of a person's life and conduct which affects only himself, or, if it also affects others, only with their free, voluntary, and undeceived consent and participation. When I say only himself, I mean directly, and in the first instance: for whatever affects himself, may affect others *through* himself; and the objection which may be grounded on this contingency, will receive consideration in the sequel. This, then, is the appropriate region of human liberty. It comprises, first, the inward domain of consciousness; demanding liberty of conscience, in the most comprehensive sense; liberty of thought and feeling; absolute freedom of opinion and sentiment on all subjects, practical or speculative, scientific, moral, or theological. The liberty of expressing and publishing opinions may seem to fall under a different principle, since it belongs to that part of the conduct of an individual which concerns other people; but, being almost of as much importance as the liberty of thought itself, and resting in great part on the same reasons, is practically inseparable from it. Secondly, the principle requires liberty of tastes and pursuits; of framing the plan of our life to suit our own character; of doing as we like, subject to such consequences as may follow; without impediment from our fellow-creatures, so long as what we do does not harm them, even though they should think our conduct foolish, perverse, or wrong. Thirdly, from this liberty of each individual, follows the liberty, within the same limits, of combination among individuals; freedom to unite, for any purpose not involving harm to others: the persons combining being supposed to be of full age, and not forced or deceived.

No society in which these liberties are not, on the whole, respected, is free, whatever may be its form of government; and none is completely free in which they do not exist absolute and unqualified. The only freedom which deserves the name, is that of pursuing our own good in our own way, so long as we do not attempt to deprive others of theirs, or impede their efforts to obtain it. Each is the proper guardian of his own health, whether bodily, or mental and spiritual. Mankind are greater gainers by suffering each other to live as seems good to themselves, than by compelling each to live as seems good to the rest.

Though this doctrine is anything but new, and, to some persons, may have the air of a truism, there is no doctrine which stands more directly opposed to the general tendency of existing opinion and practice. Society has expended fully as much effort in the attempt (according to its lights) to compel people to conform to its notions of personal, as of social excellence. The ancient commonwealths thought themselves entitled to practise, and the ancient philosophers countenanced, the regulation of every part of private conduct by public authority, on the ground that the State had a deep interest in the whole bodily and mental discipline of every one of its citizens; a mode of thinking which may have been admissible in small republics surrounded by powerful enemies, in constant peril of being subverted by foreign attack or internal commotion, and to which even a short interval of relaxed energy and self-command might so easily be fatal, that they could not afford to wait for the salutary permanent effects of freedom. In the modern world, the greater size of political communities, and above all, the separation between the spiritual and temporal authority (which placed the direction of men's consciences in other hands than those which controlled their worldly affairs), prevented so great an interference by law in the details of private life; but the engines of moral repression have been wielded more strenuously against divergence from the reigning opinion in self-regarding, than even in social matters; religion, the most powerful of the elements which have entered into the formation of moral feeling, having almost always been governed either by the ambition of a hierarchy, seeking control over every department of human conduct, or by the spirit of Puritanism. And some of those modern reformers who have placed themselves in strongest opposition to the religions of the past, have been noway behind either churches or sects in their assertion of the right of spiritual domination: M. Comte, in particular, whose social system, as unfolded in his *Traité de Politique Positive*, aims at establishing (though by moral more than by legal appliances) a despotism of society over the individual, surpassing anything contemplated in the political ideal of the most rigid disciplinarian among the ancient philosophers.

Apart from the peculiar tenets of individual thinkers, there is also in the world at large an increasing inclination to stretch unduly the powers of society over the individual, both by the force of opinion and even by that of legislation: and as the tendency of all the changes taking place in the world is to strengthen society, and diminish the power of the individual, this encroachment is not one of the evils which tend spontaneously to disappear, but, on the contrary, to grow more and more formidable. The disposition of mankind, whether as rulers, or as fellow-citizens, to impose their own opinions and inclinations as a rule of conduct on others, is so energetically supported by some of the best and by some of the worst feelings incident to human nature, that it is hardly ever kept under restraint by anything but want of power; and as the power is not declining, but growing, unless a strong barrier of moral conviction can be raised against the mischief, we must expect, in the present circumstances of the world, to see it increase.

It will be convenient for the argument, if, instead of at once entering upon the general thesis, we confine ourselves in the first instance to a single branch of it, on which the principle here stated is, if not fully, yet to a certain point, recognized by the current opinions. This one branch is the Liberty of Thought: from which it is impossible to separate the cognate liberty of speaking and of writing. Although these liberties, to some considerable amount, form part of the political morality of all countries which profess religious toleration and free institutions, the grounds, both philosophical and practical, on which they rest, are perhaps not so familiar to the general mind, nor so thoroughly appreciated by many even of the leaders of opinion, as might have been expected. Those grounds, when rightly understood, are of much wider application than to only one division of the subject, and a thorough consideration of this part of the question will be found the best introduction to the remainder. Those to whom nothing which I am about to say will be new, may therefore, I hope, excuse me, if on a subject which for now three centuries has been so often discussed, I venture on one discussion more.

CHAPTER II

OF THE LIBERTY OF THOUGHT AND DISCUSSION

THE TIME, it is to be hoped, is gone by when any defence would be necessary of the "liberty of the press" as one of the securities against corrupt or tyrannical government. No argument, we may suppose, can now be needed, against permitting a legislature or an executive, not identified in interest with the people, to prescribe opinions to them, and determine what doctrines or what arguments they shall be allowed to hear. This aspect of the question, besides, has been so often and so triumphantly enforced by preceding writers, that it needs not be specially insisted on in this place. Though the law of England, on the subject of the press, is as servile to this day as it was in the time of the Tudors, there is little danger of its being actually put in force against political discussion, except during some temporary panic, when fear of insurrection drives ministers and judges from their propriety;[1] and, speaking generally, it is not, in constitutional

---

[1] These words had scarcely been written, when, as if to give them an emphatic contradiction, occurred the Government Press Prosecutions of 1858. That ill-judged interference with the liberty of public discussion has not, however, induced me to alter a single word in the text, nor has it at all weakened my conviction that, moments of panic excepted, the era of pains and penalties for political discussion has, in our own country, passed away. For, in the first place, the prosecutions were not persisted in; and, in the second, they were never, properly speaking, political prosecutions. The offence charged was not that of criticizing institutions, or the acts or persons of rulers, but of circulating what was deemed an immoral doctrine, the lawfulness of Tyrannicide.

If the arguments of the present chapter are of any validity, there ought to exist the fullest liberty of professing and discussing, as a matter of ethical conviction, any doctrine, however immoral it may be considered. It would, therefore, be irrelevant and out of place to examine here, whether the doctrine of Tyrannicide deserves that title. I shall content myself with saying, that the subject has been at all times one of the open questions of morals; that the act of a private citizen in striking down a criminal, who, by raising himself above the law, has placed himself beyond the reach of legal punishment or control, has been accounted by whole nations, and by some of the best and wisest of men, not a crime, but an act of exalted virtue; and that, right or wrong, it is not of the nature of assassination, but of civil war. As such, I hold that the instigation to it, in a specific case, may be a proper subject of punishment, but only if an overt act has followed, and at least a probable connection can be established between the act and the instigation. Even then, it is not a foreign government, but the very government assailed, which alone, in the exercise of self-defence, can legitimately punish attacks directed against its own existence.

countries, to be apprehended, that the government, whether completely responsible to the people or not, will often attempt to control the expression of opinion, except when in doing so it makes itself the organ of the general intolerance of the public. Let us suppose, therefore, that the government is entirely at one with the people, and never thinks of exerting any power of coercion unless in agreement with what it conceives to be their voice. But I deny the right of the people to exercise such coercion, either by themselves or by their government. The power itself is illegitimate. The best government has no more title to it than the worst. It is as noxious, or more noxious, when exerted in accordance with public opinion, than when in opposition to it. If all mankind minus one, were of one opinion, and only one person were of the contrary opinion, mankind would be no more justified in silencing that one person, than he, if he had the power, would be justified in silencing mankind. Were an opinion a personal possession of no value except to the owner; if to be obstructed in the enjoyment of it were simply a private injury, it would make some difference whether the injury was inflicted only on a few persons or on many. But the peculiar evil of silencing the expression of an opinion is, that it is robbing the human race; posterity as well as the existing generation; those who dissent from the opinion, still more than those who hold it. If the opinion is right, they are deprived of the opportunity of exchanging error for truth: if wrong, they lose, what is almost as great a benefit, the clearer perception and livelier impression of truth, produced by its collision with error.

It is necessary to consider separately these two hypotheses, each of which has a distinct branch of the argument corresponding to it. We can never be sure that the opinion we are endeavoring to stifle is a false opinion; and if we were sure, stifling it would be an evil still.

First: the opinion which it is attempted to suppress by authority may possibly be true. Those who desire to suppress it, of course deny its truth; but they are not infallible. They have no authority to decide the question for all mankind, and exclude every other person from the means of judging. To refuse a hearing to an opinion, because they are sure that it is false, is to assume that *their* certainty is the same thing as *absolute* certainty. All silencing of discussion is an assumption of infallibility. Its condemnation may be allowed to rest on this common argument, not the worse for being common.

Unfortunately for the good sense of mankind, the fact of their fallibility is far from carrying the weight in their practical judgment, which is always allowed to it in theory; for while every one well knows himself to be fallible, few think it necessary to take any precautions against their own fallibility, or admit the supposition that any opinion, of which they feel very certain, may be one of the examples of the error to which they acknowledge themselves to be liable. Absolute princes, or others who are accustomed to unlimited deference, usually feel this complete confidence in their own opinions on nearly all subjects. People more happily situated, who sometimes hear their opinions disputed, and are not wholly unused to be set right when they are wrong, place the same unbounded reliance only on such of their opinions as are shared by all who surround them, or to whom they habitually defer: for in proportion to a man's want of confidence in his own solitary judgment, does he usually repose, with implicit trust, on the infallibility of "the world" in general. And the world, to each individual, means the part of it with which he comes in contact; his party, his sect, his church, his class of society: the man may be called, by comparison, almost liberal and large-minded to whom it means anything so comprehensive as his own country or his own age. Nor is his faith in this collective authority at all shaken by his being aware that other ages, countries, sects, churches, classes, and parties have thought, and even now think, the exact reverse. He devolves upon his own world the responsibility of being in the right against the dissentient worlds of other people; and it never troubles him that mere accident has decided which of these numerous worlds is the object of his reliance, and that the same causes which make him a Churchman in London, would have made him a Buddhist or a Confucian in Pekin. Yet it is as evident in itself, as any amount of argument can make it, that ages are no more infallible than individuals; every age having held many opinions which subsequent ages have deemed not only false but absurd; and it is as certain that many opinions, now general, will be rejected by future ages, as it is that many, once general, are rejected by the present.

The objection likely to be made to this argument, would

probably take some such form as the following. There is no greater assumption of infallibility in forbidding the propagation of error, than in any other thing which is done by public authority on its own judgment and responsibility. Judgment is given to men that they may use it. Because it may be used erroneously, are men to be told that they ought not to use it at all? To prohibit what they think pernicious, is not claiming exemption from error, but fulfilling the duty incumbent on them, although fallible, of acting on their conscientious conviction. If we were never to act on our opinions, because those opinions may be wrong, we should leave all our interests uncared for, and all our duties unperformed. An objection which applies to all conduct, can be no valid objection to any conduct in particular. It is the duty of governments, and of individuals, to form the truest opinions they can; to form them carefully, and never impose them upon others unless they are quite sure of being right. But when they are sure (such reasoners may say), it is not conscientiousness but cowardice to shrink from acting on their opinions, and allow doctrines which they honestly think dangerous to the welfare of mankind, either in this life or in another, to be scattered abroad without restraint, because other people, in less enlightened times, have persecuted opinions now believed to be true. Let us take care, it may be said, not to make the same mistake: but governments and nations have made mistakes in other things, which are not denied to be fit subjects for the exercise of authority: they have laid on bad taxes, made unjust wars. Ought we therefore to lay on no taxes, and, under whatever provocation, make no wars? Men, and governments, must act to the best of their ability. There is no such thing as absolute certainty, but there is assurance sufficient for the purposes of human life. We may, and must, assume our opinion to be true for the guidance of our own conduct: and it is assuming no more when we forbid bad men to pervert society by the propagation of opinions which we regard as false and pernicious.

I answer, that it is assuming very much more. There is the greatest difference between presuming an opinion to be true, because, with every opportunity for contesting it, it has not been refuted, and assuming its truth for the purpose of not permitting its refutation. Complete liberty of contradicting and disproving our opinion, is the very condition which justifies us in assuming its truth for purposes of action; and on no other terms can a being with human faculties have any rational assurance of being right.

When we consider either the history of opinion, or the ordinary conduct of human life, to what is it to be ascribed that the one and the other are no worse than they are? Not certainly to the inherent force of the human understanding; for, on any matter not self-evident, there are ninety-nine persons totally incapable of judging of it, for one who is capable; and the capacity of the hundredth person is only comparative; for the majority of the eminent men of every past generation held many opinions now known to be erroneous, and did or approved numerous things which no one will now justify. Why is it, then, that there is on the whole a preponderance among mankind of rational opinions and rational conduct? If there really is this preponderance—which there must be, unless human affairs are, and have always been, in an almost desperate state—it is owing to a quality of the human mind, the source of everything respectable in man either as an intellectual or as a moral being, namely, that his errors are corrigible. He is capable of rectifying his mistakes, by discussion and experience. Not by experience alone. There must be discussion, to show how experience is to be interpreted. Wrong opinions and practices gradually yield to fact and argument: but facts and arguments, to produce any effect on the mind, must be brought before it. Very few facts are able to tell their own story, without comments to bring out their meaning. The whole strength and value, then, of human judgment, depending on the one property, that it can be set right when it is wrong, reliance can be placed on it only when the means of setting it right are kept constantly at hand. In the case of any person whose judgment is really deserving of confidence, how has it become so? Because he has kept his mind open to criticism of his opinions and conduct. Because it has been his practice to listen to all that could be said against him; to profit by as much of it as was just, and expound to himself, and upon occasion to others, the fallacy of what was fallacious. Because he has felt, that the only way in which a human being can make some approach to knowing the whole of a subject, is by hearing what can be said about it by persons of every variety of opinion, and studying all modes in which it can be looked at by every character of mind. No wise man ever acquired his wisdom in any mode but this; nor is it in the nature of human intellect to become wise in any other manner. The steady habit of correcting and completing his own opinion by collating it with those of others, so far from causing doubt and hesitation in carrying it into practice, is the only stable foundation for a just reliance on it: for, being cognizant of all that can, at least obviously, be said against him, and having taken up his position against all gainsayers knowing that he has sought for objections and difficulties, instead of avoiding them, and has shut out no light which can be thrown upon the subject from any quarter—he has a right to think his judgment better than that of any person, or any multitude, who have not gone through a similar process.

It is not too much to require that what the wisest of mankind, those who are best entitled to trust their own judgment, find necessary to warrant their relying on it, should be submitted to by that miscellaneous collection of a few wise and many foolish individuals, called the public. The most intolerant of churches, the Roman Catholic Church, even at the canonization of a saint, admits, and listens patiently to, a "devil's advocate." The holiest of men, it appears, cannot be admitted to posthumous honors, until all that the devil could say against him is known and weighed. If even the Newtonian philosophy were not permitted to be questioned, mankind could not feel as complete assurance of its truth as they now do. The beliefs which we have most warrant for, have no safeguard to rest on, but a standing invitation to the whole world to prove them unfounded. If the challenge is not accepted, or is accepted and the attempt fails, we are far enough from certainty still; but we have done the best that the existing state of human reason admits of; we have neglected nothing that could give the truth a chance of reaching us: if the lists are kept open, we may hope that if there be a better truth, it will be found when the human mind is capable of receiving it; and in the mean time we may rely on having attained such approach to truth, as is possible in our own day. This is the amount of certainty attainable by a fallible being, and this the sole way of attaining it.

Strange it is, that men should admit the validity of the arguments for free discussion, but object to their being "pushed to an extreme;" not seeing that unless the reasons are good for an extreme case, they are not good for any case.

Strange that they should imagine that they are not assuming infallibility, when they acknowledge that there should be free discussion on all subjects which can possibly be *doubtful,* but think that some particular principle or doctrine should be forbidden to be questioned because it is *so certain,* that is, because *they are certain* that it is certain. To call any proposition certain, while there is any one who would deny its certainty if permitted, but who is not permitted, is to assume that we ourselves, and those who agree with us, are the judges of certainty, and judges without hearing the other side.

In the present age—which has been described as "destitute of faith, but terrified at scepticism,"—in which people feel sure, not so much that their opinions are true, as that they should not know what to do without them—the claims of an opinion to be protected from public attack are rested not so much on its truth, as on its importance to society. There are, it is alleged, certain beliefs, so useful, not to say indispensable to well-being, that it is as much the duty of governments to uphold those beliefs, as to protect any other of the interests of society. In a case of such necessity, and so directly in the line of their duty, something less than infallibility may, it is maintained, warrant, and even bind, governments, to act on their own opinion, confirmed by the general opinion of mankind. It is also often argued, and still oftener thought, that none but bad men would desire to weaken these salutary beliefs; and there can be nothing wrong, it is thought, in restraining bad men, and prohibiting what only such men would wish to practise. This mode of thinking makes the justification of restraints on discussion not a question of the truth of doctrines, but of their usefulness; and flatters itself by that means to escape the responsibility of claiming to be an infallible judge of opinions. But those who thus satisfy themselves, do not perceive that the assumption of infallibility is merely shifted from one point to another. The usefulness of an opinion is itself matter of opinion: as disputable, as open to discussion and requiring discussion as much, as the opinion itself. There is the same need of an infallible judge of opinions to decide an opinion to be noxious, as to decide it to be false, unless the opinion condemned has full opportunity of defending itself. And it will not do to say that the heretic may be allowed to maintain the utility or harm-

lessness of his opinion, though forbidden to maintain its truth.
The truth of an opinion is part of its utility. If we would know
whether or not it is desirable that a proposition should be
believed, is it possible to exclude the consideration of whether
or not it is true? In the opinion, not of bad men, but of the
best men, no belief which is contrary to truth can be really
useful: and can you prevent such men from urging that plea,
when they are charged with culpability for denying some
doctrine which they are told is useful, but which they believe
to be false? Those who are on the side of received opinions,
never fail to take all possible advantage of this plea; you do
not find *them* handling the question of utility as if it could be
completely abstracted from that of truth: on the contrary, it
is, above all, because their doctrine is "the truth," that the
knowledge or the belief of it is held to be so indispensable.
There can be no fair discussion of the question of usefulness,
when an argument so vital may be employed on one side, but
not on the other. And in point of fact, when law or public
feeling do not permit the truth of an opinion to be disputed,
they are just as little tolerant of a denial of its usefulness. The
utmost they allow is an extenuation of its absolute necessity,
or of the positive guilt of rejecting it.

In order more fully to illustrate the mischief of denying a
hearing to opinions because we, in our own judgment, have
condemned them, it will be desirable to fix down the discussion to a concrete case; and I choose, by preference, the
cases which are least favorable to me—in which the argument
against freedom of opinion, both on the score of truth and
on that of utility, is considered the strongest. Let the opinions
impugned be the belief in a God and in a future state, or any
of the commonly received doctrines of morality. To fight the
battle on such ground, gives a great advantage to an unfair
antagonist; since he will be sure to say (and many who have
no desire to be unfair will say it internally), Are these the
doctrines which you do not deem sufficiently certain to be
taken under the protection of law? Is the belief in a God one
of the opinions, to feel sure of which, you hold to be assuming infallibility? But I must be permitted to observe, that it
is not the feeling sure of a doctrine (be it what it may) which
I call an assumption of infallibility. It is the undertaking to
decide that question *for others*, without allowing them to hear
what can be said on the contrary side. And I denounce and

reprobate this pretension not the less, if put forth on the side of my most solemn convictions. However positive any one's persuasion may be, not only of the falsity, but of the pernicious consequences—not only of the pernicious consequences, but (to adopt expressions which I altogether condemn) the immorality and impiety of an opinion; yet if, in pursuance of that private judgment, though backed by the public judgment of his country or his contemporaries, he prevents the opinion from being heard in its defence, he assumes infallibility. And so far from the assumption being less objectionable or less dangerous because the opinion is called immoral or impious, this is the case of all others in which it is most fatal. These are exactly the occasions on which the men of one generation commit those dreadful mistakes, which excite the astonishment and horror of posterity. It is among such that we find the instances memorable in history, when the arm of the law has been employed to root out the best men and the noblest doctrines; with deplorable success as to the men, though some of the doctrines have survived to be (as if in mockery) invoked, in defence of similar conduct towards those who dissent from *them*, or from their received interpretation.

Mankind can hardly be too often reminded, that there was once a man named Socrates, between whom and the legal authorities and public opinion of his time, there took place a memorable collision. Born in an age and country abounding in individual greatness, this man has been handed down to us by those who best knew both him and the age, as the most virtuous man in it; while *we* know him as the head and prototype of all subsequent teachers of virtue, the source equally of the lofty inspiration of Plato and the judicious utilitarianism of Aristotle, "*i maëstri di color che sanno*," the two headsprings of ethical as of all other philosophy. This acknowledged master of all the eminent thinkers who have since lived—whose fame, still growing after more than two thousand years, all but outweighs the whole remainder of the names which make his native city illustrious—was put to death by his countrymen, after a judicial conviction, for impiety and immorality. Impiety, in denying the gods recognized by the State; indeed his accuser asserted (see the "Apologia") that he believed in no gods at all. Immorality, in being, by his doctrines and instructions, a "corruptor of youth." Of these charges the tribunal, there is every ground for believing, honestly found him guilty, and condemned the man who probably of all then born had deserved best of mankind, to be put to death as a criminal.

To pass from this to the only other instance of judicial iniquity, the mention of which, after the condemnation of Socrates, would not be an anti-climax: the event which took place on Calvary rather more than eighteen hundred years ago. The man who left on the memory of those who witnessed his life and conversation, such an impression of his moral grandeur, that eighteen subsequent centuries have done homage to him as the Almighty in person, was ignominiously put to death, as what? As a blasphemer. Men did not merely mistake their benefactor; they mistook him for the exact contrary of what he was, and treated him as that prodigy of impiety, which they themselves are now held to be, for their treatment of him. The feelings with which mankind now regard these lamentable transactions, especially the later of the two, render them extremely unjust in their judgment of the unhappy actors. These were, to all appearance, not bad men—not worse than men commonly are, but rather the contrary; men who possessed in a full, or somewhat more than a full measure, the religious, moral, and patriotic feelings of their time and people: the very kind of men who, in all times, our own included, have every chance of passing through life blameless and respected. The high-priest who rent his garments when the words were pronounced, which, according to all the ideas of his country, constituted the blackest guilt, was in all probability quite as sincere in his horror and indignation, as the generality of respectable and pious men now are in the religious and moral sentiments they profess; and most of those who now shudder at his conduct, if they had lived in his time, and been born Jews, would have acted precisely as he did. Orthodox Christians who are tempted to think that those who stoned to death the first martyrs must have been worse men than they themselves are, ought to remember that one of those persecutors was Saint Paul.

Let us add one more example, the most striking of all, if the impressiveness of an error is measured by the wisdom and virtue of him who falls into it. If ever any one, possessed of power, had grounds for thinking himself the best and most enlightened among his contemporaries, it was the Emperor Marcus Aurelius. Absolute monarch of the whole civilized

world, he preserved through life not only the most unblemished justice, but what was less to be expected from his
Stoical breeding, the tenderest heart. The few failings which
are attributed to him, were all on the side of indulgence:
while his writings, the highest ethical product of the ancient
mind, differ scarcely perceptibly, if they differ at all, from
the most characteristic teachings of Christ. This man, a better
Christian in all but the dogmatic sense of the word, than
almost any of the ostensibly Christian sovereigns who have
since reigned, persecuted Christianity. Placed at the summit
of all the previous attainments of humanity, with an open,
unfettered intellect, and a character which led him of himself
to embody in his moral writings the Christian ideal, he yet
failed to see that Christianity was to be a good and not an evil
to the world, with his duties to which he was so deeply penetrated. Existing society he knew to be in a deplorable state.
But such as it was, he saw or thought he saw, that it was held
together and prevented from being worse, by belief and reverence of the received divinities. As a ruler of mankind, he
deemed it his duty not to suffer society to fall in pieces; and
saw not how, if its existing ties were removed, any others
could be formed which could again knit it together. The new
religion openly aimed at dissolving these ties: unless, therefore, it was his duty to adopt that religion, it seemed to be his
duty to put it down. Inasmuch then as the theology of Christianity did not appear to him true or of divine origin, inasmuch
as this strange history of a crucified God was not credible to
him, and a system which purported to rest entirely upon a
foundation to him so wholly unbelievable, could not be fore-
seen by him to be that renovating agency which, after all
abatements, it has in fact proved to be; the gentlest and most
amiable of philosophers and rulers, under a solemn sense of
duty, authorized the persecution of Christianity. To my mind
this is one of the most tragical facts in all history. It is a bitter
thought, how different a thing the Christianity of the world
might have been, if the Christian faith had been adopted
as the religion of the empire under the auspices of Marcus
Aurelius instead of those of Constantine. But it would be
equally unjust to him and false to truth, to deny, that no
one plea which can be urged for punishing anti-Christian
teaching, was wanting to Marcus Aurelius for punishing, as
he did, the propagation of Christianity. No Christian more

firmly believes that Atheism is false, and tends to the dissolution of society, than Marcus Aurelius believed the same things of Christianity; he who, of all men then living, might have been thought the most capable of appreciating it. Unless any one who approves of punishment for the promulgation of opinions, flatters himself that he is a wiser and better man than Marcus Aurelius—more deeply versed in the wisdom of his time, more elevated in his intellect above it—more earnest in his search for truth, or more singleminded in his devotion to it when found;—let him abstain from that assumption of the joint infallibility of himself and the multitude, which the great Antoninus made with so unfortunate a result.

Aware of the impossibility of defending the use of punishment for restraining irreligious opinions, by any argument which will not justify Marcus Antoninus, the enemies of religious freedom, when hard pressed, occasionally accept this consequence, and say, with Dr. Johnson, that the persecutors of Christianity were in the right; that persecution is an ordeal through which truth ought to pass, and always passes successfully, legal penalties being, in the end, powerless against truth, though sometimes beneficially effective against mischievous errors. This is a form of the argument for religious intolerance, sufficiently remarkable not to be passed without notice.

A theory which maintains that truth may justifiably be persecuted because persecution cannot possibly do it any harm, cannot be charged with being intentionally hostile to the reception of new truths; but we cannot commend the generosity of its dealing with the persons to whom mankind are indebted for them. To discover to the world something which deeply concerns it, and of which it was previously ignorant; to prove to it that it had been mistaken on some vital point of temporal or spiritual interest, is as important a service as a human being can render to his fellow-creatures, and in certain cases, as in those of the early Christians and of the Reformers, those who think with Dr. Johnson believe it to have been the most precious gift which could be bestowed on mankind. That the authors of such splendid benefits should be requited by martyrdom; that their reward should be to be dealt with as the vilest of criminals, is not, upon this theory, a deplorable error and misfortune, for which humanity should mourn in sackcloth and ashes, but the normal and justifiable state of things. The propounder of a new truth, according to this doctrine, should stand, as stood, in the legislation of the Locrians, the proposer of a new law, with a halter round his neck, to be instantly tightened if the public assembly did not, on hearing his reasons, then and there adopt his proposition. People who defend this mode of treating benefactors, cannot be supposed to set much value on the benefit; and I believe this view of the subject is mostly confined to the sort of persons who think that new truths may have been desirable once, but that we have had enough of them now.

But, indeed, the dictum that truth always triumphs over persecution, is one of those pleasant falsehoods which men repeat after one another till they pass into commonplaces, but which all experience refutes. History teems with instances of truth put down by persecution. If not suppressed forever, it may be thrown back for centuries. To speak only of religious opinions: the Reformation broke out at least twenty times before Luther, and was put down. Arnold of Brescia was put down. Fra Dolcino was put down. Savonarola was put down. The Albigeois were put down. The Vaudois were put down. The Lollards were put down. The Hussites were put down. Even after the era of Luther, wherever persecution was persisted in, it was successful. In Spain, Italy, Flanders, the Austrian empire, Protestantism was rooted out; and, most likely, would have been so in England, had Queen Mary lived, or Queen Elizabeth died. Persecution has always succeeded, save where the heretics were too strong a party to be effectually persecuted. No reasonable person can doubt that Christianity might have been extirpated in the Roman empire. It spread, and became predominant, because the persecutions were only occasional, lasting but a short time, and separated by long intervals of almost undisturbed propagandism. It is a piece of idle sentimentality that truth, merely as truth, has any inherent power denied to error, of prevailing against the dungeon and the stake. Men are not more zealous for truth than they often are for error, and a sufficient application of legal or even of social penalties will generally succeed in stopping the propagation of either. The real advantage which truth has, consists in this, that when an opinion is true, it may be extinguished once, twice, or many times, but in the course of ages there will generally be found persons to re-

weakness in argument I suspect here

discover it, until some one of its reappearances falls on a time when from favorable circumstances it escapes persecution until it has made such head as to withstand all subsequent attempts to suppress it.

It will be said, that we do not now put to death the introducers of new opinions: we are not like our fathers who slew the prophets, we even build sepulchres to them. It is true we no longer put heretics to death; and the amount of penal infliction which modern feeling would probably tolerate, even against the most obnoxious opinions, is not sufficient to extirpate them. But let us not flatter ourselves that we are yet free from the stain even of legal persecution. Penalties for opinion, or at last for its expression, still exist by law; and their enforcement is not, even in these times, so unexampled as to make it at all incredible that they may some day be revived in full force. In the year 1857, at the summer assizes of the county of Cornwall, an unfortunate man,[2] said to be of unexceptionable conduct in all relations of life, was sentenced to twenty-one months imprisonment, for uttering, and writing on a gate, some offensive words concerning Christianity. Within a month of the same time, at the Old Bailey, two persons, on two separate occasions,[3] were rejected as jurymen, and one of them grossly insulted by the judge and by one of the counsel, because they honestly declared that they had no theological belief; and a third, a foreigner,[4] for the same reason, was denied justice against a thief. This refusal of redress took place in virtue of the legal doctrine, that no person can be allowed to give evidence in a court of justice, who does not profess belief in a God (any god is sufficient) and in a future state; which is equivalent to declaring such persons to be outlaws, excluded from the protection of the tribunals; who may not only be robbed or assaulted with impunity, if no one but themselves, or persons of similar opinions, be present; but any one else may be robbed or assaulted with impunity, if the proof of the facts depends on their evidence. The assumption on which this is grounded, is that the oath is worthless, of a person who does not believe in a future state; a proposition which betokens much ignorance of history in

[2]Thomas Pooley, Bodmin Assizes, July 31, 1857. In December following, he received a free pardon from the Crown.
[3]George Jacob Holyoake, August 17, 1857; Edward Truelove, July, 1857.
[4]Baron de Gleichen, Marlborough Street Police Court, August 4, 1857.

those who assent to it (since it is historically true that a large proportion of infidels in all ages have been persons of distinguished integrity and honor); and would be maintained by no one who had the smallest conception how many of the persons in greatest repute with the world, both for virtues and for attainments, are well known, at least to their intimates, to be unbelievers. The rule, besides, is suicidal, and cuts away its own foundation. Under pretence that atheists must be liars, it admits the testimony of all atheists who are willing to lie, and rejects only those who brave the obloquy of publicly confessing a detested creed rather than affirm a falsehood. A rule thus self-convicted of absurdity so far as regards its professed purpose, can be kept in force only as a badge of hatred, a relic of persecution; a persecution, too, having the peculiarity, that the qualification for undergoing it, is the being clearly proved not to deserve it. The rule, and the theory it implies, are hardly less insulting to believers than to infidels. For if he who does not believe in a future state, necessarily lies, it follows that they who do believe are only prevented from lying, if prevented they are, by the fear of hell. We will not do the authors and abettors of the rule the injury of supposing, that the conception which they have formed of Christian virtue is drawn from their own consciousness.

These, indeed, are but rags and remnants of persecution, and may be thought to be not so much an indication of the wish to persecute as an example of that very frequent infirmity of English minds, which makes them take a preposterous pleasure in the assertion of a bad principle, when they are no longer bad enough to desire to carry it really into practice. But unhappily there is no security in the state of the public mind, that the suspension of worse forms of legal persecution, which has lasted for about the space of a generation, will continue. In this age the quiet surface of routine is as often ruffled by attempts to resuscitate past evils, as to introduce new benefits. What is boasted of at the present time as the revival of religion, is always, in narrow and uncultivated minds, at least as much the revival of bigotry; and where there is the strong permanent leaven of intolerance in the feelings of a people, which at all times abides in the middle classes of this country, it needs but little to provoke them into actively persecuting those whom they have never ceased to think proper objects of persecution.[5] For it is this—it is the opinions men entertain, and the feelings they cherish, respecting those who disown the beliefs they deem important, which makes this country not a place of mental freedom. For a long time past, the chief mischief of the legal penalties is that they strengthen the social stigma. It is that stigma which is really effective, and so effective is it, that the profession of opinions which are under the ban of society is much less common in England, than is, in many other countries, the avowal of those which incur risk of judicial punishment. In respect to all persons but those whose pecuniary circumstances make them independent of the good will of other people, opinion, on this subject, is as efficacious as law; men might as well be imprisoned, as excluded from the means of earning their bread. Those whose bread is already secured, and who desire no favors from men in power, or from bodies of men, or from the public, have nothing to fear from the open avowal of any opinions, but to be ill-thought of and ill-spoken of, and this it ought not to require a very heroic mould to enable them to bear. There is no room for any appeal *ad misericordiam* in behalf of such persons. But though we do not now inflict so much evil on those who think differently from us, as it was formerly our custom to do, it may be that we do ourselves as much evil as ever by our treatment of them. Socrates was put to death, but the Socratic philosophy rose like the sun in heaven, and spread its illumination over the whole intellectual firmament. Christians were cast to the lions, but the Christian

---

[5]Ample warning may be drawn from the large infusion of the passions of a persecutor, which mingled with the general display of the worst parts of our national character on the occasion of the Sepoy insurrection. The ravings of fanatics or charlatans from the pulpit may be unworthy of notice; but the heads of the Evangelical party have announced as their principle, for the government of Hindoos and Mahomedans, that no schools be supported by public money in which the Bible is not taught, and by necessary consequence that no public employment be given to any but real or pretended Christians. An Under-Secretary of State, in a speech delivered to his constituents on the 12th of November, 1857, is reported to have said: "Toleration of their faith" (the faith of a hundred millions of British subjects), "the superstition which they called religion, by the British Government, had had the effect of retarding the ascendency of the British name, and preventing the salutary growth of Christianity. . . . Toleration was the great corner-stone of the religious liberties of this country; but do not let them abuse that precious word toleration. As he understood it, it meant the complete liberty to all, freedom of worship, *among Christians, who worshipped upon the same foundation.* It meant toleration of all sects and denominations of *Christians who believed in the one mediation.*" I desire to call attention to the fact, that a man who has been deemed fit to fill a high office in the government of this country, under a liberal Ministry, maintains the doctrine that all who do not believe in the divinity of Christ are beyond the pale of toleration. Who, after this imbecile display, can indulge the illusion that religious persecution has passed away never to return?

Church grew up a stately and spreading tree, overtopping the older and less vigorous growths, and stifling them by its shade. Our merely social intolerance, kills no one, roots out no opinions, but induces men to disguise them, or to abstain from any active effort for their diffusion. With us, heretical opinions do not perceptibly gain, or even lose, ground in each decade or generation; they never blaze out far and wide, but continue to smoulder in the narrow circles of thinking and studious persons among whom they originate, without ever lighting up the general affairs of mankind with either a true or a deceptive light. And thus is kept up a state of things very satisfactory to some minds, because, without the unpleasant process of fining or imprisoning anybody, it maintains all prevailing opinions outwardly undisturbed, while it does not absolutely interdict the exercise of reason by dissentients afflicted with the malady of thought. A convenient plan for having peace in the intellectual world, and keeping all things going on therein very much as they do already. But the price paid for this sort of intellectual pacification, is the sacrifice of the entire moral courage of the human mind. A state of things in which a large portion of the most active and inquiring intellects find it advisable to keep the genuine principles and grounds of their convictions within their own breasts, and attempt, in what they address to the public, to fit as much as they can of their own conclusions to premises which they have internally renounced, cannot send forth the open, fearless characters, and logical, consistent intellects who once adorned the thinking world. The sort of men who can be looked for under it, are either mere conformers to commonplace, or time-servers for truth, whose arguments on all great subjects are meant for their hearers, and are not those which have convinced themselves. Those who avoid this alternative, do so by narrowing their thoughts and interest to things which can be spoken of without venturing within the region of principles, that is, to small practical matters, which would come right of themselves, if but the minds of mankind were strengthened and enlarged, and which will never be made effectually right until then; while that which would strengthen and enlarge men's minds, free and daring speculation on the highest subjects, is abandoned.

Those in whose eyes this reticence on the part of heretics is no evil, should consider in the first place, that in consequence of it there is never any fair and thorough discussion of heretical opinions; and that such of them as could not stand such a discussion, though they may be prevented from spreading, do not disappear. But it is not the minds of heretics that are deteriorated most, by the ban placed on all inquiry which does not end in the orthodox conclusions. The greatest harm done is to those who are not heretics, and whose whole mental development is cramped, and their reason cowed, by the fear of heresy. Who can compute what the world loses in the multitude of promising intellects combined with timid characters, who dare not follow out any bold, vigorous, independent train of thought, lest it should land them in something which would admit of being considered irreligious or immoral? Among them we may occasionally see some man of deep conscientiousness, and subtle and refined understanding, who spends a life in sophisticating with an intellect which he cannot silence, and exhausts the resources of ingenuity in attempting to reconcile the promptings of his conscience and reason with orthodoxy, which yet he does not, perhaps, to the end succeed in doing. No one can be a great thinker who does not recognize, that as a thinker it is his first duty to follow his intellect to whatever conclusions it may lead. Truth gains more even by the errors of one who, with due study and preparation, thinks for himself, than by the true opinions of those who only hold them because they do not suffer themselves to think. Not that it is solely, or chiefly, to form great thinkers, that freedom of thinking is required. On the contrary, it is as much, and even more indispensable, to enable average human beings to attain the mental stature which they are capable of. There have been, and may again be, great individual thinkers, in a general atmosphere of mental slavery. But there never has been, nor ever will be, in that atmosphere, an intellectually active people. Where any people has made a temporary approach to such a character, it has been because the dread of heterodox speculation was for a time suspended. Where there is a tacit convention that principles are not to be disputed; where the discussion of the greatest questions which can occupy humanity is considered to be closed, we cannot hope to find that generally high scale of mental activity which has made some periods of history so remarkable. Never when controversy avoided the subjects which are large and important enough to kindle enthusiasm, was the mind of a people stirred up from its foundations, and the impulse given which raised even persons of the most ordinary intellect to something of the dignity of thinking beings. Of such we have had an example in the condition of Europe during the times immediately following the Reformation; another, though limited to the Continent and to a more cultivated class, in the speculative movement of the latter half of the eighteenth century; and a third, of still briefer duration, in the intellectual fermentation of Germany during the Goethian and Fichtean period. These periods differed widely in the particular opinions which they developed; but were alike in this, that during all three the yoke of authority was broken. In each, an old mental despotism had been thrown off, and no new one had yet taken its place. The impulse given at these three periods has made Europe what it now is. Every single improvement which has taken place either in the human mind or in institutions, may be traced distinctly to one or other of them. Appearances have for some time indicated that all three impulses are well-nigh spent; and we can expect no fresh start, until we again assert our mental freedom.

Let us now pass to the second division of the argument, and dismissing the supposition that any of the received opinions may be false, let us assume them to be true, and examine into the worth of the manner in which they are likely to be held, when their truth is not freely and openly canvassed. However unwillingly a person who has a strong opinion may admit the possibility that his opinion may be false, he ought to be moved by the consideration that however true it may be, if it is not fully, frequently, and fearlessly discussed, it will be held as a dead dogma, not a living truth.

There is a class of persons (happily not quite so numerous as formerly) who think it enough if a person assents undoubtingly to what they think true, though he has no knowledge whatever of the grounds of the opinion, and could not make a tenable defence of it against the most superficial objections. Such persons, if they can once get their creed taught from authority, naturally think that no good, and some harm, comes of its being allowed to be questioned. Where their influence prevails, they make it nearly impossible for the received opinion to be rejected wisely and considerately, though it may still be rejected rashly and ignorantly; for to shut out discussion entirely is seldom possible, and when it once gets in, beliefs not grounded on conviction are apt to give way before the slightest semblance of an argument. Waiving, however, this possibility—assuming that the true opinion abides in the mind, but abides as a prejudice, a belief independent of, and proof against, argument—this is not the way in which truth ought to be held by a rational being. This is not knowing the truth. Truth, thus held, is but one superstition the more, accidentally clinging to the words which enunciate a truth.

If the intellect and judgment of mankind ought to be cultivated, a thing which Protestants at least do not deny, on what can these faculties be more appropriately exercised by any one, than on the things which concern him so much that it is considered necessary for him to hold opinions on them? If the cultivation of the understanding consists in one thing more than in another, it is surely in learning the grounds of one's own opinions. Whatever people believe, on subjects on which it is of the first importance to believe rightly, they ought to be able to defend against at least the common objections. But, some one may say, "Let them be *taught* the grounds of their opinions. It does not follow that opinions must be merely parroted because they are never heard controverted. Persons who learn geometry do not simply commit the theorems to memory, but understand and learn likewise the demonstrations; and it would be absurd to say that they remain ignorant of the grounds of geometrical truths, because they never hear any one deny, and attempt to disprove them." Undoubtedly: and such teaching suffices on a subject like mathematics, where there is nothing at all to be said on the wrong side of the question. The peculiarity of the evidence of mathematical truths is, that all the argument is on one side. There are no objections, and no answers to objections. But on every subject on which difference of opinion is possible, the truth depends on a balance to be struck between two sets of conflicting reasons. Even in natural philosophy, there is always some other explanation possible of the same facts; some geocentric theory instead of heliocentric, some phlogiston instead of oxygen; and it has to be shown why that other theory cannot be the true one: and until this is shown, and until we know how it is shown, we do not understand the grounds of our opinion. But when we turn to subjects infinitely more complicated, to morals, religion, politics, social relations, and the business of life, three-fourths of the arguments for every disputed opinion consist in dispelling the appearances which favor some opinion different from it. The greatest orator, save one, of antiquity, has left it on record that he always studied his adversary's case with as great, if not with still greater, intensity than even his own. What Cicero practised as the means of forensic success, requires to be imitated by all who study any subject in order to arrive at the truth. He who knows only his own side of the case, knows little of that. His reasons may be good, and no one may have been able to refute them. But if he is equally unable to refute the reasons on the opposite side; if he does not so much as know what they are, he has no ground for preferring either opinion. The rational position for him would be suspension of judgment, and unless he contents himself with that, he is either led by authority, or adopts, like the generality of the world, the side to which he feels most inclination. Nor is it enough that he should hear the arguments of adversaries from his own teachers, presented as they state them, and accompanied by what they offer as refutations. That is not the way to do justice to the arguments, or bring them into real contact with his own mind. He must be able to hear them from persons who actually believe them; who defend them in earnest, and do their very utmost for them. He must know them in their most plausible and persuasive form; he must feel the whole force of the difficulty which the true view of the subject has to encounter and dispose of; else he will never really possess himself of the portion of truth which meets and removes that difficulty. Ninety-nine in a hundred of what are called educated men are in this condition, even of those who can argue fluently for their opinions. Their conclusion may be true, but it might be false for anything they know: they have never thrown themselves into the mental position of those who think differently from them, and considered what such persons may have to say; and consequently they do not, in any proper sense of the word, know the doctrine which they themselves profess. They do not know those parts of it which explain and justify the remainder; the considerations which show that a fact which seemingly conflicts with another is reconcilable with it, or that, of two apparently strong reasons, one and not

the other ought to be preferred. All that part of the truth
which turns the scale, and decides the judgment of a completely informed mind, they are strangers to; nor is it ever
really known, but to those who have attended equally and
impartially to both sides, and endeavored to see the reasons
of both in the strongest light. So essential is this discipline
to a real understanding of moral and human subjects, that if
opponents of all important truths do not exist, it is indispensable to imagine them, and supply them with the strongest arguments which the most skilful devil's advocate can
conjure up.

To abate the force of these considerations, an enemy of
free discussion may be supposed to say, that there is no
necessity for mankind in general to know and understand
all that can be said against or for their opinions by philosophers and theologians. That it is not needful for common
men to be able to expose all the misstatements or fallacies of
an ingenious opponent. That it is enough if there is always
somebody capable of answering them, so that nothing likely
to mislead uninstructed persons remains unrefuted. That
simple minds, having been taught the obvious grounds of the
truths inculcated on them, may trust to authority for the rest,
and being aware that they have neither knowledge nor talent
to resolve every difficulty which can be raised, may repose
in the assurance that all those which have been raised have
been or can be answered, by those who are specially trained
to the task.

Conceding to this view of the subject the utmost that can
be claimed for it by those most easily satisfied with the
amount of understanding of truth which ought to accompany
the belief of it; even so, the argument for free discussion is
no way weakened. For even this doctrine acknowledges that
mankind ought to have a rational assurance that all objections
have been satisfactorily answered; and how are they to be
answered if that which requires to be answered is not spoken?
or how can the answer be known to be satisfactory, if the
objectors have no opportunity of showing that it is unsatisfactory? If not the public, at least the philosophers and
theologians who are to resolve the difficulties, must make themselves familiar with those difficulties in their most puzzling
form; and this cannot be accomplished unless they are freely
stated, and placed in the most advantageous light which they

admit of. The Catholic Church has its own way of dealing with this embarrassing problem. It makes a broad separation between those who can be permitted to receive its doctrines on conviction, and those who must accept them on trust. Neither, indeed, are allowed any choice as to what they will accept; but the clergy, such at least as can be fully confided in, may admissibly and meritoriously make themselves acquainted with the arguments of opponents, in order to answer them, and may, therefore, read heretical books; the laity, not unless by special permission, hard to be obtained. This discipline recognizes a knowledge of the enemy's case as beneficial to the teachers, but finds means, consistent with this, of denying it to the rest of the world: thus giving to the *élite* more mental culture, though not more mental freedom, than it allows to the mass. By this device it succeeds in obtaining the kind of mental superiority which its purposes require; for though culture without freedom never made a large and liberal mind, it can make a clever *nisi prius* advocate of a cause. But in countries professing Protestantism, this resource is denied; since Protestants hold, at least in theory, that the responsibility for the choice of a religion must be borne by each for himself, and cannot be thrown off upon teachers. Besides, in the present state of the world, it is practically impossible that writings which are read by the instructed can be kept from the uninstructed. If the teachers of mankind are to be cognizant of all that they ought to know, everything must be free to be written and published without restraint.

If, however, the mischievous operation of the absence of free discussion, when the received opinions are true, were confined to leaving men ignorant of the grounds of those opinions, it might be thought that this, if an intellectual, is no moral evil, and does not affect the worth of the opinions, regarded in their influence on the character. The fact, however, is, that not only the grounds of the opinion are forgotten in the absence of discussion, but too often the meaning of the opinion itself. The words which convey it, cease to suggest ideas, or suggest only a small portion of those they were originally employed to communicate. Instead of a vivid conception and a living belief, there remain only a few phrases retained by rote; or, if any part, the shell and husk only of the meaning is retained, the finer essence being lost. The great chapter in human history which this fact occupies and fills, cannot be too earnestly studied and meditated on.

It is illustrated in the experience of almost all ethical doctrines and religious creeds. They are all full of meaning and vitality to those who originate them, and to the direct disciples of the originators. Their meaning continues to be felt in undiminished strength, and is perhaps brought out into even fuller consciousness, so long as the struggle lasts to give the doctrine or creed an ascendency over other creeds. At last it either prevails, and becomes the general opinion, or its progress stops; it keeps possession of the ground it has gained, but ceases to spread further. When either of these results has become apparent, controversy on the subject flags, and gradually dies away. The doctrine has taken its place, if not as a received opinion, as one of the admitted sects or divisions of opinion: those who hold it have generally inherited, not adopted it; and conversion from one of these doctrines to another, being now an exceptional fact, occupies little place in the thoughts of their professors. Instead of being, as at first, constantly on the alert either to defend themselves against the world, or to bring the world over to them, they have subsided into acquiescence, and neither listen, when they can help it, to arguments against their creed, nor trouble dissentients (if there be such) with arguments in its favor. From this time may usually be dated the decline in the living power of the doctrine. We often hear the teachers of all creeds lamenting the difficulty of keeping up in the minds of believers a lively apprehension of the truth which they nominally recognize, so that it may penetrate the feelings, and acquire a real mastery over the conduct. No such difficulty is complained of while the creed is still fighting for its existence: even the weaker combatants then know and feel what they are fighting for, and the difference between it and other doctrines; and in that period of every creed's existence, not a few persons may be found, who have realized its fundamental principles in all the forms of thought, have weighed and considered them in all their important bearings, and have experienced the full effect on the character, which belief in that creed ought to produce in a mind thoroughly imbued with it. But when it has come to be an hereditary creed, and to be received passively, not actively—when the mind is no longer compelled, in the same degree as at first, to exercise its vital powers on the questions which its belief presents to it, there is a progressive tendency to forget all of the belief except the formularies, or to give it a dull and torpid assent, as if accepting it on trust dispensed with the necessity of realizing it in consciousness, or testing it by personal experience; until it almost ceases to connect itself at all with the inner life of the human being. Then are seen the cases, so frequent in this age of the world as almost to form the majority, in which the creed remains as it were outside the mind, encrusting and petrifying it against all other influences addressed to the higher parts of our nature; manifesting its power by not suffering any fresh and living conviction to get in, but itself doing nothing for the mind or heart, except standing sentinel over them to keep them vacant.

To what an extent doctrines intrinsically fitted to make the deepest impression upon the mind may remain in it as dead beliefs, without being ever realized in the imagination, the feelings, or the understanding, is exemplified by the manner in which the majority of believers hold the doctrines of Christianity. By Christianity I here mean what is accounted such by all churches and sects—the maxims and precepts contained in the New Testament. These are considered sacred, and accepted as laws, by all professing Christians. Yet it is scarcely too much to say that not one Christian in a thousand guides or tests his individual conduct by reference to those laws. The standard to which he does refer it, is the custom of his nation, his class, or his religious profession. He has thus, on the one hand, a collection of ethical maxims, which he believes to have been vouchsafed to him by infallible wisdom as rules for his government; and on the other, a set of every-day judgments and practices, which go a certain length with some of those maxims, not so great a length with others, stand in direct opposition to some, and are, on the whole, a compromise between the Christian creed and the interests and suggestions of worldly life. To the first of these standards he gives his homage; to the other his real allegiance. All Christians believe that the blessed are the poor and humble, and those who are ill-used by the world; that it is easier for a camel to pass through the eye of a needle than for a rich man to enter the kingdom of heaven; that they should judge not, lest they be judged; that they should swear not at all; that they should love their neighbor as themselves; that if one take their cloak, they should give him their coat also; that they should take no thought for the morrow; that if they would be perfect, they should sell all that they have and give it to the poor. They are not insincere when they say that they believe these things. They do believe them, as people believe what they have always heard lauded and never discussed. But in the sense of that living belief which regulates conduct, they believe these doctrines just up to the point to which it is usual to act upon them. The doctrines in their integrity are serviceable to pelt adversaries with; and it is understood that they are to be put forward (when possible) as the reasons for whatever people do that they think laudable. But any one who reminded them that the maxims require an infinity of things which they never even think of doing, would gain nothing but to be classed among those very unpopular characters who affect to be better than other people. The doctrines have no hold on ordinary believers—are not a power in their minds. They have an habitual respect for the sound of them, but no feeling which spreads from the words to the things signified, and forces the mind to take *them* in, and make them conform to the formula. Whenever conduct is concerned, they look around for Mr. A and B to direct them how far to go in obeying Christ.

Now we may be well assured that the case was not thus, but far otherwise, with the early Christians. Had it been thus, Christianity never would have expanded from an obscure sect of the despised Hebrews into the religion of the Roman empire. When their enemies said, "See how these Christians love one another" (a remark not likely to be made by anybody now), they assuredly had a much livelier feeling of the meaning of their creed than they have ever had since. And to this cause, probably, it is chiefly owing that Christianity now makes so little progress in extending its domain, and after eighteen centuries, is still nearly confined to Europeans and the descendants of Europeans. Even with the strictly religious, who are much in earnest about their doctrines, and attach a greater amount of meaning to many of them than people in general, it commonly happens that the part which is thus comparatively active in their minds is that which was made by Calvin, or Knox, or some such person much nearer in character to themselves. The sayings of Christ coexist passively in their minds, producing hardly any effect beyond what is caused by mere listening to words so amiable and bland. There are many reasons, doubtless, why doctrines which are the badge of a sect retain more of their vitality than those common to all recognized sects, and why more pains are taken by teachers to keep their meaning alive; but one reason certainly is, that the peculiar doctrines are more questioned, and have to be oftener defended against open gainsayers. Both teachers and learners go to sleep at their post, as soon as there is no enemy in the field.

The same thing holds true, generally speaking, of all traditional doctrines—those of prudence and knowledge of life, as well as of morals or religion. All languages and literatures are full of general observations on life, both as to what it is, and how to conduct oneself in it; observations which everybody knows, which everybody repeats, or hears with acquiescence, which are received as truisms, yet of which most people first truly learn the meaning, when experience, generally of a painful kind, has made it a reality to them. How often, when smarting under some unforeseen misfortune or disappointment, does a person call to mind some proverb or common saying, familiar to him all his life, the meaning of which, if he had ever before felt it as he does now, would have saved him from the calamity. There are indeed reasons for this, other than the absence of discussion: there are many truths of which the full meaning *cannot* be realized, until personal experience has brought it home. But much more of the meaning even of these would have been understood and what was understood would have been far more deeply impressed on the mind, if the man had been accustomed to hear it argued *pro* and *con* by people who did understand it. The fatal tendency of mankind to leave off thinking about a thing when it is no longer doubtful, is the cause of half their errors. A cotemporary author has well spoken of "the deep slumber of a decided opinion."

But what! (it may be asked) Is the absence of unanimity an indispensable condition of true knowledge? Is it necessary that some part of mankind should persist in error, to enable any to realize the truth? Does a belief cease to be real and vital as soon as it is generally received—and is a proposition never thoroughly understood and felt unless some doubt of it remains? As soon as mankind have unanimously accepted a truth, does the truth perish within them? The highest aim and best result of improved intelligence, it has hitherto been thought, is to unite mankind more and more in the acknowledgment of all important truths: and does the intelligence only last as long as it has not achieved its object? Do the fruits of conquest perish by the very completeness of the victory?

I affirm no such thing. As mankind improve, the number of doctrines which are no longer disputed or doubted will be constantly on the increase: and the well-being of mankind may almost be measured by the number and gravity of the truths which have reached the point of being uncontested. The cessation, on one question after another, of serious controversy, is one of the necessary incidents of the consolidation of opinion; a consolidation as salutary in the case of true opinions, as it is dangerous and noxious when the opinions are erroneous. But though this gradual narrowing of the bounds of diversity of opinion is necessary in both senses of the term, being at once inevitable and indispensable, we are not therefore obliged to conclude that all its consequences must be beneficial. The loss of so important an aid to the intelligent and living apprehension of a truth, as is afforded by the necessity of explaining it to, or defending it against, opponents, though not sufficient to outweigh, is no trifling drawback from, the benefit of its universal recognition. Where this advantage can no longer be had, I confess I should like to see the teachers of mankind endeavoring to provide a substitute for it; some contrivance for making the difficulties of the question as present to the learner's consciousness, as if they were pressed upon him by a dissentient champion, eager for his conversion.

But instead of seeking contrivances for this purpose, they have lost those they formerly had. The Socratic dialectics, so magnificently exemplified in the dialogues of Plato, were a contrivance of this description. They were essentially a negative discussion of the great questions of philosophy and life, directed with consummate skill to the purpose of convincing any one who had merely adopted the commonplaces of received opinion, that he did not understand the subject—that he as yet attached no definite meaning to the doctrines he professed; in order that, becoming aware of his ignorance, he might be put in the way to attain a stable belief, resting on a clear apprehension both of the meaning of doctrines and of their evidence. The school disputations of the Middle Ages had a somewhat similar object. They were intended to make sure that the pupil understood his own opinion, and (by necessary correlation) the opinion opposed to it, and could enforce the grounds of the one and confute those of the other. These last-mentioned contests had indeed the incurable defect, that the premises appealed to were taken from authority, not from reason; and, as a discipline to the mind, they were in every respect inferior to the powerful dialectics which formed the intellects of the "Socratici viri:" but the modern mind owes far more to both than it is generally willing to admit, and the present modes of education contain nothing which in the smallest degree supplies the place either of the one or of the other. A person who derives all his instruction from teachers or books, even if he escape the besetting temptation of contenting himself with cram, is under no compulsion to hear both sides; accordingly it is far from a frequent accomplishment, even among thinkers, to know both sides; and the weakest part of what everybody says in defence of his opinion, is what he intends as a reply to antagonists. It is the fashion of the present time to disparage negative logic—that which points out weaknesses in theory or errors in practice, without establishing positive truths. Such negative criticism would indeed be poor enough as an ultimate result; but as a means to attaining any positive knowledge or conviction worthy the name, it cannot be valued too highly; and until people are again systematically trained to it, there will be few great thinkers, and a low general average of intellect, in any but the mathematical and physical departments of speculation. On any other subject no one's opinions deserve the name of knowledge, except so far as he has either had forced upon him by others, or gone through of himself, the same mental process which would have been required of him in carrying on an active controversy with opponents. That, therefore, which when absent, it is so indispensable, but so difficult, to create, how worse than absurd is it to forego, when spontaneously offering itself! If there are any persons who contest a received opinion, or who will do so if law or opinion will let them, let us thank them for it, open our minds to listen to them, and rejoice that there is some one to do for us what we otherwise ought, if we have any regard for either the certainty or the vitality of our convictions, to do with much greater labor for ourselves.

It still remains to speak of one of the principal causes which make diversity of opinion advantageous, and will continue to do so until mankind shall have entered a stage of intellectual advancement which at present seems at an incalculable distance. We have hitherto considered only two possibilities: that the received opinion may be false, and some other opinion, consequently, true; or that, the received opinion being true, a conflict with the opposite error is essential to a clear apprehension and deep feeling of its truth. But there is a commoner case than either of these; when the conflicting doctrines, instead of being one true and the other false, share the truth between them; and the nonconforming opinion is needed to supply the remainder of the truth, of which the received doctrine embodies only a part. Popular opinions, on subjects not palpable to sense, are often true, but seldom or never the whole truth. They are a part of the truth; sometimes a greater, sometimes a smaller part, but exaggerated, distorted, and disjoined from the truths by which they ought to be accompanied and limited. Heretical opinions, on the other hand, are generally some of these suppressed and neglected truths, bursting the bonds which kept them down, and either seeking reconciliation with the truth contained in the common opinion, or fronting it as enemies, and setting themselves up, with similar exclusiveness, as the whole truth. The latter case is hitherto the most frequent, as, in the human mind, one-sidedness has always been the rule, and many-sidedness the exception. Hence, even in revolutions of opinion, one part of the truth usually sets while another rises. Even progress, which ought to superadd, for the most part only substitutes one partial and incomplete truth for another; improvement consisting chiefly in this, that the new fragment of truth is more wanted, more adapted to the needs of the time, than that which it displaces. Such being the partial character of prevailing opinions, even when resting on a true foundation; every opinion which embodies somewhat of the portion of truth which the common opinion omits, ought to be considered precious, with whatever amount of error and confusion that truth may be blended. No sober judge of human affairs will feel bound to be indignant because those who force on our notice truths which we should otherwise have overlooked, overlook some of those which we see. Rather, he will think that so long as popular truth is one-sided, it is more desirable than otherwise that unpopular truth should have one-sided asserters too; such being usually the most energetic, and the most likely to compel reluctant attention to the fragment of wisdom which they proclaim as if it were the whole.

Thus, in the eighteenth century, when nearly all the instructed, and all those of the uninstructed who were led by them, were lost in admiration of what is called civilization, and of the marvels of modern science, literature, and philosophy, and while greatly overrating the amount of unlikeness between the men of modern and those of ancient times, indulged the belief that the whole of the difference was in their own favor; with what a salutary shock did the paradoxes of Rousseau explode like bombshells in the midst, dislocating the compact mass of one-sided opinion, and forcing its elements to recombine in a better form and with additional ingredients. Not that the current opinions were on the whole farther from the truth than Rousseau's were; on the contrary, they were nearer to it; they contained more of positive truth, and very much less of error. Nevertheless there lay in Rousseau's doctrine, and has floated down the stream of opinion along with it, a considerable amount of exactly those truths which the popular opinion wanted; and these are the deposit which was left behind when the flood subsided. The superior worth of simplicity of life, the enervating and demoralizing effect of the trammels and hypocrisies of artificial society, are ideas which have never been entirely absent from cultivated minds since Rousseau wrote; and they will in time produce their due effect, though at present needing to be asserted as much as ever, and to be asserted by deeds, for words, on this subject, have nearly exhausted their power.

In politics, again, it is almost a commonplace, that a party of order or stability, and a party of progress or reform, are both necessary elements of a healthy state of political life; until the one or the other shall have so enlarged its mental grasp as to be a party equally of order and of progress, knowing and distinguishing what is fit to be preserved from what ought to be swept away. Each of these modes of thinking derives its utility from the deficiencies of the other; but it is in a great measure the opposition of the other that keeps each within the limits of reason and sanity. Unless opinions favorable to democracy and to aristocracy, to property and to equality, to coöperation and to competition, to luxury and to abstinence, to sociality and individuality, to liberty and to discipline, and all the other standing antagonisms of practical life, are expressed with equal freedom, and enforced and defended with equal talent and energy, there is no chance of both elements obtaining their due; one scale is sure to go up, and the other down. Truth, in the great practical concerns of life, is so much a question of the reconciling and combining of opposites, that very few have minds sufficiently capacious and impartial to make the adjustment with an approach to correctness, and it has to be made by the rough process of a struggle between combatants fighting under hostile banners. On any of the great open questions just enumerated, if either of the two opinions has a better claim than the other, not merely to be tolerated, but to be encouraged and countenanced, it is the one which happens at the particular time and place to be in a minority. That is the opinion which, for the time being, represents the neglected interests, the side of human well-being which is in danger of obtaining less than its share. I am aware that there is not, in this country, any intolerance of differences of opinion on most of these topics. They are adduced to show, by admitted and multiplied examples, the universality of the fact, that only through diversity of opinion is there, in the existing state of human intellect, a chance of fair play to all sides of the truth. When there are persons to be found, who form an exception to the apparent unanimity of the world on any subject, even if the world is in the right, it is always probable that dissentients have something worth hearing to say for themselves, and that truth would lose something by their silence.

It may be objected, "But *some* received principles, especially on the highest and most vital subjects, are more than half-truths. The Christian morality, for instance, is the whole truth on that subject, and if any one teaches a morality which varies from it, he is wholly in error." As this is of all cases the most important in practice, none can be fitter to test the general maxim. But before pronouncing what Christian morality is or is not, it would be desirable to decide what is meant by Christian morality. If it means the morality of the New Testament, I wonder that any one who derives his knowledge of this from the book itself, can suppose that it was announced, or intended, as a complete doctrine of morals.

The Gospel always refers to a preëxisting morality, and confines its precepts to the particulars in which that morality was to be corrected, or superseded by a wider and higher; expressing itself, moreover, in terms most general, often impossible to be interpreted literally, and possessing rather the impressiveness of poetry or eloquence than the precision of legislation. To extract from it a body of ethical doctrine, has never been possible without eking it out from the Old Testament, that is, from a system elaborate indeed, but in many respects barbarous, and intended only for a barbarous people. St. Paul, a declared enemy to this Judaical mode of interpreting the doctrine and filling up the scheme of his Master, equally assumes a preëxisting morality, namely, that of the Greeks and Romans; and his advice to Christians is in a great measure a system of accommodation to that; even to the extent of giving an apparent sanction to slavery. What is called Christian, but should rather be termed theological, morality, was not the work of Christ or the Apostles, but is of much later origin, having been gradually built up by the Catholic Church of the first five centuries, and though not implicitly adopted by moderns and Protestants, has been much less modified by them than might have been expected. For the most part, indeed, they have contented themselves with cutting off the additions which had been made to it in the Middle Ages, each sect supplying the place by fresh additions, adapted to its own character and tendencies. That mankind owe a great debt to this morality, and to its early teachers, I should be the last person to deny; but I do not scruple to say of it, that it is, in many important points, incomplete and one-sided, and that unless ideas and feelings, not sanctioned by it, had contributed to the formation of European life and character, human affairs would have been in a worse condition than they now are. Christian morality (so called) has all the characters of a re-action; it is, in great part, a protest against Paganism. Its ideal is negative rather than positive; passive rather than active; Innocence rather than Nobleness; Abstinence from Evil, rather than energetic Pursuit of Good: in its precepts (as has been well said) "thou shalt not" predominates unduly over "thou shalt." In its horror of sensuality, it made an idol of asceticism, which has been gradually compromised away into one of legality. It holds out the hope of heaven and the threat of hell, as the appointed and ap-

propriate motives to a virtuous life: in this falling far below
the best of the ancients, and doing what lies in it to give to
human morality an essentially selfish character, by discon-
necting each man's feelings of duty from the interests of his
fellow-creatures, except so far as a self-interested inducement
is offered to him for consulting them. It is essentially a doctrine of passive obedience; it inculcates submission to all
authorities found established; who indeed are not to be actively
obeyed when they command what religion forbids, but who
are not to be resisted, far less rebelled against, for any
amount of wrong to ourselves. And while, in the morality
of the best Pagan nations, duty to the State holds even a
disproportionate place, infringing on the just liberty of the
individual; in purely Christian ethics, that grand department
of duty is scarely noticed or acknowledged. It is in the Koran,
not the New Testament, that we read the maxim—"A ruler who
appoints any man to an office, when there is in his dominions
another man better qualified for it, sins against God and
against the State." What little recognition the idea of obligation to the public obtains in modern morality, is derived from
Greek and Roman sources, not from Christian; as, even in the
morality of private life, whatever exists of magnanimity, high-
mindedness, personal dignity, even the sense of honor, is
derived from the purely human, not the religious part of our
education, and never could have grown out of a standard of
ethics in which the only worth, professedly recognized, is that
of obedience.

I am as far as any one from pretending that these defects
are necessarily inherent in the Christian ethics, in every
manner in which it can be conceived, or that the many
requisites of a complete moral doctrine which it does not
contain, do not admit of being reconciled with it. Far less
would I insinuate this of the doctrines and precepts of Christ
himself. I believe that the sayings of Christ are all, that I
can see any evidence of their having been intended to be;
that they are irreconcilable with nothing which a comprehensive morality requires; that everything which is excellent
in ethics may be brought within them, with no greater violence
to their language than has been done to it by all who have
attempted to deduce from them any practical system of conduct whatever. But it is quite consistent with this, to believe
that they contain, and were meant to contain, only a part

Objection to Christian ethics with the state yet desire to balance

of the truth, that many essential elements of the highest
morality are among the things which are not provided for,
nor intended to be provided for in the recorded deliverances
of the Founder of Christianity, and which have been entirely
thrown aside in the system of ethics erected on the basis of
those deliverances by the Christian Church. And this being
so, I think it a great error to persist in attempting to find in
the Christian doctrine that complete rule for our guidance,
which its author intended it to sanction and enforce, but only
partially to provide. I believe, too, that this narrow theory
is becoming a grave practical evil, detracting greatly from
the value of the moral training and instruction, which so
many well-meaning persons are now at length exerting themselves to promote. I much fear that by attempting to form
the mind and feelings on an exclusively religious type, and
discarding those secular standards (as for want of a better
name they may be called) which heretofore coexisted with
and supplemented the Christian ethics, receiving some of its
spirit, and infusing into it some of theirs, there will result,
and is even now resulting, a low, abject, servile type of
character, which, submit itself as it may to what it deems the
Supreme Will, is incapable of rising to or sympathizing in the
conception of Supreme Goodness. I believe that other ethics
than any which can be evolved from exclusively Christian
sources, must exist side by side with Christian ethics to produce the moral regeneration of mankind; and that the Christian system is no exception to the rule, that in an imperfect
state of the human mind, the interests of truth require a
diversity of opinions. It is not necessary that in ceasing to
ignore the moral truths not contained in Christianity, men
should ignore any of those which it does contain. Such prejudice, or oversight, when it occurs, is altogether an evil; but it
is one from which we cannot hope to be always exempt, and
must be regarded as the price paid for an inestimable good.
The exclusive pretension made by a part of the truth to be the
whole, must and ought to be protested against, and if a
reactionary impulse should make the protestors unjust in their
turn, this one-sidedness, like the other, may be lamented, but
must be tolerated. If Christians would teach infidels to be
just to Christianity, they should themselves be just to infidelity. It can do truth no service to blink the fact, known to
all who have the most ordinary acquaintance with literary

history, that a large portion of the noblest and most valuable moral teaching has been the work, not only of men who did not know, but of men who knew and rejected, the Christian faith.

I do not pretend that the most unlimited use of the freedom of enunciating all possible opinions would put an end to the evils of religious or philosophical sectarianism. Every truth which men of narrow capacity are in earnest about, is sure to be asserted, inculcated, and in many ways even acted on, as if no other truth existed in the world, or at all events none that could limit or qualify the first. I acknowledge that the tendency of all opinions to become sectarian is not cured by the freest discussion, but is often heightened and exacerbated thereby; the truth which ought to have been, but was not, seen, being rejected all the more violently because proclaimed by persons regarded as opponents. But it is not on the impassioned partisan, it is on the calmer and more disinterested by-stander, that this collision of opinions works its salutary effect. Not the violent conflict between parts of the truth, but the quiet suppression of half of it, is the formidable evil: there is always hope when people are forced to listen to both sides; it is when they attend only to one that errors harden into prejudices, and truth itself ceases to have the effect of truth, by being exaggerated into falsehood. And since there are few mental attributes more rare than that judicial faculty which can sit in intelligent judgment between two sides of a question, of which only one is represented by an advocate before it, truth has no chance but in proportion as every side of it, every opinion which embodies any fraction of the truth, not only finds advocates, but is so advocated as to be listened to.

We have now recognized the necessity to the mental well-being of mankind (on which all their other well-being depends) of freedom of opinion, and freedom of the expression of opinion, on four distinct grounds; which we will now briefly recapitulate.

First, if any opinion is compelled to silence, that opinion may, for aught we can certainly know, be true. To deny this is to assume our own infallibility.

Secondly, though the silenced opinion be an error, it may, and very commonly does, contain a portion of truth; and since the general or prevailing opinion on any subject is rarely or never the whole truth, it is only by the collision of adverse opinions that the remainder of the truth has any chance of being supplied.

Thirdly, even if the received opinion be not only true, but the whole truth; unless it is suffered to be, and actually is, vigorously and earnestly contested, it will, by most of those who receive it, be held in the manner of a prejudice, with little comprehension or feeling of its rational grounds. And not only this, but, fourthly, the meaning of the doctrine itself will be in danger of being lost, or enfeebled, and deprived of its vital effect on the character and conduct: the dogma becoming a mere formal profession, inefficacious for good, but cumbering the ground, and preventing the growth of any real and heartfelt conviction, from reason or personal experience.

Before quitting the subject of freedom of opinion, it is fit to take some notice of those who say, that the free expression of all opinions should be permitted, on condition that the manner be temperate, and do not pass the bounds of fair discussion. Much might be said on the impossibility of fixing where these supposed bounds are to be placed; for if the test be offence to those whose opinion is attacked, I think experience testifies that this offence is given whenever the attack is telling and powerful, and that every opponent who pushes them hard, and whom they find it difficult to answer, appears to them, if he shows any strong feeling on the subject, an intemperate opponent. But this, though an important consideration in a practical point of view, merges in a more fundamental objection. Undoubtedly the manner of asserting an opinion, even though it be a true one, may be very objectionable, and may justly incur severe censure. But the principal offences of the kind are such as it is mostly impossible, unless by accidental self-betrayal, to bring home to conviction. The gravest of them is, to argue sophistically, to suppress facts or arguments, to misstate the elements of the case, or misrepresent the opposite opinion. But all this, even to the most aggravated degree, is so continually done in perfect good faith, by persons who are not considered, and in many other respects may not deserve to be considered, ignorant or incompetent, that it is rarely possible on adequate grounds conscientiously to stamp the misrepresentation as morally culpable; and still less could law presume to interfere with this kind of controversial misconduct. With regard to what is commonly meant by intemperate discussion, namely, invective, sarcasm, personality, and the like, the denunciation of these weapons would deserve more sympathy if it were ever proposed to interdict them equally to both sides; but it is only desired to restrain the employment of them against the prevailing opinion: against the unprevailing they may not only be used without general disapproval, but will be likely to obtain for him who uses them the praise of honest zeal and righteous indignation. Yet whatever mischief arises from their use, is greatest when they are employed against the comparatively defenceless; and whatever unfair advantage can be derived by any opinion from this mode of asserting it, accrues almost exclusively to received opinions. The worst offence of this kind which can be committed by a polemic, is to stigmatize those who hold the contrary opinion as bad and immoral men. To calumny of this sort, those who hold any unpopular opinion are peculiarly exposed, because they are in general few and uninfluential, and nobody but themselves feels much interest in seeing justice done them; but this weapon is, from the nature of the case, denied to those who attack a prevailing opinion: they can neither use it with safety to themselves, nor, if they could, would it do anything but recoil on their own cause. In general, opinions contrary to those commonly received can only obtain a hearing by studied moderation of language, and the most cautious avoidance of unnecessary offence, from which they hardly ever deviate even in a slight degree without losing ground: while unmeasured vituperation employed on the side of the prevailing opinion, really does deter people from professing contrary opinions, and from listening to those who profess them. For the interest, therefore, of truth and justice, it is far more important to restrain this employment of vituperative language than the other; and, for example, if it were necessary to choose, there would be much more need to discourage offensive attacks on infidelity, than on religion. It is, however, obvious that law and authority have no business with restraining either, while opinion ought, in every instance, to determine its verdict by the circumstances of the individual case; condemning every one, on whichever side of the argument he places himself, in whose mode of advocacy either want of candor, or malignity, bigotry, or intolerance of feeling manifest themselves; but not inferring these vices from the side which a person takes, though it be the contrary side of the question to our own: and giving merited honor to every one, whatever opinion he may hold, who has calmness to see and honesty to state what his opponents and their opinions really are, exaggerating nothing to their discredit, keeping nothing back which tells, or can be supposed to tell, in their favor. This is the real morality of public discussion; and if often violated, I am happy to think that there are many controversialists who to a great extent observe it, and a still greater number who conscientiously strive towards it.

CHAPTER III

OF INDIVIDUALITY, AS ONE OF THE ELEMENTS OF WELL-BEING

SUCH BEING the reasons which make it imperative that human beings should be free to form opinions, and to express their opinions without reserve; and such the baneful consequences to the intellectual, and through that to the moral nature of man, unless this liberty is either conceded, or asserted in spite of prohibition; let us next examine whether the same reasons do not require that men should be free to act upon their opinions—to carry these out in their lives, without hindrance, either physical or moral, from their fellow-men, so long as it is at their own risk and peril. This last proviso is of course indispensable. No one pretends that actions should be as free as opinions. On the contrary, even opinions lose their immunity, when the circumstances in which they are expressed are such as to constitute their expression a positive instigation to some mischievous act. An opinion that corn-dealers are starvers of the poor, or that private property is robbery, ought to be unmolested when simply circulated through the press, but may justly incur punishment when delivered orally to an excited mob assembled before the house of a corn-dealer, or when handed about among the same mob in the form of a placard. Acts, of whatever kind, which, without justifiable cause, do harm to others, may be, and in the more important cases absolutely require to be, controlled by the unfavorable sentiments, and, when needful, by the active interference of mankind. The liberty of the individual must be thus far limited; he must not make himself a nuisance to other people. But if he refrains from molesting others in what concerns them, and merely acts according to his own inclination and judgment in things which concern himself, the same reasons which show that opinion should be free, prove also that he should be allowed, without molestation, to carry his opinions into practice at his own cost. That mankind are not infallible; that their truths, for the most part, are only half-truths; that unity of opinion, unless resulting from the fullest and freest comparison of opposite opinions, is not desirable, and diversity not an evil, but a good, until mankind are much more capable than at present of recognizing all sides of the truth, are principles applicable to men's modes of action, not less than to their opinions. As it is useful that while mankind are imperfect there should be different opinions, so is it that there should be different experiments of living; that free scope should be given to varieties of character, short of injury to others; and that the worth of different modes of life should be proved practically, when any one thinks fit to try them. It is desirable, in short, that in things which do not primarily concern others, individuality should assert itself. Where, not the person's own character, but the traditions or customs of other people are the rule of conduct, there is wanting one of the principal ingredients of human happiness, and quite the chief ingredient of individual and social progress.

In maintaining this principle, the greatest difficulty to be encountered does not lie in the appreciation of means towards an acknowledged end, but in the indifference of persons in general to the end itself. If it were felt that the free development of individuality is one of the leading essentials of well-being; that it is not only a coördinate element with all that is designated by the terms civilization, instruction, education, culture, but is itself a necessary part and condition of all those things; there would be no danger that liberty should be undervalued, and the adjustment of the boundaries between it and social control would present no extraordinary difficulty. But the evil is, that individual spontaneity is hardly recognized by the common modes of thinking as having any intrinsic worth, or deserving any regard on its own account. The majority, being satisfied with the ways of mankind as they now are (for it is they who make them what they are), cannot comprehend why those ways should not be good enough for everybody; and what is more, spontaneity forms no part of the ideal of the majority of moral and social reformers, but is rather looked on with jealousy, as a troublesome and perhaps rebellious obstruction to the general acceptance of what these reformers, in their own judgment, think would be best for mankind. Few persons, out of Germany, even comprehend the meaning of the doctrine which Wilhelm von Humboldt, so eminent both as a *savant* and as a politician, made the text of a treatise—that "the end of man, or that which is prescribed by the eternal or immutable dictates of reason, and not suggested by vague and transient desires, is the highest and most harmonious development of his powers to a complete and consistent whole;" that, therefore, the object "towards which every human being must ceaselessly direct his efforts, and on which especially those who design to influence their fellow-men must ever keep their eyes, is the individuality of power and development;" that for this there are two requisites, "freedom, and a variety of situations;" and that from the union of these arise "individual vigor and manifold diversity," which combine themselves in "originality."[6]

Little, however, as people are accustomed to a doctrine like that of Von Humboldt, and surprising as it may be to them to find so high a value attached to individuality, the question, one must nevertheless think, can only be one of degree. No one's idea of excellence in conduct is that people should do absolutely nothing but copy one another. No one would assert that people ought not to put into their mode of life, and into the conduct of their concerns, any impress whatever of their own judgment, or of their own individual character. On the other hand, it would be absurd to pretend that people ought to live as if nothing whatever had been known in the world before they came into it; as if experience had as yet done nothing towards showing that one mode of existence, or of conduct, is preferable to another. Nobody denies that people should be so taught and trained in youth, as to know and benefit by the ascertained results of human experience. But it is the privilege and proper condition of a human being, arrived at the maturity of his faculties, to use and interpret experience in his own way. It is for him to find out what part of recorded experience is properly applicable to his own circumstances and character. The traditions and customs of other people are, to a certain extent, evidence of what their experience has taught *them;* presumptive evidence, and as such, have a claim to his deference: but, in the first place, their experience may be too narrow; or they may not have interpreted it rightly. Secondly, their interpretation of experience may be correct, but unsuitable to him. Customs are made

[6]*The Sphere and Duties of Government,* from the German of Baron Wilhelm von Humboldt, pp. 11–13.

for customary circumstances, and customary characters: and his circumstances or his character may be uncustomary. Thirdly, though the customs be both good as customs, and suitable to him, yet to conform to custom, merely *as* custom, does not educate or develop in him any of the qualities which are the distinctive endowment of a human being. The human faculties of perception, judgment, discriminative feeling, mental activity, and even moral preference, are exercised only in making a choice. He who does anything because it is the custom, makes no choice. He gains no practice either in discerning or in desiring what is best. The mental and moral, like the muscular powers, are improved only by being used. The faculties are called into no exercise by doing a thing merely because others do it, no more than by believing a thing only because others believe it. If the grounds of an opinion are not conclusive to the person's own reason, his reason cannot be strengthened, but is likely to be weakened by his adopting it: and if the inducements to an act are not such as are consentaneous to his own feelings and character (where affection, or the rights of others, are not concerned), it is so much done towards rendering his feelings and character inert and torpid, instead of active and energetic.

He who lets the world, or his own portion of it, choose his plan of life for him, has no need of any other faculty than the ape-like one of imitation. He who chooses his plan for himself, employs all his faculties. He must use observation to see, reasoning and judgment to foresee, activity to gather materials for decision, discrimination to decide, and when he has decided, firmness and self-control to hold to his deliberate decision. And these qualities he requires and exercises exactly in proportion as the part of his conduct which he determines according to his own judgment and feelings is a large one. It is possible that he might be guided in some good path, and kept out of harm's way, without any of these things. But what will be his comparative worth as a human being? It really is of importance, not only what men do, but also what manner of men they are that do it. Among the works of man, which human life is rightly employed in perfecting and beautifying, the first in importance surely is man himself. Supposing it were possible to get houses built, corn grown, battles fought, causes tried, and even churches erected and prayers said, by machinery—by automatons in human form—it would be a considerable loss to exchange for these automatons even the men and women who at present inhabit the more civilized parts of the world, and who assuredly are but starved specimens of what nature can and will produce. Human nature is not a machine to be built after a model, and set to do exactly the work prescribed for it, but a tree, which requires to grow and develop itself on all sides, according to the tendency of the inward forces which make it a living thing.

It will probably be conceded that it is desirable people should exercise their understandings, and that an intelligent following of custom, or even occasionally an intelligent deviation from custom, is better than a blind and simply mechanical adhesion to it. To a certain extent it is admitted, that our understanding should be our own: but there is not the same willingness to admit that our desires and impulses should be our own likewise; or that to possess impulses of our own, and of any strength, is anything but a peril and a snare. Yet desires and impulses are as much a part of a perfect human being, as beliefs and restraints: and strong impulses are only perilous when not properly balanced; when one set of aims and inclinations is developed into strength, while others, which ought to coexist with them, remain weak and inactive. It is not because men's desires are strong that they act ill; it is because their consciences are weak. There is no natural connection between strong impulses and a weak conscience. The natural connection is the other way. To say that one person's desires and feelings are stronger and more various than those of another, is merely to say that he has more of the raw material of human nature, and is therefore capable, perhaps of more evil, but certainly of more good. Strong impulses are but another name for energy. Energy may be turned to bad uses; but more good may always be made of an energetic nature, than of an indolent and impassive one. Those who have most natural feeling, are always those whose cultivated feelings may be made the strongest. The same strong susceptibilities which make the personal impulses vivid and powerful, are also the source from whence are generated the most passionate love of virtue, and the sternest self-control. It is through the cultivation of these, that society both does its duty and protects its interests: not by rejecting the stuff of which heroes are made, because it knows not how to make them. A person whose desires and impulses are his own—are the expression of his own nature, as it has been developed and modified by his own culture—is said to have a character. One whose desires and impulses are not his own, has no character, no more than a steam-engine has a character. If, in addition to being his own, his impulses are strong, and are under the government of a strong will, he has an energetic character. Whoever thinks that individuality of desires and impulses should not be encouraged to unfold itself, must maintain that society has no need of strong natures—is not the better for containing many persons who have much character—and that a high general average of energy is not desirable.

In some early states of society, these forces might be, and were, too much ahead of the power which society then possessed of disciplining and controlling them. There has been a time when the element of spontaneity and individuality was in excess, and the social principle had a hard struggle with it. The difficulty then was, to induce men of strong bodies or minds to pay obedience to any rules which required them to control their impulses. To overcome this difficulty, law and discipline, like the Popes struggling against the Emperors, asserted a power over the whole man, claiming to control all his life in order to control his character—which society had not found any other sufficient means of binding. But society has now fairly got the better of individuality; and the danger which threatens human nature is not the excess, but the deficiency, of personal impulses and preferences. Things are vastly changed, since the passions of those who were strong by station or by personal endowment were in a state of habitual rebellion against laws and ordinances, and required to be rigorously chained up to enable the persons within their reach to enjoy any particle of security. In our times, from the highest class of society down to the lowest, every one lives as under the eye of a hostile and dreaded censorship. Not only in what concerns others, but in what concerns only themselves, the individual, or the family, do not ask themselves—what do I prefer? or, what would suit my character and disposition? or, what would allow the best and highest in me to have fair play, and enable it to grow and thrive? They ask themselves, what is suitable to my position? what is usually done by persons of my station and pecuniary circumstances? or (worse still) what is usually done by persons of a station and circumstances superior to mine? I do not mean that they choose what is customary, in preference to what suits their own inclination. It does not occur to them to have any inclination, except for what is customary. Thus the mind itself is bowed to the yoke: even in what people do for pleasure, conformity is the first thing thought of; they like in crowds; they exercise choice only among things commonly done: peculiarity of taste, eccentricity of conduct, are shunned equally with crimes: until by dint of not following their own nature, they have no nature to follow: their human capacities are withered and starved: they become incapable of any strong wishes or native pleasures, and are generally without either opinions or feelings of home growth, or properly their own. Now is this, or is it not, the desirable condition of human nature?

It is so, on the Calvinistic theory. According to that, the one great offence of man is Self-will. All the good of which humanity is capable, is comprised in Obedience. You have no choice; thus you must do, and no otherwise: "whatever is not a duty is a sin." Human nature being radically corrupt, there is no redemption for any one until human nature is killed within him. To one holding this theory of life, crushing out any of the human faculties, capacities, and susceptibilities, is no evil: man needs no capacity, but that of surrendering himself to the will of God: and if he uses any of his faculties for any other purpose but to do that supposed will more effectually, he is better without them. That is the theory of Calvinism; and it is held, in a mitigated form, by many who do not consider themselves Calvinists; the mitigation consisting in giving a less ascetic interpretation to the alleged will of God; asserting it to be his will that mankind should gratify some of their inclinations; of course not in the manner they themselves prefer, but in the way of obedience, that is, in a way prescribed to them by authority; and, therefore, by the necessary conditions of the case, the same for all.

In some such insidious form there is at present a strong tendency to this narrow theory of life, and to the pinched and hidebound type of human character which it patronizes. Many persons, no doubt, sincerely think that human beings thus cramped and dwarfed, are as their Maker designed them to be; just as many have thought that trees are a much finer thing when clipped into pollards, or cut out into figures of animals, than as nature made them. But if it be any part of religion to believe that man was made by a good Being, it is more consistent with that faith to believe, that this Being gave all human faculties that they might be cultivated and unfolded, not rooted out and consumed, and that he takes delight in every nearer approach made by his creatures to the ideal conception embodied in them, every increase in any of their capabilities of comprehension, of action, or of enjoyment. There is a different type of human excellence from the Calvinistic; a conception of humanity as having its nature bestowed on it for other purposes than merely to be abnegated. "Pagan self-assertion" is one of the elements of human worth, as well as "Christian self-denial."[7] There is a Greek ideal of self-development, which the Platonic and Christian ideal of self-government blends with, but does not supersede. It may be better to be a John Knox than an Alcibiades, but it is better to be a Pericles than either; nor would a Pericles, if we had one in these days, be without anything good which belonged to John Knox.

It is not by wearing down into uniformity all that is individual in themselves, but by cultivating it and calling it forth, within the limits imposed by the rights and interests of others, that human beings become a noble and beautiful object of contemplation; and as the works partake the character of those who do them, by the same process human life also becomes rich, diversified, and animating, furnishing more abundant aliment to high thoughts and elevating feelings, and strengthening the tie which binds every individual to the race, by making the race infinitely better worth belonging to. In proportion to the development of his individuality, each person becomes more valuable to himself, and is therefore capable of being more valuable to others. There is a greater fulness of life about his own existence, and when there is more life in the units there is more in the mass which is composed of them. As much compression as is necessary to prevent the stronger specimens of human nature from encroaching on the rights of others, cannot be dispensed with; but for this there is ample compensation even in the point of view of human development. The means of development which the individual loses by being prevented from gratifying his inclinations to the injury of others, are chiefly obtained at the expense of the development of other people.

[7] Sterling's *Essays.*

And even to himself there is a full equivalent in the better development of the social part of his nature, rendered possible by the restraint put upon the selfish part. To be held to rigid rules of justice for the sake of others, develops the feelings and capacities which have the good of others for their object. But to be restrained in things not affecting their good, by their mere displeasure, developes nothing valuable, except such force of character as may unfold itself in resisting the restraint. If acquiesced in, it dulls and blunts the whole nature. To give any fair play to the nature of each, it is essential that different persons should be allowed to lead different lives. In proportion as this latitude has been exercised in any age, has that age been noteworthy to posterity. Even despotism does not produce its worst effects, so long as Individuality exists under it; and whatever crushes individuality is despotism, by whatever name it may be called, and whether it professes to be enforcing the will of God or the injunctions of men.

Having said that Individuality is the same thing with development, and that it is only the cultivation of individuality which produces, or can produce, well-developed human beings, I might here close the argument: for what more or better can be said of any condition of human affairs, than that it brings human beings themselves nearer to the best thing they can be? or what worse can be said of any obstruction to good, than that it prevents this? Doubtless, however, these considerations will not suffice to convince those who most need convincing; and it is necessary further to show, that these developed human beings are of some use to the undeveloped—to point out to those who do not desire liberty, and would not avail themselves of it, that they may be in some intelligible manner rewarded for allowing other people to make use of it without hindrance.

In the first place, then, I would suggest that they might possibly learn something from them. It will not be denied by anybody, that originality is a valuable element in human affairs. There is always need of persons not only to discover new truths, and point out when what were once truths are true no longer, but also to commence new practices, and set the example of more enlightened conduct, and better taste and sense in human life. This cannot well be gainsaid by anybody who does not believe that the world has already attained perfection in all its ways and practices. It is true that this benefit is not capable of being rendered by everybody alike: there are but few persons, in comparison with the whole of mankind, whose experiments, if adopted by others, would be likely to be any improvement on established practice. But these few are the salt of the earth; without them, human life would become a stagnant pool. Not only is it they who introduce good things which did not before exist; it is they who keep the life in those which already existed. If there were nothing new to be done, would human intellect cease to be necessary? Would it be a reason why those who do the old things should forget why they are done, and do them like cattle, not like human beings? There is only too great a tendency in the best beliefs and practices to degenerate into the mechanical; and unless there were a succession of persons whose ever-recurring originality prevents the grounds of those beliefs and practices from becoming merely traditional, such dead matter would not resist the smallest shock from anything really alive, and there would be no reason why civilization should not die out, as in the Byzantine Empire. Persons of genius, it is true, are, and are always likely to be, a small minority; but in order to have them, it is necessary to preserve the soil in which they grow. Genius can only breathe freely in an *atmosphere* of freedom. Persons of genius are, *ex vi termini, more* individual than any other people—less capable, consequently, of fitting themselves, without hurtful compression, into any of the small number of moulds which society provides in order to save its members the trouble of forming their own character. If from timidity they consent to be forced into one of these moulds, and to let all that part of themselves which cannot expand under the pressure remain unexpanded, society will be little the better for their genius. If they are of a strong character, and break their fetters, they become a mark for the society which has not succeeded in reducing them to commonplace, to point at with solemn warning as "wild," "erratic," and the like; much as if one should complain of the Niagara river for not flowing smoothly between its banks like a Dutch canal.

I insist thus emphatically on the importance of genius, and the necessity of allowing it to unfold itself freely both in thought and in practice, being well aware that no one will deny the position in theory, but knowing also that almost every one, in reality, is totally indifferent to it. People think genius a fine thing if it enables a man to write an exciting poem, or paint a picture. But in its true sense, that of originality in thought and action, though no one says that it is not a thing to be admired, nearly all, at heart, think that they can do very well without it. Unhappily this is too natural to be wondered at. Originality is the one thing which unoriginal minds cannot feel the use of. They cannot see what it is to do for them: how should they? If they could see what it would do for them, it would not be originality. The first service which originality has to render them, is that of opening their eyes: which being once fully done, they would have a chance of being themselves original. Meanwhile, recollecting that nothing was ever yet done which some one was not the first to do, and that all good things which exist are the fruits of originality, let them be modest enough to believe that there is something still left for it to accomplish, and assure themselves that they are more in need of originality, the less they are conscious of the want.

In sober truth, whatever homage may be professed, or even paid, to real or supposed mental superiority, the general tendency of things throughout the world is to render mediocrity the ascendant power among mankind. In ancient history, in the Middle Ages, and in a diminishing degree through the long transition from feudality to the present time, the individual was a power in himself; and if he had either great talents or a high social position, he was a considerable power. At present individuals are lost in the crowd. In politics it is almost a triviality to say that public opinion now rules the world. The only power deserving the name is that of masses, and of governments while they make themselves the organ of the tendencies and instincts of masses. This is as true in the moral and social relations of private life as in public transactions. Those whose opinions go by the name of public opinion, are not always the same sort of public: in America, they are the whole white population; in England, chiefly the middle class. But they are always a mass, that is to say, collective mediocrity. And what is a still greater novelty, the mass do not now take their opinions from dignitaries in Church or State, from ostensible leaders, or from books. Their thinking is done for them by men much like themselves, addressing them or speaking in their name, on the spur of the moment, through the newspapers. I am not complaining of all this. I do not assert that anything better is compatible, as a general rule, with the present low state of the human mind. But that does not hinder the government of mediocrity from being mediocre government. No government by a democracy or a numerous aristocracy, either in its political acts or in the opinions, qualities, and tone of mind which it fosters, ever did or could rise above mediocrity, except in so far as the sovereign. Many have let themselves be guided (which in their best times they always have done) by the counsels and influence of a more highly gifted and instructed One or Few. The initiation of all wise or noble things, comes and must come from individuals; generally at first from some one individual. The honor and glory of the average man is that he is capable of following that initiative; that he can respond internally to wise and noble things, and be led to them with his eyes open. I am not countenancing the sort of "hero-worship" which applauds the strong man of genius for forcibly seizing on the government of the world and making it do his bidding in spite of itself. All he can claim is, freedom to point out the way. The power of compelling others into it, is not only inconsistent with the freedom and development of all the rest, but corrupting to the strong man himself. It does seem, however, that when the opinions of masses of merely average men are everywhere become or becoming the dominant power, the counterpoise and corrective to that tendency would be, the more and more pronounced individuality of those who stand on the higher eminences of thought. It is in these circumstances most especially, that exceptional individuals, instead of being deterred, should be encouraged in acting differently from the mass. In other times there was no advantage in their doing so, unless they acted not only differently, but better. In this age the mere example of non-conformity, the mere refusal to bend the knee to custom, is itself a service. Precisely because the tyranny of opinion is such as to make eccentricity a reproach, it is desirable, in order to break through that tyranny, that people should be eccentric. Eccentricity has always abounded when and where strength of character has abounded; and the amount of eccentricity in a society has generally been proportional to the amount of genius, mental vigor, and moral courage which it contained. That so few now dare to be eccentric, marks the chief danger of the time.

I have said that it is important to give the freest scope possible to uncustomary things, in order that it may in time appear which of these are fit to be converted into customs. But independence of action, and disregard of custom are not solely deserving of encouragement for the chance they afford that better modes of action, and customs more worthy of general adoption, may be struck out; nor is it only persons of decided mental superiority who have a just claim to carry on their lives in their own way. There is no reason that all human existences should be constructed on some one, or some small number of patterns. If a person possesses any tolerable amount of common sense and experience, his own mode of laying out his existence is the best, not because it is the best in itself, but because it is his own mode. Human beings are not like sheep; and even sheep are not undistinguishably alike. A man cannot get a coat or a pair of boots to fit him, unless they are either made to his measure, or he has a whole warehouseful to choose from: and is it easier to fit him with a life than with a coat, or are human beings more like one another in their whole physical and spiritual conformation than in the shape of their feet? If it were only that people have diversities of taste, that is reason enough for not attempting to shape them all after one model. But different persons also require different conditions for their spiritual development; and can no more exist healthily in the same moral, than all the variety of plants can in the same physical, atmosphere and climate. The same things which are helps to one person towards the cultivation of his higher nature, are hinderances to another. The same mode of life is a healthy excitement to one, keeping all his faculties of action and enjoyment in their best order, while to another it is a distracting burden, which suspends or crushes all internal life. Such are the differences among human beings in their sources of pleasure, their susceptibilities of pain, and the operation on them of different physical and moral agencies, that unless there is a corresponding diversity in their modes of life, they neither obtain their fair share of happiness, nor grow up to the mental, moral, and æsthetic stature of which their nature is capable. Why then should tolerance, as far as the public sentiment is concerned, extend only to tastes and modes of life which extort acquiescence by the multitude of their adherents? Nowhere (except in some monastic institutions) is diversity of taste entirely unrecognized; a person may without blame, either like or dislike rowing, or smoking, or music, or athletic exercises, or chess, or cards, or study, because both those who like each of these things, and those who dislike them, are too numerous to be put down. But the man, and still more the woman, who can be accused either of doing "what nobody does," or of not doing "what everybody does," is the subject of as much depreciatory remark as if he or she had committed some grave moral delinquency. Persons require to possess a title, or some other badge of rank, or the consideration of people of rank, to be able to indulge somewhat in the luxury of doing as they like without detriment to their estimation. To indulge somewhat, I repeat: for whoever allow themselves much of that indulgence, incur the risk of something worse than disparaging speeches—they are in peril of a commission *de lunatico,* and of having their property taken from them and given to their relations.[8]

There is one characteristic of the present direction of public opinion, peculiarly calculated to make it intolerant of any marked demonstration of individuality. The general average of mankind are not only moderate in intellect, but also moderate in inclinations: they have no tastes or wishes strong enough to incline them to do anything unusual, and they consequently do not understand those who have, and class all such with the wild and intemperate whom they are

[8]There is something both contemptible and frightful in the sort of evidence on which, of late years, any person can be judicially declared unfit for the management of his affairs; and after his death, his disposal of his property can be set aside, if there is enough of it to pay the expenses of litigation—which are charged on the property itself. All the minute details of his daily life are pried into, and whatever is found which, seen through the medium of the perceiving and describing faculties of the lowest of the low, bears an appearance unlike absolute commonplace, is laid before the jury as evidence of insanity, and often with success; the jurors being little, if at all, less vulgar and ignorant than the witnesses; while the judges, with that extraordinary want of knowledge of human nature and life which continually astonishes us in English lawyers, often help to mislead them. These trials speak volumes as to the state of feeling and opinion among the vulgar with regard to human liberty. So far from setting any value on individuality—so far from respecting the rights of each individual to act, in things indifferent, as seems good to his own judgment and inclinations, judges and juries cannot even conceive that a person in a state of sanity can desire such freedom. In former days, when it was proposed to burn atheists, charitable people used to suggest putting them in a madhouse instead: it would be nothing surprising now-a-days were we to see this done, and the doers applauding themselves, because, instead of persecuting for religion, they had adopted so humane and Christian a mode of treating these unfortunates, not without a silent satisfaction at their having thereby obtained their deserts.

accustomed to look down upon. Now, in addition to this fact which is general, we have only to suppose that a strong movement has set in towards the improvement of morals, and it is evident what we have to expect. In these days such a movement has set in; much has actually been effected in the way of increased regularity of conduct, and discouragement of excesses; and there is a philanthropic spirit abroad, for the exercise of which there is no more inviting field than the moral and prudential improvement of our fellow-creatures. These tendencies of the times cause the public to be more disposed than at most former periods to prescribe general rules of conduct, and endeavor to make every one conform to the approved standard. And that standard, express or tacit, is to desire nothing strongly. Its ideal of character is to be without any marked character; to maim by compression, like a Chinese lady's foot, every part of human nature which stands out prominently, and tends to make the person markedly dissimilar in outline to commonplace humanity.

As is usually the case with ideals which exclude one half of what is desirable, the present standard of approbation produces only an inferior imitation of the other half. Instead of great energies guided by vigorous reason, and strong feelings strongly controlled by a conscientious will, its result is weak feelings and weak energies, which therefore can be kept in outward conformity to rule without any strength either of will or of reason. Already energetic characters on any large scale are becoming merely traditional. There is now scarcely any outlet for energy in this country except business. The energy expended in that may still be regarded as considerable. What little is left from that employment, is expended on some hobby; which may be a useful, even a philanthropic hobby, but is always some one thing, and generally a thing of small dimensions. The greatness of England is now all collective: individually small, we only appear capable of anything great by our habit of combining; and with this our moral and religious philanthropists are perfectly contented. But it was men of another stamp than this that made England what it has been; and men of another stamp will be needed to prevent its decline.

The despotism of custom is everywhere the standing hindrance to human advancement, being in unceasing antagonism to that disposition to aim at something better than customary, which is called, according to circumstances, the spirit of liberty, or that of progress or improvement. The spirit of improvement is not always a spirit of liberty, for it may aim at forcing improvements on an unwilling people; and the spirit of liberty, in so far as it resists such attempts, may ally itself locally and temporarily with the opponents of improvement; but the only unfailing and permanent source of improvement is liberty, since by it there are as many possible independent centres of improvement as there are individuals. The progressive principle, however, in either shape, whether as the love of liberty or of improvement, is antagonistic to the sway of Custom, involving at least emancipation from that yoke; and the contest between the two constitutes the chief interest of the history of mankind. The greater part of the world has, properly speaking, no history, because the despotism of Custom is complete. This is the case over the whole East. Custom is there, in all things, the final appeal; justice and right mean conformity to custom; the argument of custom no one, unless some tyrant intoxicated with power, thinks of resisting. And we see the result. Those nations must once have had originality; they did not start out of the ground populous, lettered, and versed in many of the arts of life; they made themselves all this, and were then the greatest and most powerful nations in the world. What are they now? The subjects or dependents of tribes whose forefathers wandered in the forests when theirs had magnificent palaces and gorgeous temples, but over whom custom exercised only a divided rule with liberty and progress. A people, it appears, may be progressive for a certain length of time, and then stop: when does it stop? When it ceases to possess individuality. If a similar change should befall the nations of Europe, it will not be in exactly the same shape: the despotism of custom with which these nations are threatened is not precisely stationariness. It proscribes singularity, but it does not preclude change, provided all change together. We have discarded the fixed costumes of our forefathers; every one must still dress like other people, but the fashion may change once or twice a year. We thus take care that when there is change, it shall be for change's sake, and not from any idea of beauty or convenience; for the same idea of beauty or convenience would not strike all the world at the same moment, and be simultaneously thrown aside by all at another moment. But we are progressive as well as changeable: we continually make new inventions in mechanical things, and keep them until they are again superseded by better; we are eager for improvement in politics, in education, even in morals, though in this last our idea of improvement chiefly consists in persuading or forcing other people to be as good as ourselves. It is not progress that we object to; on the contrary, we flatter ourselves that we are the most progressive people who ever lived. It is individuality that we war against: we should think we had done wonders if we had made ourselves all alike; forgetting that the unlikeness of one person to another is generally the first thing which draws the attention of either to the imperfection of his own type, and the superiority of another, or the possibility, by combining the advantages of both, of producing something better than either. We have a warning example in China—a nation of much talent, and, in some respects, even wisdom, owing to the rare good fortune of having been provided at an early period with a particularly good set of customs, the work, in some measure, of men to whom even the most enlightened European must accord, under certain limitations, the title of sages and philosophers. They are remarkable, too, in the excellence of their apparatus for impressing, as far as possible, the best wisdom they possess upon every mind in the community, and securing that those who have appropriated most of it shall occupy the posts of honor and power. Surely the people who did this have discovered the secret of human progressiveness, and must have kept themselves steadily at the head of the movement of the world. On the contrary, they have become stationary—have remained so for thousands of years; and if they are ever to be further improved, it must be by foreigners. They have succeeded beyond all hope in what English philanthropists are so industriously working at—in making a people all alike, all governing their thoughts and conduct by the same maxims and rules; and these are the fruits. The modern *régime* of public opinion is, in an unorganized form, what the Chinese educational and political systems are in an organized; and unless individuality shall be able successfully to assert itself against this yoke, Europe, notwithstanding its noble antecedents and its professed Christianity, will tend to become another China.

What is it that has hitherto preserved Europe from this lot?

What has made the European family of nations an improving, instead of a stationary portion of mankind? Not any superior excellence in them, which when it exists, exists as the effect, not as the cause; but their remarkable diversity of character and culture. Individuals, classes, nations, have been extremely unlike one another: they have struck out a great variety of paths, each leading to something valuable; and although at every period those who travelled in different paths have been intolerant of one another, and each would have thought it an excellent thing if all the rest could have been compelled to travel his road, their attempts to thwart each other's development have rarely had any permanent success, and each has in time endured to receive the good which the others have offered. Europe is, in my judgment, wholly indebted to this plurality of paths for its progressive and many-sided development. But it already begins to possess this benefit in a considerably less degree. It is decidedly advancing towards the Chinese ideal of making all people alike. M. de Tocqueville, in his last important work, remarks how much more the Frenchmen of the present day resemble one another, than did those even of the last generation. The same remark might be made of Englishmen in a far greater degree. In a passage already quoted from Wilhelm von Humboldt, he points out two things as necessary conditions of human development, because necessary to render people unlike one another; namely, freedom, and variety of situations. The second of these two conditions is in this country every day diminishing. The circumstances which surround different classes and individuals, and shape their characters, are daily becoming more assimilated. Formerly, different ranks, different neighborhoods, different trades and professions, lived in what might be called different worlds, at present, to a great degree in the same. Comparatively speaking, they now read the same things, listen to the same things, see the same things, go to the same places, have their hopes and fears directed to the same objects, have the same rights and liberties, and the same means of asserting them. Great as are the differences of position which remain, they are nothing to those which have ceased. And the assimilation is still proceeding. All the political changes of the age promote it, since they all tend to raise the low and to lower the high. Every extension of education promotes it, because education brings people under common influences, and gives them access to the general stock of facts and sentiments. Improvements in the means of communication promote it, by bringing the inhabitants of distant places into personal contact, and keeping up a rapid flow of changes of residence between one place and another. The increase of commerce and manufactures promotes it, by diffusing more widely the advantages of easy circumstances, and opening all objects of ambition, even the highest, to general competition, whereby the desire of rising becomes no longer the character of a particular class, but of all classes. A more powerful agency than even all these, in bringing about a general similarity among mankind, is the complete establishment, in this and other free countries, of the ascendency of public opinion in the State. As the various social eminences which enabled persons entrenched on them to disregard the opinion of the multitude, gradually become levelled; as the very idea of resisting the will of the public, when it is positively known that they have a will, disappears more and more from the minds of practical politicians; there ceases to be any social support for non-conformity—any substantive power in society, which, itself opposed to the ascendency of numbers, is interested in taking under its protection opinions and tendencies at variance with those of the public.

The combination of all these causes forms so great a mass of influences hostile to Individuality, that it is not easy to see how it can stand its ground. It will do so with increasing difficulty, unless the intelligent part of the public can be made to feel its value—to see that it is good there should be differences, even though not for the better, even though, as it may appear to them, some should be for the worse. If the claims of Individuality are ever to be asserted, the time is now, while much is still wanting to complete the enforced assimilation. It is only in the earlier stages that any stand can be successfully made against the encroachment. The demand that all other people shall resemble ourselves, grows by what it feeds on. If resistance waits till life is reduced *nearly* to one uniform type, all deviations from that type will come to be considered impious, immoral, even monstrous and contrary to nature. Mankind speedily become unable to conceive diversity, when they have been for some time unaccustomed to see it.

CHAPTER IV

OF THE LIMITS TO THE AUTHORITY OF SOCIETY
OVER THE INDIVIDUAL

WHAT, THEN, is the rightful limit to the sovereignty of the individual over himself? Where does the authority of society begin? How much of human life should be assigned to individuality, and how much to society?

Each will receive its proper share, if each has that which more particularly concerns it. To individuality should belong the part of life in which it is chiefly the individual that is interested; to society, the part which chiefly interests society.

Though society is not founded on a contract, and though no good purpose is answered by inventing a contract in order to deduce social obligations from it, every one who receives the protection of society owes a return for the benefit, and the fact of living in society renders it indispensable that each should be bound to observe a certain line of conduct towards the rest. This conduct consists, first, in not injuring the interests of one another; or rather certain interests, which, either by express legal provision or by tacit understanding, ought to be considered as rights; and secondly, in each person's bearing his share (to be fixed on some equitable principle) of the labors and sacrifices incurred for defending the society or its members from injury and molestation. These conditions society is justified in enforcing, at all costs to those who endeavor to withhold fulfilment. Nor is this all that society may do. The acts of an individual may be hurtful to others, or wanting in due consideration for their welfare, without going the length of violating any of their constituted rights. The offender may then be justly punished by opinion, though not by law. As soon as any part of a person's conduct affects prejudicially the interests of others, society has jurisdiction over it, and the question whether the general welfare will or will not be promoted by interfering with it, becomes open to discussion. But there is no room for entertaining any such question when a person's conduct affects the interests of no persons besides himself, or needs not affect them unless they like (all the persons concerned being of full age, and the ordinary amount of understanding). In all such cases there should be perfect freedom, legal and social, to do the action and stand the consequences.

It would be a great misunderstanding of this doctrine, to suppose that it is one of selfish indifference, which pretends that human beings have no business with each other's conduct in life, and that they should not concern themselves about the well-doing or well-being of one another, unless their own interest is involved. Instead of any diminution, there is need of a great increase of disinterested exertion to promote the good of others. But disinterested benevolence can find other instruments to persuade people to their good, than whips and scourges, either of the literal or the metaphorical sort. I am the last person to undervalue the self-regarding virtues; they are only second in importance, if even second, to the social. It is equally the business of education to cultivate both. But even education works by conviction and persuasion as well as by compulsion, and it is by the former only that, when the period of education is past, the self-regarding virtues should be inculcated. Human beings owe to each other help to distinguish the better from the worse, and encouragement to choose the former and avoid the latter. They should be forever stimulating each other to increased exercise of their higher faculties, and increased direction of their feelings and aims towards wise instead of foolish, elevating instead of degrading, objects and contemplations. But neither one person, nor any number of persons, is warranted in saying to another human creature of ripe years, that he shall not do with his life for his own benefit what he chooses to do with it. He is the person most interested in his own well-being, the interest which any other person, except in cases of strong personal attachment, can have in it, is trifling, compared with that which he himself has; the interest which society has in him individually (except as to his conduct to others) is fractional, and altogether indirect: while, with respect to his own feelings and circumstances, the most ordinary man or woman has means of knowledge immeasurably surpassing those that can be possessed by any one else. The interference of society to overrule his judgment and purposes in what only regards himself, must be grounded on general presumptions; which may be altogether wrong, and even if right, are as likely as not to be misapplied to individual cases, by persons no better acquainted with the circumstances of such cases than those are who look at them merely from without. In this department, therefore, of human affairs, Individuality has its proper field of action. In the conduct of human beings towards one another, it is necessary that general rules should for the most part be observed, in order that people may know what they have to expect; but in each person's own concerns, his individual spontaneity is entitled to free exercise. Considerations to aid his judgment, exhortations to strengthen his will, may be offered to him, even obtruded on him, by others; but he, himself, is the final judge. All errors which he is likely to commit against advice and warning, are far outweighed by the evil of allowing others to constrain him to what they deem his good.

I do not mean that the feelings with which a person is regarded by others, ought not to be in any way affected by his self-regarding qualities or deficiencies. This is neither possible nor desirable. If he is eminent in any of the qualities which conduce to his own good, he is, so far, a proper object of admiration. He is so much the nearer to the ideal perfection of human nature. If he is grossly deficient in those qualities, a sentiment the opposite of admiration will follow. There is a degree of folly, and a degree of what may be called (though the phrase is not unobjectionable) lowness or depravation of taste, which, though it cannot justify doing harm to the person who manifests it, renders him necessarily and properly a subject of distaste, or, in extreme cases, even of contempt: a person could not have the opposite qualities in due strength without entertaining these feelings. Though doing no wrong to any one, a person may so act as to compel us to judge him, and feel to him, as a fool, or as a being of an inferior order: and since this judgment and feeling are a fact which he would prefer to avoid, it is doing him a service to warn him of it beforehand, as of any other disagreeable consequence to which he exposes himself. It would be well, indeed, if this good office were much more freely rendered than the common notions of politeness at present permit, and if one person could honestly point out to another that he thinks him in fault, without being considered unmannerly or presuming. We have a right, also, in various ways, to act upon our unfavorable opinion of any one, not to the oppression of his individuality, but in the exercise of ours. We are not bound, for example, to seek his society; we have a right to avoid it (though not to parade the avoidance), for we have a right to choose the society most acceptable to us. We have a right, and it may be our duty to caution others against him, if we think his example or conversation likely to have a pernicious effect on those with whom he associates. We may give others a preference over him in optional good offices, except those which tend to his improvement. In these various modes a person may suffer very severe penalties at the hands of others, for faults which directly concern only himself; but he suffers these penalties only in so far as they are the natural, and, as it were, the spontaneous consequences of the faults themselves, not because they are purposely inflicted on him for the sake of punishment. A person who shows rashness, obstinacy, self-conceit—who cannot live within moderate means—who cannot restrain himself from hurtful indulgences —who pursues animal pleasures at the expense of those of feeling and intellect—must expect to be lowered in the opinion of others, and to have a less share of their favorable sentiments, but of this he has no right to complain, unless he has merited their favor by special excellence in his social relations, and has thus established a title to their good offices, which is not affected by his demerits towards himself.

What I contend for is, that the inconveniences which are strictly inseparable from the unfavorable judgment of others, are the only ones to which a person should ever be subjected for that portion of his conduct and character which concerns his own good, but which does not affect the interests of others in their relations with him. Acts injurious to others require a totally different treatment. Encroachment on their rights; infliction on them of any loss or damage not justified by his own rights; falsehood or duplicity in dealing with them; unfair or ungenerous use of advantages over them; even selfish abstinence from defending them against injury—these are fit objects of moral reprobation, and, in grave cases, of moral retribution and punishment. And not only these acts, but the dispositions which lead to them, are properly immoral, and fit subjects of disapprobation which may rise to abhorrence. Cruelty of disposition; malice and ill-nature; that most anti-social and odious of all passions, envy; dissimulation and insincerity; irascibility on insufficient cause, and resentment disproportioned to the provocation; the love of domineering over others; the desire to engross more than one's share of advantages (the πλεονεξία of the Greeks); the pride which derives gratification from the abasement of others; the egotism which thinks self and its concerns more important than everything else, and decides all doubtful questions in his own favor;—these are moral vices, and constitute a bad and odious moral character: unlike the self-regarding faults previously mentioned, which are not properly immoralities, and to whatever pitch they may be carried, do not constitute wickedness. They may be proofs of any amount of folly, or want of personal dignity and self-respect; but they are only a subject of moral reprobation when they involve a breach of duty to others, for whose sake the individual is bound to have care for himself. What are called duties to ourselves are not socially obligatory, unless circumstances render them at the same time duties to others. The term duty to oneself, when it means anything more than prudence, means self-respect or self-development; and for none of these is any one accountable to his fellow-creatures, because for none of them is it for the good of mankind that he be held accountable to them.

The distinction between the loss of consideration which a person may rightly incur by defect of prudence or of personal dignity, and the reprobation which is due to him for an offence against the rights of others, is not a merely nominal distinction. It makes a vast difference both in our feelings and in our conduct towards him, whether he displeases us in things in which we think we have a right to control him, or in things in which we know that we have not. If he displeases us, we may express our distaste, and we may stand aloof from a person as well as from a thing that displeases us; but we shall not therefore feel called on to make his life uncomfortable. We shall reflect that he already bears, or will bear, the whole penalty of his error; if he spoils his life by mismanagement, we shall not, for that reason, desire to spoil it still further: instead of wishing to punish him, we shall rather endeavor to alleviate his punishment, by showing him how he may avoid or cure the evils his conduct tends to bring upon him. He may be to us an object of pity, perhaps of dislike, but not of anger or resentment; we shall not treat him like an enemy of society: the worst we shall think ourselves justified in doing is leaving him to himself, if we do not interfere benevolently by showing interest or concern for him. It is far otherwise if he has infringed the rules necessary for the protection of his fellow-creatures, individually or collectively. The evil consequences of his acts do not then fall on himself, but on others; and society, as the protector of all its members, must retaliate on him; must inflict pain on him for the express purpose of punishment, and must take care that it be sufficiently severe. In the one case, he is an offender at our bar, and we are called on not only to sit in judgment on him, but, in one shape or another, to execute our own sentence: in the other case, it is not our part to inflict any suffering on him, except what may incidentally follow from our using the same liberty in the regulation of our own affairs, which we allow to him in his.

The distinction here pointed out between the part of a person's life which concerns only himself, and that which concerns others, many persons will refuse to admit. How (it may be asked) can any part of the conduct of a member of society be a matter of indifference to the other members? No person is an entirely isolated being; it is impossible for a person to do anything seriously or permanently hurtful to himself, without mischief reaching at least to his near connections, and often far beyond them. If he injures his property, he does harm to those who directly or indirectly derived support from it, and usually diminishes, by a greater or less amount, the general resources of the community. If he deteriorates his bodily or mental faculties, he not only brings evil upon all who depended on him for any portion of their happiness, but disqualifies himself for rendering the services which he owes to his fellow-creatures generally; perhaps becomes a burden on their affection or benevolence; and if such conduct were very frequent, hardly any offence that is committed would detract more from the general sum of good. Finally, if by his vices or follies a person does no direct harm to others, he is nevertheless (it may be said) injurious by his example; and ought to be compelled to control himself, for the sake of those whom the sight or knowledge of his conduct might corrupt or mislead.

And even (it will be added) if the consequences of misconduct could be confined to the vicious or thoughtless individual, ought society to abandon to their own guidance those who are manifestly unfit for it? If protection against themselves is confessedly due to children and persons under age, is not society equally bound to afford it to persons of mature years who are equally incapable of self-government? If gambling, or drunkenness, or incontinence, or idleness, or uncleanliness, are as injurious to happiness, and as great a hindrance to improvement, as many or most of the acts prohibited by law, why (it may be asked) should not law, so far as is consistent with practicability and social convenience, endeavor to repress these also? And as a supplement to the unavoidable imperfections of law, ought not opinion at least to organize a powerful police against these vices, and visit rigidly with social penalties those who are known to practise them? These is no question here (it may be said) about restricting individuality, or impeding the trial of new and original experiments in living. The only things it is sought to prevent are things which have been tried and condemned from the beginning of the world until now; things which experience has shown not to be useful or suitable to any person's individuality. There must be some length of time and amount of experience, after which a moral or prudential truth may be regarded as established: and it is merely desired to prevent generation after generation from falling over the same precipice which has been fatal to their predecessors.

I fully admit that the mischief which a person does to himself, may seriously affect, both through their sympathies and their interests, those nearly connected with him, and in a minor degree, society at large. When, by conduct of this sort, a person is led to violate a distinct and assignable obligation to any other person or persons, the case is taken out of the self-regarding class, and becomes amenable to moral disapprobation in the proper sense of the term. If, for example, a man, through intemperance or extravagance, becomes unable to pay his debts, or, having undertaken the moral responsibility of a family, becomes from the same cause incapable of supporting or educating them, he is deservedly reprobated, and might be justly punished; but it is for the breach of duty to his family or creditors, not for the extravagance. If the resources which ought to have been devoted to them, had been diverted from them for the most prudent investment, the moral culpability would have been the same. George Barnwell murdered his uncle to get money for his mistress, but if he had done it to set himself up in business, he would equally have been hanged. Again, in the frequent case of a man who causes grief to his family by addiction to bad habits, he deserves reproach for his unkindness or ingratitude; but so he may for cultivating habits not in themselves vicious, if they are painful to those with whom he passes his life, or who from personal ties are dependent on him for their comfort. Whoever fails in the consideration generally due to the interests and feelings of others, not being compelled by some more imperative duty, or justified by allowable self-preference, is a subject of moral disapprobation for that failure, but not for the cause of it, nor for the errors, merely personal to himself, which may have remotely led to it. In like manner, when a person disables himself, by conduct purely self-regarding, from the performance of some definite duty incumbent on him to the public, he is guilty of a social offence. No person ought to be punished simply for being drunk; but a soldier or a policeman should be punished for being drunk on duty. Whenever, in short, there is a definite damage, or a definite risk of damage, either to an individual or to the public, the case is taken out of the province of liberty, and placed in that of morality or law.

But with regard to the merely contingent, or, as it may be called, constructive injury which a person causes to society, by conduct which neither violates any specific duty to the public, nor occasions perceptible hurt to any assignable individual except himself; the inconvenience is one which society can afford to bear, for the sake of the greater good of human freedom. If grown persons are to be punished for not taking proper care of themselves, I would rather it were for their own sake, than under pretence of preventing them from impairing their capacity of rendering to society benefits which society does not pretend it has a right to exact. But I cannot consent to argue the point as if society had no means of bringing its weaker members up to its ordinary standard of rational conduct, except waiting till they do something irrational, and then punishing them, legally or morally, for it. Society has had absolute power over them during all the early portion of their existence: it has had the whole period of childhood and nonage in which to try whether it could make them capable of rational conduct in life. The existing generation is master both of the training and the entire circumstances of the generation to come; it cannot indeed make them perfectly wise and good, because it is itself so lamentably deficient in goodness and wisdom; and its best efforts are not always, in individual cases, its most successful ones; but it is perfectly well able to make the rising generation, as a whole, as good as, and a little better than, itself. If society lets any considerable number of its members grow up mere children, incapable of being acted on by rational consideration of distant motives, society has itself to blame for the consequences. Armed not only with all the powers of education, but with the ascendency which the authority of a received opinion always exercises over the minds who are least fitted to judge for themselves; and aided by the *natural* penalties which cannot be prevented from falling on those who incur the distaste or the contempt of those who know them; let not society pretend that it needs, besides all this, the power to issue commands and enforce obedience in the personal concerns of individuals, in which, on all principles of justice and policy, the decision ought to rest with those who are to abide the consequences. Nor is there anything which tends more to discredit and frustrate the better means of influencing conduct, than a resort to the worse. If there be among those whom it is attempted to coerce into prudence or temperance, any of the material of which vigorous and independent characters are made, they will infallibly rebel against the yoke. No such person will ever feel that others have a right to control him in his concerns, such as they have to prevent him from injuring them in theirs; and it easily comes to be considered a mark of spirit and courage to fly in the face of such usurped authority, and do with ostentation the exact opposite of what it enjoins; as in the fashion of grossness which succeeded, in the time of Charles II, to the fanatical moral intolerance of the Puritans. With respect to what is said of the necessity of protecting society from the bad example set to others by the vicious or the self-indulgent; it is true that bad example may have a pernicious effect, especially the example of doing wrong to others with impunity to the wrongdoer. But we are now speaking of conduct which, while it does no wrong to others, is supposed to do great harm to the agent himself: and I do not see how those who believe this, can think otherwise than that the example, on the whole, must be more salutary than hurtful, since, if it displays the misconduct, it displays also the painful or degrading consequences which, if the conduct is justly censured, must be supposed to be in all or most cases attendant on it.

But the strongest of all the arguments against the interference of the public with purely personal conduct, is that when it does interfere, the odds are that it interferes wrongly, and in the wrong place. On questions of social morality, of duty to others, the opinion of the public, that is, of an overruling majority, though often wrong, is likely to be still oftener right; because on such questions they are only required to judge of their own interests; of the manner in which some mode of conduct, if allowed to be practised, would affect themselves. But the opinion of a similar majority, imposed as a law on the minority, on questions of self-regarding conduct, is quite as likely to be wrong as right; for in these cases public opinion means, at the best, some people's opinion of what is good or bad for other people; while very often it does not even mean that; the public, with the most perfect indifference, passing over the pleasure or convenience of those whose conduct they censure, and considering only their own preference. There are many who consider as an injury to themselves any conduct which they have a distaste for, and resent it as an outrage to their feelings; as a religious bigot, when charged with disregarding the religious feelings of others, has been known to retort that they disregard his feelings, by persisting in their abominable worship or creed. But there is no parity between the feeling of a person for his own opinion, and the feeling of another who is offended at his holding it; no more than between the desire of a thief to take a purse, and the desire of the right owner to keep it. And a person's taste is as much his own peculiar concern as his opinion or his purse. It is easy for any one to imagine an ideal public, which leaves the freedom and choice of individuals in all uncertain matters undisturbed, and only requires them to abstain from modes of conduct which universal experience has condemned. But where has there been seen a public which set any such limit to its censorship? or when does the public trouble itself about universal experience? In its interferences with personal conduct it is seldom thinking of anything but the enormity of acting or feeling differently from itself; and this standard of judgment, thinly disguised, is held up to mankind as the dictate of religion and philosophy, by nine tenths of all moralists and speculative writers. These teach that things are right because they are right; because we feel them to be so. They tell us to search in our own minds and hearts for laws of conduct binding on ourselves and on all others. What can the poor public do but apply these instructions, and make their own personal feelings of good and evil, if they are tolerably unanimous in them, obligatory on all the world?

The evil here pointed out is not one which exists only in theory; and it may perhaps be expected that I should specify the instances in which the public of this age and country improperly invests its own preferences with the character of moral laws. I am not writing an essay on the aberrations of existing moral feeling. That is too weighty a subject to be discussed parenthetically, and by way of illustration. Yet examples are necessary, to show that the principle I maintain is of serious and practical moment, and that I am not endeavoring to erect a barrier against imaginary evils. And it is not difficult to show, by abundant instances, that to extend the bounds of what may be called moral police, until it encroaches on the most unquestionably legitimate liberty of the individual, is one of the most universal of all human propensities.

As a first instance, consider the antipathies which men cherish on no better grounds than that persons whose religious opinions are different from theirs, do not practise their religious observances, especially their religious abstinences. To cite a rather trivial example, nothing in the creed or practice of Christians does more to envenom the hatred of Mahomedans against them, than the fact of their eating pork. There are few acts which Christians and Europeans regard with more unaffected disgust, than Mussulmans regard this particular mode of satisfying hunger. It is, in the first place, an offence against their religion; but this circumstance by no means explains either the degree or the kind of their repugnance; for wine also is forbidden by their religion, and to partake of it is by all Mussulmans accounted wrong, but not disgusting. Their aversion to the flesh of the "unclean beast" is, on the contrary, of that peculiar character, resembling an instinctive antipathy, which the idea of uncleanness, when once it thoroughly sinks into the feelings, seems always to excite even in those whose personal habits are anything but scrupulously cleanly, and of which the sentiment of religious impurity, so intense in the Hindoos, is a remarkable example. Suppose now that in a people, of whom the majority were Mussulmans, that majority should insist upon not permitting pork to be eaten within the limits of the country. This would be nothing new in Mahomedan countries.[9] Would it be a legitimate exercise of the moral authority of public opinion? and if not, why not? The practice is really revolting to such a public. They also sincerely think that it is forbidden and abhorred by the Deity. Neither could the prohibition be censured as religious persecution. It might be religious in its origin, but it would not be persecution for religion, since nobody's religion makes it a duty to eat pork. The only tenable ground of condemnation would be, that with the personal tastes and self-regarding concerns of individuals the public has no business to interfere.

To come somewhat nearer home: the majority of Spaniards consider it a gross impiety, offensive in the highest degree to the Supreme Being, to worship him in any other manner than the Roman Catholic; and no other public worship is lawful on Spanish soil. The people of all Southern Europe look upon a married clergy as not only irreligious, but unchaste, indecent, gross, disgusting. What do Protestants think of these perfectly sincere feelings, and of the attempt to enforce them against non-Catholics? Yet, if mankind are justified in interfering with each other's liberty in things which do not concern the interests of others, on what principle is it possible consistently to exclude these cases? or who can blame people for desiring to suppress what they regard as a scandal in the

---

[9]The case of the Bombay Parsees is a curious instance in point. When this industrious and enterprising tribe, the descendants of the Persian fire-worshippers, flying from their native country before the Caliphs, arrived in Western India, they were admitted to toleration by the Hindoo sovereigns, on condition of not eating beef. When those regions afterwards fell under the dominion of Mahomedan conquerors, the Parsees obtained from them a continuance of indulgence, on condition of refraining from pork. What was at first obedience to authority became a second nature, and the Parsees to this day abstain both from beef and pork. Though not required by their religion, the double abstinence has had time to grow into a custom of their tribe; and custom, in the East, is a religion.

sight of God and man? No stronger case can be shown for
prohibiting anything which is regarded as a personal immorality, than is made out for suppressing these practices in
the eyes of those who regard them as impieties; and unless
we are willing to adopt the logic of persecutors, and to say that
we may persecute others because we are right, and that they
must not persecute us because they are wrong, we must be-
ware of admitting a principle of which we should resent as a
gross injustice the application to ourselves.

The preceding instances may be objected to, although
unreasonably, as drawn from contingencies impossible among
us: opinion, in this country, not being likely to enforce abstinence from meats, or to interfere with people for worshipping,
and for either marrying or not marrying, according to their
creed or inclination. The next example, however, shall be
taken from an interference with liberty which we have by
no means passed all danger of. Wherever the Puritans have
been sufficiently powerful, as in New England, and in Great
Britain at the time of the Commonwealth, they have endeavored, with considerable success, to put down all public, and
nearly all private, amusements: especially music, dancing,
public games, or other assemblages for purposes of diversion,
and the theatre. There are still in this country large bodies
of persons by whose notions of morality and religion these
recreations are condemned; and those persons belonging
chiefly to the middle class, who are the ascendant power in
the present social and political condition of the kingdom, it
is by no means impossible that persons of these sentiments
may at some time or other command a majority in Parliament.
How will the remaining portion of the community like to
have the amusements that shall be permitted to them regulated by the religious and moral sentiments of the stricter
Calvinists and Methodists? Would they not, with considerable
peremptoriness, desire these intrusively pious members of
society to mind their own business? This is precisely what
should be said to every government and every public, who
have the pretension that no person shall enjoy any pleasure
which they think wrong. But if the principle of the pretension
be admitted, no one can reasonably object to its being acted
on in the sense of the majority, or other preponderating power
in the country; and all persons must be ready to conform to
the idea of a Christian commonwealth, as understood by the

early settlers in New England, if a religious profession similar to theirs should ever succeed in regaining its lost ground, as religions supposed to be declining have so often been known to do.

To imagine another contingency, perhaps more likely to be realized than the one last mentioned. There is confessedly a strong tendency in the modern world towards a democratic constitution of society, accompanied or not by popular political institutions. It is affirmed that in the country where this tendency is most completely realized—where both society and the government are most democratic—the United States—the feeling of the majority, to whom any appearance of a more showy or costly style of living than they can hope to rival is disagreeable, operates as a tolerably effectual sumptuary law, and that in many parts of the Union it is really difficult for a person possessing a very large income, to find any mode of spending it, which will not incur popular disapprobation. Though such statements as these are doubtless much exaggerated as a representation of existing facts, the state of things they describe is not only a conceivable and possible, but a probable result of democratic feeling, combined with the notion that the public has a right to a veto on the manner in which individuals shall spend their incomes. We have only further to suppose a considerable diffusion of Socialist opinions, and it may become infamous in the eyes of the majority to possess more property than some very small amount, or any income not earned by manual labor. Opinions similar in principle to these, already prevail widely among the artisan class, and weigh oppressively on those who are amenable to the opinion chiefly of that class, namely, its own members. It is known that the bad workmen who form the majority of the operatives in many branches of industry, are decidedly of opinion that bad workmen ought to receive the same wages as good, and that no one ought to be allowed, through piecework or otherwise, to earn by superior skill or industry more than others can without it. And they employ a moral police, which occasionally becomes a physical one, to deter skilful workmen from receiving, and employers from giving, a larger remuneration for a more useful service. If the public have any jurisdiction over private concerns, I cannot see that these people are in fault, or that any individual's particular public can be blamed for asserting the same authority over his individual conduct, which the general public asserts over people in general.

But, without dwelling upon supposititious cases, there are, in our own day, gross usurpations upon the liberty of private life actually practised, and still greater ones threatened with some expectation of success, and opinions proposed which assert an unlimited right in the public not only to prohibit by law everything which it thinks wrong, but in order to get at what it thinks wrong, to prohibit any number of things which it admits to be innocent.

Under the name of preventing intemperance, the people of one English colony, and of nearly half the United States, have been interdicted by law from making any use whatever of fermented drinks, except for medical purposes: for prohibition of their sale is in fact, as it is intended to be, prohibition of their use. And though the impracticability of executing the law has caused its repeal in several of the States which had adopted it, including the one from which it derives its name, an attempt has notwithstanding been commenced, and is prosecuted with considerable zeal by many of the professed philanthropists, to agitate for a similar law in this country. The association, or "Alliance" as it terms itself, which has been formed for this purpose, has acquired some notoriety through the publicity given to a correspondence between its Secretary and one of the very few English public men who hold that a politician's opinions ought to be founded on principles. Lord Stanley's share in this correspondence is calculated to strengthen the hopes already built on him, by those who know how rare such qualities as are manifested in some of his public appearances, unhappily are among those who figure in political life. The organ of the Alliance, who would "deeply deplore the recognition of any principle which could be wrested to justify bigotry and persecution," undertakes to point out the "broad and impassable barrier" which divides such principles from those of the association. "All matters relating to thought, opinion, conscience, appear to me," he says, "to be without the sphere of legislation; all pertaining to social act, habit, relation, subject only to a discretionary power vested in the State itself, and not in the individual, to be within it." No mention is made of a third class, different from either of these, viz., acts and habits which are not social, but individual; although it is to this class, surely, that the act of drinking fermented liquors belongs. Selling fermented liquors, however, is trading, and trading is a social act. But the infringement complained of is not on the liberty of the seller, but on that of the buyer and consumer; since the State might just as well forbid him to drink wine, as purposely make it impossible for him to obtain it. The Secretary, however, says, "I claim, as a citizen, a right to legislate whenever my social rights are invaded by the social act of another." And now for the definition of these "social rights." "If anything invades my social rights, certainly the traffic in strong drink does. It destroys my primary right of security, by constantly creating and stimulating social disorder. It invades my right of equality, by deriving a profit from the creation of a misery, I am taxed to support. It impedes my right to free moral and intellectual development, by surrounding my path with dangers, and by weakening and demoralizing society, from which I have a right to claim mutual aid and intercourse." A theory of "social rights," the like of which probably never before found its way into distinct language—being nothing short of this— that it is the absolute social right of every individual, that every other individual shall act in every respect exactly as he ought; that whosoever fails thereof in the smallest particular, violates my social right, and entitles me to demand from the legislature the removal of the grievance. So monstrous a principle is far more dangerous than any single interference with liberty; there is no violation of liberty which it would not justify; it acknowledges no right to any freedom whatever, except perhaps to that of holding opinions in secret, without ever disclosing them: for the moment an opinion which I consider noxious, passes any one's lips, it invades all the "social rights" attributed to me by the Alliance. The doctrine ascribes to all mankind a vested interest in each other's moral, intellectual, and even physical perfection, to be defined by each claimant according to his own standard.

Another important example of illegitimate interference with the rightful liberty of the individual, not simply threatened, but long since carried into triumphant effect, is Sabbatarian legislation. Without doubt, abstinence on one day in the week, so far as the exigencies of life permit, from the usual daily occupation, though in no respect religiously binding on any except Jews, is a highly beneficial custom. And inasmuch as this custom cannot be observed without a general consent to that effect among the industrious classes, therefore, in so far as some persons by working may impose the same necessity on others, it may be allowable and right that the law should guarantee to each, the observance by others of the custom, by suspending the greater operations of industry on a particular day. But this justification, grounded on the direct interest which others have in each individual's observance of the practice, does not apply to the self-chosen occupations in which a person may think fit to employ his leisure; nor does it hold good, in the smallest degree, for the legal restrictions on amusements. It is true that the amusement of some is the day's work of others; but the pleasure, not to say the useful recreation, of many, is worth the labor of a few, provided the occupation is freely chosen, and can be freely resigned. The operatives are perfectly right in thinking that if all worked on Sunday seven days' work would have to be given for six days' wages: but so long as the great mass of employments are suspended, the small number who for the enjoyment of others must still work, obtain a proportional increase of earnings; and they are not obliged to follow those occupations, if they prefer leisure to emolument. If a further remedy is sought, it might be found in the establishment by custom of a holiday on some other day of the week for those particular classes of persons. The only ground, therefore, on which restrictions on Sunday amusements can be defended, must be that they are religiously wrong; a motive of legislation which never can be too earnestly protested again. *Deorum injuriæ Diis curæ*. It remains to be proved that society or any of its officers holds a commission from on high to avenge any supposed offence to Omnipotence, which is not also a wrong to our fellow-creatures. The notion that it is one man's duty that another should be religious, was the foundation of all the religious persecutions ever perpetrated, and if admitted, would fully justify them. Though the feeling which breaks out in the repeated attempts to stop railway travelling on Sunday, in the resistance to the opening of Museums, and the like, has not the cruelty of the old persecutors, the state of mind indicated by it is fundamentally the same. It is a determination not to tolerate others in doing what is permitted by their religion, because it is not permitted by the persecutor's religion. It is a belief that God not only abominates the act of the misbeliever, but will not hold us guiltless if we leave him unmolested.

I cannot refrain from adding to these examples of the little account commonly made of human liberty, the language of downright persecution which breaks out from the press of this country, whenever it feels called on to notice the remarkable phenomenon of Mormonism. Much might be said on the unexpected and instructive fact, that an alleged new revelation, and a religion founded on it, the product of palpable imposture, not even supported by the *prestige* of extraordinary qualities in its founder, is believed by hundreds of thousands, and has been made the foundation of a society, in the age of newspapers, railways, and the electric telegraph. What here concerns us is, that this religion, like other and better religions, has its martyrs; that its prophet and founder was, for his teaching, put to death by a mob; that others of its adherents lost their lives by the same lawless violence; that they were forcibly expelled, in a body, from the country in which they first grew up; while, now that they have been chased into a solitary recess in the midst of a desert, many in this country openly declare that it would be right (only that it is not convenient) to send an expedition against them, and compel them by force to conform to the opinions of other people. The article of the Mormonite doctrine which is the chief provocative to the antipathy which thus breaks through the ordinary restraints of religious tolerance, is its sanction of polygamy; which, though permitted to Mahomedans, and Hindoos, and Chinese, seems to excite unquenchable animosity when practised by persons who speak English, and profess to be a kind of Christians. No one has a deeper disapprobation than I have of this Mormon institution; both for other reasons, and because, far from being in any way countenanced by the principle of liberty, it is a direct infraction of that principle, being a mere riveting of the chains of one half of the community, and an emancipation of the other from reciprocity of obligation towards them. Still, it must be remembered that this relation is as much voluntary on the part of the women concerned in it, and who may be deemed the sufferers by it, as is the case with any other form of the marriage institution; and however surprising this fact may appear, it has its explanation in the common ideas and customs of the world, which teaching women to think marriage the one thing needful, make it intelligible that many a woman should prefer being one of several wives, to not being a wife at all. Other countries are not asked to recognize such unions, or release any portion of their inhabitants from their own laws on the score of Mormonite opinions. But when the dissentients have conceded to the hostile sentiments of others, far more than could justly be demanded; when they have left the countries to which their doctrines were unacceptable, and established themselves in a remote corner of the earth, which they have been the first to render habitable to human beings; it is difficult to see on what principles but those of tyranny they can be prevented from living there under what laws they please, provided they commit no aggression on other nations, and allow perfect freedom of departure to those who are dissatisfied with their ways. A recent writer, in some respects of considerable merit, proposes (to use his own words,) not a crusade, but a *civilizade*, against this polygamous community, to put an end to what seems to him a retrograde step in civilization. It also appears so to me, but I am not aware that any community has a right to force another to be civilized. So long as the sufferers by the bad law do not invoke assistance from other communities, I cannot admit that persons entirely unconnected with them ought to step in and require that a condition of things with which all who are directly interested appear to be satisfied, should be put an end to because it is a scandal to persons some thousands of miles distant, who have no part or concern in it. Let them send missionaries, if they please, to preach against it; and let them, by any fair means (of which silencing the teachers is not one,) oppose the progress of similar doctrines among their own people. If civilization has got the better of barbarism when barbarism had the world to itself, it is too much to profess to be afraid lest barbarism, after having been fairly got under, should revive and conquer civilization. A civilization that can thus succumb to its vanquished enemy must first have become so degenerate, that neither its appointed priests and teachers, nor anybody else, has the capacity, or will take the trouble, to stand up for it. If this be so, the sooner such a civilization receives notice to quit, the better. It can only go on from bad to worse, until destroyed and regenerated (like the Western Empire) by energetic barbarians.

CHAPTER V

APPLICATIONS

THE PRINCIPLES asserted in these pages must be more generally admitted as the basis for discussion of details, before a consistent application of them to all the various departments of government and morals can be attempted with any prospect of advantage. The few observations I propose to make on questions of detail, are designed to illustrate the principles, rather than to follow them out to their consequences. I offer, not so much applications, as specimens of application; which may serve to bring into greater clearness the meaning and limits of the two maxims which together form the entire doctrine of this Essay, and to assist the judgment in holding the balance between them, in the cases where it appears doubtful which of them is applicable to the case.

The maxims are, first, that the individual is not accountable to society for his actions, in so far as these concern the interests of no person but himself. Advice, instruction, persuasion, and avoidance by other people, if thought necessary by them for their own good, are the only measures by which society can justifiably express its dislike or disapprobation of his conduct. Secondly, that for such actions as are prejudicial to the interests of others, the individual is accountable, and may be subjected either to social or to legal punishments, if society is of opinion that the one or the other is requisite for its protection.

In the first place, it must by no means be supposed, because damage, or probability of damage, to the interests of others, can alone justify the interference of society, that therefore it always does justify such interference. In many cases, an individual, in pursuing a legitimate object, necessarily and therefore legitimately causes pain or loss to others, or intercepts a good which they had a reasonable hope of obtaining. Such oppositions of interest between individuals often arise from bad social institutions, but are unavoidable while those institutions last; and some would be unavoidable under any institutions. Whoever succeeds in an overcrowded profession, or in a competitive examination; whoever is preferred to another in any contest for an object which both desire, reaps benefit from the loss of others, from their wasted exertion and their disappointment. But it is, by common admission, better for the general interest of mankind, that persons should pursue their objects undeterred by this sort of consequences. In other words, society admits no right, either legal or moral, in the disappointed competitors, to immunity from this kind of suffering; and feels called on to interfere, only when means of success have been employed which it is contrary to the general interest to permit—namely, fraud or treachery, and force.

Again, trade is a social act. Whoever undertakes to sell any description of goods to the public, does what affects the interest of other persons, and of society in general; and thus his conduct, in principle, comes within the jurisdiction of society: accordingly, it was once held to be the duty of governments, in all cases which were considered of importance, to fix prices, and regulate the processes of manufacture. But it is now recognized, though not till after a long struggle, that both the cheapness and the good quality of commodities are most effectually provided for by leaving the producers and sellers perfectly free, under the sole check of equal freedom to the buyers for supplying themselves elsewhere. This is the so-called doctrine of Free Trade, which rests on grounds different from, though equally solid with, the principle of individual liberty asserted in this Essay. Restrictions on trade, or on production for purposes of trade, are indeed restraints; and all restraint, *quâ* restraint, is an evil: but the restraints in question affect only that part of conduct which society is competent to restrain, and are wrong solely because they do not really produce the results which it is desired to produce by them. As the principle of individual liberty is not involved in the doctrine of Free Trade, so neither is it in most of the questions which arise respecting the limits of that doctrine: as for example, what amount of public control is admissible for the prevention of fraud by adulteration; how far sanitary precautions, or arrangements to protect work-people employed in dangerous occupations, should be enforced on employers. Such questions involve considerations of liberty, only in so far as leaving people to themselves is always better, *cæteris paribus*, than controlling them: but that they may be legitimately controlled for these ends, is in principle undeniable. On the other hand, there are questions relating to interference with trade, which are essentially questions of liberty; such as the Maine Law, already touched upon; the prohibition of the importation of opium into China; the restriction of the sale of poisons; all cases, in short, where the object of the interference is to make it impossible or difficult to obtain a particular commodity. These interferences are objectionable, not as infringements on the liberty of the producer or seller, but on that of the buyer.

One of these examples, that of the sale of poisons, opens a new question; the proper limits of what may be called the functions of police; how far liberty may legitimately be invaded for the prevention of crime, or of accident. It is one of the undisputed functions of government to take precautions against crime before it has been committed, as well as to detect and punish it afterwards. The preventive function of government, however, is far more liable to be abused, to the prejudice of liberty, than the punitory function; for there is hardly any part of the legitimate freedom of action of a human being which would not admit of being represented, and fairly too, as increasing the facilities for some form or other of delinquency. Nevertheless, if a public authority, or even a private person, sees any one evidently preparing to commit a crime, they are not bound to look on inactive until the crime is committed, but may interfere to prevent it. If poisons were never bought or used for any purpose except the commission of murder, it would be right to prohibit their manufacture and sale. They may, however, be wanted not only for innocent but for useful purposes, and restrictions cannot be imposed in the one case without operating in the other. Again, it is a proper office of public authority to guard against accidents. If either a public officer or any one else saw a person attempting to cross a bridge which had been ascertained to be unsafe, and there were not time to warn him of his danger, they might seize him and turn him back, without any real infringement of his liberty; for liberty consists in doing what one desires, and he does not desire to fall into the river. Nevertheless, when there is not a certainty, but only a danger of mischief, no one but the person himself can judge of the sufficiency of the motive which may prompt him to incur the risk: in this case, therefore, (unless he is a child, or delirious, or in some state of excitement or absorption incompatible with the full use of the reflecting faculty), he ought, I conceive, to be only warned of the danger; not forcibly prevented from exposing himself to it. Similar considerations, applied to such a question as the sale of poisons, may enable us to decide which among the possible modes of regulation are or are not contrary to principle. Such a precaution, for example, as that of labelling the drug with some word expressive of its dangerous character, may be enforced without violation of liberty: the buyer cannot wish not to know that the thing he possesses has poisonous qualities. But to require in all cases the certificate of a medical practitioner, would make it sometimes impossible, always expensive, to obtain the article for legitimate uses. The only mode apparent to me, in which difficulties may be thrown in the way of crime committed through this means, without any infringement, worth taking into account, upon the liberty of those who desire the poisonous substance for other purposes, consists in providing what, in the apt language of Bentham, is called "preappointed evidence." This provision is familiar to every one in the case of contracts. It is usual and right that the law, when a contract is entered into, should require as the condition of its enforcing performance, that certain formalities should be observed, such as signatures, attestation of witnesses, and the like, in order that in case of subsequent dispute, there may be evidence to prove that the contract was really entered into, and that there was nothing in the circumstance to render it legally invalid: the effect being, to throw great obstacles in the way of fictitious contracts, or contracts made in circumstances which, if known, would destroy their validity. Precautions of a similar nature might be enforced in the sale of articles adapted to be instruments of crime. The seller, for example, might be required to enter in a register the exact time of the transaction, the name and address of the buyer, the precise quality and quantity sold; to ask the purpose for which it was wanted, and record the answer he received. When there was no medical prescription, the presence of some third person might be required, to bring home the fact to the purchaser, in case there should afterwards be reason to believe that the article had been applied to criminal purposes. Such regulations would in general be no material impediment to obtaining the article, but a very considerable one to making an improper use of it without detection.

The right inherent in society, to ward off crimes against itself by antecedent precautions, suggests the obvious limitations to the maxim, that purely self-regarding misconduct cannot properly be meddled with in the way of prevention or punishment. Drunkenness, for example, in ordinary cases, is not a fit subject for legislative interference; but I should deem it perfectly legitimate that a person, who had once been convicted of any act of violence to others under the influence of drink, should be placed under a special legal restriction, personal to himself; that if he were afterwards found drunk, he should be liable to a penalty, and that if when in that state he committed another offence, the punishment to which he would be liable for that other offence should be increased in severity. The making himself drunk, in a person whom drunkenness excites to do harm to others, is a crime against others. So, again, idleness, except in a person receiving support from the public, or except when it constitutes a breach of contract, cannot without tyranny be made a subject of legal punishment; but if either from idleness or from any other avoidable cause, a man fails to perform his legal duties to others, as for instance to support his children, it is no tyranny to force him to fulfil that obligation, by compulsory labor, if no other means are available.

Again, there are many acts which, being directly injurious only to the agents themselves, ought not to be legally interdicted, but which, if done publicly, are a violation of good manners, and coming thus within the category of offences against others, may rightfully be prohibited. Of this kind are offences against decency; on which it is unnecessary to dwell, the rather as they are only connected indirectly with our subject, the objection to publicity being equally strong in the case of many actions not in themselves condemnable, nor supposed to be so.

There is another question to which an answer must be found, consistent with the principles which have been laid down. In cases of personal conduct supposed to be blameable, but which respect for liberty precludes society from preventing or punishing, because the evil directly resulting falls wholly on the agent; what the agent is free to do, ought other persons to be equally free to counsel or instigate? This question is not free from difficulty. The case of a person who solicits another to do an act, is not strictly a case of self-regarding conduct. To give advice or offer inducements to any one, is a social act, and may therefore, like actions in general which affect others, be supposed amenable to social control. But a little reflection corrects the first impression, by showing that if the case is not strictly within the definition of individual liberty, yet the reasons on which the principle of individual liberty is grounded, are applicable to it. If people must be allowed, in whatever concerns only themselves, to act as seems best to themselves at their own peril, they must equally be free to consult with one another about what is fit to be so done; to exchange opinions, and give and receive suggestions. Whatever it is permitted to do, it must be permitted to advise to do. The question is doubtful, only when the instigator derives a personal benefit from his advice; when he makes it his occupation, for subsistence or pecuniary gain, to promote what society and the State consider to be an evil. Then, indeed, a new element of complication is introduced; namely, the existence of classes of persons with an interest opposed to what is considered as the public weal, and whose mode of living is grounded on the counter-action of it. Ought this to be interfered with, or not? Fornication, for example, must be tolerated, and so must gambling; but should a person be free to be a pimp, or to keep a gambling-house? The case is one of those which lie on the exact boundary line between two principles, and it is not at once apparent to which of the two it properly belongs. There are arguments on both sides. On the side of toleration it may be said, that the fact of following anything as an occupation, and living or profiting by the practice of it, cannot make that criminal which would otherwise be admissible; that the act should either be consistently permitted or consistently prohibited; that if the principles which we have hitherto defended are true, society has no business, *as* society, to decide anything to be wrong which concerns only the individual; that it cannot go beyond dissuasion, and that one person should be as free to persuade, as another to dissuade. In opposition to this it may be contended, that although the public, or the State, are not warranted in authoritatively deciding, for purposes of repression or punishment, that such or such conduct affecting only the interests of the individual is good or bad, they are fully justified in assuming, if they regard it as bad, that its being so or not is at least a disputable question: That, this being supposed, they cannot be acting wrongly in endeavoring to exclude the influence of solicitations which are not disinterested, of instigators who cannot possibly be impartial—who have a direct personal interest on one side, and that side the one which the State believes to be wrong, and who confessedly promote it for personal objects only. There can surely, it may be urged, be nothing lost, no sacrifice of good, by so ordering matters that persons shall make their election, either wisely or foolishly, on their own prompting, as free as possible from the arts of persons who stimulate their inclinations for interested purposes of their own. Thus, (it may be said) though the statutes respecting unlawful games are utterly indefensible—though all persons should be free to gamble in their own or each other's houses, or in any place of meeting established by their own subscriptions, and open only to the members and their visitors—yet public gambling-houses should not be permitted. It is true that the prohibition is never effectual, and that whatever amount of tyrannical power is given to the police, gambling-houses can always be maintained under other pretences; but they may be compelled to conduct their operations with a certain degree of secrecy and mystery, so that nobody knows anything about them but those who seek them; and more than this, society ought not to aim at. There is considerable force in these arguments. I will not venture to decide whether they are sufficient to justify the moral anomaly of punishing the accessary, when the principal is (and must be) allowed to go free; of fining or imprisoning the procurer, but not the fornicator, the gambling-house keeper, but not the gambler. Still less ought the common operations of buying and selling to be interfered with on analogous grounds. Almost every article which is bought and sold may be used in excess, and the sellers have a pecuniary interest in encouraging that excess; but no argument can be founded on this, in favor, for instance, of the Maine Law; because the class of dealers in strong drinks, though interested in their abuse, are indispensably required for the sake of their legitimate use. The interest, however, of these dealers in promoting intemperance is a real evil, and justifies the State in imposing restrictions and requiring guarantees, which but for that justification would be infringements of legitimate liberty.

A further question is, whether the State, while it permits, should nevertheless indirectly discourage conduct which it deems contrary to the best interests of the agent; whether, for example, it should take measures to render the means of drunkenness more costly, or add to the difficulty of procuring them, by limiting the number of the places of sale. On this as on most other practical questions, many distinctions require to be made. To tax stimulants for the sole purpose of making them more difficult to be obtained, is a measure differing only in degree from their entire prohibition; and would be justifiable only if that were justifiable. Every increase of cost is a prohibition, to those whose means do not come up to the augmented price; and to those who do, it is a penalty laid on them for gratifying a particular taste. Their choice of pleasures, and their mode of expending their income, after satisfying their legal and moral obligations to the State and to individuals, are their own concern, and must rest with their own judgment. These considerations may seem at first sight to condemn the selection of stimulants as special subjects of taxation for purposes of revenue. But it must be remembered that taxation for fiscal purposes is absolutely inevitable; that in most countries it is necessary that a considerable part of that taxation should be indirect; that the State, therefore, cannot help imposing penalties, which to some persons may be prohibitory, on the use of some articles of consumption. It is hence the duty of the State to consider, in the imposition of taxes, what commodities the consumers can best spare; and à fortiori, to select in preference those of which it deems the use, beyond a very moderate quantity, to be positively injurious. Taxation, therefore, of stimulants, up to the point which produces the largest amount of revenue (supposing that the State needs all the revenue which it yields) is not only admissible, but to be approved of.

The question of making the sale of these commodities a

more or less exclusive privilege, must be answered differently, according to the purposes to which the restriction is intended to be subservient. All places of public resort require the restraint of a police, and places of this kind peculiarly, because offences against society are especially apt to originate there. It is, therefore, fit to confine the power of selling these commodities (at least for consumption on the spot) to persons of known or vouched-for respectability of conduct; to make such regulations respecting hours of opening and closing as may be requisite for public surveillance, and to withdraw the license if breaches of the peace repeatedly take place through the connivance or incapacity of the keeper of the house, or if it becomes a rendezvous for concocting and preparing offences against the law. Any further restriction I do not conceive to be, in principle, justifiable. The limitation in number, for instance, of beer and spirit-houses, for the express purpose of rendering them more difficult of access, and diminishing the occasions of temptation, not only exposes all to an inconvenience because there are some by whom the facility would be abused, but is suited only to a state of society in which the laboring classes are avowedly treated as children or savages, and placed under an education of restraint, to fit them for future admission to the privileges of freedom. This is not the principle on which the laboring classes are professedly governed in any free country; and no person who sets due value on freedom will give his adhesion to their being so governed, unless after all efforts have been exhausted to educate them for freedom and govern them as freemen, and it has been definitively proved that they can only be governed as children. The bare statement of the alternative shows the absurdity of supposing that such efforts have been made in any case which needs be considered here. It is only because the institutions of this country are a mass of inconsistencies, that things find admittance into our practice which belong to the system of despotic, or what is called paternal, government, while the general freedom of our institutions precludes the exercise of the amount of control necessary to render the restraint of any real efficacy as a moral education.

It was pointed out in an early part of this Essay, that the liberty of the individual, in things wherein the individual is alone concerned, implies a corresponding liberty in any number of individuals to regulate by mutual agreement such things as regard them jointly, and regard no persons but themselves. This question presents no difficulty, so long as the will of all the persons implicated remains unaltered; but since that will may change, it is often necessary, even in things in which they alone are concerned, that they should enter into engagements with one another; and when they do, it is fit, as a general rule, that those engagements should be kept. Yet in the laws, probably, of every country, this general rule has some exceptions. Not only persons are not held to engagements which violate the rights of third parties, but it is sometimes considered a sufficient reason for releasing them from an engagement, that it is injurious to themselves. In this and most other civilized countries, for example, an engagement by which a person should sell himself, or allow himself to be sold, as a slave, would be null and void; neither enforced by law nor by opinion. The ground for thus limiting his power of voluntarily disposing of his own lot in life, is apparent, and is very clearly seen in this extreme case. The reason for not interfering, unless for the sake of others, with a person's voluntary acts, is consideration for his liberty. His voluntary choice is evidence that what he so chooses is desirable, or at the least endurable, to him, and his good is on the whole best provided for by allowing him to take his own means of pursuing it. But by selling himself for a slave, he abdicates his liberty; he foregoes any future use of it, beyond that single act. He therefore defeats, in his own case, the very purpose which is the justification of allowing him to dispose of himself. He is no longer free; but is thenceforth in a position which has no longer the presumption in its favor, that would be afforded by his voluntarily remaining in it. The principle of freedom cannot require that he should be free not to be free. It is not freedom, to be allowed to alienate his freedom. These reasons, the force of which is so conspicuous in this peculiar case, are evidently of far wider application; yet a limit is everywhere set to them by the necessities of life, which continually require, not indeed that we should resign our freedom, but that we should consent to this and the other limitation of it. The principle, however, which demands uncontrolled freedom of action in all that concerns only the agents themselves, requires that those who have become bound to one another, in things which concern no third party, should be able to release one another from the engagement: and even without such voluntary release, there are perhaps no contracts or engagements, except those that relate to money or money's worth, of which one can venture to say that there ought to be no liberty whatever of retractation. Baron Wilhelm von Humboldt, in the excellent Essay from which I have already quoted, states it as his conviction, that engagements which involve personal relations or services, should never be legally binding beyond a limited duration of time; and that the most important of these engagements, marriage, having the peculiarity that its objects are frustrated unless the feelings of both the parties are in harmony with it, should require nothing more than the declared will of either party to dissolve it. This subject is too important, and too complicated, to be discussed in a parenthesis, and I touch on it only so far as is necessary for purposes of illustration. If the conciseness and generality of Baron Humboldt's dissertation had not obliged him in this instance to content himself with enunciating his conclusion without discussing the premises, he would doubtless have recognized that the question cannot be decided on grounds so simple as those to which he confines himself. When a person, either by express promise or by conduct, has encouraged another to rely upon his continuing to act in a certain way—to build expectations and calculations, and stake any part of his plan of life upon that supposition, a new series of moral obligations arises on his part towards that person, which may possibly be overruled, but cannot be ignored. And again, if the relation between two contracting parties has been followed by consequences to others; if it has placed third parties in any peculiar position, or, as in the case of marriage, has even called third parties into existence, obligations arise on the part of both the contracting parties towards those third persons, the fulfilment of which, or at all events the mode of fulfilment, must be greatly affected by the continuance or disruption of the relation between the original parties to the contract. It does not follow, nor can I admit, that these obligations extend to requiring the fulfilment of the contract at all costs to the happiness of the reluctant party; but they are a necessary element in the question; and even if, as Von Humboldt maintains, they ought to make no difference in the *legal* freedom of the parties to release themselves from the engagement (and I also hold that they ought not to make *much* difference), they necessarily make a great difference in the *moral* freedom. A person is bound to take all these circumstances into account, before resolving on a step which may affect such important interests of others; and if he does not allow proper weight to those interests, he is morally responsible for the wrong. I have made these obvious remarks for the better illustration of the general principle of liberty, and not because they are at all needed on the particular question, which, on the contrary, is usually discussed as if the interest of children was everything, and that of grown persons nothing.

I have already observed that, owing to the absence of any recognized general principles, liberty is often granted where it should be withheld, as well as withheld where it should be granted; and one of the cases in which, in the modern European world, the sentiment of liberty is the strongest, is a case where, in my view, it is altogether misplaced. A person should be free to do as he likes in his own concerns; but he ought not to be free to do as he likes in acting for another under the pretext that the affairs of another are his own affairs. The State, while it respects the liberty of each in what specially regards himself, is bound to maintain a vigilant control over his exercise of any power which it allows him to possess over others. This obligation is almost entirely disregarded in the case of the family relations, a case, in its direct influence on human happiness, more important than all others taken together. The almost despotic power of husbands over wives needs not be enlarged upon here, because nothing more is needed for the complete removal of the evil, than that wives should have the same rights, and should receive the protection of law in the same manner, as all other persons; and because, on this subject, the defenders of established injustice do not avail themselves of the plea of liberty, but stand forth openly as the champions of power. It is in the case of children, that misapplied notions of liberty are a real obstacle to the fulfilment by the State of its duties. One would almost think that a man's children were supposed to be literally, and not metaphorically, a part of himself, so jealous is opinion of the smallest interference of law with his absolute and exclusive control over them; more jealous than of almost any interference with his own freedom of action: so much less do the generality of mankind value liberty than power. Consider, for example, the case of education. Is it not almost a self-evident axiom, that the State should require and compel the education, up to a certain standard, of every human being who is born its citizen? Yet who is there that is not afraid to recognize and assert this truth? Hardly any one indeed will deny that it is one of the most sacred duties of the parents (or, as law and usage now stand, the father), after summoning a human being into the world, to give to that being an education fitting him to perform his part well in life towards others and towards himself. But while this is unanimously declared to be the father's duty, scarcely anybody, in this country, will bear to hear of obliging him to perform it. Instead of his being required to make any exertion or sacrifice for securing education to the child, it is left to his choice to accept it or not when it is provided gratis! It still remains unrecognized, that to bring a child into existence without a fair prospect of being able, not only to provide food for its body, but instruction and training for its mind, is a moral crime, both against the unfortunate offspring and against society; and that if the parent does not fulfil this obligation, the State ought to see it fulfilled at the charge, as far as possible, of the parent.

Were the duty of enforcing universal education once admitted, there would be an end to the difficulties about what the State should teach, and how it should teach, which now convert the subject into a mere battle-field for sects and parties, causing the time and labor which should have been spent in educating, to be wasted in quarrelling about education. If the government would make up its mind to *require* for every child a good education, it might save itself the trouble of *providing* one. It might leave to parents to obtain the education where and how they pleased, and content itself with helping to pay the school fees of the poorer classes of children, and defraying the entire school expenses of those who have no one else to pay for them. The objections which are urged with reason against State education, do not apply to the enforcement of education by the State, but to the State's taking upon itself to direct that education: which is a totally different thing. That the whole or any large part of the education of the people should be in State hands, I go as far as any one in deprecating. All that has been said of

the importance of individuality of character, and diversity in
opinions and modes of conduct, involves, as of the same un-
speakable importance, diversity of education. A general State
education is a mere contrivance for moulding people to be exactly like one another: and as the mould in which it casts
them is that which pleases the predominant power in the
government, whether this be a monarch, a priesthood, an
aristocracy, or the majority of the existing generation, in proportion as it is efficient and successful, it establishes a despotism over the mind, leading by natural tendency to one
over the body. An education established and controlled
by the State, should only exist, if it exist at all, as one among
many competing experiments, carried on for the purpose of
example and stimulus, to keep the others up to a certain
standard of excellence. Unless, indeed, when society in general is in so backward a state that it could not or would not
provide for itself any proper institutions of education, unless the government undertook the task; then, indeed, the
government may, as the less of two great evils, take upon
itself the business of schools and universities, as it may that of
joint-stock companies, when private enterprise, in a shape
fitted for undertaking great works of industry, does not exist
in the country. But in general, if the country contains a
sufficient number of persons qualified to provide education
under government auspices, the same persons would be
able and willing to give an equally good education on the
voluntary principle, under the assurance of remuneration
afforded by a law rendering education compulsory, combined with State aid to those unable to defray the expense.

The instrument for enforcing the law could be no other
than public examinations, extending to all children, and
beginning at an early age. An age might be fixed at which every
child must be examined, to ascertain if he (or she) is able
to read. If a child proves unable, the father, unless he has
some sufficient ground of excuse, might be subjected to a
moderate fine, to be worked out, if necessary, by his labor,
and the child might be put to school at his expense. Once
in every year the examination should be renewed, with a
gradually extending range of subjects, so as to make the universal acquisition, and what is more, retention, of a certain
minimum of general knowledge, virtually compulsory. Beyond
that minimum, there should be voluntary examinations on

all subjects, at which all who come up to a certain standard of proficiency might claim a certificate. To prevent the State from exercising through these arrangements, an improper influence over opinion, the knowledge required for passing an examination (beyond the merely instrumental parts of knowledge, such as languages and their use) should, even in the higher class of examinations, be confined to facts and positive science exclusively. The examinations on religion, politics, or other disputed topics, should not turn on the truth or falsehood of opinions, but on the matter of fact that such and such an opinion is held, on such grounds, by such authors, or schools, or churches. Under this system, the rising generation would be no worse off in regard to all disputed truths, than they are at present; they would be brought up either churchmen or dissenters as they now are, the State merely taking care that they should be instructed churchmen, or instructed dissenters. There would be nothing to hinder them from being taught religion, if their parents chose, at the same schools where they were taught other things. All attempts by the State to bias the conclusions of its citizens on disputed subjects, are evil; but it may very properly offer to ascertain and certify that a person possesses the knowledge, requisite to make his conclusions, on any given subject, worth attending to. A student of philosophy would be the better for being able to stand an examination both in Locke and in Kant, whichever of the two he takes up with, or even if with neither: and there is no reasonable objection to examining an atheist in the evidences of Christianity, provided he is not required to profess a belief in them. The examinations, however, in the higher branches of knowledge should, I conceive, be entirely voluntary. It would be giving too dangerous a power to governments, were they allowed to exclude any one from professions, even from the profession of teacher, for alleged deficiency of qualifications: and I think, with Wilhelm von Humboldt, that degrees, or other public certificates of scientific or professional acquirements, should be given to all who present themselves for examination, and stand the test; but that such certificates should confer no advantage over competitors, other than the weight which may be attached to their testimony by public opinion.

It is not in the matter of education only, that misplaced notions of liberty prevent moral obligations on the part of parents from being recognized, and legal obligations from being imposed, where there are the strongest grounds for the former always, and in many cases for the latter also. The fact itself, of causing the existence of a human being, is one of the most responsible actions in the range of human life. To undertake this responsibility—to bestow a life which may be either a curse or a blessing—unless the being on whom it is to be bestowed will have at least the ordinary chances of a desirable existence, is a crime against that being. And in a country either over-peopled, or threatened with being so, to produce children, beyond a very small number, with the effect of reducing the reward of labor by their competition, is a serious offence against all who live by the remuneration of their labor. The laws which, in many countries on the Continent, forbid marriage unless the parties can show that they have the means of supporting a family, do not exceed the legitimate powers of the State: and whether such laws be expedient or not (a question mainly dependent on local circumstances and feelings), they are not objectionable as violations of liberty. Such laws are interferences of the State to prohibit a mischievous act—an act injurious to others, which ought to be a subject of reprobation, and social stigma, even when it is not deemed expedient to superadd legal punishment. Yet the current ideas of liberty, which bend so easily to real infringements of the freedom of the individual, in things which concern only himself, would repel the attempt to put any restraint upon his inclinations when the consequence of their indulgence is a life, or lives, of wretchedness and depravity to the offspring, with manifold evils to those sufficiently within reach to be in any way affected by their actions. When we compare the strange respect of mankind for liberty, with their strange want of respect for it, we might imagine that a man had an indispensable right to do harm to others, and no right at all to please himself without giving pain to any one.

I have reserved for the last place a large class of questions respecting the limits of government interference, which, though closely connected with the subject of this Essay, do not, in strictness, belong to it. These are cases in which the reasons against interference do not turn upon the principle of liberty: the question is not about restraining the actions of individuals, but about helping them: it is asked whether the government should do, or cause to be done, something for their benefit, instead of leaving it to be done by themselves, individually, or in voluntary combination.

The objections to government interference, when it is not such as to involve infringement of liberty, may be of three kinds.

The first is, when the thing to be done is likely to be better done by individuals than by the government. Speaking generally, there is no one so fit to conduct any business, or to determine how or by whom it shall be conducted, as those who are personally interested in it. This principle condemns the interferences, once so common, of the legislature, or the officers of government, with the ordinary processes of industry. But this part of the subject has been sufficiently enlarged upon by political economists, and is not particularly related to the principles of this Essay.

The second objection is more nearly allied to our subject. In many cases, though individuals may not do the particular thing so well, on the average, as the officers of government, it is nevertheless desirable that it should be done by them, rather than by the government, as a means to their own mental education—a mode of strengthening their active faculties, exercising their judgment, and giving them a familiar knowledge of the subjects with which they are thus left to deal. This is a principal, though not the sole, recommendation of jury trial (in cases not political); of free and popular local and municipal institutions; of the conduct of industrial and philanthropic enterprises by voluntary associations. These are not questions of liberty, and are connected with that subject only by remote tendencies; but they are questions of development. It belongs to a different occasion from the present to dwell on these things as parts of national education; as being, in truth, the peculiar training of a citizen, the practical part of the political education of a free people, taking them out of the narrow circle of personal and family selfishness, and accustoming them to the comprehension of joint interests, the management of joint concerns—habituating them to act from public or semi-public motives, and guide their conduct by aims which unite instead of isolating them from one another. Without these habits and powers, a free constitution can neither be worked nor preserved, as is exemplified by the too-often transitory nature of political freedom in countries where it does not rest upon a sufficient basis of local liberties.

The management of purely local business by the localities, and of the great enterprises of industry by the union of those who voluntarily supply the pecuniary means, is further recommended by all the advantages which have been set forth in this Essay as belonging to individuality of development, and diversity of modes of action. Government operations tend to be everywhere alike. With individuals and voluntary associations, on the contrary, there are varied experiments, and endless diversity of experience. What the State can usefully do, is to make itself a central depository, and active circulator and diffuser, of the experience resulting from many trials. Its business is to enable each experimentalist to benefit by the experiments of others, instead of tolerating no experiments but its own.

The third, and most cogent reason for restricting the interference of government, is the great evil of adding unnecessarily to its power. Every function superadded to those already exercised by the government, causes its influence over hopes and fears to be more widely diffused, and converts, more and more, the active and ambitious part of the public into hangers-on of the government, or of some party which aims at becoming the government. If the roads, the railways, the banks, the insurance offices, the great joint-stock companies, the universities, and the public charities, were all of them branches of the government; if, in addition, the municipal corporations and local boards, with all that now devolves on them, became departments of the central administration; if the employés of all these different enterprises were appointed and paid by the government, and looked to the government for every rise in life; not all the freedom of the press and popular constitution of the legislature would make this or any other country free otherwise than in name. And the evil would be greater, the more efficiently and scientifically the administrative machinery was constructed—the more skilful the arrangements for obtaining the best qualified hands and heads with which to work it. In England it has of late been proposed that all the members of the civil service of government should be selected by competitive examination, to obtain for those employments the most intelligent and instructed persons procurable; and much has been said and written for and against this proposal. One of the arguments most insisted on by its opponents, is that the occupation of a permanent official servant of the State does not hold out sufficient prospects of emolument and importance to attract the highest talents, which will always be able to find a more inviting career in the professions, or in the service of companies and other public bodies. One would not have been surprised if this argument had been used by the friends of the proposition, as an answer to its principal difficulty. Coming from the opponents it is strange enough. What is urged as an objection is the safety-valve of the proposed system. If indeed all the high talent of the country *could* be drawn into the service of the government, a proposal tending to bring about that result might well inspire uneasiness. If every part of the business of society which required organized concert, or large and comprehensive views, were in the hands of the government, and if government offices were universally filled by the ablest men, all the enlarged culture and practised intelligence in the country, except the purely speculative, would be concentrated in a numerous bureaucracy, to whom alone the rest of the community would look for all things: the multitude for direction and dictation in all they had to do; the able and aspiring for personal advancement. To be admitted into the ranks of this bureaucracy, and when admitted, to rise therein, would be the sole objects of ambition. Under this régime, not only is the outside public ill-qualified, for want of practical experience, to criticize or check the mode of operation of the bureaucracy, but even if the accidents of despotic or the natural working of popular institutions occasionally raise to the summit a ruler or rulers of reforming inclinations, no reform can be effected which is contrary to the interest of the bureaucracy. Such is the melancholy condition of the Russian empire, as is shown in the accounts of those who have had sufficient opportunity of observation. The Czar himself is powerless against the bureaucratic body; he can send any one of them to Siberia, but he cannot govern without them, or against their will. On every decree of his they have a tacit veto, by merely refraining from carrying it into effect. In countries of more advanced civilization and of a more insurrectionary spirit, the public, accustomed to expect everything to be done for them by the State, or at least to do nothing for themselves without asking from the State not only leave to do it, but even how it is to be done, naturally hold the State responsible for all evil which befalls them, and when the evil exceeds their amount of patience, they rise against the government and make what is called a revolution; whereupon somebody else, with or without legitimate authority from the nation, vaults into the seat, issues his orders to the bureaucracy, and everything goes on much as it did before; the bureaucracy being unchanged, and nobody else being capable of taking their place.

A very different spectacle is exhibited among a people accustomed to transact their own business. In France, a large part of the people having been engaged in military service, many of whom have held at least the rank of noncommissioned officers, there are in every popular insurrection several persons competent to take the lead, and improvise some tolerable plan of action. What the French are in military affairs, the Americans are in every kind of civil business; let them be left without a government, every body of Americans is able to improvise one, and to carry on that or any other public business with a sufficient amount of intelligence, order, and decision. This is what every free people ought to be: and a people capable of this is certain to be free; it will never let itself be enslaved by any man or body of men because these are able to seize and pull the reins of the central administration. No bureaucracy can hope to make such a people as this do or undergo anything that they do not like. But where everything is done through the bureaucracy, nothing to which the bureaucracy is really adverse can be done at all. The constitution of such countries is an organization of the experience and practical ability of the nation, into a disciplined body for the purpose of governing the rest; and the more perfect that organization is in itself, the more successful in drawing to itself and educating for itself the persons of greatest capacity from all ranks of the community, the more complete is the bondage of all, the members of the bureaucracy included. For the governors are as much the slaves of their organization and discipline, as the governed are of the governors. A Chinese mandarin is as much the tool and creature of a despotism as the humblest cultivator. An individual Jesuit is to the utmost degree of abasement the slave of his order though the order itself exists for the collective power and importance of its members.

It is not, also, to be forgotten, that the absorption of all the principal ability of the country into the governing body is fatal, sooner or later, to the mental activity and progressiveness of the body itself. Banded together as they are—working a system which, like all systems, necessarily proceeds in a great measure by fixed rules—the official body are under the constant temptation of sinking into indolent routine, or, if they now and then desert that mill-horse round, of rushing into some half-examined crudity which has struck the fancy of some leading member of the corps: and the sole check to these closely allied, though seemingly opposite, tendencies, the only stimulus which can keep the ability of the body itself up to a high standard, is liability to the watchful criticism of equal ability outside the body. It is indispensable, therefore, that the means should exist, independently of the government, of forming such ability, and furnishing it with the opportunities and experience necessary for a correct judgment of great practical affairs. If we would possess permanently a skilful and efficient body of functionaries—above all, a body able to originate and willing to adopt improvements; if we would not have our bureaucracy degenerate into a pedantocracy, this body must not engross all the occupations which form and cultivate the faculties required for the government of mankind.

To determine the point at which evils, so formidable to human freedom and advancement, begin, or rather at which they begin to predominate over the benefits attending the collective application of the force of society, under its recognized chiefs, for the removal of the obstacles which stand in the way of its well-being, to secure as much of the advantages of centralized power and intelligence, as can be had without turning into governmental channels too great a proportion of the general activity, is one of the most difficult and complicated questions in the art of government. It is, in a great measure, a question of detail, in which many and various considerations must be kept in view, and no absolute rule can be laid down. But I believe that the practical principle in which safety resides, the ideal to be kept in view, the standard by which to test all arrangements intended for overcoming the difficulty, may be conveyed in these words: the greatest dissemination of power consistent with efficiency; but the greatest possible centralization of information, and diffusion of it from the centre. Thus, in municipal administration, there would be, as in the New

England States, a very minute division among separate officers, chosen by the localities, of all business which is not better left to the persons directly interested; but besides this, there would be, in each department of local affairs, a central superintendence, forming a branch of the general government. The organ of this superintendence would concentrate, as in a focus, the variety of information and experience derived from the conduct of that branch of public business in all the localities, from everything analogous which is done in foreign countries, and from the general principles of political science. This central organ should have a right to know all that is done, and its special duty should be that of making the knowledge acquired in one place available for others. Emancipated from the petty prejudices and narrow views of a locality by its elevated position and comprehensive sphere of observation, its advice would naturally carry much authority; but its actual power, as a permanent institution, should, I conceive, be limited to compelling the local officers to obey the laws laid down for their guidance. In all things not provided for by general rules, those officers should be left to their own judgment, under responsibility to their constituents. For the violation of rules, they should be responsible to law, and the rules themselves should be laid down by the legislature; the central administrative authority only watching over their execution, and if they were not properly carried into effect, appealing, according to the nature of the case, to the tribunal to enforce the law, or to the constituencies to dismiss the functionaries who had not executed it according to its spirit. Such, in its general conception, is the central superintendence which the Poor Law Board is intended to exercise over the administrators of the Poor Rate throughout the country. Whatever powers the Board exercises beyond this limit, were right and necessary in that peculiar case, for the cure of rooted habits of mal-administration in matters deeply affecting not the localities merely, but the whole community; since no locality has a moral right to make itself by mismanagement a nest of pauperism, necessarily overflowing into other localities, and impairing the moral and physical condition of the whole laboring community. The powers of administrative coercion and subordinate legislation possessed by the Poor Law Board (but which, owing to the state of opinion on the subject, are very scantily exercised by them), though perfectly justifiable in a case of a first-rate national interest, would be wholly out of place in the superintendence of interests purely local. But a central organ of information and instruction for all the localities, would be equally valuable in all departments of administration. A government cannot have too much of the kind of activity which does not impede, but aids and stimulates, individual exertion and development. The mischief begins when, instead of calling forth the activity and powers of individuals and bodies, it substitutes its own activity for theirs; when, instead of informing, advising, and, upon occasion, denouncing, it makes them work in fetters, or bids them stand aside and does their work instead of them. The worth of a State, in the long run, is the worth of the individuals composing it; and a State which postpones the interests of *their* mental expansion and elevation, to a little more of administrative skill, or that semblance of it which practice gives, in the details of business; a State which dwarfs its men, in order that they may be more docile instruments in its hands even for beneficial purposes, will find that with small men no great thing can really be accomplished; and that the perfection of machinery to which it has sacrificed everything, will in the end avail it nothing, for want of the vital power which, in order that the machine might work more smoothly, it has preferred to banish.

Utilitarianism

CHAPTER I

GENERAL REMARKS

THERE ARE FEW circumstances, among those which make up the present condition of human knowledge, more unlike what might have been expected, or more significant of the backward state in which speculation on the most important subjects still lingers, than the little progress which has been made in the decision of the controversy respecting the criterion of right and wrong. From the dawn of philosophy, the question concerning the *summum bonum,* or, what is the same thing, concerning the foundation of morality, has been accounted the main problem in speculative thought, has occupied the most gifted intellects, and divided them into sects and schools, carrying on a vigorous warfare against one another. And, after more than two thousand years, the same discussions continue, philosophers are still ranged under the same contending banners, and neither thinkers nor mankind at large seem nearer to being unanimous on the subject than when the youth Socrates listened to the old Protagoras, and asserted (if Plato's dialogue be grounded on a real conversation) the theory of utilitarianism against the popular morality of the so-called spohist.

It is true, that similar confusion and uncertainty, and in some cases similar discordance, exist respecting the first principles of all the sciences, not excepting that which is deemed the most certain of them,—mathematics; without much impairing, generally indeed without impairing at all, the trustworthiness of the conclusions of those sciences. An apparent anomaly, the explanation of which is, that the detailed doctrines of a science are not usually deduced from, nor depend for their evidence upon, what are called its first principles. Were it not so, there would be no science more precarious, or whose conclusions were more insufficiently made out, than algebra; which derives none of its certainty from what are commonly taught to learners as its elements; since these, as laid down by some of its most eminent teachers, are as full of fictions as English law, and of mysteries as theology. The truths which are ultimately accepted as the first principles of a science are really the last results of metaphysical analysis, practised on the elementary notions with which the science is conversant; and their relation to the science is not that of foundations to an edifice, but of roots to a tree, which may perform their office equally well though they be never dug down to and exposed to light. But, though in science the particular truths precede the general theory, the contrary might be expected to be the case with a practical art, such as morals or legislation. All action is for the sake of some end; and rules of action, it seems natural to suppose, must take their whole character and color from the end to which they are subservient. When we engage in a pursuit, a clear and precise conception of what we are pursuing would seem to be the first thing we need, instead of the last we are to look forward to. A test of right and wrong must be the means, one would think, of ascertaining what is right or wrong, and not a consequence of having already ascertained it.

The difficulty is not avoided by having recourse to the popular theory of a natural faculty, a sense or instinct, informing us of right and wrong. For, besides that the existence of such a moral instinct is itself one of the matters in dispute, those believers in it who have any pretensions to philosophy have been obliged to abandon the idea that it discerns what is right or wrong in the particular case in hand, as our other senses discern the sight or sound actually present. Our moral faculty, according to all those of its interpreters who are entitled to the name of thinkers, supplies us only with the general principles of moral judgments: it is a branch of our reason, not of our sensitive faculty; and must be looked to for the abstract doctrines of morality, not for perception of it in the concrete. The intuitive, no less than what may be termed the inductive, school of ethics, insists on the necessity of general laws. They both agree that the morality of an individual action is not a question of direct perception, but of the application of a law to an individual case. They recognize also, to a great extent, the same moral laws, but differ as to their evidence, and the source from which they derive their authority. According to the one opinion, the principles of morals are evident *à priori;* requiring nothing to command assent, except that the meaning of the terms be understood. According to the other doctrine, right and wrong, as well as truth and falsehood, are questions of observation and experience. But both hold equally, that morality must be deduced from principles; and the intuitive school affirm, as strongly as the inductive, that there is a science of morals. Yet they seldom attempt to make out a list of the *à priori* principles which are to serve as the premises of the science; still more rarely do they make any effort to reduce those various principles to one first principle, or common ground of obligation. They either assume the ordinary precepts of morals as of *à priori* authority, or they lay down as the common groundwork of those maxims some generality much less obviously authoritative than the maxims themselves, and which has never succeeded in gaining popular acceptance. Yet, to support their pretensions, there ought either to be some one fundamental principle or law at the root of all morality; or, if there be several, there should be a determinate order of precedence among them; and the one principle, or the rule for deciding between the various principles when they conflict, ought to be self-evident.

To inquire how far the bad effects of this deficiency have been mitigated in practice, or to what extent the moral beliefs of mankind have been vitiated or made uncertain by the absence of any distinct recognition of an ultimate standard, would imply a complete survey and criticism of past and present ethical doctrine. It would, however, be easy to show that whatever steadiness or consistency these moral beliefs have attained has been mainly due to the tacit influence of a standard not recognized. Although the non-existence of an acknowledged first principle has made ethics not so much a guide as a consecration of men's actual sentiments, still, as men's sentiments, both of favor and of aversion, are greatly influenced by what they suppose to be the effects of things upon their happiness, the principle of utility, or, as Bentham latterly called it, the greatest-happiness principle, has had a large share in forming the moral doctrines even of those who most scornfully reject its authority. Nor is there any school of thought which refuses to admit that the influence of actions on happiness is a most material and even predominant consideration in many of the details of morals, however unwilling to acknowledge it as the fundamental principle of morality and the source of moral obligation. I might go much further, and say, that, to all those *à priori* moralists who deem it necessary to argue at all, utilitarian arguments are indispensable. It is not my present purpose to criticise these thinkers; but I cannot help referring, for illustration, to a systematic treatise by one of the most illustrious of them,—the "Metaphysics of Ethics," by Kant. This remarkable man, whose system of thought will long remain one of the landmarks in the history of philosophical speculation, does, in the treatise in question, lay down an universal first principle as the origin and ground of moral obligation. It is this: "So act, that the rule on which thou actest would admit of being adopted as a law by all rational beings." But, when he begins to deduce from this precept any of the actual duties of morality, he fails, almost grotesquely, to show that there would be any contradiction, any logical (not to say physical) impossibility, in the adoption by all rational beings of the most outrageously immoral rules of conduct. All he shows is, that the *consequences* of their universal adoption would be such as no one would choose to incur.

On the present occasion, I shall, without further discussion of the other theories, attempt to contribute something towards the understanding and appreciation of the Utilitarian or Happiness theory, and towards such proof as it is susceptible of. It is evident that this cannot be proof in the ordinary and popular meaning of the term. Questions of ultimate ends are not amenable to direct proof. Whatever can be proved to be good, must be so by being shown to be a means to something admitted to be good without proof. The medical art is proved to be good by its conducing to health; but how is it possible to prove that health is good? The art of music is good, for the reason, among others, that it produces pleasure; but what proof is it possible to give that pleasure is good? If, then, it is asserted that there is a comprehensive formula, including all things which are in themselves good, and that whatever else is good is not so as an end, but as a mean, the formula may be accepted or rejected, but is not a subject of what is commonly understood by proof. We are not, however, to infer that its acceptance or rejection must depend on blind impulse or arbitrary choice. There is a larger meaning of the word "proof," in which this question is as amenable to it as any other of the disputed questions of philosophy. The subject is within the cognizance of the rational faculty, and neither does that faculty deal with it solely in the way of intuition. Considerations may be presented capable of determining the intellect either to give or withhold its assent to the doctrine; and this is equivalent to proof.

We shall examine presently of what nature are these considerations; in what manner they apply to the case; and what rational grounds, therefore, can be given for accepting or rejecting the utilitarian formula. But it is a preliminary condition of rational acceptance or rejection, that the formula should be correctly understood. I believe that the very imperfect notion ordinarily formed of its meaning is the chief obstacle which impedes its reception; and that, could it be cleared even from only the grosser misconceptions, the question would be greatly simplified, and a large proportion of its difficulties removed. Before, therefore, I attempt to enter into the philosophical grounds which can be given for assenting to the utilitarian standard, I shall offer some illustrations of the doctrine itself, with the view of showing more clearly what it is, distinguishing it from what it is not, and disposing of such of the practical objections to it as either originate in, or are closely connected with, mistaken interpretations of its meaning. Having thus prepared the ground, I shall afterwards endeavor to throw such light as I can upon the question, considered as one of philosophical theory.

CHAPTER II

WHAT UTILITARIANISM IS

A PASSING REMARK is all that needs be given to the ignorant blunder of supposing that those who stand up for utility, as the test of right and wrong, use the term in that restricted and merely colloquial sense in which utility is opposed to pleasure. An apology is due to the philosophical opponents of utilitarianism for even the momentary appearance of confounding them with any one capable of so absurd a misconception; which is the more extraordinary, inasmuch as the contrary accusation, of referring every thing to pleasure, and that, too, in its grossest form, is another of the common charges against utilitarianism: and, as has been pointedly remarked by an able writer, the same sort of persons, and often the very same persons, denounce the theory "as impracticably dry when the word 'utility' precedes the word 'pleasure,' and as too practicably voluptuous when the word 'pleasure' precedes the word 'utility.'" Those who know any thing about the matter are aware, that every writer, from Epicurus to Bentham, who maintained the theory of utility, meant by it, not something to be contradistinguished from pleasure, but pleasure itself, together with exemption from pain; and, instead of opposing the useful to the agreeable or the ornamental, have always declared that the useful means these, among other things. Yet the common herd, including the herd of writers, not only in newspapers and periodicals, but in books of weight and pretension, are perpetually falling into this shallow mistake. Having caught up the word "utilitarian," while knowing nothing whatever about it but its sound, they habitually express by it the rejection or the neglect of pleasure in some of its forms; of beauty, of ornament, or of amusement. Nor is the term thus ignorantly misapplied solely in disparagement, but occasionally in compliment; as though it implied superiority to frivolity and the mere pleasures of the moment. And this perverted use is the only one in which the word is popularly known, and the one from which the new generation are acquiring their sole notion of its meaning. Those who introduced the word, but who had for many years discontinued it as a distinctive appellation, may well feel themselves called upon to resume it, if by doing so they can hope to contribute any thing towards rescuing it from this utter degradation.[1]

The creed which accepts, as the foundation of morals, Utility, or the Greatest-happiness Principle, holds that actions are right in proportion as they tend to promote happiness, wrong as they tend to produce the reverse of happiness. By happiness is intended pleasure and the absence of pain; by unhappiness, pain and the privation of pleasure. To give a clear view of the moral standard set up by the theory, much more requires to be said; in particular, what things it includes in the ideas of pain and pleasure, and to what extent this is left an open question. But these supplementary explanations do not affect the theory of life on which this theory of morality is grounded,—namely, that pleasure, and freedom from pain, are the only things desirable as ends; and that all desirable things (which are as numerous in the utilitarian as in any other scheme) are desirable either for the pleasure inherent in themselves, or as means to the promotion of pleasure and the prevention of pain.

Now, such a theory of life excites in many minds, and among them in some of the most estimable in feeling and purpose, inveterate dislike. To suppose that life has (as they express it) no higher end than pleasure,—no better and nobler object of desire and pursuit,—they designate as utterly mean and grovelling; as a doctrine worthy only of swine, to whom the followers of Epicurus were, at a very early period, contemptuously likened: and modern holders of the doctrine

[1]The author of this essay has reason for believing himself to be the first person who brought the word "utilitarian" into use. He did not invent it, but adopted it from a passing expression in Mr. Galt's Annals of the Parish. After using it as a designation for several years, he and others abandoned it from a growing dislike to any thing resembling a badge or watchword of sectarian distinction. But as a name for one single opinion, not a set of opinions,—to denote the recognition of utility as a standard, not any particular way of applying it,—the term supplies a want in the language, and offers, in many cases, a convenient mode of avoiding tiresome circumlocution.

are occasionally made the subject of equally polite comparisons by its German, French, and English assailants.

When thus attacked, the Epicureans have always answered, that it is not they, but their accusers, who represent human nature in a degrading light, since the accusation supposes human beings to be capable of no pleasures except those of which swine are capable. If this supposition were true, the charge could not be gainsaid, but would then be no longer an imputation; for, if the sources of pleasure were precisely the same to human beings and to swine, the rule of life which is good enough for the one would be good enough for the other. The comparison of the Epicurean life to that of beasts is felt as degrading, precisely because a beast's pleasures do not satisfy a human being's conceptions of happiness. Human beings have faculties more elevated than the animal appetites; and, when once made conscious of them, do not regard any thing as happiness which does not include their gratification. I do not, indeed, consider the Epicureans to have been by any means faultless in drawing out their scheme of consequences from the utilitarian principle. To do this in any sufficient manner, many Stoic as well as Christian elements require to be included. But there is no known Epicurean theory of life which does not assign to the pleasures of the intellect, of the feelings and imagination, and of the moral sentiments, a much higher value as pleasures than to those of mere sensation. It must be admitted, however, that utilitarian writers in general have placed the superiority of mental over bodily pleasures chiefly in the greater permanency, safety, uncostliness, &c., of the former,—that is, in their circumstantial advantages rather than in their intrinsic nature. And, on all these points, utilitarians have fully proved their case; but they might have taken the other, and, as it may be called, higher ground, with entire consistency. It is quite compatible with the principle of utility to recognize the fact, that some *kinds* of pleasure are more desirable and more valuable than others. It would be absurd, that while, in estimating all other things, quality is considered as well as quantity, the estimation of pleasures should be supposed to depend on quantity alone.

If I am asked what I mean by difference of quality in pleasures, or what makes one pleasure more valuable than another, merely as a pleasure, except its being greater in amount, there is but one possible answer. Of two pleasures, if there be one to which all or almost all who have experience of both give a decided preference, irrespective of any feeling of moral obligation to prefer it, that is the more desirable pleasure. If one of the two is, by those who are competently acquainted with both, placed so far above the other that they prefer it, even though knowing it to be attended with a greater amount of discontent, and would not resign it for any quantity of the other pleasure which their nature is capable of, we are justified in ascribing to the preferred enjoyment a superiority in quality, so far outweighing quantity, as to render it, in comparison, of small account.

Now, it is an unquestionable fact, that those who are equally acquainted with and equally capable of appreciating and enjoying both do give a most marked preference to the manner of existence which employs their higher faculties. Few human creatures would consent to be changed into any of the lower animals, for a promise of the fullest allowance of a beast's pleasures: no intelligent human being would consent to be a fool, no instructed person would be an ignoramus, no person of feeling and conscience would be selfish and base, even though they should be persuaded that the fool, the dunce, or the rascal is better satisfied with his lot than they are with theirs. They would not resign what they possess more than he for the most complete satisfaction of all the desires which they have in common with him. If they ever fancy they would, it is only in cases of unhappiness so extreme, that, to escape from it, they would exchange their lot for almost any other, however undesirable in their own eyes. A being of higher faculties requires more to make him happy, is capable probably of more acute suffering, and certainly accessible to it at more points, than one of an inferior type; but, in spite of these liabilities, he can never really wish to sink into what he feels to be a lower grade of existence. We may give what explanation we please of this unwillingness; we may attribute it to pride, a name which is given indiscriminately to some of the most and to some of the least estimable feelings of which mankind are capable; we may refer it to the love of liberty and personal independence,—an appeal to which was with the Stoics one of the most effective means for the inculcation of it; to the love of power, or to the love of excitement, both of which do really enter into and contribute to it: but its most appropriate appellation is a sense of dignity, which all human beings possess in one form or other, and in some, though by no means in exact, proportion to their higher faculties, and which is so essential a part of the happiness of those in whom it is strong, that nothing which conflicts with it could be, otherwise than momentarily, an object of desire to them. Whoever supposes that this preference takes place at a sacrifice of happiness; that the superior being, in any thing like equal circumstances, is not happier than the inferior,—confounds the two very different ideas of happiness and content. It is indisputable, that the being whose capacities of enjoyment are low has the greatest chance of having them fully satisfied; and a highly endowed being will always feel that any happiness which he can look for, as the world is constituted, is imperfect. But he can learn to bear its imperfections, if they are at all bearable; and they will not make him envy the being who is indeed unconscious of the imperfections, but only because he feels not at all the good which those imperfections qualify. It is better to be a human being dissatisfied, than a pig satisfied; better to be Socrates dissatisfied, than a fool satisfied. And if the fool or the pig are of a different opinion, it is because they only know their own side of the question. The other party to the comparison knows both sides.

It may be objected, that many who are capable of the higher pleasures, occasionally, under the influence of temptation, postpone them to the lower. But this is quite compatible with a full appreciation of the intrinsic superiority of the higher. Men often, from infirmity of character, make their election for the nearer good, though they know it to be the less valuable, and this no less when the choice is between two bodily pleasures than when it is between bodily and mental. They pursue sensual indulgences to the injury of health, though perfectly aware that health is the greater good. It may be further objected, that many who begin with youthful enthusiasm for every thing noble, as they advance in years sink into indolence and selfishness. But I do not believe that those who undergo this very common change voluntarily choose the lower description of pleasures in preference to the higher. I believe, that, before they devote themselves exclusively to the one, they have already become incapable of the other. Capacity for the nobler feelings is in most natures a very tender plant, easily killed, not only by hostile influences, but by mere want of sustenance; and, in the majority of young persons, it speedily dies away if the occupations to which their position in life has devoted them, and the society into which it has thrown them, are not favorable to keeping that higher capacity in exercise. Men lose their high aspirations as they lose their intellectual tastes, because they have not time or opportunity for indulging them; and they addict themselves to inferior pleasures, not because they deliberately prefer them, but because they are either the only ones to which they have access, or the only ones which they are any longer capable of enjoying. It may be questioned, whether any one, who has remained equally susceptible to both classes of pleasures, ever knowingly and calmly preferred the lower; though many in all ages have broken down in an ineffectual attempt to combine both.

From this verdict of the only competent judges, I apprehend there can be no appeal. On a question, which is the best worth having of two pleasures, or which of two modes of existence is the most grateful to the feelings, apart from its moral attributes and from its consequences, the judgment of those who are qualified by knowledge of both, or, if they differ, that of the majority among them, must be admitted as final. And there needs be the less hesitation to accept this judgment respecting the quality of pleasures, since there is no other tribunal to be referred to even on the question of quantity. What means are there of determining which is the acutest of two pains, or the intensest of two pleasurable sensations, except the general suffrage of those who are familiar with both? Neither pains nor pleasures are homogeneous, and pain is always heterogeneous with pleasure. What is there to decide whether a particular pleasure is worth purchasing at the cost of a particular pain, except the feelings and judgment of the experienced? When, therefore, those feelings and judgment declare the pleasures derived from the higher faculties to be preferable *in kind*, apart from the question of intensity, to those of which the animal nature, disjoined from the higher faculties, is susceptible, they are entitled on this subject to the same regard.

I have dwelt on this point, as being a necessary part of a perfectly just conception of Utility or Happiness, considered as the directive rule of human conduct. But it is by no means an indispensable condition to the acceptance of the utilitarian standard; for that standard is not the agent's own greatest happiness, but the greatest amount of happiness altogether: and, if it may possibly be doubted whether a noble character is always the happier for its nobleness, there can be no doubt that it makes other people happier, and that the world in general is immensely a gainer by it. Utilitarianism, therefore, could only attain its end by the general cultivation of nobleness of character, even if each individual were only benefited by the nobleness of others, and his own, so far as happiness is concerned, were a sheer deduction from the benefit. But the bare enunciation of such an absurdity as this last renders refutation superfluous.

According to the Greatest-happiness Principle, as above explained, the ultimate end, with reference to and for the sake of which all other things are desirable (whether we are considering our own good or that of other people), is an existence exempt as far as possible from pain, and as rich as possible in enjoyments, both in point of quantity and quality; the test of quality, and the rule for measuring it against quantity, being the preference felt by those, who in their opportunities of experience, to which must be added their habits of self-consciousness and self-observation, are best furnished with the means of comparison. This, being, according to the utilitarian opinion, the end of human action, is necessarily also the standard of morality: which may accordingly be defined, the rules and precepts for human conduct, by the observance of which an existence such as has been described might be, to the greatest extent possible, secured to all mankind; and not to them only, but, so far as the nature of things admits, to the whole sentient creation.

Against this doctrine, however, arises another class of objectors, who say that happiness, in any form, cannot be the rational purpose of human life and action; because, in the first place, it is unattainable: and they contemptuously ask, What right hast thou to be happy? a question which Mr. Carlyle clinches by the addition, What right, a short time ago, hadst thou even *to be*? Next, they say that men can do *without* happiness; that all noble human beings have felt this, and could not have become noble but by learning the lesson of Entsagen, or renunciation; which lesson, thoroughly learnt and submitted to, they affirm to be the beginning and necessary condition of all virtue.

The first of these objections would go to the root of the matter, were it well founded; for, if no happiness is to be had at all by human beings, the attainment of it cannot be the end of morality, or of any rational conduct. Though, even in that case, something might still be said for the utilitarian theory; since utility includes not solely the pursuit of happiness, but the prevention or mitigation of unhappiness: and, if the former aim be chimerical, there will be all the greater scope and more imperative need for the latter, so long at least as mankind think fit to live, and do not take refuge in the simultaneous act of suicide recommended under certain conditions by Novalis. When, however, it is thus positively asserted to be impossible that human life should be happy, the assertion, if not something like a verbal quibble, is at least an exaggeration. If by happiness be meant a continuity of highly pleasurable excitement, it is evident enough that this is impossible. A state of exalted pleasure lasts only moments, or in some cases, and with some intermissions, hours or days; and is the occasional brilliant flash of enjoyment, not its permanent and steady flame. Of this the philosophers who have taught that happiness is the end of life were as fully aware as those who taunt them. The happiness which they meant was not a life of rapture, but moments of such, in an existence made up of few and transitory pains, many and various pleasures, with a decided predominance of the active over the passive, and having, as the foundation of the whole, not to expect more from life than it is capable of bestowing. A life thus composed, to those who have been fortunate enough to obtain it, has always appeared worthy of the name of "happiness." And such an existence is even now the lot of many, during some considerable portion of their lives. The present wretched education and wretched social arrangements are the only real hinderance to its being attainable by almost all.

The objectors, perhaps, may doubt whether human beings, if taught to consider happiness as the end of life, would be satisfied with such a moderate share of it. But great numbers of mankind have been satisfied with much less. The main constituents of a satisfied life appear to be two, either of which by itself is often found sufficient for the purpose,—tranquillity and excitement. With much tranquillity, many find that they can be content with very little pleasure; with much excitement, many can reconcile themselves to a considerable quantity of pain. There is assuredly no inherent impossibility in enabling even the mass of mankind to unite both; since the two are so far from being incompatible, that they are in natural alliance; the prolongation of either being a preparation for, and exciting a wish for, the other. It is only those in whom indolence amounts to a vice, that do not desire excitement after an interval of repose; it is only those in whom the need of excitement is a disease, that feel the tranquillity which follows excitement dull and insipid, instead of pleasurable in direct proportion to the excitement which preceded it. When people who are tolerably fortunate in their outward lot do not find in life sufficient enjoyment to make it valuable to them, the cause generally is, caring for nobody but themselves. To those who have neither public nor private affections, the excitements of life are much curtailed, and, in any case, dwindle in value as the time approaches when all selfish interests must be terminated by death; while those who leave after them objects of personal affection, and especially those who have also cultivated a fellow-feeling with the collective interests of mankind, retain as lively an interest in life on the eve of death as in the vigor of youth and health. Next to selfishness, the principal cause which makes life unsatisfactory is want of mental cultivation. A cultivated mind—I do not mean that of a philosopher, but any mind to which the fountains of knowledge have been opened, and which has been taught, in any tolerable degree, to exercise its faculties —finds sources of inexhaustible interest in all that surrounds it; in the objects of nature, the achievements of art, the imaginations of poetry, the incidents of history, the ways of mankind past and present, and their prospects in the future. It is possible, indeed, to become indifferent to all this, and that, too, without having exhausted a thousandth part of it; but only when one has had from the beginning no moral or human interest in these things, and has sought in them only the gratification of curiosity.

Now, there is absolutely no reason in the nature of things why an amount of mental culture sufficient to give an intelligent interest in these objects of contemplation should not be the inheritance of every one born in a civilized country. As

little is there an inherent necessity that any human being
should be a selfish egotist, devoid of every feeling or care but
those which centre in his own miserable individuality. Something far superior to this is sufficiently common even now to
give ample earnest of what the human species may be made.
Genuine private affections, and a sincere interest in the public
good, are possible, though in unequal degrees, to every rightly
brought up human being. In a world in which there is so
much to interest, so much to enjoy, and so much also to correct and improve, every one who has this moderate amount of
moral and intellectual requisites is capable of an existence
which may be called enviable; and unless such a person,
through bad laws, or subjection to the will of others, is denied
the liberty to use the sources of happiness within his reach,
he will not fail to find this enviable existence, if he escapes
the positive evils of life, the great sources of physical and
mental suffering,—such as indigence, disease, and the unkindness, worthlessness, or premature loss, of objects of affection.
The main stress of the problem lies, therefore, in the contest
with these calamities, from which it is a rare good fortune entirely to escape; which, as things now are, cannot be obviated,
and often cannot be, in any material degree, mitigated. Yet
no one, whose opinion deserves a moment's consideration,
can doubt that most of the great positive evils of the world
are in themselves removable, and will, if human affairs continue to improve, be in the end reduced within narrow limits.
Poverty, in any sense implying suffering, may be completely
extinguished by the wisdom of society, combined with the
good sense and providence of individuals. Even that most in-
tractable of enemies, disease, may be indefinitely reduced in
dimensions by good physical and moral education, and proper control of noxious influences; while the progress of science
holds out a promise for the future of still more direct con-
quests over this detestable foe. And every advance in that direction relieves us from some, not only of the chances which
cut short our own lives, but, what concerns us still more, which
deprive us of those in whom our happiness is wrapped up.
As for vicissitudes of fortune, and other disappointments connected with worldly circumstances, these are principally the
effect either of gross imprudence, or ill-regulated desires, or
of bad or imperfect social institutions. All the grand sources,
in short, of human suffering, are in a great degree, many of

them almost entirely, conquerable by human care and effort: and though their removal is grievously slow; though a long succession of generations will perish in the breach before the conquest is completed, and this world becomes all that, if will and knowledge were not wanting, it might easily be made, —yet every mind sufficiently intelligent and generous to bear a part, however small and unconspicuous, in the endeavor, will draw a noble enjoyment from the contest itself, which he would not, for any bribe in the form of selfish indulgence, consent to be without.

And this leads to the true estimation of what is said by the objectors concerning the possibility and the obligation of learning to do without happiness. Unquestionably, it is possible to do without happiness: it is done involuntarily by nineteen-twentieths of mankind, even in those parts of our present world which are least deep in barbarism; and it often has to be done voluntarily by the hero or the martyr, for the sake of something which he prizes more than his individual happiness. But this something—what is it, unless the happiness of others, or some of the requisites of happiness? It is noble to be capable of resigning entirely one's own portion of happiness, or chances of it: but, after all, this self-sacrifice must be for some end; it is not its own end; and if we are told that its end is not happiness, but virtue, which is better than happiness, I ask, Would the sacrifice be made if the hero or martyr did not believe that it would earn for others immunity from similar sacrifices? Would it be made if he thought that his renunciation of happiness for himself would produce no fruit for any of his fellow-creatures but to make their lot like his, and place them also in the condition of persons who have renounced happiness? All honor to those who can abnegate for themselves the personal enjoyment of life, when by such renunciation they contribute worthily to increase the amount of happiness in the world; but he who does it, or professes to do it, for any other purpose, is no more deserving of admiration than the ascetic mounted on his pillar. He may be an inspiriting proof of what men *can* do, but assuredly not an example of what they *should*.

Though it is only in a very imperfect state of the world's arrangements that any one can best serve the happiness of others by the absolute sacrifice of his own, yet, so long as the world is in that imperfect state, I fully acknowledge that the readiness to make such a sacrifice is the highest virtue which can be found in man. I will add, that in this condition of the world, paradoxical as the assertion may be, the conscious ability to do without happiness gives the best prospect of realizing such happiness as is attainable. For nothing except that consciousness can raise a person above the chances of life, by making him feel, that, let fate and fortune do their worst, they have not power to subdue him; which, once felt, frees him from excess of anxiety concerning the evils of life, and enables him, like many a Stoic in the worst times of the Roman Empire, to cultivate in tranquillity the sources of satisfaction accessible to him, without concerning himself about the uncertainty of their duration, any more than about their inevitable end.

Meanwhile, let utilitarians never cease to claim the morality of self-devotion as a possession which belongs by as good a right to them as either to the Stoic or to the Transcendentalist. The utilitarian morality does recognize in human beings the power of sacrificing their own greatest good for the good of others. It only refuses to admit that the sacrifice is itself a good. A sacrifice which does not increase, or tend to increase, the sum total of happiness, it considers as wasted. The only self-renunciation which it applauds is devotion to the happiness, or to some of the means of happiness, of others, either of mankind collectively, or of individuals within the limits imposed by the collective interests of mankind.

I must again repeat, what the assailants of utilitarianism seldom have the justice to acknowledge, that the happiness which forms the utilitarian standard of what is right in conduct is not the agent's own happiness, but that of all concerned; as between his own happiness and that of others, utilitarianism requires him to be as strictly impartial as a disinterested and benevolent spectator. In the golden rule of Jesus of Nazareth, we read the complete spirit of the ethics of utility. To do as you would be done by, and to love your neighbor as yourself, constitute the ideal perfection of utilitarian morality. As the means of making the nearest approach to this ideal, utility would enjoin, first, that laws and social arrangements should place the happiness or (as, speaking practically, it may be called) the interest of every individual as nearly as possible in harmony with the interest of the whole; and, secondly, that education and opinion, which have so vast a power over human character, should so use that power as to establish in the mind of every individual an indissoluble association between his own happiness and the good of the whole,—especially between his own happiness, and the practice of such modes of conduct, negative and positive, as regard for the universal happiness prescribes,—so that not only he may be unable to conceive the possibility of happiness to himself, consistently with conduct opposed to the general good, but also that a direct impulse to promote the general good may be in every individual one of the habitual motives of action, and the sentiments connected therewith may fill a large and prominent place in every human being's sentient existence. If the impugners of the utilitarian morality represented it to their own minds in this its true character, I know not what recommendation possessed by any other morality they could possibly affirm to be wanting to it; what more beautiful or more exalted developments of human nature any other ethical system can be supposed to foster; or what springs of action, not accessible to the utilitarian, such systems rely on for giving effect to their mandates.

The objectors to utilitarianism cannot always be charged with representing it in a discreditable light. On the contrary, those among them who entertain any thing like a just idea of its disinterested character sometimes find fault with its standard as being too high for humanity. They say it is exacting too much to require that people shall always act from the inducement of promoting the general interests of society. But this is to mistake the very meaning of a standard of morals, and confound the rule of action with the motive of it. It is the business of ethics to tell us what are our duties, or by what test we may know them; but no system of ethics requires that the sole motive of all we do shall be a feeling of duty: on the contrary, ninety-nine hundredths of all our actions are done from other motives, and rightly so done, if the rule of duty does not condemn them. It is the more unjust to utilitarianism that this particular misapprehension should be made a ground of objection to it, inasmuch as utilitarian moralists have gone beyond almost all others in affirming that the motive has nothing to do with the morality of the action, though much with the worth of the agent. He who saves a fellow-creature from drowning does what is morally right, whether his motive be duty, or the hope of being paid for his trouble: he who betrays the friend that trusts him is guilty of a crime, even if his object be to serve another friend to whom he is under greater obligations. But to speak only of actions done from the motive of duty, and in direct obedience to principle: it is a misapprehension of the utilitarian mode of thought to conceive it as implying that people should fix their minds upon so wide a generality as the world or society at large. The great majority of good actions are intended, not for the benefit of the world, but for that of individuals, of which the good of the world is made up; and the thoughts of the most virtuous man need not on these occasions travel beyond the particular persons concerned, except so far as is necessary to assure himself, that, in benefiting them, he is not violating the rights—that is, the legitimate and authorized expectations—of any one else. The multiplication of happiness is, according to the utilitarian ethics, the object of virtue: the occasions on which any person (except one in a thousand) has it in his power to do this on an extended scale—in other words, to be a public benefactor—are but exceptional; and on these occasions alone is he called on to consider public utility: in every other case, private utility, the interest or happiness of some few persons, is all he has to attend to. Those alone, the influence of whose actions extends to society in general, need concern themselves habitually about so large an object. In the case of abstinences indeed,—of things which people forbear to do from moral considerations, though the consequences in the particular case might be beneficial,—it would be unworthy of an intelligent agent not to be consciously aware that the action is of a class, which, if practised generally, would be generally injurious, and that this is the ground of the obligation to abstain from it. The amount of regard for the public interest implied in this recognition is no greater than is demanded by every system of morals; for they all enjoin to abstain from whatever is manifestly pernicious to society.

The same considerations dispose of another reproach against the doctrine of utility, founded on a still grosser misconception of the purpose of a standard of morality, and of the very meaning of the words "right" and "wrong." It is often affirmed, that utilitarianism renders men cold and unsympathizing; that it chills their moral feelings towards individuals; that it makes them regard only the dry and hard consideration of the consequences of actions, not taking into their moral estimate the qualities from which those actions emanate. If the assertion means that they do not allow their judgment respecting the rightness or wrongness of an action to be influenced by their opinion of the qualities of the person who does it, this is a complaint, not against utilitarianism, but against having any standard of morality at all: for certainly no known ethical standard decides an action to be good or bad because it is done by a good or a bad man; still less because done by an amiable, a brave, or a benevolent man, or the contrary. These considerations are relevant, not to the estimation of actions, but of persons; and there is nothing in the utilitarian theory inconsistent with the fact, that there are other things which interest us in persons besides the rightness and wrongness of their actions. The Stoics indeed, with the paradoxical misuse of language which was part of their system, and by which they strove to raise themselves above all concern about any thing but virtue, were fond of saying, that he who has that, has every thing; that he, and only he, is rich, is beautiful, is a king. But no claim of this description is made for the virtuous man by the utilitarian doctrine. Utilitarians are quite aware that there are other desirable possessions and qualities besides virtue, and are perfectly willing to allow to all of them their full worth. They are also aware that a right action does not necessarily indicate a virtuous character; and that actions which are blamable often proceed from qualities entitled to praise. When this is apparent in any particular case, it modifies their estimation, not certainly of the act, but of the agent. I grant that they are, notwithstanding, of opinion, that, in the long-run, the best proof of a good character is good actions; and resolutely refuse to consider any mental disposition as good, of which the predominant tendency is to produce bad conduct. This makes them unpopular with many people: but it is an unpopularity which they must share with every one who regards the distinction between right and wrong in a serious light; and the reproach is not one which a conscientious utilitarian need be anxious to repel.

If no more be meant by the objection than that many utilitarians look on the morality of actions, as measured by the utilitarian standard, with too exclusive a regard, and do not lay sufficient stress upon the other beauties of character which go towards making a human being lovable or admirable, this may be admitted. Utilitarians who have cultivated their moral feelings, but not their sympathies nor their artistic perceptions, do fall into this mistake; and so do all other moralists under the same conditions. What can be said in excuse for other moralists is equally available for them; namely, that, if there is to be any error, it is better that it should be on that side. As a matter of fact, we may affirm that among utilitarians, as among adherents of other systems, there is every imaginable degree of rigidity and of laxity in the application of their standard: some are even puritanically rigorous, while others are as indulgent as can possibly be desired by sinner or by sentimentalist. But, on the whole, a doctrine which brings prominently forward the interest that mankind have in the repression and prevention of conduct which violates the moral law, is likely to be inferior to no other in turning the sanctions of opinion against such violations. It is true, the question, What does violate the moral law? is one on which those who recognize different standards of morality are likely now and then to differ. But difference of opinion on moral questions was not first introduced into the world by utilitarianism; while that doctrine does supply, if not always an easy, at all events a tangible and intelligible, mode of deciding such differences.

It may not be superfluous to notice a few more of the common misapprehensions of utilitarian ethics, even those which are so obvious and gross that it might appear impossible for any person of candor and intelligence to fall into them; since persons even of considerable mental endowments often give themselves so little trouble to understand the bearings of any opinion against which they entertain a prejudice, and men are in general so little conscious of this voluntary ignorance as a defect, that the vulgarest misunderstandings of ethical doctrines are continually met with in the deliberate writings of persons of the greatest pretensions both to high principle and to philosophy. We not uncommonly hear the doctrine of utility inveighed against as a *godless* doctrine. If it be necessary to say any thing at all against so mere an assumption, we may say that the question depends upon what idea we have formed of the moral character of the Deity. If it be a true belief, that God desires, above all things, the happiness of his creatures, and that this was his purpose in their creation, utility is not only not a godless doctrine, but more profoundly religious than any other. If it be meant that utilitarianism does not recognize the revealed will of God as the supreme law of morals, I answer, that an utilitarian, who believes in the perfect goodness and wisdom of God, necessarily believes that whatever God has thought fit to reveal on the subject of morals must fulfil the requirements of utility in a supreme degree. But others besides utilitarians have been of opinion, that the Christian revelation was intended, and is fitted, to inform the hearts and minds of mankind with a spirit which should enable them to find for themselves what is right, and incline them to do it when found, rather than to tell them, except in a very general way, what it is; and that we need a doctrine of ethics, carefully followed out, to *interpret* to us the will of God. Whether this opinion is correct or not, it is superfluous here to discuss; since whatever aid religion, either natural or revealed, can afford to ethical investigation, is as open to the utilitarian moralist as to any other. He can use it as the testimony of God to the usefulness or hurtfulness of any given course of action, by as good a right as others can use it for the indication of a transcendental law, having no connection with usefulness or with happiness.

Again: Utility is often summarily stigmatized as an immoral doctrine by giving it the name of Expediency, and, taking advantage of the popular use of that term, to contrast it with Principle. But the Expedient, in the sense in which it is opposed to the Right, generally means that which is expedient for the particular interest of the agent himself; as when a minister sacrifices the interests of his country to keep himself in place. When it means any thing better than this, it means that which is expedient for some immediate object, some temporary purpose, but which violates a rule whose observance is expedient in a much higher degree. The Expedient, in this sense, instead of being the same thing with the useful, is a branch of the hurtful. Thus it would often be expedient, for the purpose of getting over some momentary embarrassment, or attaining some object immediately useful to ourselves or others, to tell a lie. But inasmuch as the cultivation in ourselves of a sensitive feeling on the subject of veracity is one of the most useful, and the enfeeblement of that feeling one of the most hurtful, things to which our conduct can be instrumental; and inasmuch as any, even un-intentional, deviation from truth does that much towards weakening the trustworthiness of human assertion, which is not only the principal support of all present social well-being, but the insufficiency of which does more than any one thing that can be named to keep back civilization, virtue, every thing on which human happiness on the largest scale depends,—we feel that the violation, for a present advantage, of a rule of such transcendent expediency, is not expedient; and that he, who, for the sake of a convenience to himself or to some other individual, does what depends on him to deprive mankind of the good, and inflict upon them the evil, involved in the greater or less reliance which they can place in each other's word, acts the part of one of their worst enemies. Yet that even this rule, sacred as it is, admits of possible exceptions, is acknowledged by all moralists; the chief of which is, when the witholding of some fact (as of information from a malefactor, or bad news from a person dangerously ill) would save an individual (especially an individual other than one's self) from great and unmerited evil, and when the withholding can only be effected by denial. But in order that the exception may not extend itself beyond the need, and may have the least possible effect in weakening reliance on veracity, it ought to be recognized, and, if possible, its limits defined; and, if the principle of utility is good for any thing, it must be good for weighing these conflicting utilities against one another, and marking out the region within which one or the other preponderates.

Again: defenders of utility often find themselves called upon to reply to such objections as this,—that there is not time, previous to action, for calculating and weighing the effects of any line of conduct on the general happiness. This is exactly as if any one were to say that it is impossible to guide our conduct by Christianity, because there is not time, on every occasion on which any thing has to be done, to read through the Old and New Testaments. The answer to the objection is, that there has been ample time; namely, the whole past duration of the human species. During all that time, mankind have been learning by experience the tend-encies of actions, on which experience all the prudence as well as all the morality of life are dependent. People talk as if the commencement of this course of experience had hitherto been put off, and as if, at the moment when some man feels tempted to meddle with the property or life of another, he had to begin considering for the first time whether murder and theft are injurious to human happiness. Even then, I do not think that he would find the question very puzzling; but, at all events, the matter is now done to his hand. It is truly a whimsical supposition, that, if mankind were agreed in considering utility to be the test of morality, they would remain without any agreement as to what *is* useful, and would take no measures for having their notions on the subject taught to the young, and enforced by law and opinion. There is no difficulty in proving any ethical standard whatever to work ill, if we suppose universal idiocy to be conjoined with it: but, on any hypothesis short of that, mankind must by this time have acquired positive beliefs as to the effects of some actions on their happiness; and the beliefs which have thus come down are the rules of morality for the multitude, and for the philosopher, until he has succeeded in finding better. That philosophers might easily do this, even now, on many subjects; that the received code of ethics is by no means of divine right; and that mankind have still much to learn as to the effects of actions on the general happiness,—I admit, or, rather, earnestly maintain. The corollaries from the principle of utility, like the precepts of every practical art, admit of indefinite improvement; and, in a progressive state of the human mind, their improvement is perpetually going on. But to consider the rules of morality as improvable is one thing; to pass over the intermediate generalizations entirely, and endeavor to test each individual action directly by the first principle, is another. It is a strange notion, that the acknowledgment of a first principle is inconsistent with the admission of secondary ones. To inform a traveller respecting the place of his ultimate destination is not to forbid the use of landmarks and direction-posts on the way. The proposition that happiness is the end and aim of morality does not mean that no road ought to be laid down to that goal, or that persons going thither should not be advised to take one direction rather than another. Men really ought to leave off talking a kind of nonsense on this subject which they would neither talk nor listen to on other matters of practical concernment. Nobody argues that the art of navigation is not founded on astronomy, because sailors cannot wait to calculate the "Nautical Almanac." Being rational creatures, they go to sea with it ready calculated; and all rational creatures go out upon the sea of life with their minds made up on the common questions of right and wrong, as well as on many of the far more difficult questions of wise and foolish. And this, as long as foresight is a human quality, it is to be presumed they will continue to do. Whatever we adopt as the fundamental principle of morality, we require subordinate principles to apply it by: the impossibility of doing without them, being common to all systems, can afford no argument against any one in particular; but gravely to argue as if no such secondary principles could be had, and as if mankind had remained till now, and always must remain, without drawing any general conclusions from the experience of human life, is as high a pitch, I think, as absurdity has ever reached in philosophical controversy.

The remainder of the stock arguments against utilitarianism mostly consist in laying to its charge the common infirmities of human nature, and the general difficulties which embarrass conscientious persons in shaping their course through life. We are told that an utilitarian will be apt to make his own particular case an exception to moral rules; and, when under temptation, will see an utility in the breach of a rule greater than he will see in its observance. But is utility the only creed which is able to furnish us with excuses for evil-doing, and means of cheating our own conscience? They are afforded in abundance by all doctrines which recognize as a fact in morals the existence of conflicting considerations; which all doctrines do that have been believed by sane persons. It is not the fault of any creed, but of the complicated nature of human affairs, that rules of conduct cannot be so framed as to require no exceptions, and that hardly any kind of action can safely be laid down as either always obligatory or always condemnable. There is no ethical creed which does not temper the rigidity of its laws by giving a certain latitude, under the moral responsibility of the agent, for accommodation to peculiarities of circumstances; and under every creed, at the opening thus made, self-deception and dishonest casuistry get in. There exists no moral system under which there do not arise unequivocal cases of conflicting obligation. These are the real difficulties; the knotty points both in the theory of ethics, and in the conscientious guidance of personal conduct. They are overcome practically with greater or with less success according to the intellect and virtue of the individual; but it can hardly be pretended that any one will be the less qualified for dealing with them, from possessing an ultimate standard to which conflicting rights and duties can be referred. If utility is the ultimate source of moral obligations, utility may be invoked to decide between them when their demands are incompatible. Though the application of the standard may be difficult, it is better than none at all: while in other systems, the moral laws all claiming independent authority, there is no common umpire entitled to interfere between them; their claims to precedence one over another rest on little better than sophistry; and unless determined, as they generally are, by the unacknowledged influence of considerations of utility, afford a free scope for the action of personal desires and partialities. We must remember that only in these cases of conflict between secondary principles is it requisite that first principles should be appealed to. There is no case of moral obligation in which some secondary principle is not involved; and, if only one, there can seldom be any real doubt which one it is, in the mind of any person by whom the principle itself is recognized.

CHAPTER III

OF THE ULTIMATE SANCTION OF THE PRINCIPLE OF UTILITY

THE QUESTION is often asked, and properly so, in regard to any supposed moral standard, What is its sanction? what are the motives to obey it? or, more specifically, what is the source of its obligation? whence does it derive its binding force? It is a necessary part of moral philosophy to provide the answer to this question; which, though frequently assuming the shape of an objection to the utilitarian morality, as if it had some special applicability to that above others, really arises in regard to all standards. It arises, in fact, whenever a person is called on to *adopt* a standard, or refer morality to any basis on which he has not been accustomed to rest it. For the customary morality, that which education and opinion have consecrated, is the only one which presents itself to the mind with the feeling of being *in itself* obligatory: and, when a person is asked to believe that this morality *derives* its obligation from some general principle round which custom has not thrown the same halo, the assertion is to him a paradox; the supposed corollaries seem to have a more binding force than the original theorem; the superstructure seems to stand better without than with what is represented as its foundation. He says to himself, "I feel that I am bound not to rob or murder, betray or deceive; but why am I bound to promote the general happiness? If my own happiness lies in something else, why may I not give that the preference?"

If the view adopted by the utilitarian philosophy of the nature of the moral sense be correct, this difficulty will always present itself, until the influences which form moral character have taken the same hold of the principle which they have taken of some of the consequences; until, by the improvement of education, the feeling of unity with our fellow-creatures shall be (what it cannot be denied that Christ intended it to be) as deeply rooted in our character, and, to our own consciousness, as completely a part of our nature, as the horror of crime is in an ordinarily well brought up young person. In the mean time, however, the difficulty has no peculiar application to the doctrine of utility, but is inherent in every attempt to analyze morality, and reduce it to principles; which, unless the principle is already in men's minds invested with as much sacredness as any of its applications, always seems to divest them of a part of their sanctity.

The principle of utility either has, or there is no reason why it might not have, all the sanctions which belong to any other system of morals. Those sanctions are either external or internal. Of the external sanctions it is not necessary to speak at any length. They are, the hope of favor and the fear of displeasure from our fellow-creatures, or from the Ruler of the universe, along with whatever we may have of sympathy or affection for them; or of love and awe of him, inclining us to do his will independently of selfish consequences. There is evidently no reason why all these motives for observance should not attach themselves to the utilitarian morality as completely and as powerfully as to any other. Indeed, those of them which refer to our fellow-creatures are sure to do so, in proportion to the amount of general intelligence: for, whether there be any other ground of moral obligation than the general happiness or not, men do desire happiness; and, however imperfect may be their own practice, they desire and commend all conduct in others towards themselves by which they think their happiness is promoted. With regard to the religious motive, if men believe, as most profess to do, in the goodness of God, those who think that conduciveness to the general happiness is the essence, or even only the criterion, of good, must necessarily believe that it is also that which God approves. The whole force, therefore, of external reward and punishment, whether physical or moral, and whether proceeding from God or from our fellow-men, together with all that the capacities of human nature admit of disinterested devotion to either, become available to enforce the utilitarian morality, in proportion as that morality is recognized; and the more powerfully, the more the appliances of education and general cultivation are bent to the purpose.

So far as to external sanctions. The internal sanction of duty, whatever our standard of duty may be, is one and the same,—a feeling in our own mind; a pain, more or less intense, attendant on violation of duty, which, in properly cultivated moral natures, rises in the more serious cases into shrinking from it as an impossibility. This feeling, when disinterested, and connecting itself with the pure idea of duty, and not with some particular form of it, or with any of the merely accessory circumstances, is the essence of Conscience: though in that complex phenomenon, as it actually exists, the simple fact is, in general, all incrusted over with collateral associations, derived from sympathy, from love, and still more from fear; from all the forms of religious feeling; from the recollections of childhood, and of all our past life; from self-esteem, desire of the esteem of others, and occasionally even self-abasement. This extreme complication is, I apprehend, the origin of the sort of mystical character, which, by a tendency of the human mind of which there are many other examples, is apt to be attributed to the idea of moral obligation, and which leads people to believe that the idea cannot possibly attach itself to any other objects than those which, by a supposed mysterious law, are found in our present experience to excite it. Its binding force, however, consists in the existence of a mass of feeling which must be broken through in order to do what violates our standard of right; and which, if we do nevertheless violate that standard, will probably have to be encountered afterwards in the form of remorse. Whatever theory we have of the nature or origin of conscience, this is what essentially constitutes it.

The ultimate sanction, therefore, of all morality (external motives apart) being a subjective feeling in our own minds, I see nothing embarrassing, to those whose standard is utility, in the question, What is the sanction of that particular standard? We may answer, The same as of all other moral standards,—the conscientious feelings of mankind. Undoubtedly this sanction has no binding efficacy on those who do not possess the feelings it appeals to; but neither will these persons be more obedient to any other moral principle than to the utilitarian one. On them, morality of any kind has no hold but through the external sanctions. Meanwhile the feelings exist,—a fact in human nature, the reality of which, and the great power with which they are capable of acting on those in whom they have been duly cultivated, are proved by experience. No reason has ever been shown why they may not be cultivated to as great intensity in connection with the utilitarian as with any other rule of morals.

There is, I am aware, a disposition to believe that a person who sees in moral obligation a transcendental fact, an objective reality belonging to the province of "things in themselves," is likely to be more obedient to it than one who believes it to be entirely subjective, having its seat in human consciousness only. But, whatever a person's opinion may be on this point of ontology, the force he is really urged by is his own subjective feeling, and is exactly measured by its strength. No one's belief that Duty is an objective reality is stronger than the belief that God is so; yet the belief in God, apart from the expectation of actual reward and punishment, only operates on conduct through, and in proportion to, the subjective religious feeling. The sanction, so far as it is disinterested, is always in the mind itself: and the notion, therefore, of the transcendental moralists must be, that this sanction will not exist *in* the mind, unless it is believed to have its root out of the mind; and that if a person is able to say to himself, "This which is restraining me, and which is called my conscience, is only a feeling in my own mind," he may possibly draw the conclusion, that, when the feeling ceases, the obligation ceases; and that, if he find the feeling inconvenient, he may disregard it, and endeavor to get rid of it. But is this danger confined to the utilitarian morality? Does the belief that moral obligation has its seat outside the mind make the feeling of it too strong to be got rid of? The fact is so far otherwise, that all moralists admit and lament the ease with which, in the generality of minds, conscience can be silenced or stifled. The question, Need I obey my conscience? is quite as often put to themselves by persons who never heard of the principle of utility as by its adherents. Those whose conscientious feelings are so weak as to allow of their asking this question, if they answer it affirmatively, will not do so because they believe in the transcendental theory, but because of the external sanctions.

It is not necessary, for the present purpose, to decide whether the feeling of duty is innate or implanted. Assuming it to be innate, it is an open question to what objects it naturally attaches itself; for the philosophic supporters of that theory are now agreed that the intuitive perception is of principles of morality, and not of the details. If there be any thing innate in the matter, I see no reason why the feeling which is innate should not be that of regard to the pleasures and pains of others. If there is any principle of morals which is intuitively obligatory, I should say it must be that. If so, the intuitive ethics would coincide with the utilitarian, and there would be no further quarrel between them. Even as it is, the intuitive moralists, though they believe that there are other intuitive moral obligations, do already believe this to be one; for they unanimously hold that a large *portion* of morality turns upon the consideration due to the interests of our fellow-creatures. Therefore, if the belief in the transcendental origin of moral obligation gives any additional efficacy to the internal sanction, it appears to me that the utilitarian principle has already the benefit of it.

On the other hand, if, as is my own belief, the moral feelings are not innate, but acquired, they are not for that reason the less natural. It is natural to man to speak, to reason, to build cities, to cultivate the ground, though these are acquired faculties. The moral feelings are not indeed a part of our nature, in the sense of being in any perceptible degree present in all of us; but this, unhappily, is a fact admitted by those who believe the most strenuously in their transcendental origin. Like the other acquired capacities above referred to, the moral faculty, if not a part of our nature, is a natural outgrowth from it; capable like them, in a certain small degree, of springing up spontaneously, and susceptible of being brought by cultivation to a high degree of development. Unhappily, it is also susceptible, by a sufficient use of the external sanctions and of the force of early impressions, of being cultivated in almost any direction; so that there is hardly any thing so absurd or so mischievous that it may not, by means of these influences, be made to act on the human mind with all the authority of conscience. To doubt that the same potency might be given by the same means to the principle of utility, even if it had no foundation in human nature, would be flying in the face of all experience.

But moral associations which are wholly of artificial creation, when intellectual culture goes on, yield by degrees to the dissolving force of analysis: and if the feeling of duty, when associated with utility, would appear equally arbitrary;

if there were no leading department of our nature, no powerful class of sentiments, with which that association would harmonize, which would make us feel it congenial, and incline us not only to foster it in others (for which we have abundant interested motives), but also to cherish it in ourselves; if there were not, in short, a natural basis of sentiment for utilitarian morality,—it might well happen that this association also, even after it had been implanted by education, might be analyzed away.

But there *is* this basis of powerful natural sentiment; and this it is, which, when once the general happiness is recognized as the ethical standard, will constitute the strength of the utilitarian morality. This firm foundation is that of the social feelings of mankind; the desire to be in unity with our fellow-creatures, which is already a powerful principle in human nature, and happily one of those which tend to become stronger, even without express inculcation from the influences of advancing civilization. The social state is at once so natural, so necessary, and so habitual to man, that except in some unusual circumstances, or by an effort of voluntary abstraction, he never conceives himself otherwise than as a member of a body; and this association is riveted more and more as mankind are further removed from the state of savage independence. Any condition, therefore, which is essential to a state of society, becomes more and more an inseparable part of every person's conception of the state of things which he is born into, and which is the destiny of a human being. Now, society between human beings, except in the relation of master and slave, is manifestly impossible on any other footing than that the interests of all are to be consulted. Society between equals can only exist on the understanding that the interests of all are to be regarded equally. And since, in all states of civilization, every person except an absolute monarch has equals, every one is obliged to live on these terms with somebody; and, in every age, some advance is made towards a state in which it will be impossible to live permanently on other terms with anybody. In this way, people grow up unable to conceive as possible to them a state of total disregard of other people's interests. They are under a necessity of conceiving themselves as at least abstaining from all the grosser injuries, and (if only for their own protection) living in a state of constant protest against them. They are also

familiar with the fact of co-operating with others, and propos-
ing to themselves a collective, not an individual, interest as
the aim (at least for the time being) of their actions. So long
as they are co-operating, their ends are identified with those
of others: there is at least a temporary feeling that the interests
of others are their own interests. Not only does all strengthening of social ties, and all healthy growth of society, give to
each individual a stronger personal interest in practically consulting the welfare of others: it also leads him to identify his
feelings more and more with their good, or at least with an
ever greater degree of practical consideration for it. He comes,
as though instinctively, to be conscious of himself as a being
who *of course* pays regard to others. The good of others
becomes to him a thing naturally and necessarily to be attended to, like any of the physical conditions of our existence.
Now, whatever amount of this feeling a person has, he is
urged by the strongest motives, both of interest and of sympathy, to demonstrate it, and, to the utmost of his power, encourage it in others; and, even if he has none of it himself, he
is as greatly interested as any one else that others should
have it. Consequently, the smallest germs of the feeling are
laid hold of and nourished by the contagion of sympathy
and the influences of education, and a complete web of cor-
roborative association is woven round it by the powerful
agency of the external sanctions. This mode of conceiving
ourselves and human life, as civilization goes on, is felt to
be more and more natural. Every step in political improvement renders it more so, by removing the sources of opposition
of interest, and levelling those inequalities of legal privilege
between individuals or classes, owing to which there are large
portions of mankind whose happiness it is still practicable to
disregard. In an improving state of the human mind, the influences are constantly on the increase which tend to generate
in each individual a feeling of unity with all the rest, which,
if perfect, would make him never think of or desire any beneficial condition for himself, in the benefits of which they are
not included. If we now suppose this feeling of unity to be
taught as a religion, and the whole force of education, of
institutions, and of opinion, directed, as it once was in the case
of religion, to make every person grow up from infancy surrounded on all sides both by the profession and the practice of
it, I think that no one who can realize this conception will

feel any misgiving about the sufficiency of the ultimate sanction for the Happiness morality. To any ethical student who finds the realization difficult, I recommend, as a means of facilitating it, the second of M. Comte's two principal works, the "Traité de Politique Positive." I entertain the strongest objections to the system of politics and morals set forth in that treatise: but I think it has superabundantly shown the possibility of giving to the service of humanity, even without the aid of belief in a Providence, both the psychological power and the social efficacy of a religion; making it take hold of human life, and color all thought, feeling, and action, in a manner of which the greatest ascendency ever exercised by any religion may be but a type and foretaste, and of which the danger is, not that it should be insufficient, but that it should be so excessive as to interfere unduly with human freedom and individuality.

Neither is it necessary to the feeling which constitutes the binding force of the utilitarian morality on those who recognize it, to wait for those social influences which would make its obligation felt by mankind at large. In the comparatively early state of human advancement in which we now live, a person cannot indeed feel that entireness of sympathy with all others which would make any real discordance in the general direction of their conduct in life impossible; but already a person in whom the social feeling is at all developed cannot bring himself to think of the rest of his fellow-creatures as struggling rivals with him for the means of happiness, whom he must desire to see defeated in their object in order that he may succeed in his. The deeply rooted conception which every individual even now has of himself as a social being tends to make him feel it one of his natural wants, that there should be harmony between his feelings and aims and those of his fellow-creatures. If differences of opinion and of mental culture make it impossible for him to share many of their actual feelings,—perhaps make him denounce and defy those feelings,—he still needs to be conscious that his real aim and theirs do not conflict; that he is not opposing himself to what they really wish for,—namely, their own good,—but is, on the contrary, promoting it. This feeling in most individuals is much inferior in strength to their selfish feelings, and is often wanting altogether. But, to those who have it, it possesses all the characters of a natural feeling. It does not present itself to their minds as a superstition of education, or a law despotically imposed by the power of society, but as an attribute which it would not be well for them to be without. This conviction is the ultimate sanction of the greatest-happiness morality. This it is which makes any mind of well-developed feelings work with, and not against, the outward motives to care for others, afforded by what I have called the external sanctions; and when those sanctions are wanting, or act in an opposite direction, constitutes in itself a powerful internal binding force, in proportion to the sensitiveness and thoughtfulness of the character: since few but those whose mind is a moral blank could bear to lay out their course of life on the plan of paying no regard to others, except so far as their own private interest compels.

CHAPTER IV

IT HAS ALREADY been remarked, that questions of ultimate ends do not admit of proof, in the ordinary acceptation of the term. To be incapable of proof by reasoning is common to all first principles; to the first premises of our knowledge, as well as to those of our conduct. But the former, being matters of fact, may be the subject of a direct appeal to the faculties which judge of fact; namely, our senses, and our internal consciousness. Can an appeal be made to the same faculties on questions of practical ends? Or by what other faculty is cognizance taken of them?

Questions about ends are, in other words, questions of what things are desirable. The utilitarian doctrine is, that happiness is desirable, and the only thing desirable, as an end; all other things being only desirable as means to that end. What ought to be required of this doctrine—what conditions is it requisite that the doctrine should fulfil—to make good its claim to be believed?

The only proof capable of being given that an object is visible, is that people actually see it; the only proof that a sound is audible, is that people hear it: and so of the other sources of our experience. In like manner, I apprehend, the sole evidence it is possible to produce that any thing is desirable, is that people do actually desire it. If the end which the utilitarian doctrine proposes to itself were not, in theory and in practice, acknowledged to be an end, nothing could ever convince any person that it was so. No reason can be given why the general happiness is desirable, except that each person, so far as he believes it to be attainable, desires his own happiness. This, however, being a fact, we have

273

not only all the proof which the case admits of, but all which it is possible to require, that happiness is a good; that each person's happiness is a good to that person; and the general happiness, therefore, a good to the aggregate of all persons. Happiness has made out its title as *one* of the ends of conduct, and consequently one of the criteria of morality.

But it had not, by this alone, proved itself to be the sole criterion. To do that, it would seem, by the same rule, necessary to show, not only that people desire happiness, but that they never desire any thing else. Now, it is palpable that they do desire things, which, in common language, are decidedly distinguished from happiness. They desire, for example, virtue and the absence of vice, no less really than pleasure and the absence of pain. The desire of virtue is not as universal, but it is as authentic a fact, as the desire of happiness; and hence the opponents of the utilitarian standard deem that they have a right to infer that there are other ends of human action besides happiness, and that happiness is not the standard of approbation and disapprobation.

But does the utilitarian doctrine deny that people desire virtue, or maintain that virtue is not a thing to be desired? The very reverse. It maintains not only that virtue is to be desired, but that it is to be desired disinterestedly, for itself. Whatever may be the opinion of utilitarian moralists as to the original conditions by which virtue is made virtue; however they may believe (as they do) that actions and dispositions are only virtuous because they promote another end than virtue,—yet this being granted, and it having been decided, from considerations of this description, what *is* virtuous, they not only place virtue at the very head of the things which are good as means to the ultimate end, but they also recognize, as a psychological fact, the possibility of its being, to the individual, a good in itself, without looking to any end beyond it; and hold that the mind is not in a right state, not in a state conformable to utility, not in the state most conducive to the general happiness, unless it does love virtue in this manner,—as a thing desirable in itself, even although, in the individual instance, it should not produce those other desirable consequences which it tends to produce, and on account of which it is held to be virtue. This opinion is not, in the smallest degree, a departure from the Happiness principle. The ingredients of happiness are very various, and each of them is desirable in itself, and not merely when considered as swelling an aggregate. The principle of utility does not mean that any given pleasure—as music, for instance—or any given exemption from pain—as, for example, health—are to be looked upon as means to a collective something termed happiness, and to be desired on that account. They are desired and desirable in and for themselves: besides being means, they are a part of the end. Virtue, according to the utilitarian doctrine, is not naturally and originally part of the end, but it is capable of becoming so, and, in those who love it disinterestedly, it has become so, and is desired and cherished, not as a means to happiness, but as a part of their happiness.

To illustrate this further: we may remember that virtue is not the only thing, originally a means, and which, if it were not a means to any thing else, would be and remain indifferent, but which, by association with what it is a means to, comes to be desired for itself, and that, too, with the utmost intensity. What, for example, shall we say of the love of money? There is nothing originally more desirable about money than about any heap of glittering pebbles. Its worth is solely that of the things which it will buy; the desires for other things than itself, which it is a means of gratifying. Yet the love of money is not only one of the strongest moving forces of human life, but money is, in many cases, desired in and for itself: the desire to possess it is often stronger than the desire to use it, and goes on increasing when all the desires which point to ends beyond it, to be compassed by it, are falling off. It may, then, be said truly, that money is desired, not for the sake of an end, but as part of the end. From being a means to happiness, it has come to be itself a principal ingredient of the individual's conception of happiness. The same may be said of the majority of the great objects of human life,—power, for example, or fame; except that to each of these there is a certain amount of immediate pleasure annexed, which has at least the semblance of being naturally inherent in them: a thing which cannot be said of money. Still, however, the strongest natural attraction, both of power and of fame, is the immense aid they give to the attainment of our other wishes; and it is the strong association thus generated between them and all our objects of desire which gives to the direct desire of them the intensity it often assumes, so as in some characters to surpass in strength all other desires. In these cases, the means have become a part of the end, and a more important part of it than any of the things which they are means to. What was once desired as an instrument for the attainment of happiness has come to be desired for its own sake. In being desired for its own sake, it is, however, desired as *part* of happiness. The person is made, or thinks he would be made, happy by its mere possession, and is made unhappy by failure to obtain it. The desire of it is not a different thing from the desire of happiness, any more than the love of music or the desire of health. They are included in happiness. They are some of the elements of which the desire of happiness is made up. Happiness is not an abstract idea, but a concrete whole; and these are some of its parts. And the utilitarian standard sanctions and approves their being so. Life would be a poor thing, very ill provided with sources of happiness, if there were not this provision of nature, by which things originally indifferent, but conducive to, or otherwise associated with, the satisfaction of our primitive desires, become in themselves sources of pleasure more valuable than the primitive pleasures, both in permanency, in the space of human existence that they are capable of covering, and even in intensity.

Virtue, according to the utilitarian conception, is a good of this description. There was no original desire of it, or motive to it, save its conduciveness to pleasure, and especially to protection from pain. But, through the association thus formed, it may be felt a good in itself, and desired as such with as great intensity as any other good; and with this difference between it and the love of money, of power, or of fame,—that all of these may, and often do, render the individual noxious to the other members of the society to which he belongs, whereas there is nothing which makes him so much a blessing to them as the cultivation of the disinterested love of virtue. And consequently the utilitarian standard, while it tolerates and approves those other acquired desires, up to the point beyond which they would be more injurious to the general happiness than promotive of it, enjoins and requires the cultivation of the love of virtue up to the greatest strength possible, as being above all things important to the general happiness.

It results from the preceding considerations, that there is in reality nothing desired except happiness. Whatever is desired otherwise than as a means to some end beyond itself, and ultimately to happiness, is desired as itself a part of happiness, and is not desired for itself until it has become so. Those who desire virtue for its own sake, desire it either because the consciousness of it is a pleasure, or because the consciousness of being without it is a pain, or for both reasons united: as in truth the pleasure and pain seldom exist separately, but almost always together; the same person feeling pleasure in the degree of virtue attained, and pain in not having attained more. If one of these gave him no pleasure, and the other no pain, he would not love or desire virtue, or would desire it only for the other benefits which it might produce to himself or to persons whom he cared for.

We have now, then, an answer to the question, of what sort of proof the principle of utility is susceptible. If the opinion which I have now stated is psychologically true; if human nature is so constituted as to desire nothing which is not either a part of happiness or a means of happiness,— we can have no other proof, and we require no other, that these are the only things desirable. If so, happiness is the sole end of human action, and the promotion of it the test by which to judge of all human conduct; from whence it necessarily follows that it must be the criterion of morality, since a part is included in the whole.

And, now, to decide whether this is really so; whether mankind do desire nothing for itself but that which is a pleasure to them, or of which the absence is a pain,—we have evidently arrived at a question of fact and experience, dependent, like all similar questions, upon evidence. It can only be determined by practised self-consciousness and self-observation, assisted by observation of others. I believe that these sources of evidence, impartially consulted, will declare that desiring a thing and finding it pleasant, aversion to it and thinking of it as painful, are phenomena entirely inseparable, or rather two parts of the same phenomenon,—in strictness of language, two different modes of naming the same psychological fact; that to think of an object as desirable (unless for the sake of its consequences), and to think of it as pleasant, are one and the same thing; and that to desire any thing, except in proportion as the idea of it is pleasant, is a physical and metaphysical impossibility.

So obvious does this appear to me, that I expect it will hardly be disputed: and the objection made will be, not that

desire can possibly be directed to any thing ultimately except pleasure, and exemption from pain, but that the will is a
different thing from desire; that a person of confirmed virtue,
or any other person whose purposes are fixed, carries out his
purposes without any thought of the pleasure he has in contemplating them, or expects to derive from their fulfilment;
and persists in acting on them, even though these pleasures
are much diminished by changes in his character, or decay of
his passive sensibilities, or are outweighed by the pains which
the pursuit of the purposes may bring upon him. All this
I fully admit, and have stated it elsewhere as positively and
emphatically as any one. Will, the active phenomenon, is a
different thing from desire, the state of passive sensibility,
and, though originally an offshoot from it, may in time take
root, and detach itself from the parent stock; so much so,
that in the case of an habitual purpose, instead of willing
the thing because we desire it, we often desire it only because we will it. This, however, is but an instance of that
familiar fact, the power of habit, and is nowise confined to the
case of virtuous actions. Many indifferent things, which men
originally did from a motive of some sort, they continue to
do from habit. Sometimes this is done unconsciously, the consciousness coming only after the action; at other times with
conscious volition, but volition which has become habitual,
and is put in operation by the force of habit, in opposition, perhaps, to the deliberate preference, as often happens with
those who have contracted habits of vicious or hurtful indulgence. Third and last comes the case in which the habitual
act of will in the individual instance is not in contradiction to
the general intention prevailing at other times, but in fulfilment of it; as in the case of the person of confirmed virtue,
and of all who pursue deliberately and consistently any
determinate end. The distinction between will and desire, thus
understood, is an authentic and highly important psychological
fact; but the fact consists solely in this,—that will, like all other
parts of our constitution, is amenable to habit, and that we
may will from habit what we no longer desire for itself,
or desire only because we will it. It is not the less true, that
will, in the beginning, is entirely produced by the desire; including in that term the repelling influence of pain, as well
as the attractive one of pleasure. Let us take into consideration
no longer the person who has a confirmed will to do right,

but him in whom that virtuous will is still feeble, conquerable by temptation, and not to be fully relied on: by what means can it be strengthened? How can the will to be virtuous, where it does not exist in sufficient force, be implanted or awakened? Only by making the person *desire* virtue; by making him think of it in a pleasurable light, or of its absence in a painful one. It is by associating the doing right with pleasure, or the doing wrong with pain, or by eliciting and impressing and bringing home to the person's experience the pleasure naturally involved in the one or the pain in the other, that it is possible to call forth that will to be virtuous, which, when confirmed, acts without any thought of either pleasure or pain. Will is the child of desire, and passes out of the dominion of its parent only to come under that of habit. That which is the result of habit affords no presumption of being intrinsically good; and there would be no reason for wishing that the purpose of virtue should become independent of pleasure and pain, were it not that the influence of the pleasurable and painful associations which prompt to virtue is not sufficiently to be depended on for unerring constancy of action until it has acquired the support of habit. Both in feeling and in conduct, habit is the only thing which imparts certainty; and it is because of the importance to others of being able to rely absolutely on one's feelings and conduct, and to one's self of being able to rely on one's own, that the will to do right ought to be cultivated into this habitual independence. In other words, this state of the will is a means to good, not intrinsically a good; and does not contradict the doctrine, that nothing is a good to human beings but in so far as it is either itself pleasurable, or a means of attaining pleasure or averting pain.

But, if this doctrine be true, the principle of utility is proved. Whether it is so or not, must now be left to the consideration of the thoughtful reader.

CHAPTER V

ON THE CONNECTION BETWEEN JUSTICE AND UTILITY

IN ALL AGES of speculation, one of the strongest obstacles to the reception of the doctrine, that Utility or Happiness is the criterion of right and wrong, has been drawn from the idea of Justice. The powerful sentiment and apparently clear perception which that word recalls, with a rapidity and certainty resembling an instinct, have seemed to the majority of thinkers to point to an inherent quality in things; to show that the Just must have an existence in nature as something absolute, generically distinct from every variety of the Expedient, and, in idea, opposed to it, though (as is commonly acknowledged) never, in the long-run, disjoined from it in fact.

In the case of this, as of our other moral sentiments, there is no necessary connection between the question of its origin and that of its binding force. That a feeling is bestowed on us by nature does not necessarily legitimate all its promptings. The feeling of justice might be a peculiar instinct, and might yet require, like our other instincts, to be controlled and enlightened by a higher reason. If we have intellectual instincts leading us to judge in a particular way, as well as animal instincts that prompt us to act in a particular way, there is no necessity that the former should be more infallible in their sphere than the latter in theirs: it may as well happen that wrong judgments are occasionally suggested by those, as wrong actions by these. But though it is one thing to believe that we have natural feelings of justice, and another to acknowledge them as an ultimate criterion of conduct, these two opinions are very closely connected in point of fact. Mankind are always predisposed to believe that any subjective feeling, not otherwise accounted for, is a revelation of some objective reality. Our present object is to determine whether the reality, to which the feeling of justice corresponds, is one which needs any such special revelation; whether the justice or injustice of an action is a thing intrinsically peculiar, and distinct from all its other qualities, or only a combination of certain of those qualities, presented under a peculiar aspect. For the purpose of this inquiry, it is practically important to consider, whether the feeling itself, of justice and injustice, is *sui generis* like our sensations of color and taste, or a derivative feeling, formed by a combination of others. And this it is the more essential to examine, as people are in general willing enough to allow, that, objectively, the dictates of Justice coincide with a part of the field of General Expediency; but inasmuch as the subjective mental feeling of Justice is different from that which commonly attaches to simple expediency, and, except in the extreme cases of the latter, is far more imperative in its demands, people find it difficult to see, in Justice, only a particular kind or branch of general utility, and think that its superior binding force requires a totally different origin.

To throw light upon this question, it is necessary to attempt to ascertain what is the distinguishing character of justice, or of injustice; what is the quality, or whether there is any quality, attributed in common to all modes of conduct designated as unjust (for justice, like many other moral attributes, is best defined by its opposite), and distinguishing them from such modes of conduct as are disapproved, but without having that particular epithet of disapprobation applied to them. If, in every thing which men are accustomed to characterize as just or unjust, some one common attribute, or collection of attributes, is always present, we may judge whether this particular attribute, or combination of attributes, would be capable of gathering round it a sentiment of that peculiar character and intensity by virtue of the general laws of our emotional constitution; or whether the sentiment is inexplicable, and requires to be regarded as a special provision of nature. If we find the former to be the case, we shall, in resolving this question, have resolved also the main problem; if the latter, we shall have to seek for some other mode of investigating it.

To find the common attributes of a variety of objects, it is necessary to begin by surveying the objects themselves

in the concrete. Let us therefore advert successively to the
various modes of action, and arrangements of human affairs,
which are classed, by universal or widely spread opinion, as
Just or as Unjust. The things well known to excite the sentiments associated with those names are of a very multifarious
character. I shall pass them rapidly in review, without studying any particular arrangement.

In the first place, it is mostly considered unjust to deprive
any one of his personal liberty, his property, or any other
thing which belongs to him by law. Here, therefore, is one
instance of the application of the terms Just and Unjust in
a perfectly definite sense; namely, that it is just to respect,
unjust to violate, the *legal rights* of any one. But this judgment admits of several exceptions, arising from the other
forms in which the notions of justice and injustice present
themselves. For example: the person who suffers the dep-
rivation may (as the phrase is) have *forefeited* the rights
which he is so deprived of; a case to which we shall return
presently. But also,—

Secondly, The legal rights of which he is deprived may
be rights which *ought* not to have belonged to him: in other
words, the law which confers on him these rights may be
a bad law. When it is so, or when (which is the same thing for
our purpose) it is supposed to be so, opinions will differ as to
the justice or injustice of infringing it. Some maintain that no
law, however bad, ought to be disobeyed by an individual
citizen; that his opposition to it, if shown at all, should only
be shown in endeavoring to get it altered by competent authority. This opinion (which condemns many of the most illustrious benefactors of mankind, and would often protect pernicious institutions against the only weapons, which, in the
state of things existing at the time, have any chance of succeeding against them) is defended, by those who hold it, on
grounds of expediency; principally on that of the importance,
to the common interests of mankind, of maintaining inviolate
the sentiment of submission to law. Other persons, again,
hold the directly contrary opinion, that any law, judged to
be bad, may blamelessly be disobeyed, even though it be not
judged to be unjust, but only inexpedient; while others would
confine the license of disobedience to the case of unjust laws.
But, again, some say that all laws which are inexpedient are
unjust, since every law imposes some restriction on the natural

liberty of mankind; which restriction is an injustice, unless legitimated by tending to their good. Among these diversities of opinion, it seems to be universally admitted that there may be unjust laws, and that law, consequently, is not the ultimate criterion of justice, but may give to one person a benefit, or impose on another an evil, which justice condemns. When, however, a law is thought to be unjust, it seems always to be regarded as being so in the same way in which a breach of law is unjust,—namely, by infringing somebody's right; which, as it cannot in this case be a legal right, receives a different appellation, and is called a moral right. We may say, therefore, that a second case of injustice consists in taking or withholding from any person that to which he has a *moral right*.

Thirdly, It is universally considered just, that each person should obtain that (whether good or evil) which he *deserves;* and unjust, that he should obtain a good, or be made to undergo an evil, which he does not deserve. This is, perhaps, the clearest and most emphatic form in which the idea of justice is conceived by the general mind. As it involves the notion of desert, the question arises, What constitutes desert? Speaking in a general way, a person is understood to deserve good if he does right; evil, if he does wrong: and, in a more particular sense, to deserve good from those to whom he does or has done good, and evil from those to whom he does or has done evil. The precept of returning good for evil has never been regarded as a case of the fulfilment of justice, but as one in which the claims of justice are waived, in obedience to other considerations.

Fourthly, It is confessedly unjust to *break faith* with any one; to violate an engagement, either express or implied; or disappoint expectations raised by our own conduct, at least if we have raised those expectations knowingly and voluntarily. Like the other obligations of justice already spoken of, this one is not regarded as absolute, but as capable of being overruled by a stronger obligation of justice on the other side, or by such conduct on the part of the person concerned as is deemed to absolve us from our obligation to him, and to constitute a *forfeiture* of the benefit which he has been led to expect.

Fifthly, It is, by universal admission, inconsistent with justice to be *partial;* to show favor or preference to one person over another in matters to which favor and preference do not properly apply. Impartiality, however, does not seem to be regarded as a duty in itself, but rather as instrumental to some other duty; for it is admitted that favor and preference are not always censurable, and indeed the cases in which they are condemned are rather the exception than the rule. A person would be more likely to be blamed than applauded for giving his family or friends no superiority in good offices over strangers, when he could do so without violating any other duty; and no one thinks it unjust to seek one person in preference to another as a friend, connection, or companion. Impartiality, where rights are concerned, is of course obligatory; but this is involved in the more general obligation of giving to every one his right. A tribunal, for example, must be impartial, because it is bound to award, without regard to any other consideration, a disputed object to the one of two parties who has the right to it. There are other cases in which impartiality means, being solely influenced by desert; as with those who, in the capacity of judges, preceptors, or parents, administer reward and punishment as such. There are cases, again, in which it means being solely influenced by consideration for the public interest; as in making a selection among candidates for a government employment. Impartiality, in short, as an obligation of justice, may be said to mean being exclusively influenced by the considerations which it is supposed ought to influence the particular case in hand, and resisting the solicitation of any motives which prompt to conduct different from what those considerations would dictate.

Nearly allied to the idea of impartiality is that of *equality;* which often enters as a component part both into the conception of justice and into the practice of it, and, in the eyes of many persons, constitutes its essence. But, in this still more than in any other case, the notion of justice varies in different persons, and always conforms in its variations to their notion of utility. Each person maintains that equality is the dictate of justice, except where he thinks that expediency requires inequality. The justice of giving equal protection to the rights of all is maintained by those who support the most outrageous inequality in the rights themselves. Even in slave countries, it is theoretically admitted that the rights of the slave, such as they are, ought to be as sacred as those of the master, and that a tribunal which fails to enforce them with equal strictness is wanting in justice; while, at the same time, institutions which leave to the slave scarcely any rights to enforce are not deemed unjust, because they are not deemed inexpedient. Those who think that utility requires distinctions of rank do not consider it unjust that riches and social privileges should be unequally dispensed; but those who think this inequality inexpedient think it unjust also. Whoever thinks that government is necessary sees no injustice in as much inequality as is constituted by giving to the magistrate powers not granted to other people. Even among those who hold levelling doctrines, there are as many questions of justice as there are differences of opinion about expediency. Some Communists consider it unjust that the produce of the labor of the community should be shared on any other principle than that of exact equality; others think it just that those should receive most whose wants are greatest; while others hold that those who work harder, or who produce more, or whose services are more valuable to the community, may justly claim a larger quota in the division of the produce. And the sense of natural justice may be plausibly appealed to in behalf of every one of these opinions.

Among so many diverse applications of the term Justice, which yet is not regarded as ambiguous, it is a matter of some difficulty to seize the mental link which holds them together, and on which the moral sentiment adhering to the term essentially depends. Perhaps, in this embarrassment, some help may be derived from the history of the word, as indicated by its etymology.

In most, if not in all languages, the etymology of the word which corresponds to Just points distinctly to an origin connected with the ordinances of law. *Justum* is a form of *jussum,*—that which has been ordered. Δίκαιον comes directly from δίκη, a suit at law. *Recht,* from which came *right* and *righteous,* is synonymous with law. The courts of justice, the administration of justice, are the courts and the administration of law. *La justice,* in French, is the established term for judicature. I am not committing the fallacy imputed with some show of truth to Horne Tooke, of assuming that a word must still continue to mean what it originally meant. Etymology is slight evidence of what the idea now signified is, but the very best evidence of how it sprang up. There can, I think, be no doubt that the *idée mère*, the primitive element, in the formation of the notion of justice, was conformity to law. It constituted the entire idea among the Hebrews up to the birth of Christianity; as might be expected in the case of a people whose laws attempted to embrace all subjects on which precepts were required, and who believed those laws to be a direct emanation from the Supreme Being. But other nations, and in particular the Greeks and Romans, who knew that their laws had been made originally, and still continued to be made, by men, were not afraid to admit that those men might make bad laws; might do, by law, the same things, and from the same motives, which, if done by individuals without the sanction of law, would be called unjust. And hence the sentiment of injustice came to be attached, not to all violations of law, but only to violations of such laws as *ought* to exist, including such as ought to exist, but do not; and to laws themselves, if supposed to be contrary to what ought to be law. In this manner, the idea of law and of its injunctions was still predominant in the notion of justice, even when the laws actually in force ceased to be accepted as the standard of it.

It is true that mankind consider the idea of justice and its obligations as applicable to many things which neither are, nor is it desired that they should be, regulated by law. Nobody desires that laws should interfere with the whole detail of private life; yet every one allows, that, in all daily conduct, a person may and does show himself to be either just or unjust. But, even here, the idea of the breach of what ought to be law still lingers in a modified shape. It would always give us pleasure, and chime in with our feelings of fitness, that acts which we deem unjust should be punished, though we do not always think it expedient that this should be done by the tribunals. We forego that gratification on account of incidental inconveniences. We should be glad to see just conduct enforced, and injustice repressed, even in the minutest details, if we were not with reason afraid of trusting the magistrate with so unlimited an amount of power over individuals. When we think that a person is bound in justice to do a thing, it is an ordinary form of language to say, that he ought to be compelled to do it. We should be gratified to see the obligation enforced by anybody who had the power. If we see that its enforcement by law would be inexpedient, we lament the impossibility, we consider the impunity given to injustice as an evil, and strive to make amends for it by bringing a strong expression of our own and the public disapprobation to bear upon the offender. Thus the idea of legal constraint is still the generating idea of the notion of justice, though undergoing several transformations before that notion, as it exists in an advanced state of society, becomes complete.

The above is, I think, a true account, as far as it goes, of the origin and progressive growth of the idea of justice. But we must observe, that it contains, as yet, nothing to distinguish that obligation from moral obligation in general. For the truth is, that the idea of penal sanction, which is the essence of law, enters not only into the conception of injustice, but into that of any kind of wrong. We do not call any thing wrong, unless we mean to imply that a person ought to be punished in some way or other for doing it; if not by law, by the opinion of his fellow-creatures; if not by opinion, by the reproaches of his own conscience. This seems the real turning-point of the distinction between morality and simple expediency. It is a part of the notion of Duty in every one of its forms, that a person may rightfully be compelled to fulfil it. Duty is a thing which may be *exacted* from a person, as one exacts a debt. Unless we think that it may be exacted from him, we do not call it his duty. Reasons of prudence, or the interest of other people, may militate against actually exacting it; but the person himself, it is clearly understood, would not be entitled to complain. There are other things, on the contrary, which we wish that people should do, which we like or admire them for doing, perhaps dislike or despise them for not doing, but yet admit that they are not bound to do: it is not a case of moral obligation: we do not blame them; that is, we do not think that they are proper objects of punishment. How we come by these ideas of deserving and not deserving punishment, will appear, perhaps, in the sequel: but I think there is no doubt that this distinction lies at the bottom of the notions of right and wrong; that we call any conduct wrong, or employ instead some other term of dislike or disparagement, according as we think that the person ought, or ought not, to be punished for it; and we say it would be right to do so and so, or merely that it would be desirable or laudable, according as we would wish to see the person whom it concerns compelled, or only persuaded and exhorted, to act in that manner.[2]

This, therefore, being the characteristic difference which marks off, not justice, but morality in general, from the remaining provinces of Expediency and Worthiness, the character is still to be sought which distinguishes justice from other branches of morality. Now, it is known that ethical writers divide moral duties into two classes, denoted by the ill-chosen expressions, duties of perfect and of imperfect obligation: the latter being those in which, though the act is obligatory, the particular occasions of performing it are left to our choice; as in the case of charity or beneficence, which we are indeed bound to practise, but not towards any definite person, nor at any prescribed time. In the more precise language of philosophic jurists, duties of perfect obligation are those duties in virtue of which a correlative *right* resides in some person or persons: duties of imperfect obligation are those moral obligations which do not give birth to any right. I think it will be found that this distinction exactly coincides with that which exists between justice and the other obligations of morality. In our survey of the various popular acceptations of justice, the term appeared generally to involve the idea of a personal right,—a claim on the part of one or more individuals, like that which the law gives when it confers a proprietary or other legal right. Whether the injustice consists in depriving a person of a possession, or in breaking faith with him, or in treating him worse than he deserves, or worse than other people who have no greater claims, in each case the supposition implies two things,—a wrong done, and some assignable person who is wronged. Injustice may also be done by treating a person better than others; but the wrong in this case is to his competitors, who are also assignable persons. It seems to me that this feature in the case—a right in some person, correlative to the moral obligation—constitutes the specific difference between justice, and generosity or beneficence. Justice implies something which it is not only right to do, and wrong not to do, but which some individual person can claim from us as his moral right. No one has a moral right to our generosity or beneficence, because we are not

[2]See this point enforced and illustrated by Professor Bain, in an admirable chapter (entitled "The Ethical Emotions, or the Moral Sense") of the second of the two treatises composing his elaborate and profound work on the Mind.

morally bound to practise those virtues towards any given individual. And it will be found, with respect to this as to every correct definition, that the instances which seem to conflict with it are those which most confirm it; for if a moralist attempts, as some have done, to make out that mankind generally, though not any given individual, have a right to all the good we can do them, he at once, by that thesis, includes generosity and beneficence within the category of justice. He is obliged to say that our utmost exertions are *due* to our fellow-creatures, thus assimilating them to a debt; or that nothing less can be a sufficient *return* for what society does for us, thus classing the case as one of gratitude; both of which are acknowledged cases of justice. Wherever there is a right, the case is one of justice, and not of the virtue of beneficence; and whoever does not place the distinction between justice and morality in general where we have now placed it will be found to make no distinction between them at all, but to merge all morality in justice.

Having thus endeavored to determine the distinctive elements which enter into the composition of the idea of justice, we are ready to enter on the inquiry, whether the feeling which accompanies the idea is attached to it by a special dispensation of nature, or whether it could have grown up by any known laws out of the idea itself; and, in particular, whether it can have originated in considerations of general expediency.

I conceive that the sentiment itself does not arise from any thing which would commonly or correctly be termed an idea of expediency; but that, though the sentiment does not, whatever is moral in it does.

We have seen that the two essential ingredients in the sentiment of justice are the desire to punish a person who has done harm, and the knowledge or belief that there is some definite individual or individuals to whom harm has been done.

Now, it appears to me that the desire to punish a person who has done harm to some individual is a spontaneous outgrowth from two sentiments, both in the highest degree natural, and which either are or resemble instincts,—the impulse of self-defence, and the feeling of sympathy.

It is natural to resent, and to repel or retaliate, any harm done or attempted against ourselves, or against those with whom we sympathize. The origin of this sentiment it is not necessary here to discuss. Whether it be an instinct, or a result of intelligence, it is, we know, common to all animal nature; for every animal tries to hurt those who have hurt, or who it thinks are about to hurt, itself or its young. Human beings, on this point, only differ from other animals in two particulars: first, in being capable of sympathizing, not solely with their offspring, or, like some of the more noble animals, with some superior animal who is kind to them, but with all human, and even with all sentient beings; secondly, in having a more developed intelligence, which gives a wider range to the whole of their sentiments, whether self-regarding or sympathetic. By virtue of his superior intelligence, even apart from his superior range of sympathy, a human being is capable of apprehending a community of interest between himself and the human society of which he forms a part, such that any conduct which threatens the security of the society generally is threatening to his own, and calls forth his instinct (if instinct it be) of self-defence. The same superiority of intelligence, joined to the power of sympathizing with human beings generally, enables him to attach himself to the collective idea of his tribe, his country, or mankind, in such a manner that any act hurtful to them raises his instinct of sympathy, and urges him to resistance.

The sentiment of justice, in that one of its elements which consists of the desire to punish, is thus, I conceive, the natural feeling of retaliation, or vengeance, rendered by intellect and sympathy applicable to those injuries—that is, to those hurts —which wound us through, or in common with, society at large. This sentiment in itself has nothing moral in it: what is moral is, the exclusive subordination of it to the social sympathies, so as to wait on and obey their call. For the natural feeling would make us resent indiscriminately whatever any one does that is disagreeable to us; but, when moralized by the social feeling, it only acts in the directions conformable to the general good: just persons resenting a hurt to society, though not otherwise a hurt to themselves, and not resenting a hurt to themselves, however painful, unless it be of the kind which society has a common interest with them in the repression of.

It is no objection against this doctrine to say, that, when

we feel our sentiment of justice outraged, we are not thinking of society at large, or of any collective interest, but only of the individual case. It is common enough, certainly, though the reverse of commendable, to feel resentment merely because we have suffered pain; but a person whose resentment is really a moral feeling,—that is, who considers whether an act is blamable before he allows himself to resent it,—such a person, though he may not say expressly to himself that he is standing up for the interest of society, certainly does feel that he is asserting a rule which is for the benefit of others as well as for his own. If he is not feeling this; if he is regarding the act solely as it affects him individually,—he is not consciously just; he is not concerning himself about the justice of his actions. This is admitted even by anti-utilitarian moralists. When Kant (as before remarked) propounds as the fundamental principle of morals, "So act that thy rule of conduct might be adopted as a law by all rational beings," he virtually acknowledges that the interest of mankind collectively, or at least of mankind indiscriminately, must be in the mind of the agent when conscientiously deciding on the morality of the act. Otherwise he uses words without a meaning; for that a rule even of utter selfishness could not *possibly* be adopted by all rational beings—that there is any insuperable obstacle in the nature of things to its adoption—cannot be even plausibly maintained. To give any meaning to Kant's principle, the sense put upon it must be, that we ought to shape our conduct by a rule which all rational beings might adopt *with benefit to their collective interest.*

To recapitulate: the idea of justice supposes two things,—a rule of conduct, and a sentiment which sanctions the rule. The first must be supposed common to all mankind, and intended for their good: the other (the sentiment) is a desire that punishment may be suffered by those who infringe the rule. There is involved, in addition, the conception of some definite person who suffers by the infringement; whose rights (to use the expression appropriated to the case) are violated by it. And the sentiment of justice appears to me to be, the animal desire to repel or retaliate a hurt or damage to one's self, or to those with whom one sympathizes, widened so as to include all persons, by the human capacity of enlarged sympathy, and the human conception of intelligent self-interest. From the latter elements, the feeling derives its morality; from the former, its peculiar impressiveness and energy of self-assertion.

I have, throughout, treated the idea of a *right* residing in the injured person, and violated by the injury, not as a separate element in the composition of the idea and sentiment, but as one of the forms in which the other two elements clothe themselves. These elements are, a hurt to some assignable person or persons on the one hand, and a demand for punishment on the other. An examination of our own minds, I think, will show that these two things include all that we mean when we speak of violation of a right. When we call any thing a person's right, we mean that he has a valid claim on society to protect him in the possession of it, either by the force of law, or by that of education and opinion. If he has what we consider a sufficient claim, on whatever account, to have something guaranteed to him by society, we say that he has a right to it. If we desire to prove that any thing does not belong to him by right, we think this done as soon as it is admitted that society ought not to take measures for securing it to him, but should leave him to chance, or to his own exertions. Thus a person is said to have a right to what he can earn in fair professional competition, because society ought not to allow any other person to hinder him from endeavoring to earn in that manner as much as he can. But he has not a right to three hundred a year, though he may happen to be earning it, because society is not called on to provide that he shall earn that sum. On the contrary, if he owns ten thousand pounds three-percent stock, he *has* a right to three hundred a year, because society has come under an obligation to provide him with an income of that amount.

To have a right, then, is, I conceive, to have something which society ought to defend me in the possession of. If the objector goes on to ask why it ought, I can give him no other reason than general utility. If that expression does not seem to convey a sufficient feeling of the strength of the obligation, nor to account for the peculiar energy of the feeling, it is because there goes to the composition of the sentiment, not a rational only, but also an animal element,—the thirst for retaliation; and this thirst derives its intensity, as well as its moral justification, from the extraordinarily important and impressive kind of utility which is concerned. The interest in-

volved is that of security; to every one's feelings, the most
vital of all interests. All other earthly benefits are needed by
one person, not needed by another; and many of them can,
if necessary, be cheerfully foregone, or replaced by something
else. But security no human being can possibly do without:
on it we depend for all our immunity from evil, and for the
whole value of all and every good, beyond the passing
moment; since nothing but the gratification of the instant
could be of any worth to us if we could be deprived of every
thing the next instant by whoever was momentarily stronger
than ourselves. Now, this most indispensable of all necessaries,
after physical nutriment, cannot be had, unless the machinery
for providing it is kept unintermittedly in active play. Our
notion, therefore, of the claim we have on our fellow-creatures
to join in making safe for us the very groundwork of our
existence, gathers feelings around it so much more intense
than those concerned in any of the more common cases of
utility, that the difference in degree (as is often the case in
psychology) becomes a real difference in kind. The claim
assumes that character of absoluteness, that apparent infinity, and incommensurability with all other considerations,
which constitute the distinction between the feeling of right
and wrong and that of ordinary expediency and inexpediency.
The feelings concerned are so powerful, and we count so
positively on finding a responsive feeling in others (all being
alike interested), that *ought* and *should* grow into *must*, and
recognized indispensability becomes a moral necessity, analogous to physical, and often not inferior to it in binding force.

If the preceding analysis, or something resembling it, be
not the correct account of the notion of justice; if justice be
totally independent of utility, and be a standard *per se*, which
the mind can recognize by simple introspection of itself,—
it is hard to understand why that internal oracle is so ambiguous, and why so many things appear either just or unjust,
according to the light in which they are regarded.

We are continually informed that Utility is an uncertain
standard, which every different person interprets differently;
and that there is no safety but in the immutable, ineffaceable,
and unmistakable dictates of Justice, which carry their evidence in themselves, and are independent of the fluctuations
of opinion. One would suppose from this, that, on questions of

justice, there could be no controversy; that, if we take that for our rule, its application to any given case could leave us in as little doubt as a mathematical demonstration. So far is this from being the fact, that there is as much difference of opinion and as much discussion about what is just as about what is useful to society. Not only have different nations and individuals different notions of justice, but, in the mind of one and the same individual, justice is not some one rule, principle, or maxim, but many, which do not always coincide in their dictates, and, in choosing between which, he is guided either by some extraneous standard, or by his own personal predilections.

For instance: there are some who say that it is unjust to punish any one for the sake of example to others; that punishment is just, only when intended for the good of the sufferer himself. Others maintain the extreme reverse; contending that to punish persons who have attained years of discretion, for their own benefit, is despotism and injustice; since, if the matter at issue is solely their own good, no one has a right to control their own judgment of it; but that they may justly be punished to prevent evil to others, this being the exercise of the legitimate right of self-defence. Mr. Owen, again, affirms that it is unjust to punish at all; for the criminal did not make his own character: his education, and the circumstances which surrounded him, have made him a criminal; and for these he is not responsible. All these opinions are extremely plausible; and so long as the question is argued as one of justice simply, without going down to the principles which lie under justice, and are the source of its authority, I am unable to see how any of these reasoners can be refuted. For, in truth, every one of the three builds upon rules of justice confessedly true. The first appeals to the acknowledged injustice of singling out an individual, and making him a sacrifice, without his consent, for other people's benefit. The second relies on the acknowledged justice of self-defence, and the admitted injustice of forcing one person to conform to another's notions of what constitutes his good. The Owenite invokes the admitted principle, that it is unjust to punish any one for what he cannot help. Each is triumphant so long as he is not compelled to take into consideration any other maxims of justice than the one he has selected; but, as soon as their several maxims are brought face to face, each disputant seems to have exactly as much to say for himself as the others. No one of them can carry out his own notion of justice without trampling upon another equally binding. These are difficulties; they have always been felt to be such; and many devices have been invented to turn rather than to overcome them. As a refuge from the last of the three, men imagined what they called the "freedom of the will;" fancying that they could not justify punishing a man whose will is in a thoroughly hateful state, unless it be supposed to have come into that state through no influence of anterior circumstances. To escape from the other difficulties, a favorite contrivance has been the fiction of a contract, whereby at some unknown period all the members of society engaged to obey the laws, and consented to be punished for any disobedience to them; thereby giving to their legislators the right, which it is assumed they would not otherwise have had, of punishing them, either for their own good or for that of society. This happy thought was considered to get rid of the whole difficulty, and to legitimate the infliction of punishment, in virtue of another received maxim of justice, *Volenti non fit injuria*, "That is not unjust which is done with the consent of the person who is supposed to be hurt by it." I need hardly remark, that, even if the consent were not a mere fiction, this maxim is not superior in authority to the others which it is brought in to supersede. It is, on the contrary, an instructive specimen of the loose and irregular manner in which supposed principles of justice grow up. This particular one evidently came into use as a help to the coarse exigencies of courts of law, which are sometimes obliged to be content with very uncertain presumptions, on account of the greater evils which would often arise from any attempt on their part to cut finer. But even courts of law are not able to adhere consistently to the maxim; for they allow voluntary engagements to be set aside on the ground of fraud, and sometimes on that of mere mistake or misinformation.

Again: when the legitimacy of inflicting punishment is admitted, how many conflicting conceptions of justice come to light in discussing the proper apportionment of punishments to offences! No rule on the subject recommends itself so strongly to the primitive and spontaneous sentiment of justice, as the *lex talionis*, "An eye for an eye, and a tooth for a tooth." Though this principle of the Jewish and of the Mahometan law has been generally abandoned in Europe as a practical maxim, there is, I suspect, in most minds, a secret hankering after it; and, when retribution accidentally falls on an offender in that precise shape, the general feeling of satisfaction evinced bears witness how natural is the sentiment to which this repayment in kind is acceptable. With many, the test of justice in penal infliction is that the punishment should be proportioned to the offence,—meaning that it should be exactly measured by the moral guilt of the culprit (whatever be their standard for measuring moral guilt); the consideration, what amount of punishment is necessary to deter from the offence, having nothing to do with the question of justice, in their estimation: while there are others to whom that consideration is all in all; who maintain that it is not just, at least for man, to inflict on a fellow-creature, whatever may be his offences, any amount of suffering beyond the least that will suffice to prevent him from repeating, and others from imitating, his misconduct.

To take another example from a subject already once referred to. In a co-operative industrial association, is it just or not that talent or skill should give a title to superior remuneration? On the negative side of the question it is argued, that whoever does the best he can deserves equally well, and ought not in justice to be put in a position of inferiority for no fault of his own; that superior abilities have already advantages more than enough, in the admiration they excite, the personal influence they command, and the internal sources of satisfaction attending them, without adding to these a superior share of the world's goods; and that society is bound in justice rather to make compensation to the less favored, for this unmerited inequality of advantages, than to aggravate it. On the contrary side it is contended, that society receives more from the more efficient laborer; that, his services being more useful, society owes him a larger return for them; that a greater share of the joint result is actually his work, and not to allow his claim to it is a kind of robbery; that, if he is only to receive as much as others, he can only be justly required to produce as much, and to give a smaller amount of time and exertion, proportioned to his superior efficiency. Who shall decide between these appeals to conflicting principles of justice? Justice has in this case two sides to it, which it is impossible to bring into harmony; and the two disputants have chosen opposite sides: the one looks to what it is just that the individual should receive; the other, to what it is just that the community should give. Each, from his own point of view, is unanswerable; and any choice between them, on grounds of justice, must be perfectly arbitrary. Social utility alone can decide the preference.

How many, again, and how irreconcilable, are the standards of justice to which reference is made in discussing the repartition of taxation! One opinion is, that payment to the State should be in numerical proportion to pecuniary means. Others think that justice dictates what they term "graduated taxation,"—taking a higher percentage from those who have more to spare. In point of natural justice, a strong case might be made for disregarding means altogether, and taking the same absolute sum (whenever it could be got) from every one; as the subscribers to a mess, or to a club, all pay the same sum for the same privileges, whether they can all equally afford it or not. Since the protection (it might be said) of law and government is afforded to and is equally required by all, there is no injustice in making all buy it at the same price. It is reckoned justice, not injustice, that a dealer should charge to all customers the same price for the same article; not a price varying according to their means of payment. This doctrine, as applied to taxation, finds no advocates, because it conflicts so strongly with man's feelings of humanity and of social expediency; but the principle of justice which it invokes is as true and as binding as those which can be appealed to against it. Accordingly, it exerts a tacit influence on the line of defence employed for other modes of assessing taxation. People feel obliged to argue that the State does more for the rich than for the poor, as a justification for its taking more from them: though this is in reality not true; for the rich would be far better able to protect themselves, in the absence of law or government, than the poor, and indeed would probably be successful in converting the poor into their slaves. Others, again, so far defer to the same conception of justice as to maintain that all should pay an equal capitation-tax for the protection of their persons (these being of equal value to all), and an unequal tax for the protection of their property, which is unequal. To this others reply, that the all of one man is as valuable to him as the all of another. From these confusions, there is no other mode of extrication than the utilitarian.

Is, then, the difference between the Just and the Expedient a merely imaginary distinction? Have mankind been under a delusion in thinking that justice is a more sacred thing than policy, and that the latter ought only to be listened to after the former has been satisfied? By no means. The exposition we have given of the nature and origin of the sentiment recognizes a real distinction; and no one of those who profess the most sublime contempt for the consequences of actions as an element in their morality attaches more importance to the distinction than I do. While I dispute the pretensions of any theory which sets up an imaginary standard of justice not grounded on utility, I account the justice which is grounded on utility to be the chief part, and incomparably the most sacred and binding part, of all morality. Justice is a name for certain classes of moral rules which concern the essentials of human well-being more nearly, and are therefore of more absolute obligation, than any other rules for the guidance of life; and the notion which we have found to be of the essence of the idea of justice, that of a right residing in an individual, implies and testifies to this more binding obligation.

The moral rules which forbid mankind to hurt one another (in which we must never forget to include wrongful interference with each other's freedom) are more vital to human well-being than any maxims, however important, which only point out the best mode of managing some department of human affairs. They have also the peculiarity, that they are the main element in determining the whole of the social feelings of mankind. It is their observance which alone preserves peace among human beings: if obedience to them were not the rule, and disobedience the exception, every one would see in every one else an enemy, against whom he must be perpetually guarding himself. What is hardly less important, these are the precepts which mankind have the strongest and the most direct inducements for impressing upon one another. By merely giving to each other prudential instruction or exhortation, they may gain, or think they gain, nothing; in inculcating on each other the duty of positive beneficence, they have an unmistakable interest, but far less in degree: a person may possibly not need the benefits of others; but he always needs that they should not do him hurt. Thus the moralities which protect every individual from being harmed by others, either directly or by being hindered in his freedom of pursuing his own good, are at once those which he himself has most at heart, and those which he has the strongest interest in publishing and enforcing by word and deed. It is by a person's observance of these, that his fitness to exist as one of the fellowship of human beings is tested and decided; for on that depends his being a nuisance or not to those with whom he is in contact. Now, it is these moralities, primarily, which compose the obligations of justice. The most marked cases of injustice, and those which give the tone to the feeling of repugnance which characterizes the sentiment, are acts of wrongful aggression, or wrongful exercise of power over some one; the next are those which consist in wrongfully withholding from him something which is his due: in both cases inflicting on him a positive hurt, either in the form of direct suffering, or of the privation of some good which he had reasonable ground, either of a physical or of a social kind, for counting upon.

The same powerful motives which command the observance of these primary moralities enjoin the punishment of those who violate them; and as the impulses of self-defence, of defence of others, and of vengeance, are all called forth against such persons, retribution, or evil for evil, becomes closely connected with the sentiment of justice, and is universally included in the idea. Good for good is also one of the dictates of justice; and this, though its social utility is evident, and though it carries with it a natural human feeling, has not at first sight that obvious connection with hurt or injury, which, existing in the most elementary cases of just and unjust, is the source of the characteristic intensity of the sentiment. But the connection, though less obvious, is not less real. He who accepts benefits, and denies a return of them when needed, inflicts a real hurt, by disappointing one of the most natural and reasonable of expectations, and one which he must at least tacitly have encouraged, otherwise the benefits would seldom have been conferred. The important rank, among human evils and wrongs, of the disappointment of expectation, is shown in the fact, that it constitutes the principal criminality of two such highly immoral acts as a breach of friendship and a breach of promise. Few hurts which human beings can sustain are greater, and none wound more, than when that on which they habitually and with full assurance relied fails them in the hour of need; and few wrongs are greater than this mere withholding of good: none excite more resentment, either in the person suffering, or in a sympathizing spectator. The principle, therefore, of giving to each what they deserve,—that is, good for good, as well as evil for evil,—is not only included within the idea of Justice as we have defined it, but is a proper object of that intensity of sentiment which places the Just, in human estimation, above the simply Expedient.

Most of the maxims of justice current in the world, and commonly appealed to in its transactions, are simply instrumental to carrying into effect the principles of justice which we have now spoken of. That a person is only responsible for what he has done voluntarily, or could voluntarily have avoided; that it is unjust to condemn any person unheard; that the punishment ought to be proportioned to the offence, and the like,— are maxims intended to prevent the just principle of evil for evil from being perverted to the infliction of evil without that justification. The greater part of these common maxims have come into use from the practice of courts of justice, which have been naturally led to a more complete recognition and elaboration than was likely to suggest itself to others, of the rules necessary to enable them to fulfil their double function, of inflicting punishment when due, and of awarding to each person his right.

That first of judicial virtues, impartiality, is an obligation of justice, partly for the reason last mentioned, as being a necessary condition of the fulfilment of the other obligations of justice. But this is not the only source of the exalted rank, among human obligations, of those maxims of equality and impartiality, which, both in popular estimation and in that of the most enlightened, are included among the precepts of justice. In one point of view, they may be considered as corollaries from the principles already laid down. If it is a duty to do to each according to his deserts, returning good for good as well as repressing evil by evil, it necessarily follows that we should treat all equally well (when no higher duty forbids) who have deserved equally well of *us;* and that society should treat all equally well who have deserved equally well of *it,* —that is, who have deserved equally well absolutely. This is the highest abstract standard of social and distributive justice, towards which all institutions, and the efforts of all virtuous citizens, should be made in the utmost possible degree to converge. But this great moral duty rests upon a still deeper foundation; being a direct emanation from the first principle of morals, and not a mere logical corollary from secondary or derivative doctrines. It is involved in the very meaning of Utility, or the Greatest-happiness Principle. That principle is a mere form of words without rational signification, unless one person's happiness, supposed equal in degree (with the proper allowance made for kind), is counted for exactly as much as another's. Those conditions being supplied, Bentham's dictum, "Everybody to count for one, nobody for more than one," might be written under the principle of utility as an explanatory commentary.[3] The equal claim of everybody to happiness, in the estimation of the moralist and the legislator, involves an equal claim to all the means of happiness, except in so far as the inevitable conditions of human life, and the general interest, in which that of every individual is included, set limits to the maxim; and those limits ought to be strictly construed. As every other maxim of justice, so this, is by no means applied or held applicable universally: on the contrary, as I have already remarked, it bends to every person's ideas of social expediency. But, in whatever case it is deemed applicable at all, it is held to be the dictate of jus-

---

[3]This implication, in the first principle of the utilitarian scheme of perfect impartiality between persons, is regarded by Mr. Herbert Spencer (in his "Social Statics") as a disproof of the pretensions of utility to be a sufficient guide to right; since (he says) the principle of utility presupposes the anterior principle, that everybody has an equal right to happiness. It may be more correctly described as supposing that equal amounts of happiness are equally desirable, whether felt by the same or by different persons. This, however, is not a *pre*supposition; not a premise needful to support the principle of utility, but the very principle itself: for what is the principle of utility, if it be not that "happiness" and "desirable" are synonymous terms? If there is any anterior principle implied, it can be no other than this,—that the truths of arithmetic are applicable to the valuation of happiness, as of all other measurable quantities.

[Mr. Herbert Spencer, in a private communication on the subject of the preceding note, objects to being considered an opponent of Utilitarianism, and states that he regards happiness as the ultimate end of morality; but deems that end only partially attainable by empirical generalizations from the observed results of conduct, and completely attainable only by deducing, from the laws of life and the conditions of existence, what kinds of action necessarily tend to produce happiness, and what kinds to produce unhappiness. With the exception of the word "necessarily," I have no dissent to express from this doctrine; and (omitting that word) I am not aware that any modern advocate of utilitarianism is of a different opinion. Bentham certainly, to whom, in the "Social Statics," Mr. Spencer particularly referred, is, least of all writers, chargeable with unwillingness to deduce the effect of actions on happiness from the laws of human nature and the universal conditions of human life. The common charge against him is of relying too exclusively upon such deductions, and declining altogether to be bound by the generalizations from specific experience which Mr. Spencer thinks that utilitarians generally confine themselves to. My own opinion (and, as I collect, Mr. Spencer's) is, that in ethics, as in all other branches of scientific study, the consilience of the results of both these processes, each corroborating and verifying the other, is requisite to give to any general proposition the kind and degree of evidence which constitutes scientific proof.]

tice. All persons are deemed to have a *right* to equality of treatment, except when some recognized social expediency requires the reverse. And hence all social inequalities, which have ceased to be considered expedient, assume the character, not of simple inexpediency, but of injustice, and appear so tyrannical, that people are apt to wonder how they ever could have been tolerated; forgetful that they themselves perhaps tolerate other inequalities under an equally mistaken notion of expediency, the correction of which would make that which they approve seem quite as monstrous as what they have at last learnt to condemn. The entire history of social improvement has been a series of transitions, by which one custom or institution after another, from being a supposed primary necessity of social existence, has passed into the rank of an universally stigmatized injustice and tyranny. So it has been with the distinctions of slaves and freemen, nobles and serfs, patricians and plebeians; and so it will be, and in part already is, with the aristocracies of color, race, and sex.

It appears, from what has been said, that justice is a name for certain moral requirements, which, regarded collectively, stand higher in the scale of social utility, and are therefore of more paramount obligation, than any others; though particular cases may occur in which some other social duty is so important as to overrule any one of the general maxims of justice. Thus, to save a life, it may not only be allowable, but a duty, to steal, or take by force, the necessary food or medicine, or to kidnap, and compel to officiate, the only qualified medical practitioner. In such cases, as we do not call any thing justice which is not a virtue, we usually say, not that justice must give way to some other moral principle, but that what is just in ordinary cases is, by reason of that other principle, not just in the particular case. By this useful accommodation of language, the character of indefeasibility attributed to justice is kept up, and we are saved from the necessity of maintaining that there can be laudable injustice.

The considerations which have now been adduced, resolve, I conceive, the only real difficulty in the utilitarian theory of morals. It has always been evident that all cases of justice are also cases of expediency: the difference is in the peculiar sentiment which attaches to the former, as contradistinguished from the latter. If this characteristic sentiment has been sufficiently accounted for; if there is no necessity to assume for it any peculiarity of origin; if it is simply the natural feeling of resentment, moralized by being made co-extensive with the demands of social good; and if this feeling not only does but ought to exist in all the classes of cases to which the idea of justice corresponds,—that idea no longer presents itself as a stumbling-block to the utilitarian ethics. Justice remains the appropriate name for certain social utilities which are vastly more important, and therefore more absolute and imperative, than any others are as a class (though not more so than others may be in particular cases), and which therefore ought to be, as well as naturally are, guarded by a sentiment not only different in degree, but also in kind; distinguished from the milder feeling which attaches to the mere idea of promoting human pleasure or convenience, at once by the more definite nature of its commands, and by the sterner character of its sanctions.

Inaugural Address
at Saint Andrews[1]

[1]Delivered to the University of St. Andrews, February 1, 1867. VOL. IV.

In complying with the custom which prescribes that the person whom you have called by your suffrages to the honorary presidency of your University should embody in an Address a few thoughts on the subjects which most nearly concern a seat of liberal education, let me begin by saying, that this usage appears to me highly commendable. Education, in its larger sense, is one of the most inexhaustible of all topics. Though there is hardly any subject on which so much has been written, by so many of the wisest men, it is as fresh to those who come to it with a fresh mind, a mind not hopelessly filled full with other people's conclusions, as it was to the first explorers of it; and notwithstanding the great mass of excellent things which have been said respecting it, no thoughtful person finds any lack of things both great and small still waiting to be said, or waiting to be developed and followed out to their consequences. Education, moreover, is one of the subjects which most essentially require to be considered by various minds, and from a variety of points of view. For, of all many-sided subjects, it is the one which has the greatest number of sides. Not only does it include whatever we do for ourselves, and whatever is done for us by others, for the express purpose of bringing us somewhat nearer to the perfection of our nature; it does more: in its largest acceptation, it comprehends even the indirect effects produced on character and on the human faculties, by things of which the direct purposes are quite different; by laws, by forms of government, by the industrial arts, by modes of social life; nay, even by physical facts not dependent on human will; by climate, soil, and local position. Whatever helps to shape the human being—to make the individual what he is, or hinder him from being what he is not—is part of his education. And a very bad education it often is, requiring all that can be done by cultivated intelligence and will, to counteract its tendencies. To take an obvious instance: the niggardliness of Nature in some places, by engrossing the whole energies of the human being in the mere preservation of life, and her over-bounty in others, affording a sort of brutish subsistence on too easy terms, with hardly any exertion of the human faculties, are both hostile to the spontaneous growth and development of the mind; and it is at those two extremes of the scale that we find human societies in the state of most unmitigated savagery. I shall confine myself, however, to education in the narrower sense; the culture which each generation purposely gives to those who are to be its successors, in order to qualify them for at least keeping up, and if possible for raising, the level of improvement which has been attained. Nearly all here present are daily occupied either in receiving or in giving this sort of education; and the part of it which most concerns you at present is that in which you are yourselves engaged—the stage of education which is the appointed business of a national University.

The proper function of a University in national education is tolerably well understood. At least there is a tolerably general agreement about what a University is not. It is not a place of professional education. Universities are not intended to teach the knowledge required to fit men for some special mode of gaining their livelihood. Their object is not to make skilful lawyers, or physicians, or engineers, but capable and cultivated human beings. It is very right that there should be public facilities for the study of professions. It is well that there should be Schools of Law, and of Medicine, and it would be well if there were schools of engineering, and the industrial arts. The countries which have such institutions are greatly the better for them; and there is something to be said for having them in the same localities, and under the same general superintendence, as the establishments devoted to education properly so called. But these things are no part of what every generation owes to the next, as that on which its civilization and worth will principally depend. They are needed only by a comparatively few, who are under the strongest private inducements to acquire them by their own efforts; and even those few do not require them until after their education, in the ordinary sense, has been completed. Whether those whose speciality they are, will learn them as a branch of intelligence or as a mere trade, and whether, having learned them, they will make a wise and conscientious use of them or the reverse, depends less on the manner in which they are taught their profession, than upon what sort of minds they bring to it—what kind of intelligence, and of conscience, the general system of education has developed in them. Men are men before they are lawyers, or physicians, or merchants, or manufacturers; and if you make them capable and sensible men, they will make themselves capable and sensible lawyers or physicians. What professional men should carry away with them from a University, is not professional knowledge, but that which should direct the use of their professional knowledge, and bring the light of general culture to illuminate the technicalities of a special pursuit. Men may be competent lawyers without general education, but it depends on general education to make them philosophic lawyers—who demand, and are capable of apprehending, principles, instead of merely cramming their memory with details. And so of all other useful pursuits, mechanical included. Education makes a man a more intelligent shoemaker, if that be his occupation, but not by teaching him how to make shoes; it does so by the mental exercise it gives, and the habits it impresses.

This, then, is what a mathematician would call the higher limit of University education: its province ends where education, ceasing to be general, branches off into departments adapted to the individual's destination in life. The lower limit is more difficult to define. A University is not concerned with elementary instruction: the pupil is supposed to have acquired that before coming here. But where does elementary instruction end, and the higher studies begin? Some have given a very wide extension to the idea of elementary instruction. According to them, it is not the office of a University to give instruction in single branches of knowledge from the commencement. What the pupil should be taught here (they think), is to methodize his knowledge: to look at every separate part of it in its relation to the other parts, and to the whole; combining the partial glimpses which he has obtained of the field of human knowledge at different points, into a general map, if I may so speak, of the entire region; observing how all knowledge is connected, how we ascend to one branch by means of another, how the higher modifies the lower, and the lower helps us to understand the higher; how every existing reality is a compound of many properties, of which each science or distinct mode of study reveals but a small part, but the whole of which must be included to enable us to know it truly as a fact in Nature, and not as a mere abstraction.

This last stage of general education, destined to give the pupil a comprehensive and connected view of the things which he has already learned separately, includes a philosophic study of the Methods of the sciences; the modes in which the human intellect proceeds from the known to the unknown. We must be taught to generalize our conception of the resources which the human mind possesses for the exploration of nature; to understand how man discovers the real facts of the world, and by what tests he can judge whether he has really found them. And doubtless this is the crown and consummation of a liberal education: but before we restrict a University to this highest department of instruction—before we confine it to teaching, not knowledge, but the philosophy of knowledge—we must be assured that the knowledge itself has been acquired elsewhere. Those who take this view of the function of a University are not wrong in thinking that the schools, as distinguished from the Universities, ought to be adequate to teaching every branch of general instruction required by youth, so far as it can be studied apart from the rest. But where are such schools to be found? Since science assumed its modern character, nowhere; and in these islands less even than elsewhere. This ancient kingdom, thanks to its great religious reformers, had the inestimable advantage, denied to its southern sister, of excellent parish schools, which gave, really and not in pretence, a considerable amount of valuable literary instruction to the bulk of the population, two centuries earlier than in any other country. But schools of a still higher description have been, even in Scotland, so few and inadequate, that the Universities have had to perform largely the functions which ought to be performed by schools; receiving students at an early age, and undertaking not only the work for which the schools should have prepared them, but much of the preparation itself. Every Scottish University is not a University only, but a High School, to supply the deficiency of other schools. And if the English Universities do not do the same, it is not because the same need does not exist, but because it is disregarded. Youths come to the Scottish Universities ignorant, and are there taught. The majority of those who come to the English Universities come still more ignorant, and ignorant they go away.

In point of fact, therefore, the office of a Scottish University comprises the whole of a liberal education, from the foundations upwards. And the scheme of your Universities has, almost from the beginning, really aimed at including the whole, both in depth and in breadth. You have not, as the English Universities so long did, confined all the stress of your teaching, all your real effort to teach, within the limits of two subjects, the classical languages and mathematics. You did not wait till the last few years to establish a Natural Science and a Moral Science Tripos. Instruction in both those departments was organized long ago; and your teachers of those subjects have not been nominal professors, who did not lecture: some of the greatest names in physical and in moral science have taught in your Universities, and by their teaching contributed to form some of the most distinguished intellects of the last and present centuries. To comment upon the course of education at the Scottish Universities is to pass in review every essential department of general culture. The best use, then, which I am able to make of the present occasion, is to offer a few remarks on each of those departments, considered in its relation to human cultivation at large; adverting to the nature of the claims which each has to a place in liberal education; in what special manner they each conduce to the improvement of the individual mind and the benefit of the race; and how they all conspire to the common end, the strengthening, exalting, purifying, and beautifying of our common nature, and the fitting out of mankind with the necessary mental implements for the work they have to perform through life.

Let me first say a few words on the great controversy of the present day with regard to the higher education, the difference which most broadly divides educational reformers and conservatives; the vexed question between the ancient languages, and the modern sciences and arts; whether general education should be classical—let me use a wider expression, and say literary—or scientific. A dispute as endlessly, and often

as fruitlessly agitated as that old controversy which it re-
sembles, made memorable by the names of Swift and Sir
William Temple in England, and Fontenelle in France—the
contest for superiority between the ancients and the moderns.
This question, whether we should be taught the classics or
the sciences, seems to me, I confess, very like a dispute
whether painters should cultivate drawing or coloring, or,
to use a more homely illustration, whether a tailor should
make coats or trousers. I can only reply by the question, Why
not both? Can anything deserve the name of a good education which does not include literature and science too? If
there were no more to be said than that scientific education
teaches us to think, and literary education to express our
thoughts, do we not require both? and is not any one a poor,
maimed, lopsided fragment of humanity who is deficient in
either? We are not obliged to ask ourselves whether it is
more important to know the languages or the sciences. Short
as life is, and shorter still as we make it by the time we waste
on things which are neither business, nor meditation, nor
pleasure, we are not so badly off that our scholars need be
ignorant of the laws and properties of the world they live in,
or our scientific men destitute of poetic feeling and artistic
cultivation. I am amazed at the limited conception which
many educational reformers have formed to themselves of a
human being's power of acquisition. The study of science,
they truly say, is indispensable: our present education neg-
lects it: there is truth in this too, though it is not all truth:
and they think it impossible to find room for the studies which
they desire to encourage, but by turning out, at least from
general education, those which are now chiefly cultivated.
How absurd, they say, that the whole of boyhood should be
taken up in acquiring an imperfect knowledge of two dead
languages. Absurd indeed: but is the human mind's capacity
to learn, measured by that of Eton and Westminster to
teach? I should prefer to see these reformers pointing their
attacks against the shameful inefficiency of the schools, public
and private, which pretend to teach these two languages and
do not. I should like to hear them denounce the wretched
methods of teaching, and the criminal idleness and supineness,
which waste the entire boyhood of the pupils without really
giving to most of them more than a smattering, if even that,
of the only kind of knowledge which is even pretended to

be cared for. Let us try what conscientious and intelligent teaching can do, before we presume to decide what cannot be done.

Scotland has on the whole, in this respect, been considerably more fortunate than England. Scotch youths have never found it impossible to leave school or the University having learned somewhat of other things besides Greek and Latin; and why? Because Greek and Latin have been better taught. A beginning of classical instruction has all along been made in the common schools; and the common schools of Scotland, like her Universities, have never been the mere shams that the English Universities were during the last century, and the greater part of the English classical schools still are. The only tolerable Latin Grammars for school purposes that I know of, which had been produced in these islands until very lately, were written by Scotchmen. Reason, indeed, is beginning to find its way by gradual infiltration even into English schools, and to maintain a contest, though as yet a very unequal one, against routine. A few practical reformers of school tuition, of whom Arnold was the most eminent, have made a beginning of amendment in many things; but reforms, worthy of the name, are always slow, and reform even of governments and churches is not so slow as that of schools, for there is the great preliminary difficulty of fashioning the instruments; of teaching the teachers. If all the improvements in the mode of teaching languages which are already sanctioned by experience, were adopted into our classical schools, we should soon cease to hear of Latin and Greek as studies which must engross the school years, and render impossible any other acquirements. If a boy learned Greek and Latin on the same principle on which a mere child learns with such ease and rapidity any modern language, namely, by acquiring some familiarity with the vocabulary by practice and repetition, before being troubled with grammatical rules,—those rules being acquired with tenfold greater facility when the cases to which they apply are already familiar to the mind,—an average schoolboy, long before the age at which schooling terminates, would be able to read fluently and with intelligent interest any ordinary Latin or Greek author in prose or verse, would have a competent knowledge of the grammatical structure of both languages, and have had time besides for an ample amount of scientific instruction. I might go much farther; but I am as unwilling to speak out all that I think practicable in this matter, as George Stephenson was about railways, when he calculated the average speed of a train at ten miles an hour, because if he had estimated it higher, the practical men would have turned a deaf ear to him, as that most unsafe character in their estimation, an enthusiast and a visionary. The results have shown, in that case, who was the real practical man. What the results would show in the other case, I will not attempt to anticipate. But I will say confidently, that if the two classical languages were properly taught, there would be no need whatever for ejecting them from the school course, in order to have sufficient time for every thing else that need be included therein.

Let me say a few words more on this strangely limited estimate of what it is possible for human beings to learn, resting on a tacit assumption that they are already as efficiently taught as they ever can be. So narrow a conception not only vitiates our idea of education, but actually, if we receive it, darkens our anticipations as to the future progress of mankind. For if the inexorable conditions of human life make it useless for one man to attempt to know more than one thing, what is to become of the human intellect as facts accumulate? In every generation, and now more rapidly than ever, the things which it is necessary that somebody should know are more and more multiplied. Every department of knowledge becomes so loaded with details, that one who endeavors to know it with minute accuracy, must confine himself to a smaller and smaller portion of the whole extent: every science and art must be cut up into subdivisions, until each man's portion, the district which he thoroughly knows, bears about the same ratio to the whole range of useful knowledge that the art of putting on a pin's head does to the field of human industry. Now, if, in order to know that little completely, it is necessary to remain wholly ignorant of all the rest, what will soon be the worth of a man, for any human purpose except his own infinitesimal fraction of human wants and requirements? His state will be even worse than that of simple ignorance. Experience proves that there is no one study or pursuit, which, practised to the exclusion of all others, does not narrow and pervert the mind; breeding in it a class of prejudices special to that pursuit, besides a general prejudice, common to all narrow specialities, against large views, from an incapacity to take in and appreciate the grounds of them. We should have to expect that human nature would be more and more dwarfed, and unfitted for great things, by its very proficiency in small ones. But matters are not so bad with us: there is no ground for so dreary an anticipation. It is not the utmost limit of human acquirement to know only one thing, but to combine a minute knowledge of one or a few things with a general knowledge of many things. By a general knowledge I do not mean a few vague impressions. An eminent man, one of whose writings is part of the course of this University, Archbishop Whately, has well discriminated between a general knowledge and a superficial knowledge. To have a general knowledge of a subject is to know only its leading truths, but to know these not superficially but thoroughly, so as to have a true conception of the subject in its great features; leaving the minor details to those who require them for the purposes of their special pursuit. There is no incompatibility between knowing a wide range of subjects up to this point, and some one subject with the completeness required by those who make it their principal occupation. It is this combination which gives an enlightened public: a body of cultivated intellects, each taught by its attainments in its own province what real knowledge is, and knowing enough of other subjects to be able to discern who are those that know them better. The amount of knowledge is not to be lightly estimated, which qualifies us for judging to whom we may have recourse for more. The elements of the more important studies being widely diffused, those who have reached the higher summits find a public capable of appreciating their superiority, and prepared to follow their lead. It is thus, too, that minds are formed capable of guiding and improving public opinion on the greater concerns of practical life. Government and civil society are the most complicated of all subjects accessible to the human mind; and he who would deal competently with them as a thinker, and not as a blind follower of a party, requires not only a general knowledge of the leading facts of life, both moral and material, but an understanding exercised and disciplined in the principles and rules of sound thinking, up to a point which neither the experience of life, nor any one science or branch of knowledge, affords. Let us understand, then, that it should be our aim in learning, not merely to know the one thing which is to be our principal occupation, as well as it can be known, but to do this and also to know something of all the great subjects of human interest; taking care to know that something accurately; marking well the dividing line between what we know accurately and what we do not; and remembering that our object should be to obtain a true view of nature and life in their broad outline, and that it is idle to throw away time upon the details of any thing which is to form no part of the occupation of our practical energies.

It by no means follows, however, that every useful branch of general, as distinct from professional, knowledge, should be included in the curriculum of school or University studies. There are things which are better learned out of school, or when the school years, and even those usually passed in a Scottish University, are over. I do not agree with those reformers who would give a regular and prominent place in the school or University course to modern languages. This is not because I attach small importance to the knowledge of them. No one can in our age be esteemed a well-instructed person who is not familiar with at least the French language, so as to read French books with ease; and there is great use in cultivating a familiarity with German. But living languages are so much more easily acquired by intercourse with those who use them in daily life; a few months in the country itself, if properly employed, go so much farther than as many years of school lessons; that it is really waste of time for those to whom that easier mode is attainable, to labor at them with no help but that of books and masters: and it will in time be made attainable, through international schools and colleges, to many more than at present. Universities do enough to facilitate the study of modern languages, if they give a mastery over that ancient language which is the foundation of most of them, and the possession of which makes it easier to learn four or five of the continental languages than it is to learn one of them without it. Again, it has always seemed to me a great absurdity that history and geography should be taught in schools; except in elementary schools for the children of the laboring classes, whose subsequent access to books is limited. Who ever really learned history and geography except by private reading? and what an utter failure a system of education must be, if it has not given the pupil a sufficient taste for reading to seek for himself those most attractive and easily intelligible of all kinds of knowledge! Besides, such history and geography as can be taught in schools exercise none of the faculties of the intelligence except the memory. A University is indeed the place where the student should be introduced to the Philosophy of History; where professors who not merely know the facts, but have exercised their minds on them, should initiate him into the causes and explanations, so far as within our reach, of the past life of mankind in its principal features. Historical criticism also—the tests of historical truth—are a subject to which his attention may well be drawn in this stage of his education. But of the mere facts of history, as commonly accepted, what educated youth of any mental activity does not learn as much as is necessary, if he is simply turned loose into an historical library? What he needs on this, and on most other matters of common information, is, not that he should be taught it in boyhood, but that abundance of books should be accessible to him.

The only languages, then, and the only literature, to which I would allow a place in the ordinary curriculum, are those of the Greeks and Romans; and to these I would preserve the position in it which they at present occupy. That position is justified, by the great value, in education, of knowing well some other cultivated language and literature than one's own, and by the peculiar value of those particular languages and literatures.

There is one purely intellectual benefit from a knowledge of languages, which I am specially desirous to dwell on. Those who have seriously reflected on the causes of human error, have been deeply impressed with the tendency of mankind to mistake words for things. Without entering into the metaphysics of the subject, we know how common it is to use words glibly and with apparent propriety, and to accept them confidently when used by others, without ever having had any distinct conception of the things denoted by them. To quote again from Archbishop Whately, it is the habit of mankind to mistake familiarity for accurate knowledge. As we seldom think of asking the meaning of what we see every day, so when our ears are used to the sound of a word or a phrase, we do not suspect that it conveys no clear idea to our minds, and that we should have the utmost difficulty in defining it, or expressing, in any other words, what we think we understand by it. Now, it is obvious in what manner this *linguistic analysis needed !*

bad habit tends to be corrected by the practice of translating with accuracy from one language to another, and hunting out the meanings expressed in a vocabulary with which we have not grown familiar by early and constant use. I hardly know any greater proof of the extraordinary genius of the Greeks, than that they were able to make such brilliant achievements in abstract thought, knowing, as they generally did, no language but their own. But the Greeks did not escape the effects of this deficiency. Their greatest intellects, those who laid the foundation of philosophy and of all our intellectual culture, Plato and Aristotle, are continually led away by words; mistaking the accidents of language for real relations in nature, and supposing that things which have the same name in the Greek tongue must be the same in their own essence. There is a well-known saying of Hobbes, the far-reaching significance of which you will more and more appreciate in proportion to the growth of your own intellect: "Words are the counters of wise men, but the money of fools." With the wise man a word stands for the fact which it represents; to the fool it is itself the fact. To carry on Hobbes's metaphor, the counter is far more likely to be taken for merely what it is, by those who are in the habit of using many different kinds of counters. But, besides the advantage of possessing another cultivated language, there is a further consideration equally important. Without knowing the language of a people, we never really know their thoughts, their feelings, and their type of character: and unless we do possess this knowledge, of some other people than ourselves, we remain, to the hour of our death, with our intellects only half expanded. Look at a youth who has never been out of his family circle: he never dreams of any other opinions or ways of thinking than those he has been bred up in; or, if he has heard of any such, attributes them to some moral defect, or inferiority of nature or education. If his family are Tory, he cannot conceive the possibility of being a Liberal; if Liberal, of being a Tory. What the notions and habits of a single family are to a boy who has had no intercourse beyond it, the notions and habits of his own country are to him who is ignorant of every other. Those notions and habits are to him human nature itself; whatever varies from them is an unaccountable aberration which he cannot mentally realize: the idea that any other ways can be right, or as near an approach to right) as some of his own, is inconceivable to him. This does not merely close his eyes to the many things which every country still has to learn from others: it hinders every country from reaching the improvement which it could otherwise attain by itself. We are not likely to correct any of our opinions or mend any of our ways, unless we begin by conceiving that they are capable of amendment: but merely to know that foreigners think differently from ourselves, without understanding why they do so, or what they really do think, does but confirm us in our self-conceit, and connect our national vanity with the preservation of our own peculiarities. Improvement consists in bringing our opinions into nearer agreement with facts; and we shall not be likely to do this while we look at facts only through glasses colored by those very opinions. But since we cannot divest ourselves of preconceived notions, there is no known means of eliminating their influence but by frequently using the differently colored glasses of other people: and those of other nations, as the most different, are the best.

But if it is so useful, on this account, to know the language and literature of any other cultivated and civilized people, the most valuable of all to us in this respect are the languages and literature of the ancients. No nations of modern and civilized Europe are so unlike one another, as the Greeks and Romans are unlike all of us; yet without being, as some remote Orientals are, so totally dissimilar, that the labor of a life is required to enable us to understand them. Were this the only gain to be derived from a knowledge of the ancients, it would already place the study of them in a high rank among enlightening and liberalizing pursuits. It is of no use saying that we may know them through modern writings. We may know something of them in that way; which is much better than knowing nothing. But modern books do not teach us ancient thought; they teach us some modern writer's notion of ancient thought. Modern books do not show us the Greeks and Romans; they tell us some modern writer's opinions about the Greeks and Romans. Translations are scarcely better. When we want really to know what a person thinks or says, we seek it at first hand from himself. We do not trust to another person's impression of his meaning, given in another person's words; we refer to his own. Much more is it necessary to do so when his words are in one language, and those of his reporter in another. Modern phraseology never conveys the exact meaning of a Greek writer; it cannot do so, except by a diffuse explanatory circumlocution which no translator dares use. We must be able, in a certain degree, to think in Greek, if we would represent to ourselves how a Greek thought; and this not only in the abstruse region of metaphysics, but about the political, religious, and even domestic concerns of life. I will mention a further aspect of this question, which, though I have not the merit of originating it, I do not remember to have seen noticed in any book. There is no part of our knowledge which it is more useful to obtain at first hand—to go to the fountain head for—than our knowledge of history. Yet this, in most cases, we hardly ever do. Our conception of the past is not drawn from its own records, but from books written about it, containing not the facts, but a view of the facts which has shaped itself in the mind of somebody of our own or a very recent time. Such books are very instructive and valuable; they help us to understand history, to interpret history, to draw just conclusions from it; at the worst, they set us the example of trying to do all this; but they are not themselves history. The knowledge they give is upon trust, and even when they have done their best, it is not only incomplete, but partial, because confined to what a few modern writers have seen in the materials, and have thought worth picking out from among them. How little we learn of our own ancestors from Hume, or Hallam, or Macaulay, compared with what we know if we add to what these tell us, even a little reading of contemporary authors and documents! The most recent historians are so well aware of this, that they fill their pages with extracts from the original materials, feeling that these extracts are the real history, and their comments and thread of narrative are only helps towards understanding it. Now, it is part of the great worth to us of our Greek and Latin studies, that in them we do read history in the original sources. We are in actual contact with contemporary minds; we are not dependent on hearsay; we have something by which we can test and check the representations and theories of modern historians. It may be asked, Why then not study the original materials of modern history? I answer, It is highly desirable to do so; and let me remark by the way, that even this requires a dead language; nearly all the documents prior to the Reformation, and many subsequent to it, being written in Latin. But the exploration of these documents, though a most useful pursuit, cannot be a branch of education. Not to speak of their vast extent, and the fragmentary nature of each, the strongest reason is, that in learning the spirit of our own past ages, until a comparatively recent period, from contemporary writers, we learn hardly anything else. Those authors, with a few exceptions, are little worth reading on their own account. While, in studying the great writers of antiquity, we are not only learning to understand the ancient mind, but laying in a stock of wise thought and observation, still valuable to ourselves; and at the same time making ourselves familiar with a number of the most perfect and finished literary compositions which the human mind has produced—compositions which, from the altered conditions of human life, are likely to be seldom paralleled, in their sustained excellence, by the times to come.

Even as mere languages, no modern European language is so valuable a discipline to the intellect as those of Greece and Rome, on account of their regular and complicated structure. Consider for a moment what grammar is. It is the most elementary part of logic. It is the beginning of the analysis of the thinking process. The principles and rules of grammar are the means by which the forms of language are made to correspond with the universal forms of thought. The distinctions between the various parts of speech, between the cases of nouns, the moods and tenses of verbs, the functions of particles, are distinctions in thought, not merely in words. Single nouns and verbs express objects and events, many of which can be cognized by the senses: but the modes of putting nouns and verbs together, express the relations of objects and events, which can be cognized only by the intellect; and each different mode corresponds to a different relation. The structure of every sentence is a lesson in logic. The various rules of syntax oblige us to distinguish between the subject and predicate of a proposition, between the agent, the action, and the thing acted upon; to mark when an idea is intended to modify or qualify, or merely to unite with, some other idea; what assertions are categorical, what only conditional; whether the intention is to express similarity or contrast, to make a plurality of assertions conjunctively or disjunctively; what portions of a sentence, though grammatically complete within themselves, are mere members or subordinate parts of the assertion made by the entire sentence. Such things form the subject-matter of universal grammar; and the languages which teach it best are those which have the most definite rules, and which provide distinct forms for the greatest number of distinctions in thought, so that if we fail to attend precisely and accurately to any of these, we cannot avoid committing a solecism in language. In these qualities the classical languages have an incomparable superiority over every modern language, and over all languages, dead or living, which have a literature worth being generally studied.

But the superiority of the literature itself, for purposes of education, is still more marked and decisive. Even in the substantial value of the matter of which it is the vehicle, it is very far from having been superseded. The discoveries of the ancients in science have been greatly surpassed, and as much of them as is still valuable loses nothing by being incorporated in modern treatises: but what does not so well admit of being transferred bodily, and has been very imperfectly carried off even piecemeal, is the treasure which they accumulated of what may be called the wisdom of life; the rich store of experience of human nature and conduct, which the acute and observing minds of those ages, aided in their observations by the greater simplicity of manners and life, consigned to their writings, and most of which retains all its value. The speeches in Thucydides; the Rhetoric, Ethics, and Politics of Aristotle; the Dialogues of Plato; the Orations of Demosthenes; the Satires, and especially the Epistles of Horace; all the writings of Tacitus; the great work of Quintilian, a repertory of the best thoughts of the ancient world on all subjects connected with education; and, in a less formal manner, all that is left to us of the ancient historians, orators, philosophers, and even dramatists, are replete with remarks and maxims of singular good sense and penetration, applicable both to political and to private life: and the actual truths we find in them are even surpassed in value by the encouragement and help they give us in the pursuit of truth. Human invention has never produced anything so valuable, in the way both of stimulation and of discipline to the inquiring intellect, as the dialectics of the ancients, of which many of the works of Aristotle illustrate the theory, and those of Plato exhibit the practice. No modern writings come near to these, in teaching, both by precept and example, the way to investigate truth, on those subjects, so vastly important to us, which remain matters of controversy, from the difficulty or impossibility of bringing them to a directly experimental test. To question all things; never to turn away from any difficulty; to accept no doctrine either from ourselves or from other people without a rigid scrutiny by negative criticism, letting no fallacy, or incoherence, or confusion of thought, slip by unperceived; above all, to insist upon having the meaning of a word clearly understood before using it, and the meaning of a proposition before assenting to it; these are the lessons we learn from the ancient dialecticians. With all this vigorous management of the negative element, they inspire no scepticism about the reality of truth, or indifference to its pursuit. The noblest enthusiasm, both for the search after truth and for applying it to its highest uses, pervades these writers, Aristotle no less than Plato, though Plato has incomparably the greater power of imparting those feelings to others. In cultivating, therefore, the ancient languages as our best literary education, we are all the while laying an admirable foundation for ethical and philosophical culture. In purely literary excellence—in perfection of form—the pre-eminence of the ancients is not disputed. In every department which they attempted,—and they attempted almost all,—their composition, like their sculpture, has been to the greatest modern artists an example, to be looked up to with hopeless admiration, but of inappreciable value as a light on high, guiding their own endeavors. In prose and in poetry, in epic, lyric, or dramatic, as in historical, philosophical, and oratorical art, the pinnacle on which they stand is equally eminent. I am now speaking of the form, the artistic perfection of treatment; for, as regards substance, I consider modern poetry to be superior to ancient, in the same manner, though in a less degree, as modern science: it enters deeper into nature. The feelings of the modern mind are more various, more complex and manifold, than those of the ancients ever were. The modern mind is, what the ancient mind was not, brooding and self-conscious; and its meditative self-consciousness has discovered depths in the human soul which the Greeks and Romans did not dream of, and would not have understood. But what they had got to express, they expressed in a manner which few even of the greatest moderns have seriously attempted to rival. It must be remembered that they had more time, and that they wrote chiefly for a select class, possessed of leisure. To us who write in a hurry for people who read in a hurry, the attempt to give an equal degree of finish would be loss of time. But to be familiar with perfect models is not the less important to us because the element in which we work precludes even the effort to equal them. They show us at least what excellence is, and make us desire it, and strive to get as near to it as is within our reach. And this is the value to us of the ancient writers, all the more emphatically, because their excellence does not admit of being copied, or directly imitated. It does not consist in a trick which can be learned, but in the perfect adaptation of means to ends. The secret of the style of the great Greek and Roman authors is, that it is the perfection of good sense. In the first place, they never use a word without a meaning, or a word which adds nothing to the meaning. They always (to begin with) had a meaning; they knew what they wanted to say; and their whole purpose was to say it with the highest degree of exactness and completeness, and bring it home to the mind with the greatest possible clearness and vividness. It never entered into their thoughts to conceive of a piece of writing as beautiful in itself, abstractedly from what it had to express: its beauty must all be subservient to the most perfect expression of the sense. The *curiosa felicitas* which their critics ascribed in a pre-eminent degree to Horace, expresses the standard at which they all aimed. Their style is exactly described by Swift's definition, "the right words in the right places." Look at an oration of Demosthenes; there is nothing in it which calls attention to itself as style at all: it is only after a close examination we perceive that every word is what it should be, and where it should be, to lead the hearer smoothly and imperceptibly into the state of mind which the orator wishes to produce. The perfection of the workmanship is only visible in the total absence of any blemish or fault, and of anything which checks the flow of thought and feeling, anything which even momentarily distracts the mind from the main purpose. But then (as has been well said) it was not the object of Demosthenes to make the Athenians cry out, "What a splendid speaker!" but to make them say, "Let us march against Philip!" It was only in the decline of ancient literature that ornament began to be cultivated merely as ornament. In the time of its maturity, not the merest epithet was put in because it was thought beautiful in itself; nor even for a merely descriptive purpose, for epithets purely descriptive were one of the corruptions of style which abound in Lucan, for example: the word had no business there unless it brought out some feature which was wanted, and helped to place the object in the light which the purpose of the composition required. These conditions being complied with, then indeed the intrinsic beauty of the means used was a source of additional effect, of which it behooved them to avail themselves, like rhythm and melody of versification. But these great writers knew that ornament for the sake of ornament, ornament which attracts attention to itself, and shines by its own beauties, only does so by calling off the mind from the main object, and thus not only interferes with the higher purpose of human discourse, which ought, and generally professes, to have some matter to communicate, apart from the mere excitement of the moment, but also spoils the perfection of the composition as a piece of fine art, by destroying the unity of effect. This, then, is the first great lesson in composition to be learned from the classical authors. The second is, not to be prolix. In a single paragraph, Thucydides can give a clear and vivid representation of a battle, such as a reader who has once taken it into his mind can seldom forget. The most powerful and affecting piece of narrative perhaps in all historical literature, is the account of the Sicilian catastrophe in his seventh book; yet how few pages does it fill! The ancients were concise, because of the extreme pains they took with their compositions; almost all moderns are prolix, because they do not. The great ancients could express a thought so perfectly in a few words or sentences, that they did not need to add any more: the moderns, because they cannot bring it out clearly and completely at once, return again and again, heaping sentence upon sentence, each adding a little more elucidation, in hopes that, though no single sentence expresses the full meaning, the whole together may give a sufficient notion of it. In this respect I am afraid we are growing worse, instead of better, for want of time and patience, and from the necessity we are in of addressing almost all writings to a busy and imperfectly prepared public. The demands of modern life are such, the work to be done, the mass to be worked upon, are so vast, that those who have anything particular to say—who have, as the phrase goes, any message to deliver—cannot afford to devote their time to the production of masterpieces. But they would do far worse than they do, if there had never been masterpieces, or if they had never known them. Early familiarity with the perfect makes our most imperfect production far less bad than it otherwise would be. To have a high standard of excellence often makes the whole difference of rendering our work good when it would otherwise be mediocre.

For all these reasons I think it important to retain these two languages and literatures in the place they occupy, as a part of liberal education, that is, of the education of all who are not obliged by their circumstances to discontinue their scholastic studies at a very early age. But the same reasons which vindicate the place of classical studies in general education, show also the proper limitation of them. They should be carried as far as is sufficient to enable the pupil, in after life, to read the great works of ancient literature with ease. Those who have leisure and inclination to make scholarship, or ancient history, or general philology, their pursuit, of course require much more; but there is no room for more in general education. The laborious idleness in which the schooltime is wasted away in the English classical schools deserves the severest reprehension. To what purpose should the most precious years of early life be irreparably squandered in learning to write bad Latin and Greek verses? I do not see that we are much the better even for those who end by writing good ones. I am often tempted to ask the favorites of nature and fortune, whether all the serious and important work of the world is done, that their time and energy can be spared for these *nugæ difficiles*. I am not blind to the utility of composing in a language, as a means of learning it accurately. I hardly know any other means equally effectual. But why should not prose composition suffice? What need is there of original composition at all? if that can be called original which unfortunate school-boys, without any thoughts to express, hammer out on compulsion from mere memory, acquiring the pernicious habit which a teacher should consider it one of his first duties to repress—that of merely stringing together borrowed phrases? The exercise in composition, most suitable to the requirements of learners, is that most valuable one, of retranslating from translated passages of a good author: and to this might be added, what still exists in many Continental places of education, occasional practice in talking Latin. There would be something to be said for the time spent in the manufacture of verses, if such practice were necessary for the enjoyment of ancient poetry; though it would be better to lose that enjoyment than to purchase it at so extravagant a price. But the beauties of a great poet would be a far poorer thing than they are, if they only impressed us through a knowledge of the technicalities of his art. The poet needed those technicalities: they are not necessary to us. They are essential for criticising a poem, but not for enjoying it. All that is wanted is sufficient familiarity with the language, for its meaning to reach us without any sense of effort, and clothed with the associations on which the poet counted for producing his effect. Whoever has this familiarity, and a practised ear, can have as keen a relish of the music of Virgil and Horace, as of Gray, or Burns, or Shelley, though he know not the metrical rules of a common Sapphic or Alcaic. I do not say that these rules ought not to be taught, but I would have a class apart for them, and would make the appropriate exercises an optional, not a compulsory part of the school teaching.

Much more might be said respecting classical instruction, and literary cultivation in general, as a part of liberal education. But it is time to speak of the uses of scientific instruction; or rather its indispensable necessity, for it is recommended by every consideration which pleads for any high order of intellectual education at all.

The most obvious part of the value of scientific instruction —the mere information that it gives—speaks for itself. We are born into a world which we have not made; a world whose phenomena take place according to fixed laws, of which we do not bring any knowledge into the world with us. In such a world we are appointed to live, and in it all our work is to be done. Our whole working power depends on knowing the laws of the world—in other words, the properties of the things which we have to work with, and to work among, and to work upon. We may and do rely, for the greater part of this knowledge, on the few who in each department make its acquisition their main business in life. But unless an elementary knowledge of scientific truths is diffused among the public, they never know what is certain and what is not, or who are entitled to speak with authority and who are not: and they either have no faith at all in the testimony of science, or are the ready dupes of charlatans and impostors. They alternate between ignorant distrust, and blind, often misplaced, confidence. Besides, who is there who would not wish to understand the meaning of the common physical facts that take place under his eye? Who would not wish to know why a pump raises water, why a lever moves heavy weights, why it is hot at the tropics and cold at the poles, why the moon is sometimes dark and sometimes bright, what is the cause of the tides? Do we not feel that he who is totally ignorant of these things, let him be ever so skilled in a special profession, is not an educated man, but an ignoramus? It is surely no small part of education to put us in intelligent possession of the most important and most universally interesting facts of the universe, so that the world which surrounds us may not be a sealed book to us, uninteresting because unintelligible. This, however, is but the simplest and most obvious part of the utility of science, and the part which, if neglected in youth, may be the most easily made up for afterwards. It is more important to understand the value of scientific instruction as a training and disciplining process, to fit the intellect for the proper work of a human being. Facts are the materials of our knowledge, but the mind itself is the instrument; and it is easier to acquire facts, than to judge what they prove, and how, through the facts which we know, to get to those which we want to know.

The most incessant occupation of the human intellect throughout life is the ascertainment of truth. We are always needing to know what is actually true about something or other. It is not given to us all to discover great general truths that are a light to all men and to future generations; though with a better general education the number of those who could do so would be far greater than it is. But we all require the ability to judge between the conflicting opinions which are offered to us as vital truths; to choose what doctrines we will receive in the matter of religion, for example; to judge whether we ought to be Tories, Whigs, or Radicals, or to what length it is our duty to go with each; to form a rational conviction on great questions of legislation and internal policy, and on the manner in which our country should behave to dependencies and to foreign nations. And the need we have of knowing how to discriminate truth, is not confined to the larger truths. All through life it is our most pressing interest to find out the truth about all the matters we are concerned with. If we are farmers we want to find what will truly improve our soil; if merchants, what will truly influence the markets of our commodities; if judges, or jurymen, or advocates, who it was that truly did an unlawful act, or to whom a disputed right truly belongs. Every time we have to make a new resolution or alter an old one, in any situation in life, we shall go wrong unless we know the truth about the facts on which our resolution depends. Now, however different these searches for truth may look, and however unlike they really are in their subject-matter, the methods of getting at truth, and the tests of truth, are in all cases much the same. There are but two roads by which truth can be discovered—observation and reasoning; observation, of course, including experiment. We all observe, and we all reason, and therefore, more or less successfully, we all ascertain truths: but most of us do it very ill, and could not get on at all were we not able to fall back on others who do it better. If we could not do it in any degree, we should be mere instruments in the hands of those who could; they would be able to reduce us to slavery. Then how shall we best learn to do this? By being shown the way in which it has already been successfully done. The processes by which truth is attained, reasoning and observation, have been carried to their greatest known perfection in the physical sciences. As classical literature furnishes the most perfect types of the art of expression, so do the physical sciences those of the art of thinking. Mathematics, and its application to astronomy and natural philosophy, are the most complete example of the discovery of truths by reasoning; experimental science, of their discovery by direct observation. In all these cases we know that we can trust the operation, because the conclusions to which it has led have been found true by subsequent trial. It is by the study of these, then, that we may hope to qualify ourselves for distinguishing truth, in cases where there do not exist the same ready means of verification.

In what consists the principal and most characteristic difference between one human intellect and another? In their ability to judge correctly of evidence. Our direct perceptions of truth are so limited,—we know so few things by immediate intuition, or, as it used to be called, by simple apprehension,—that we depend, for almost all our valuable knowledge, on evidence external to itself; and most of us are very unsafe hands at estimating evidence, where an appeal cannot be made to actual eyesight. The intellectual part of our education has nothing more important to do than to correct or mitigate this almost universal infirmity—this summary and substance of nearly all purely intellectual weakness. To do this with effect needs all the resources which the most perfect system of intellectual training can command. Those resources, as every teacher knows, are but of three kinds: first, models; secondly, rules; thirdly, appropriate practice. The models of the art of estimating evidence are furnished by science; the rules are suggested by science; and the study of science is the most fundamental portion of the practice.

Take, in the first instance, mathematics. It is chiefly from mathematics we realize the fact that there actually is a road to truth by means of reasoning; that anything real, and which will be found true when tried, can be arrived at by a mere operation of the mind. The flagrant abuse of mere reasoning in the days of the schoolmen, when men argued confidently to supposed facts of outward nature without properly establishing their premises, or checking the conclusions by observation, created a prejudice in the modern, and especially in the English mind, against deductive reasoning altogether, as a mode of investigation. The prejudice lasted long, and was upheld by the misunderstood authority of Lord Bacon; until the prodigious applications of mathematics to physical science—to the discovery of the laws of external nature—slowly and tardily restored the reasoning process to the place which belongs to it as a source of real knowledge. Mathematics, pure and applied, are still the great conclusive example of what can be done by reasoning. Mathematics also habituates us to several of the principal precautions for the safety of the process. Our first studies in geometry teach us two invaluable lessons. One is, to lay down at the beginning, in express and clear terms, all the premises from which we intend to reason. The other is, to keep every step in the reasoning distinct and separate from all the other steps, and to make each step safe before proceeding to another; expressly stating to ourselves, at every joint in the reasoning, what new premise we there introduce. It is not necessary that we should do this at all times, in all our reasonings. But we must be always able and ready to do it. If the validity of our argument is denied, or if we doubt it ourselves, that is the way to check it. In this way we are often enabled to detect at once the exact place where paralogism or confusion get in: and after sufficient practice we may be able to keep them out from the beginning. It is to mathematics, again, that we owe our first notion of a connected body of truth; truths which grow out of one another, and hang together so that each implies all the rest; that no one of them can be questioned without contradicting another or others, until in the end it appears that no part of the system can be false unless the whole is so. Pure mathematics first gave us this conception; applied mathematics extends it to the realm of physical nature. Applied mathematics shows us that not only the truths of abstract number and extension, but the external facts of the universe, which we apprehend by our senses, form, at least in a large part of all nature, a web similarly held together. We are able, by reasoning from a few fundamental truths, to explain and predict the phenomena of material objects: and what is still more remarkable, the fundamental truths were themselves found out by reasoning; for they are not such as are obvious to the senses, but had to be inferred by a mathematical process from a mass of minute details, which alone came within the direct reach of human observation. When Newton, in this manner, discovered the laws of the solar system, he created, for all posterity, the true idea of science. He gave the most perfect example we are ever likely to have, of that union of reasoning and observation, which by means of facts that can be directly observed, ascends to laws which govern multitudes of other facts—laws which not only explain and account for what we see, but give us assurance beforehand of much that we do not see, much that we never could have found out by observation, though, having been found out, it is always verified by the result.

While mathematics, and the mathematical sciences, supply us with a typical example of the ascertainment of truth by reasoning,—those physical sciences which are not mathematical, such as chemistry, and purely experimental physics, show us in equal perfection the other mode of arriving at certain truth, by observation, in its most accurate form—that of experiment. The value of mathematics in a logical point of view is an old topic with mathematicians, and has even been insisted on so exclusively as to provoke a counter-exaggeration, of which a well-known essay by Sir William Hamilton is an example: but the logical value of experimental science is comparatively a new subject; yet there is no intellectual discipline more important than that which the experimental sciences afford. Their whole occupation consists in doing well, what all of us, during the whole of life, are engaged in doing, for the most part badly. All men do not affect to be reasoners, but all profess, and really attempt, to draw inferences from experience: yet hardly any one, who has not been a student of the physical sciences, sets out with any just idea of what the process of interpreting experience really is. If a fact has occurred once or oftener, and another fact has followed it, people think they have got an experiment, and are well on the road towards showing that the one fact is the cause of the other. If they did but know the immense amount of precaution necessary to a scientific experiment; with what sedulous care the accompanying circumstances are contrived and varied, so as to exclude every agency but that which is the subject of the experiment—or, when disturbing agencies cannot be excluded, the minute accuracy with which their influence is calculated and allowed for, in order that the residue may contain nothing but what is due to the one agency under examination; if these things were attended to, people would be much less easily satisfied that their opinions have the evidence of experience; many popular notions and generalizations which are in all mouths, would be thought a great deal less certain than they are supposed to be; but we should begin to lay the foundation of really experimental knowledge on things which are now the subjects of mere vague discussion, where one side finds as much to say and says it as confidently as another, and each person's opinion is less determined by evidence than by his accidental interest or prepossession. In politics, for instance, it is evident to whoever comes to the study from that of the experimental sciences, that no political conclusions of any value for practice can be arrived at by direct experience. Such specific experience as we can have serves only to verify, and even that insufficiently, the conclusions of reasoning. Take any active force you please in politics; take the liberties of England, or free trade: how should we know that either of these things conduced to prosperity, if we could discern no tendency in the things themselves to produce it? If we had only the evidence of what is called our experience, such prosperity as we enjoy might be owing to a hundred other causes, and might have been obstructed, not promoted, by these. All true political science is, in one sense of the phrase, *à priori*, being deduced from the tendencies of things—tendencies known either through our general experience of human nature, or as the result of an analysis of the course of history, considered as a progressive evolution. It requires, therefore, the union of induction and deduction, and the mind that is equal to it must have been well disciplined in both. But familiarity with scientific experiment at least does the useful service of inspiring a wholesome scepticism about the conclusions which the mere surface of experience suggests.

The study, on the one hand, of mathematics and its applications, on the other, of experimental science, prepares us for the principal business of the intellect, by the practice of it in the most characteristic cases, and by familiarity with the most perfect and successful models of it. But in great things as in small, examples and models are not sufficient: we want rules as well. Familiarity with the correct use of a language in conversation and writing does not make rules of grammar unnecessary; nor does the amplest knowledge of sciences of reasoning and experiment dispense with rules of logic. We may have heard correct reasonings and seen skilful experiments all our lives—we shall not learn by mere imitation to do the like, unless we pay careful attention to how it is done. It is much easier in these abstract matters, than in purely mechanical ones, to mistake bad work for good. To mark out the difference between them is the province of logic. Logic lays down the general principles and laws of the search after truth; the conditions which, whether recognized or not, must actually have been observed if the mind has done its work rightly. Logic is the intellectual complement of mathematics and physics. Those sciences give the practice, of which Logic is the theory. It declares the principles, rules, and precepts, of which they exemplify the observance.

The science of Logic has two parts; ratiocinative and inductive logic. The one helps to keep us right in reasoning from premises, the other in concluding from observation. Ratiocinative logic is much older than inductive, because reasoning in the narrower sense of the word is an easier process than induction, and the science which works by mere reasoning, pure mathematics, had been carried to a considerable height while the sciences of observation were still in the purely empirical period. The principles of ratiocination, therefore, were the earliest understood and systematized, and the logic of ratiocination is even now suitable to an earlier stage in education than that of induction. The principles of induction cannot be properly understood without some previous study of the inductive sciences; but the logic of reasoning, which was already carried to a high degree of perfection by Aristotle, does not absolutely require even a knowledge of mathematics, but can be sufficiently exemplified and illustrated from the practice of daily life.

Of Logic I venture to say, even if limited to that of mere ratiocination, the theory of names, propositions, and the syllogism, that there is no part of intellectual education which is of greater value, or whose place can so ill be supplied by any thing else. Its uses, it is true, are chiefly negative; its function is, not so much to teach us to go right, as to keep us from going wrong. But in the operations of the intellect it is so much easier to go wrong than right; it is so utterly impossible for even the most vigorous mind to keep itself in the path but by maintaining a vigilant watch against all deviations, and noting all the byways by which it is possible to go astray—that the chief difference between one reasoner and another consists in their less or greater liability to be misled. Logic points out all the possible ways in which, starting from true premises, we may draw false conclusions. By its analysis of the reasoning process, and the forms it supplies for stating and setting forth our reasonings, it enables us to guard the points at which a fallacy is in danger of slipping in, or to lay our fingers upon the place where it has slipped in. When I consider how very simple the theory of reasoning is, and how short a time is sufficient for acquiring a thorough knowledge of its principles and rules, and even considerable expertness in applying them, I can find no excuse for omission to study it on the part of any one who aspires to succeed in any intellectual pursuit. Logic is the great disperser of hazy and confused thinking: it clears up the fogs which hide from us our own ignorance, and make us believe that we understand a subject when we do not. We must not be led away by talk about inarticulate giants who do great deeds without knowing how, and see into the most recondite truths without any of the ordinary helps, and without being able to explain to other people how they reach their conclusions, nor consequently to convince any other people of the truth of them. There may be such men, as there are deaf and dumb persons who do clever things; but for all that, speech and hearing are faculties by no means to be dispensed with. If you want to know whether you are thinking rightly, put your thoughts into words. In the very attempt to do this you will find yourselves, consciously or unconsciously, using logical forms. Logic compels us to throw our meaning into distinct propositions, and our reasonings into distinct steps. It makes us conscious of all the implied assumptions on which we are proceeding, and which, if not true, vitiate the entire process. It makes us aware what extent of doctrine we commit ourselves to by any course of reasoning, and obliges us to look the implied premises in the face, and make up our minds whether we can stand to them. It makes our opinions consistent with themselves and with one another, and forces us to think clearly, even when it cannot make us think correctly. It is true that error may be consistent and systematic as well as truth; but this is not the common case. It is no small advantage to see clearly the principles and consequences involved in our opinions, and which we must either accept, or else abandon those opinions. We are much nearer to finding truth when we search for it in broad daylight. Error, pursued rigorously to all that is implied in it, seldom fails to get detected by coming into collision with some known and admitted fact.

You will find abundance of people to tell you that logic is no help to thought, and that people cannot be taught to think by rules. Undoubtedly rules by themselves, without practice, go but a little way in teaching anything. But if the practice of thinking is not improved by rules, I venture to say it is the only difficult thing done by human beings that is not so. A man learns to saw wood principally by practice, but there are rules for doing it, grounded on the nature of the operation, and if he is not taught the rules, he will not saw well until he has discovered them for himself. Wherever there is a right way and a wrong, there must be a difference between them, and it must be possible to find out what the difference is; and when found out and expressed in words, it is a rule for the operation. If any one is inclined to disparage rules, I say to him, try to learn anything which there are rules for, without knowing the rules, and see how you succeed. To those who think lightly of the school logic, I say, take the trouble to learn it. You will easily do so in a few weeks, and you will see whether it is of no use to you in making your mind clear, and keeping you from stumbling in the dark over the most outrageous fallacies. Nobody, I believe, who has really learned it, and who goes on using his mind, is insensible to its benefits, unless he started with a prejudice, or, like some eminent English and Scottish thinkers of the past century, is under the influence of a reaction against the exaggerated pretensions made by the schoolmen, not so much in behalf of logic as of the reasoning process itself. Still more highly must the use of logic be estimated, if we include in it, as we ought to do, the principles and rules of Induction as well as of Ratiocination. As the one logic guards us against bad deduction, so does the other against bad generalization, which is a still more universal error. If men easily err in arguing from one general proposition to another, still more easily do they go wrong in interpreting the observations made by themselves and others. There is nothing in which an untrained mind shows itself more hopelessly incapable, than in drawing the proper general conclusions from its own experience. And even trained minds, when all their training is on a special subject, and does not extend to the general principles of induction, are only kept right when there are ready opportunities of verifying their inferences by facts. Able scientific men, when they venture upon subjects in which they have no facts to check them, are often found drawing conclusions or making generalizations from their experimental knowledge, such as any sound theory of induction would show to be utterly unwarranted. So true is it that practice alone, even of a good kind, is not sufficient without principles and rules. Lord Bacon had the great merit of seeing that rules were necessary, and conceiving, to a very considerable extent, their true character. The defects of his conception were such as were inevitable while the inductive sciences were only in the earliest stage of their progress, and the highest efforts of the human mind in that direction had not yet been made. Inadequate as the Baconian view of induction was, and rapidly as the practice outgrew it, it is only within a generation or two that any considerable improvement has been made in the theory; very much through the impulse given by two of the many distinguished men who have adorned the Scottish Universities—Dugald Stewart and Brown.

I have given a very incomplete and summary view of the educational benefits derived from instruction in the more perfect sciences, and in the rules for the proper use of the intellectual faculties which the practice of those sciences has suggested. There are other sciences, which are in a more backward state, and tax the whole powers of the mind in its mature years, yet a beginning of which may be beneficially made in university studies, while a tincture of them is valuable even to those who are never likely to proceed farther. The first is physiology; the science of the laws of organic and animal life, and especially of the structure and functions of the human body. It would be absurd to pretend that a profound knowledge of this difficult subject can be acquired in youth, or as a part of general education. Yet an acquaintance with its leading truths is one of those acquirements which ought not to be the exclusive property of a particular profession. The value of such knowledge for daily uses has been made familiar to us all by the sanitary discussions of late years. There is hardly one among us who may not, in some position of authority, be required to form an opinion and take part in public action on sanitary subjects. And the importance of understanding the true conditions of health and disease—of knowing how to acquire and preserve that healthy habit of body which the most tedious and costly medical treatment so often fails to restore when once lost—should secure a place in general education for the principal maxims of hygiene, and some of those even of practical medicine. For those who aim at high intellectual cultivation, the study of physiology has still greater recommendations, and is, in the present state of advancement of the higher studies, a real necessity. The practice which it gives in the study of nature is such as no other physical science affords in the same kind, and is the best introduction to the difficult questions of politics and social life. Scientific education, apart from professional objects, is but a preparation for judging rightly of Man, and of his requirements and interests. But to this final pursuit, which has been called *par excellence* the proper study of mankind, physiology is the most serviceable of the sciences, because it is the nearest. Its subject is already Man: the same complex and manifold being, whose properties are not independent of circumstance, and immovable from age to age, like those of the ellipse and hyperbola, or of sulphur and phosphorus, but

342 / Six Great Humanistic Essays

are infinitely various, indefinitely modifiable by art or accident, graduating by the nicest shades into one another, and reacting upon one another in a thousand ways, so that they are seldom capable of being isolated and observed separately. With the difficulties of the study of a being so constituted, the physiologist, and he alone among scientific inquirers, is already familiar. Take what view we will of man as a spiritual being, one part of his nature is far more like another than either of them is like anything else. In the organic world we study nature under disadvantages very similar to those which affect the study of moral and political phenomena: our means of making experiments are almost as limited, while the extreme complexity of the facts makes the conclusions of general reasoning unusually precarious, on account of the vast number of circumstances that conspire to determine every result. Yet, in spite of these obstacles, it is found possible in physiology to arrive at a considerable number of well-ascertained and important truths. This, therefore, is an excellent school in which to study the means of overcoming similar difficulties elsewhere. It is in physiology, too, that we are first introduced to some of the conceptions which play the greatest part in the moral and social sciences, but which do not occur at all in those of inorganic nature; as, for instance, the idea of predisposition, and of predisposing causes, as distinguished from exciting causes. The operation of all moral forces is immensely influenced by predisposition: without that element, it is impossible to explain the commonest facts of history and social life. Physiology is also the first science in which we recognize the influence of habit—the tendency of something to happen again merely because it has happened before. From physiology, too, we get our clearest notion of what is meant by development or evolution. The growth of a plant or animal from the first germ is the typical specimen of a phenomenon which rules through the whole course of the history of man and society—increase of function, through expansion and differentiation of structure by internal forces. I cannot enter into the subject at greater length; it is enough if I throw out hints which may be germs of further thought in yourselves. Those who aim at high intellectual achievements may be assured that no part of their time will be less wasted, than that which they employ in becoming familiar with the methods and with the main conceptions of the science of organization and life.

Physiology, at its upper extremity, touches on Psychology, or the Philosophy of Mind: and without raising any disputed questions about the limits between Matter and Spirit, the nerves and brain are admitted to have so intimate a connection with the mental operations, that the student of the last cannot dispense with a considerable knowledge of the first. The value of psychology itself need hardly be expatiated upon in a Scottish University; for it has always been there studied with brilliant success. Almost everything which has been contributed from these islands towards its advancement since Locke and Berkeley, has until very lately, and much of it even in the present generation, proceeded from Scottish authors and Scottish professors. Psychology, in truth, is simply the knowledge of the laws of human nature. If there is anything that deserves to be studied by man, it is his own nature and that of his fellow-men: and if it is worth studying at all, it is worth studying scientifically, so as to reach the fundamental laws which underlie and govern all the rest. With regard to the suitableness of this subject for general education, a distinction must be made. There are certain observed laws of our thoughts and of our feelings which rest upon experimental evidence, and, once seized, are a clew to the interpretation of much that we are conscious of in ourselves, and observe in one another. Such, for example, are the laws of association. Psychology, so far as it consists of such laws,— I speak of the laws themselves, not of their disputed applications,—is as positive and certain a science as chemistry, and fit to be taught as such. When, however, we pass beyond the bounds of these admitted truths, to questions which are still in controversy among the different philosophical schools—how far the higher operations of the mind can be explained by association, how far we must admit other primary principles— what faculties of the mind are simple, what complex, and what is the composition of the latter—above all, when we embark upon the sea of metaphysics properly so called, and inquire, for instance, whether time and space are real existences, as is our spontaneous impression, or forms of our sensitive faculty, as is maintained by Kant, or complex ideas generated by association; whether matter and spirit are conceptions merely relative to our faculties, or facts existing *per se*, and

344 / Six Great Humanistic Essays

in the latter case, what is the nature and limit of our knowledge of them; whether the will of man is free or determined by causes, and what is the real difference between the two doctrines; matters on which the most thinking men, and those who have given most study to the subjects, are still divided; it is neither to be expected nor desired that those who do not specially devote themselves to the higher departments of speculation should employ much of their time in attempting to get to the bottom of these questions. But it is a part of liberal education to know that such controversies exist, and, in a general way, what has been said on both sides of them. It is instructive to know the failures of the human intellect as well as its successes, its imperfect as well as its perfect attainments; to be aware of the open questions, as well as of those which have been definitively resolved. A very summary view of these disputed matters may suffice for the many; but a system of education is not intended solely for the many; it has to kindle the aspirations and aid the efforts of those who are destined to stand forth as thinkers above the multitude: and for these there is hardly to be found any discipline comparable to that which these metaphysical controversies afford. For they are essentially questions about the estimation of evidence; about the ultimate grounds of belief; the conditions required to justify our most familiar and intimate convictions; and the real meaning and import of words and phrases which we have used from infancy as if we understood all about them, which are even at the foundation of human language, yet of which no one except a metaphysician has rendered to himself a complete account. Whatever philosophical opinions the study of these questions may lead us to adopt, no one ever came out of the discussion of them without increased vigor of understanding, an increased demand for precision of thought and language, and a more careful and exact appreciation of the nature of proof. There never was any sharpener of the intellectual faculties superior to the Berkeleian controversy. There is even now no reading more profitable to students—confining myself to writers in our own language, and notwithstanding that so many of their speculations are already obsolete—than Hobbes and Locke, Reid and Stewart, Hume, Hartley, and Brown; on condition that these great thinkers are not read passively, as masters to be followed, but actively, as supplying materials and incentives to thought.

To come to our own contemporaries, he who has mastered Sir William Hamilton and your own lamented Ferrier as distinguished representatives of one of the two great schools of philosophy, and an eminent Professor in a neighboring University, Professor Bain, probably the greatest living authority in the other, has gained a practice in the most searching methods of philosophic investigation applied to the most arduous subjects, which is no inadequate preparation for any intellectual difficulties that he is ever likely to be called on to resolve.

In this brief outline of a complete scientific education, I have said nothing about direct instruction in that which it is the chief of all the ends of intellectual education to qualify us for—the exercise of thought on the great interests of mankind as moral and social beings—ethics and politics, in the largest sense. These things are not, in the existing state of human knowledge, the subject of a science, generally admitted and accepted. Politics cannot be learned once for all, from a text-book, or the instructions of a master. What we require to be taught on that subject, is to be our own teachers. It is a subject on which we have no masters to follow; each must explore for himself, and exercise an independent judgment. Scientific politics do not consist in having a set of conclusions ready made, to be applied everywhere indiscriminately, but in setting the mind to work in a scientific spirit to discover in each instance the truths applicable to the given case. And this, at present, scarcely any two persons do in the same way. Education is not entitled, on this subject, to recommend any set of opinions as resting on the authority of established science. But it can supply the student with materials for his own mind, and helps to use them. It can make him acquainted with the best speculations on the subject, taken from different points of view; none of which will be found complete, while each embodies some considerations really relevant, really requiring to be taken into the account. Education may also introduce us to the principal facts which have a direct bearing on the subject, namely, the different modes or stages of civilization that have been found among mankind, and the characteristic properties of each. This is the true purpose of historical studies, as prosecuted in a University. The leading facts of ancient and modern history should be known by the student from his private reading: if that knowledge be wanting, it cannot possibly be supplied here. What a Professor of History has to teach, is the meaning of those facts. His office is to help the student in collecting from history what are the main differences between human beings, and between the institutions of society, at one time or place and at another; in picturing to himself human life and the human conception of life, as they were at the different stages of human development; in distinguishing between what is the same in all ages and what is progressive, and forming some incipient conception of the causes and laws of progress. All these things are as yet very imperfectly understood even by the most philosophic inquirers, and are quite unfit to be taught dogmatically. The object is to lead the student to attend to them; to make him take interest in history not as a mere narrative, but as a chain of causes and effects still unwinding itself before his eyes, and full of momentous consequences to himself and his descendants; the unfolding of a great epic or dramatic action, to terminate in the happiness or misery, the elevation or degradation, of the human race; an unremitting conflict between good and evil powers, of which every act done by any of us, insignificant as we are, forms one of the incidents; a conflict in which even the smallest of us cannot escape from taking part, in which whoever does not help the right side is helping the wrong, and for our share in which, whether it be greater or smaller, and let its actual consequences be visible or in the main invisible, no one of us can escape the responsibility. Though education cannot arm and equip its pupils for this fight with any complete philosophy either of politics or of history, there is much positive instruction that it can give them, having a direct bearing on the duties of citizenship. They should be taught the outlines of the civil and political institutions of their own country, and in a more general way, of the more advanced of the other civilized nations. Those branches of politics, or of the laws of social life, in which there exists a collection of facts or thoughts sufficiently sifted and methodized to form the beginning of a science, should be taught *ex professo*. Among the chief of these is Political Economy; the sources and conditions of wealth and material prosperity for aggregate bodies of human beings. This study approaches nearer to the rank of a science, in the sense in which we apply that name to the physical sciences, than anything else connected with politics yet does. I need not enlarge

on the important lessons which it affords for the guidance
of life, and for the estimation of laws and institutions, or on
the necessity of knowing all that it can teach in order to have
true views of the course of human affairs, or form plans for
their improvement which will stand actual trial. The same
persons who cry down Logic will generally warn you against
Political Economy. It is unfeeling, they will tell you. It
recognizes unpleasant facts. For my part, the most unfeeling
thing I know of is the law of gravitation: it breaks the neck
of the best and most amiable person without scruple, if he
forgets for a single moment to give heed to it. The winds and
waves too are very unfeeling. Would you advise those who go
to sea to deny the winds and waves—or to make use of them,
and find the means of guarding against their dangers? My
advice to you is to study the great writers on Political
Economy, and hold firmly by whatever in them you find
true; and depend upon it that if you are not selfish or hard-
hearted already, Political Economy will not make you so. Of
no less importance than Political Economy is the study of
what is called Jurisprudence; the general principles of law;
the social necessities which laws are required to meet; the
features common to all systems of law, and the differences
between them; the requisites of good legislation, the proper
mode of constructing a legal system, and the best constitution
of courts of justice and modes of legal procedure. These things
are not only the chief part of the business of government, but
the vital concern of every citizen; and their improvement affords a wide scope for the energies of any duly prepared
mind, ambitious of contributing towards the better condition
of the human race. For this, too, admirable helps have been
provided by writers of our own or of a very recent time. At
the head of them stands Bentham, undoubtedly the greatest
master who ever devoted the labor of a life to let in light on
the subject of law, and who is the more intelligible to non-
professional persons, because, as his way is, he builds up the
subject from its foundation in the facts of human life, and
shows, by careful consideration of ends and means, what law
might and ought to be, in deplorable contrast with what it is.
Other enlightened jurists have followed with contributions of
two kinds, as the type of which I may take two works, equally
admirable in their respective times. Mr. Austin, in his Lec-
tures on Jurisprudence, takes for his basis the Roman law, the

most elaborately consistent legal system which history has shown us in actual operation, and that which the greatest number of accomplished minds have employed themselves in harmonizing. From this he singles out the principles and distinctions which are of general applicability, and employs the powers and resources of a most precise and analytic mind to give to those principles and distinctions a philosophic basis, grounded in the universal reason of mankind, and not in mere technical convenience. Mr. Maine, in his treatise on Ancient Law in its relations to Modern Thought, shows from the history of law, and from what is known of the primitive institutions of mankind, the origin of much that has lasted till now, and has a firm footing both in the laws and in the ideas of modern times; showing that many of these things never originated in reason, but are relics of the institutions of barbarous society, modified more or less by civilization, but kept standing by the persistency of ideas which were the off-spring of those barbarous institutions, and have survived their parent. The path opened by Mr. Maine has been followed up by others, with additional illustrations of the influence of obsolete ideas on modern institutions, and of obsolete institutions on modern ideas; an action and reaction which perpetuate, in many of the greatest concerns, a mitigated barbarism; things being continually accepted as dictates of nature and necessities of life, which, if we knew all, we should see to have originated in artificial arrangements of society, long since abandoned and condemned.

To these studies I would add International Law; which I decidedly think should be taught in all Universities, and should form part of all liberal education. The need of it is far from being limited to diplomatists and lawyers: it extends to every citizen. What is called the Law of Nations is not properly law, but a part of ethics; a set of moral rules, accepted as authoritative by civilized states. It is true that these rules neither are nor ought to be of eternal obligation, but do and must vary more or less from age to age, as the consciences of nations become more enlightened and the exigencies of political society undergo change. But the rules mostly were at their origin, and still are, an application of the maxims of honesty and humanity to the intercourse of states. They were introduced by the moral sentiments of mankind, or by their sense of the general interest, to mitigate the crimes and sufferings of a state of war, and to restrain governments and nations from unjust or dishonest conduct towards one another in time of peace. Since every country stands in numerous and various relations with the other countries of the world, and many, our own among the number, exercise actual authority over some of these, a knowledge of the established rules of international morality is essential to the duty of every nation, and therefore of every person in it who helps to make up the nation, and whose voice and feeling form a part of what is called public opinion. Let not any one pacify his conscience by the delusion that he can do no harm if he takes no part, and forms no opinion. Bad men need nothing more to compass their ends, than that good men should look on and do nothing. He is not a good man who, without a protest, allows wrong to be committed in his name, and with the means which he helps to supply, because he will not trouble himself to use his mind on the subject. It depends on the habit of attending to and looking into public transactions, and on the degree of information and solid judgment respecting them that exists in the community, whether the conduct of the nation as a nation, both within itself and towards others, shall be selfish, corrupt, and tyrannical, or rational and enlightened, just and noble.

Of these more advanced studies, only a small commencement can be made at schools and Universities; but even this is of the highest value, by awakening an interest in the subjects, by conquering the first difficulties, and inuring the mind to the kind of exertion which the studies require, by implanting a desire to make further progress, and directing the student to the best tracks and the best helps. So far as these branches of knowledge have been acquired, we have learned, or been put into the way of learning, our duty, and our work in life. Knowing it, however, is but half the work of education; it still remains, that what we know, we shall be willing and determined to put in practice. Nevertheless, to know the truth is already a great way towards disposing us to act upon it. What we see clearly and apprehend keenly, we have a natural desire to act out. "To see the best, and yet the worst pursue," is a possible but not a common state of mind; those who follow the wrong have generally first taken care to be voluntarily ignorant of the right. They have silenced their conscience. but they are not knowingly disobeying it. If you take an average human mind while still young, before the objects it has chosen in life have given it a turn in any bad direction, you will generally find it desiring what is good, right, and for the benefit of all; and if that season is properly used to implant the knowledge and give the training which shall render rectitude of judgment more habitual than sophistry, a serious barrier will have been erected against the inroads of selfishness and falsehood. Still, it is a very imperfect education which trains the intelligence only, but not the will. No one can dispense with an education directed expressly to the moral as well as the intellectual part of his being. Such education, so far as it is direct, is either moral or religious; and these may either be treated as distinct, or as different aspects of the same thing. The subject we are now considering is not education as a whole, but scholastic education, and we must keep in view the inevitable limitations of what schools and Universities can do. It is beyond their power to educate morally or religiously. Moral and religious education consists in training the feelings and the daily habits; and these are, in the main, beyond the sphere and inaccessible to the control of public education. It is the home, the family, which gives us the moral or religious education we really receive: and this is completed, and modified, sometimes for the better, often for the worse, by society, and the opinions and feelings with which we are there surrounded. The moral or religious influence which a University can exercise, consists less in any express teaching, than in the pervading tone of the place. Whatever it teaches, it should teach as penetrated by a sense of duty; it should present all knowledge as chiefly a means to worthiness of life, given for the double purpose of making each of us practically useful to his fellow-creatures, and of elevating the character of the species itself; exalting and dignifying our nature. There is nothing which spreads more contagiously from teacher to pupil than elevation of sentiment: often and often have students caught from the living influence of a professor a contempt for mean and selfish objects, and a noble ambition to leave the world better than they found it, which they have carried with them throughout life. In these respects, teachers of every kind have natural and peculiar means of doing with effect what every one who mixes with his fellow-beings, or addresses himself to them in any character, should feel bound to do to the extent of his capacity and opportunities. What is special to a University on these subjects belongs chiefly, like the rest of its work, to the intellectual department. A University exists for the purpose of laying open to each succeeding generation, as far as the conditions of the case admit, the accumulated treasure of the thoughts of mankind. As an indispensable part of this, it has to make known to them what mankind at large, their own country, and the best and wisest individual men, have thought on the great subjects of morals and religion. There should be, and there is in most Universities, professorial instruction in moral philosophy; but I could wish that this instruction were of a somewhat different type from what is ordinarily met with. I could wish that it were more expository, less polemical, and above all less dogmatic. The learner should be made acquainted with the principal systems of moral philosophy which have existed and been practically operative among mankind, and should hear what there is to be said for each: the Aristotelian, the Epicurean, the Stoic, the Judaic, the Christian in the various modes of its interpretation, which differ almost as much from one another as the teachings of those earlier schools. He should be made familiar with the different standards of right and wrong which have been taken as the basis of ethics; general utility, natural justice, natural rights, a moral sense, principles of practical reason, and the rest. Among all these, it is not so much the teacher's business to take a side, and fight stoutly for some one against the rest, as it is to direct them all towards the establishment and preservation of the rules of conduct most advantageous to mankind. There is not one of these systems which has not its good side; not one from which there is not something to be learned by the votaries of the others; not one which is not suggested by a keen, though it may not always be a clear, perception of some important truths, which are the prop of the system, and the neglect or undervaluing of which in other systems, is their characteristic infirmity. A system which may be as a whole erroneous, is still valuable, until it has forced upon mankind a sufficient attention to the portion of truth which suggested it. The ethical teacher does his part best, when he points out how each system may be strengthened even on its own basis, by taking into more complete account the truths which other systems have realized more fully and made more prominent. I do not mean that he should encourage an essentially sceptical eclecticism. While placing every system in the best aspect it admits of, and endeavoring to draw from all of them the most salutary consequences compatible with their nature, I would by no means debar him from enforcing by his best arguments his own preference for some one of the number. They cannot be all true; though those which are false as theories may contain particular truths, indispensable to the completeness of the true theory. But on this subject, even more than on any of those I have previously mentioned, it is not the teacher's business to impose his own judgment, but to inform and discipline that of his pupil.

And this same clew, if we keep hold of it, will guide us through the labyrinth of conflicting thought into which we enter when we touch the great question of the relation of education to religion. As I have already said, the only really effective religious education is the parental—that of home and childhood. All that social and public education has in its power to do, further than by a general pervading tone of reverence and duty, amounts to little more than the information which it can give; but this is extremely valuable. I shall not enter into the question which has been debated with so much vehemence in the last and present generation, whether religion ought to be taught at all in Universities and public schools, seeing that religion is the subject of all others on which men's opinions are most widely at variance. On neither side of this controversy do the disputants seem to me to have sufficiently freed their minds from the old notion of education, that it consists in the dogmatic inculcation from authority, of what the teacher deems true. Why should it be impossible, that information of the greatest value, on subjects connected with religion, should be brought before the student's mind; that he should be made acquainted with so important a part of the national thought, and of the intellectual labors of past generations, as those relating to religion, without being taught dogmatically the doctrines of any church or sect? Christianity being an historical religion, the sort of religious instruction which seems to me most appropriate to a University is the study of ecclesiastical history. If teaching, even on matters of scientific certainty, should aim quite as much at showing how the results are arrived at, as at teaching the results themselves, far more, then, should this be the case on subjects where there is the widest diversity of opinion among men of equal ability, and who have taken equal pains to arrive at the truth. This diversity should of itself be a warning to a conscientious teacher that he has no right to impose his opinion authoritatively upon a youthful mind. His teaching should not be in the spirit of dogmatism, but in that of inquiry. The pupil should not be addressed as if his religion had been chosen for him, but as one who will have to choose it for himself. The various Churches, established and unestablished, are quite competent to the task which is peculiarly theirs—that of teaching each its own doctrines, as far as necessary, to its own rising generation. The proper business of a University is different; not to tell us from authority what we ought to believe, and make us accept the belief as a duty, but to give us information and training, and help us to form our own belief in a manner worthy of intelligent beings, who seek for truth at all hazards, and demand to know all the difficulties, in order that they may be better qualified to find, or recognize, the most satisfactory mode of resolving them. The vast importance of these questions—the great results as regards the conduct of our lives, which depend upon our choosing one belief or another—are the strongest reasons why we should not trust our judgment when it has been formed in ignorance of the evidence, and why we should not consent to be restricted to a one-sided teaching, which informs us of what a particular teacher or association of teachers receive as true doctrine and sound argument, but of nothing more.

I do not affirm that a University, if it represses free thought and inquiry, must be altogether a failure, for the freest thinkers have often been trained in the most slavish seminaries of learning. The great Christian reformers were taught in Roman Catholic Universities; the sceptical philosophers of France were mostly educated by the Jesuits. The human mind is sometimes impelled all the more violently in one direction, by an over-zealous and demonstrative attempt to drag it in the opposite. But this is not what Universities are appointed for—to drive men from them, even into good, by excess of evil. A University ought to be a place of free speculation. The more diligently it does its duty in all other respects, the more certain it is to be that. The old English Universities, in the present generation, are doing better work than they have done within human memory in teaching the ordinary studies of their curriculum; and one of the consequences has been, that whereas they formerly seemed to exist mainly for the repression of independent thought, and the chaining up of the individual intellect and conscience, they are now the great foci of free and manly inquiry, to the higher and professional classes, south of the Tweed. The ruling minds of those ancient seminaries have at last remembered that to place themselves in hostility to the free use of the understanding, is to abdicate their own best privilege, that of guiding it. A modest deference, at least provisional, to the united authority of the specially instructed, is becoming in a youthful and imperfectly formed mind; but when there is no united authority—when the specially instructed are so divided and scattered that almost any opinion can boast of some high authority, and no opinion whatever can claim all; when, therefore, it can never be deemed extremely improbable that one who uses his mind freely may see reason to change his first opinion; then, whatever you do, keep, at all risks, your minds open: do not barter away your freedom of thought. Those of you who are destined for the clerical profession are, no doubt, so far held to a certain number of doctrines, that, if they ceased to believe them, they would not be justified in remaining in a position in which they would be required to teach insincerely. But use your influence to make those doctrines as few as possible. It is not right that men should be bribed to hold out against conviction—to shut their ears against objections, or, if the objections penetrate, to continue professing full and unfaltering belief when their confidence is already shaken. Neither is it right that, if men honestly profess to have changed some of their religious opinions, their honesty should as a matter of course exclude them from taking a part for which they may be admirably qualified, in the spiritual instruction of the nation. The tendency of the age, on both sides of the ancient Border, is towards the relaxation of formularies, and a less rigid construction of articles. This very circumstance, by making the limits of orthodoxy less definite, and obliging every one to draw the line for himself, is an embarrassment to consciences. But I hold entirely with those clergymen who elect to remain in the national church, so long as they are able to accept its articles and confessions in any sense or with any interpretation consistent with common honesty, whether it be the generally received interpretation or not. If all were to desert the church who put a large and liberal construction on its terms of communion, or who would wish to see those terms widened, the national provision for religious teaching and worship would be left utterly to those who take the narrowest, the most literal, and purely textual view of the formularies; who, though by no means necessarily bigots, are under the great disadvantage of having the bigots for their allies, and who, however great their merits may be,—and they are often very great,—yet, if the church is improvable, are not the most likely persons to improve it. Therefore, if it were not an impertinence in me to tender advice in such a matter, I should say, let all who conscientiously can, remain in the church. A church is far more easily improved from within than from without. Almost all the illustrious reformers of religion began by being clergymen; but they did not think that their profession as clergymen was inconsistent with being reformers. They mostly indeed ended their days outside the churches in which they were born; but it was because the churches, in an evil hour for themselves, cast them out. They did not think it any business of theirs to withdraw. They thought they had a better right to remain in the fold, than those had who expelled them.

I have now said what I had to say on the two kinds of education which the system of schools and Universities is intended to promote—intellectual education and moral education; knowledge and the training of the knowing faculty, conscience and that of the moral faculty. These are the two main ingredients of human culture; but they do not exhaust the whole of it. There is a third division, which, if subordinate, and owing allegiance to the two others, is barely inferior to them, and not less needful to the completeness of the human being; I mean the æsthetic branch; the culture which comes through poetry and art, and may be described as the education of the feelings, and the cultivation of the beautiful. This department of things deserves to be regarded in a far more serious light than is the custom of these countries. It is only of late, and chiefly by a superficial imitation of foreigners, that we have begun to use the word Art by itself, and to speak of Art as we speak of Science, or Government, or Religion: we used to talk of the Arts, and more specifically of the Fine Arts: and even by them were vulgarly meant only two forms of art, Painting and Sculpture, the two which as a people we cared least about—which were regarded even by the more cultivated among us as little more than branches of domestic ornamentation, a kind of elegant upholstery. The very words "Fine Arts" called up a notion of frivolity, of great pains expended on a rather trifling object—on something which differed from the cheaper and commoner arts of producing pretty things, mainly by being more difficult, and by giving fops an opportunity of pluming themselves on caring for it, and on being able to talk about it. This estimate extended in no small degree, though not altogether, even to poetry, the queen of arts, but, in Great Britain, hardly included under the name. It cannot exactly be said that poetry was little thought of; we were proud of our Shakespeare and Milton, and in one period at least of our history, that of Queen Anne, it was a high literary distinction to be a poet; but poetry was hardly looked upon in any serious light, or as having much value except as an amusement or excitement, the superiority of which over others principally consisted in being that of a more refined order of minds. Yet the celebrated saying of Fletcher of Saltoun, "Let who will make the laws of a people if I write their songs," might have taught us how great an instrument for acting on the human mind we were undervaluing. It would be difficult for anybody to imagine that "Rule Britannia," for example, or "Scots wha hae," had no permanent influence on the higher region of human character: some of Moore's songs have done more for Ireland than all Grattan's speeches: and songs are far from being the highest or most impressive form of poetry. On these subjects, the mode of thinking and feeling of other countries was not only not intelligible, but not credible, to an average Englishman.

To find Art ranking on a complete equality, in theory at least, with Philosophy, Learning, and Science—as holding an equally important place among the agents of civilization and among the elements of the worth of humanity; to find even painting and sculpture treated as great social powers, and the art of a country as a feature, in its character and condition, little inferior in importance to either its religion or its government; all this only did not amaze and puzzle Englishmen, because it was too strange for them to be able to realize it, or, in truth, to believe it possible: and the radical difference of feeling on this matter between the British people and those of France, Germany, and the Continent generally, is one among the causes of that extraordinary inability to understand one another, which exists between England and the rest of Europe, while it does not exist to anything like the same degree between one nation of Continental Europe and another. It may be traced to the two influences which have chiefly shaped the British character since the days of the Stuarts: commercial money-getting business, and religious Puritanism. Business, demanding the whole of the faculties, and whether pursued from duty or the love of gain, regarding as a loss of time whatever does not conduce directly to the end; Puritanism, which, looking upon every feeling of human nature, except fear and reverence for God, as a snare, if not as partaking of sin, looked coldly, if not disapprovingly, on the cultivation of the sentiments. Different causes have produced different effects in the Continental nations; among whom it is even now observable that virtue and goodness are generally for the most part an affair of the sentiments, while with us they are almost exclusively an affair of duty. Accordingly, the kind of advantage which we have had over many other countries in point of morals—I am not sure that we are not losing it—has consisted in greater tenderness of conscience. In this we have had on the whole a real superiority, though one principally negative; for conscience is with most men a power chiefly in the way of restraint—a power which acts rather in staying our hands from any great wickedness, than by the direction it gives to the general course of our desires and sentiments. One of the commonest types of character among us is that of a man all whose ambition is self-regarding; who has no higher purpose in life than to enrich or raise in the world himself and his family; who never dreams of making the good of his fellow-creatures or of his country an habitual object, further than giving away, annually or from time to time, certain sums in charity; but who has a conscience sincerely alive to whatever is generally considered wrong, and would scruple to use any very illegitimate means for attaining his self-interested objects. While it will often happen in other countries that men whose feelings and whose active energies point strongly in an unselfish direction, who have the love of their country, of human improvement, of human freedom, even of virtue, in great strength, and of whose thoughts and activity a large share is devoted to disinterested objects, will yet, in the pursuit of these or of any other objects that they strongly desire, permit themselves to do wrong things which the other man, though intrinsically, and taking the whole of his character, farther removed from what a human being ought to be, could not bring himself to commit. It is of no use to debate which of these two states of mind is the best, or rather the least bad. It is quite possible to cultivate the conscience and the sentiments too. Nothing hinders us from so training a man that he will not, even for a disinterested purpose, violate the moral law, and also feeding and encouraging those high feelings, on which we mainly rely for lifting men above low and sordid objects, and giving them a higher conception of what constitutes success in life. If we wish men to practise virtue, it is worth while trying to make them love virtue, and feel it an object in itself, and not a tax paid for leave to pursue other objects. It is worth training them to feel, not only actual wrong or actual meanness, but the absence of noble aims and endeavors, as not merely blamable but also degrading; to have a feeling of the miserable smallness of mere self in the face of this great universe, of the collective mass of our fellow-creatures, in the face of past history and of the indefinite future—the poorness and insignificance of human life if it is to be all spent in making things comfortable for ourselves and our kin, and raising ourselves and them a step or two on the social ladder.

Thus feeling, we learn to respect ourselves only so far as we feel capable of nobler objects: and if unfortunately those by whom we are surrounded do not share our aspirations, perhaps disapprove the conduct to which we are prompted by them—to sustain ourselves by the ideal sympathy of the great characters in history, or even in fiction, and by the contemplation of an idealized posterity: shall I add, of ideal perfection embodied in a Divine Being? Now, of this elevated tone of mind the great source of inspiration is poetry, and all literature so far as it is poetical and artistic. We may imbibe exalted feelings from Plato, or Demosthenes, or Tacitus, but it is in so far as those great men are not solely philosophers, or orators, or historians, but poets and artists. Nor is it only loftiness, only the heroic feelings, that are bred by poetic cultivation. Its power is as great in calming the soul as in elevating it—in fostering the milder emotions, as the more exalted. It brings home to us all those aspects of life which take hold of our nature on its unselfish side, and lead us to identify our joy and grief with the good or ill of the system of which we form a part; and all those solemn or pensive feelings, which, without having any direct application to conduct, incline us to take life seriously, and predispose us to the reception of anything which comes before us in the shape of duty. Who does not feel a better man after a course of Dante, or of Wordsworth, or, I will add, of Lucretius or the Georgics, or after brooding over Gray's Elegy, or Shelley's Hymn to Intellectual Beauty? I have spoken of poetry, but all the other modes of art produce similar effects in their degree. The races and nations whose senses are naturally finer and their sensuous perceptions more exercised than ours, receive the same kind of impressions from painting and sculpture; and many of the more delicately organized among themselves do the same. All the arts of expression tend to keep alive and in activity the feelings they express. Do you think that the great Italian painters would have filled the place they did in the European mind, would have been universally ranked among the greatest men of their time, if their productions had done nothing for it but to serve as the decoration of a public hall or a private *salon*? Their Nativities and Crucifixions, their glorious Madonnas and Saints, were to their susceptible Southern countrymen the great school not only of devotional, but of all the elevated and all the imaginative feelings. We colder Northerns may approach to a conception of this function of art when we listen to an oratorio of Handel, or give ourselves up to the emotions excited by a Gothic cathedral. Even apart from any specific emotional expression, the mere contemplation of beauty of a high order produces in no small degree this elevating effect on the character. The power of natural scenery addresses itself to the same region of human nature which corresponds to Art. There are few capable of feeling the sublimer order of natural beauty, such as your own Highlands and other mountain regions afford, who are not, at least temporarily, raised by it above the littlenesses of humanity, and made to feel the puerility of the petty objects which set men's interests at variance, contrasted with the nobler pleasures which all might share. To whatever avocations we may be called in life, let us never quash these susceptibilities within us, but carefully seek the opportunities of maintaining them in exercise. The more prosaic our ordinary duties, the more necessary it is to keep up the tone of our minds by frequent visits to that higher region of thought and feeling, in which every work seems dignified in proportion to the ends for which, and the spirit in which, it is done; where we learn, while eagerly seizing every opportunity of exercising higher faculties and performing higher duties, to regard all useful and honest work as a public function, which may be ennobled by the mode of performing it—which has not properly any other nobility than what that gives—and which, if ever so humble, is never mean but when it is meanly done, and when the motives from which it is done are mean motives.

There is, besides, a natural affinity between goodness and the cultivation of the Beautiful, when it is real cultivation, and not a mere unguided instinct. He who has learned what beauty is, if he be of a virtuous character, will desire to realize it in his own life—will keep before himself a type of perfect beauty in human character, to light his attempts at self-culture. There is a true meaning in the saying of Goethe, though liable to be misunderstood and perverted, that the Beautiful is greater than the Good; for it includes the Good, and adds something to it: it is the Good made perfect, and fitted with all the collateral perfections which make it a finished and completed thing. Now, this sense of perfection, which would make us demand from every creation of man the very utmost that it ought to give, and render us intolerant of the smallest fault in ourselves or in anything we do, is one of the results of Art cultivation. No other human productions come so near to perfection as works of pure Art. In all other things, we are, and may reasonably be, satisfied if the degree of excellence is as great as the object immediately in view seems to us to be worth: but in Art, the perfection is itself the object. If I were to define Art, I should be inclined to call it, the endeavor after perfection in execution. If we meet with even a piece of mechanical work which bears the marks of being done in this spirit—which is done as if the workman loved it, and tried to make it as good as possible, though something less good would have answered the purpose for which it was ostensibly made—we say that he has worked like an artist. Art, when really cultivated, and not merely practised empirically, maintains, what it first gave the conception of, an ideal Beauty, to be eternally aimed at, though surpassing what can be actually attained; and by this idea it trains us never to be com-

pletely satisfied with imperfection in what we ourselves do
and are: to idealize, as much as possible, every work we do,
and most of all, our own characters and lives.

And now, having travelled with you over the whole range
of the materials and training which a University supplies as
a preparation for the higher uses of life, it is almost needless
to add any exhortation to you to profit by the gift. Now is
your opportunity for gaining a degree of insight into subjects
larger and far more ennobling than the minutiæ of a business
or a profession, and for acquiring a facility of using your
minds on all that concerns the higher interests of man, which
you will carry with you into the occupations of active life,
and which will prevent even the short intervals of time which
that may leave you, from being altogether lost for noble
purposes. Having once conquered the first difficulties, the
only ones of which the irksomeness surpasses the interest;
having turned the point beyond which what was once a task
becomes a pleasure; in even the busiest after-life, the higher
powers of your mind will make progress imperceptibly, by the
spontaneous exercise of your thoughts, and by the lessons you
will know how to learn from daily experience. So, at least,
it will be if in your earlier studies you have fixed your eyes
upon the ultimate end from which those studies take their chief
value—that of making you more effective combatants in the
great fight which never ceases to rage between Good and
Evil, and more equal to coping with the ever new problems
which the changing course of human nature and human society
present to be resolved. Aims like these commonly retain the
footing which they have once established in the mind; and
their presence in our thoughts keeps our higher faculties in
exercise, and makes us consider the acquirements and powers
which we store up at any time of our lives, as a mental
capital, to be freely expended in helping forward any mode
which presents itself of making mankind in any respect wiser
or better, or placing any portion of human affairs on a more
sensible and rational footing than its existing one. There is
not one of us who may not qualify himself so to improve the
average amount of opportunities, as to leave his fellow-creatures some little the better for the use he has known how to
make of his intellect. To make this little greater, let us strive
to keep ourselves acquainted with the best thoughts that are
brought forth by the original minds of the age; that we may

know what movements stand most in need of our aid, and that, as far as depends on us, the good seed may not fall on a rock, and perish without reaching the soil in which it might have germinated and flourished. You are to be a part of the public who are to welcome, encourage, and help forward the future intellectual benefactors of humanity; and you are, if possible, to furnish your contingent to the number of those benefactors. Nor let any one be discouraged by what may seem, in moments of despondency, the lack of time and of opportunity. Those who know how to employ opportunities will often find that they can create them: and what we achieve depends less on the amount of time we possess, than on the use we make of our time. You and your like are the hope and resource of your country in the coming generation. All great things which that generation is destined to do, have to be done by some like you; several will assuredly be done by persons for whom society has done much less, to whom it has given far less preparation, than those whom I am now addressing. I do not attempt to instigate you by the prospect of direct rewards, either earthly or heavenly; the less we think about being rewarded in either way, the better for us. But there is one reward which will not fail you, and which may be called disinterested, because it is not a consequence, but is inherent in the very fact of deserving it; the deeper and more varied interest you will feel in life: which will give it tenfold its value, and a value which will last to the end. All merely personal objects grow less valuable as we advance in life: this not only endures, but increases.

[handwritten marginal note:] complication of his opinion on utility

The Folger Shakespeare Library Editions

THE FOLGER LIBRARY SHAKESPEARE

All of Shakespeare's comedies, tragedies, histories, and the collected sonnets, each in a single volume featuring authoritative explanatory notes keyed by line number facing each page of text, extensive background material on Shakespeare, his work and his theatre, a key to famous lines, as well as illustrations from the Folger Collection.

SHAKESPEARE FOR EVERYMAN

An exciting and informative introduction to Shakespeare and the qualities upon which his reputation is based, including extensive material on the Elizabethan stage, anti-Shakespeare cults, guidance in selecting materials for further study and bibliographies, written by Louis B. Wright, Director of the Folger Shakespeare Library, 1948-1968.

THE FOLGER SHAKESPEARE RECORDINGS
A New Series

Now available, the complete text of *Romeo and Juliet*, including narrated stage directions, sound effects, and musical score on four long-playing records. Recorded for the first time by an all-American cast under the supervision of Louis B. Wright and Virginia A. LaMar.

A complete brochure of these materials is available free upon request from Washington Square Press, Inc., Educational Department, 630 Fifth Avenue, New York, N.Y. 10020.

WSP 2/68